黒鷺死体宅配便
the KUROSAGI corpse delivery service

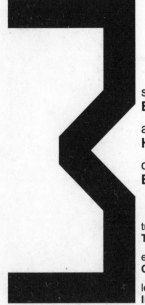

story
EIJI OTSUKA

art
HOUSUI YAMAZAKI

original cover design
BUNPEI YORIFUJI

translation
TOSHIFUMI YOSHIDA

editor and english adaptation
CARL GUSTAV HORN

lettering and touch-up
IHL

contents

tie
a
b
b
body
bowel

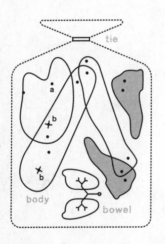

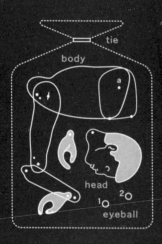

tie

body

a

head

¹O   ²O

eyeball

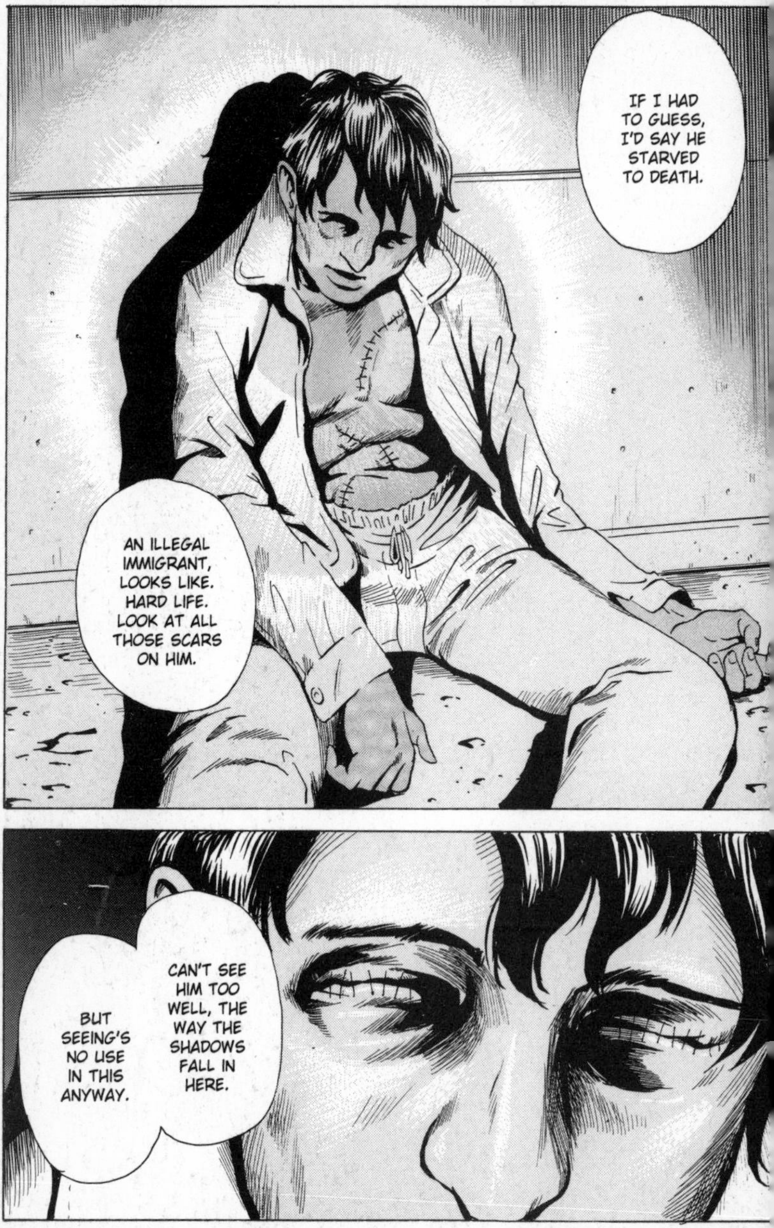
IF I HAD TO GUESS, I'D SAY HE STARVED TO DEATH.
AN ILLEGAL IMMIGRANT, LOOKS LIKE. HARD LIFE. LOOK AT ALL THOSE SCARS ON HIM.
CAN'T SEE HIM TOO WELL, THE WAY THE SHADOWS FALL IN HERE.
BUT SEEING'S NO USE IN THIS ANYWAY.

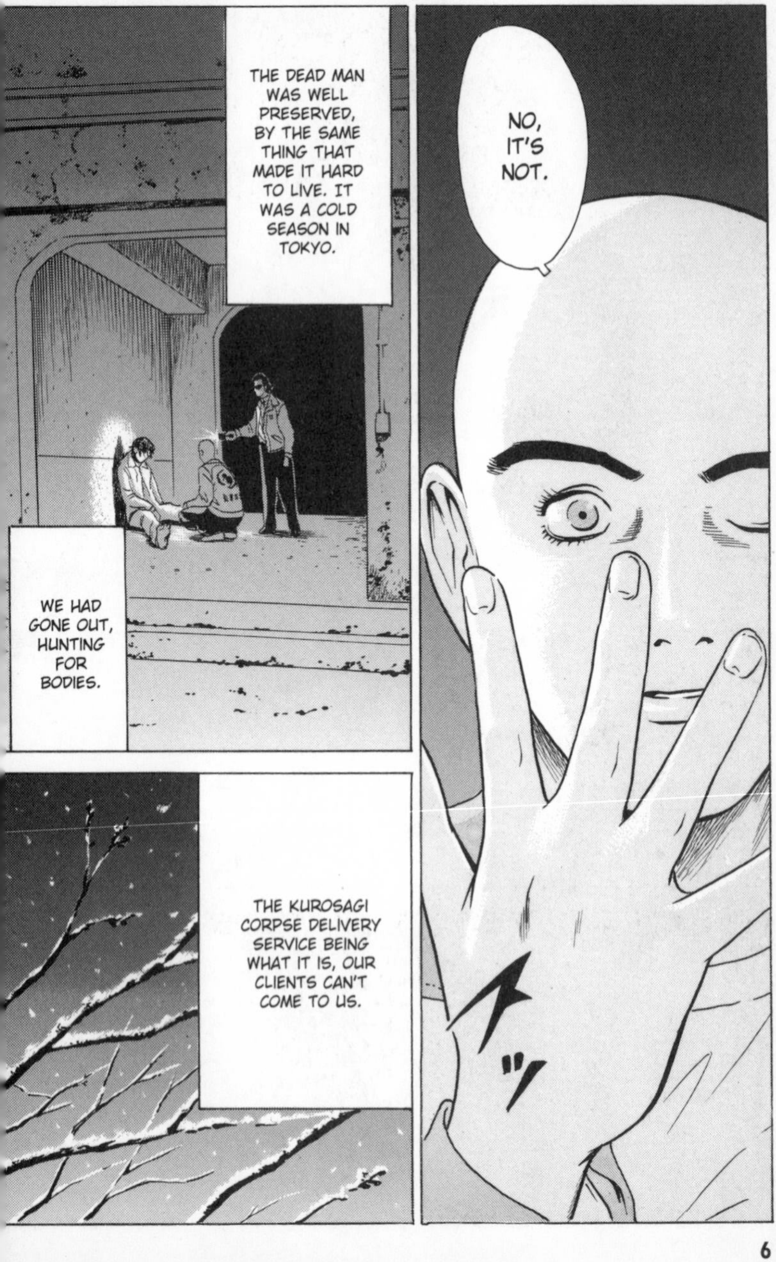
NO, IT'S NOT.
スッ
THE DEAD MAN WAS WELL PRESERVED, BY THE SAME THING THAT MADE IT HARD TO LIVE. IT WAS A COLD SEASON IN TOKYO.
WE HAD GONE OUT, HUNTING FOR BODIES.
THE KUROSAGI CORPSE DELIVERY SERVICE BEING WHAT IT IS, OUR CLIENTS CAN'T COME TO US.

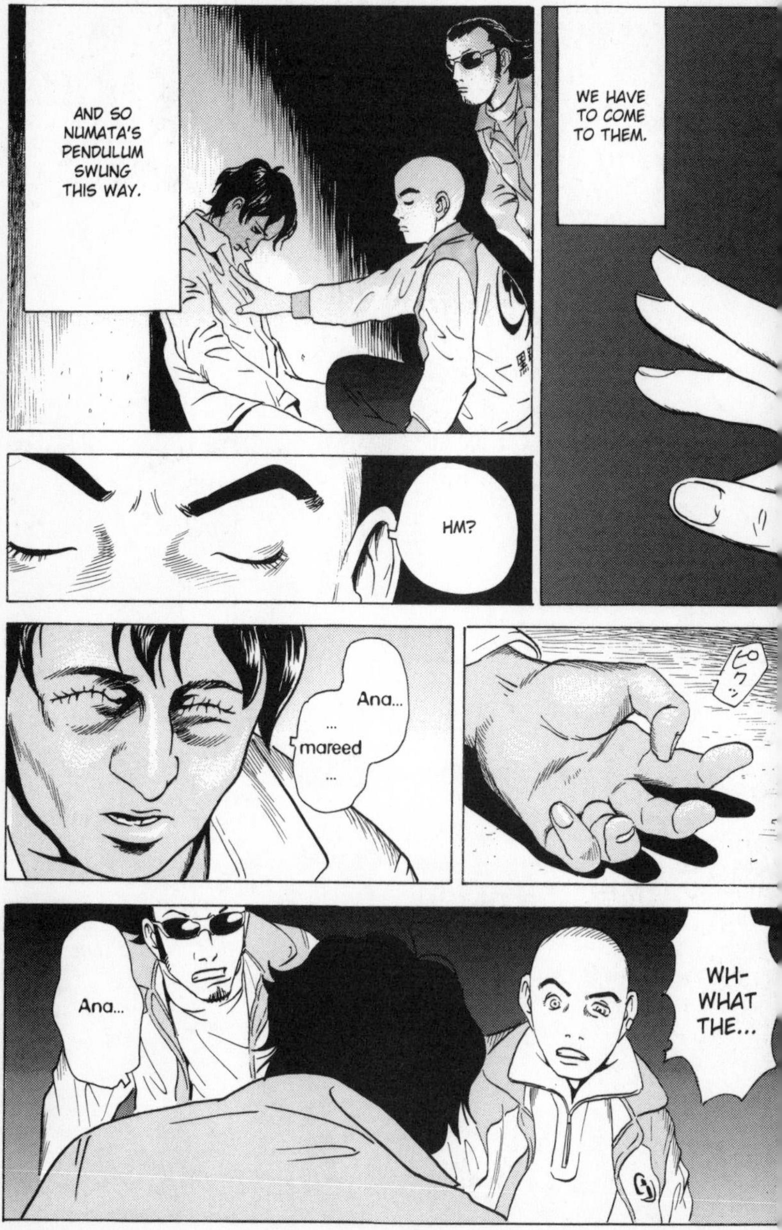
WE HAVE TO COME TO THEM.
AND SO NUMATA'S PENDULUM SWUNG THIS WAY.
HM?
ピクッ
Ana... ... mareed ...
WH- WHAT THE...
Ana...

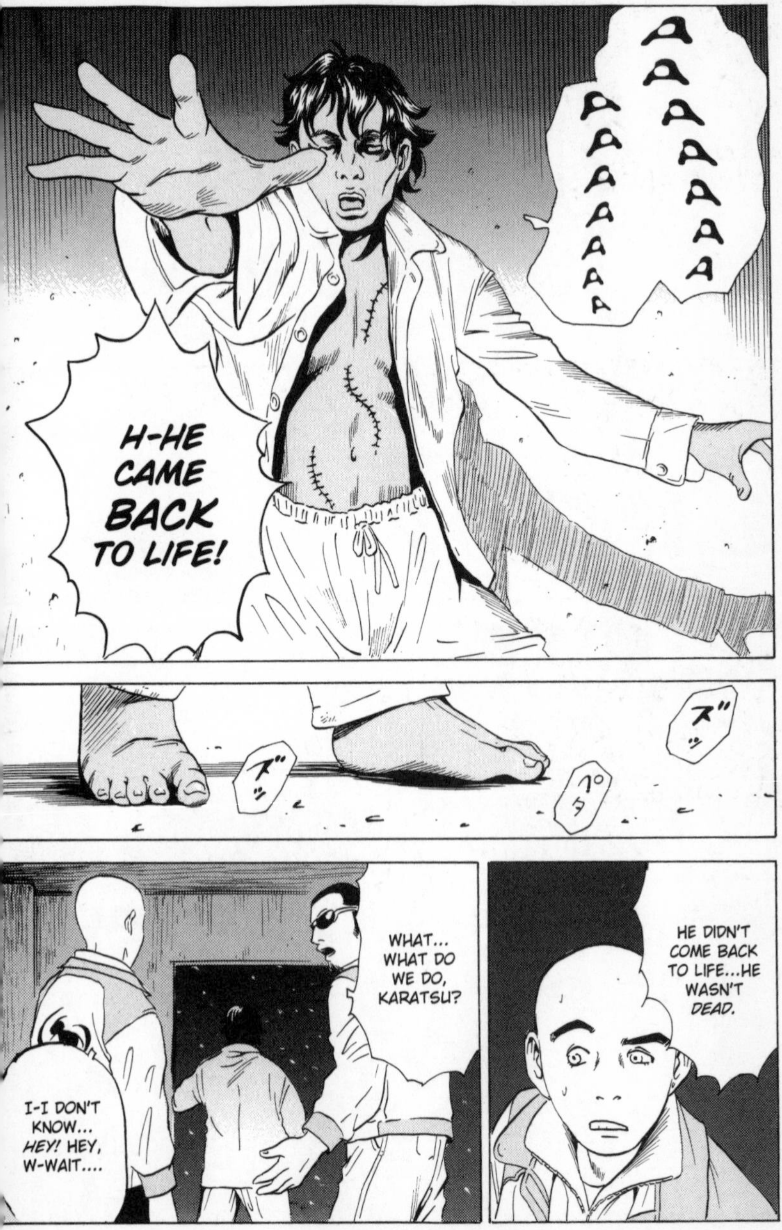
AAAAAAAAAAAAAAAAA
H-HE CAME BACK TO LIFE!
ズッ
ペタ
ズッ
HE DIDN'T COME BACK TO LIFE...HE WASN'T *DEAD*.
WHAT... WHAT DO WE DO, KARATSU?
I-I DON'T KNOW... *HEY!* HEY, W-WAIT....

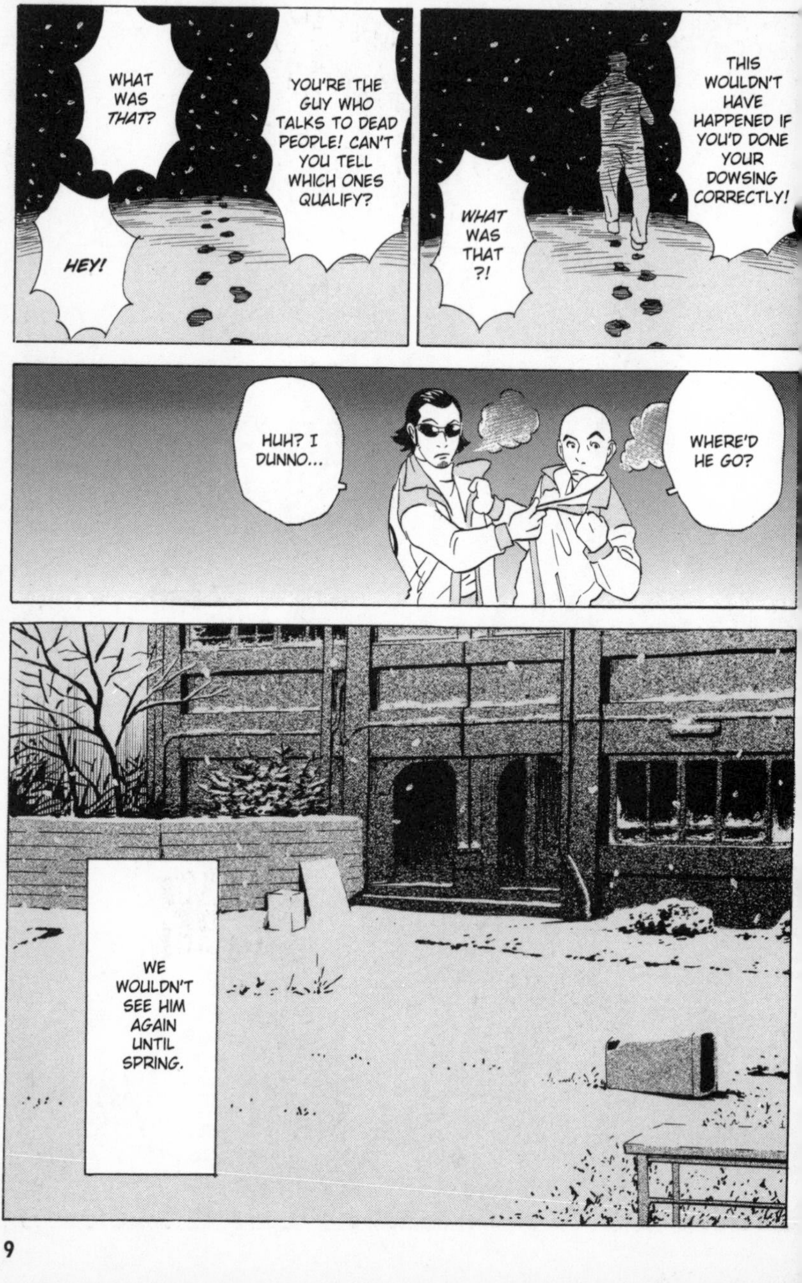
THIS WOULDN'T HAVE HAPPENED IF YOU'D DONE YOUR DOWSING CORRECTLY!
WHAT WAS THAT ?!
YOU'RE THE GUY WHO TALKS TO DEAD PEOPLE! CAN'T YOU TELL WHICH ONES QUALIFY?
WHAT WAS *THAT?*
HEY!
WHERE'D HE GO?
HUH? I DUNNO...
WE WOULDN'T SEE HIM AGAIN UNTIL SPRING.

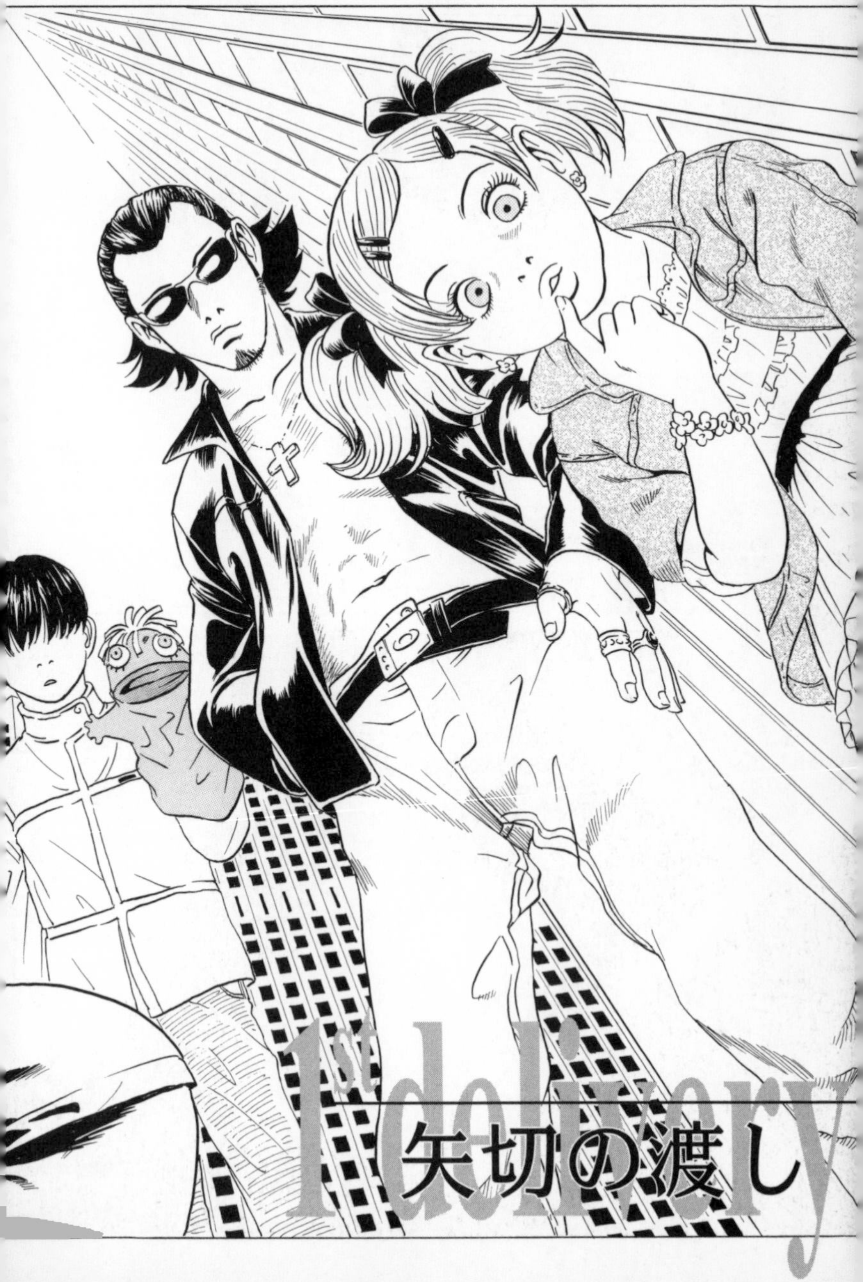
1st delivery
矢切の渡し

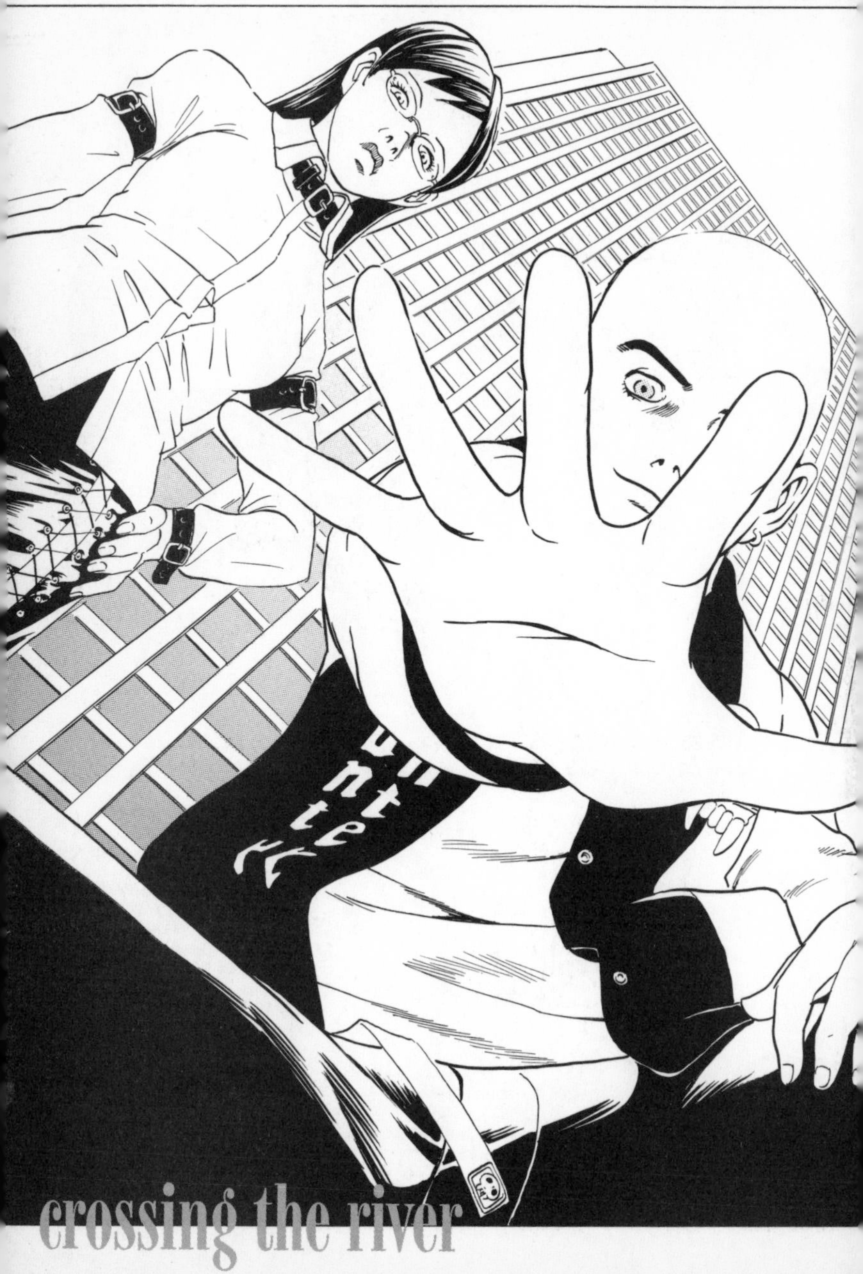

crossing the river

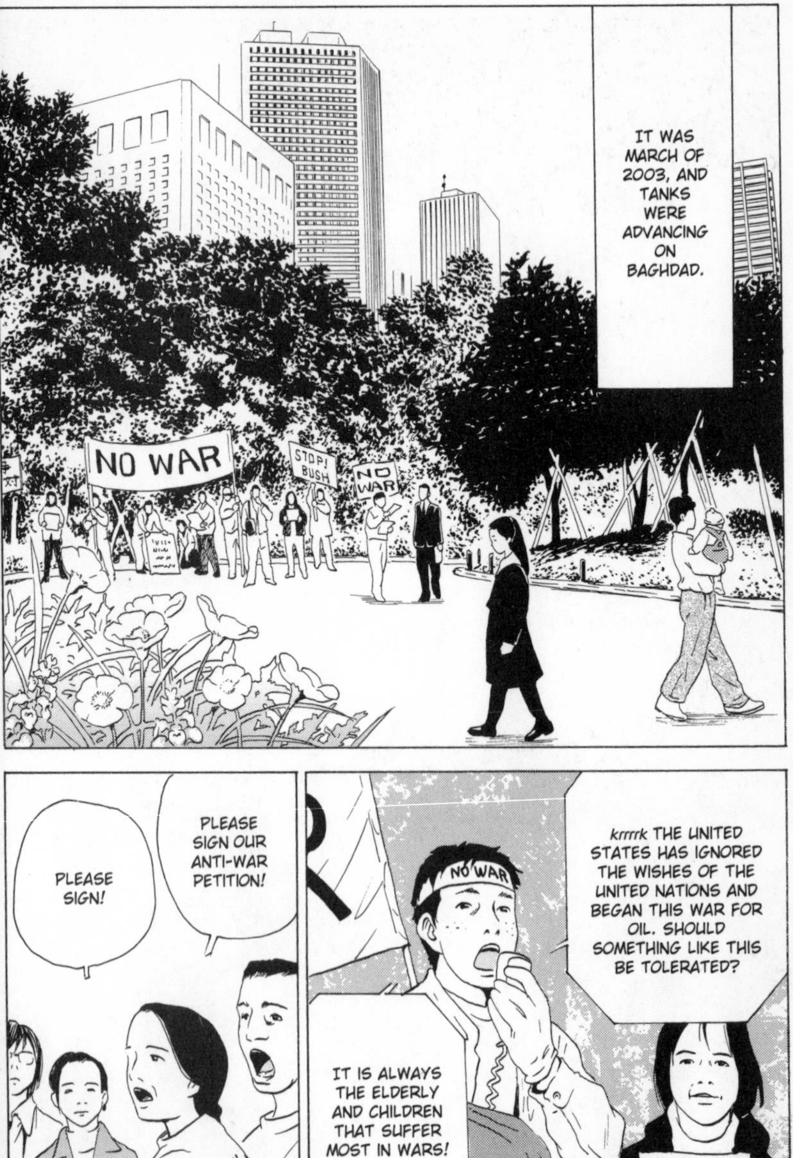
IT WAS MARCH OF 2003, AND TANKS WERE ADVANCING ON BAGHDAD.
NO WAR
STOP! BUSH
NO WAR
NO WAR
krrrk THE UNITED STATES HAS IGNORED THE WISHES OF THE UNITED NATIONS AND BEGAN THIS WAR FOR OIL. SHOULD SOMETHING LIKE THIS BE TOLERATED?
IT IS ALWAYS THE ELDERLY AND CHILDREN THAT SUFFER MOST IN WARS!
STOP
PLEASE SIGN OUR ANTI-WAR PETITION!
PLEASE SIGN!

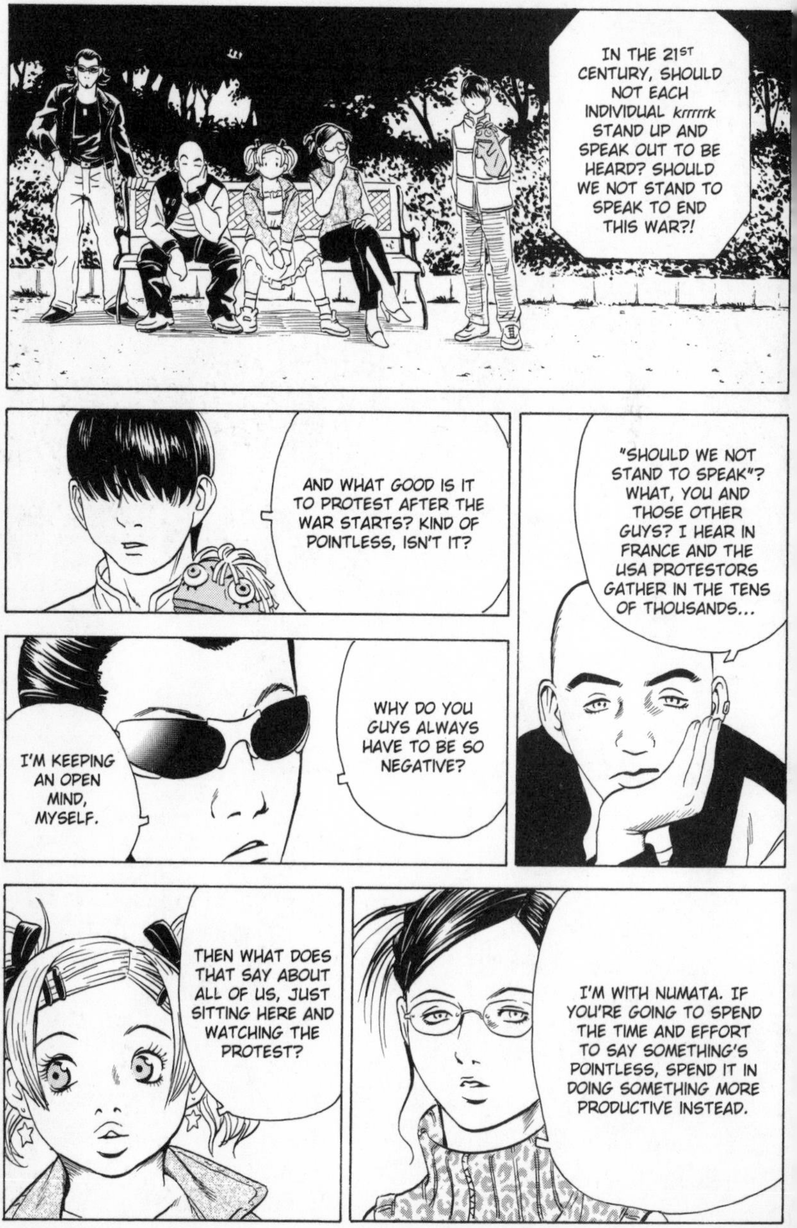
IN THE 21ST CENTURY, SHOULD NOT EACH INDIVIDUAL krrrrrk STAND UP AND SPEAK OUT TO BE HEARD? SHOULD WE NOT STAND TO SPEAK TO END THIS WAR?!
"SHOULD WE NOT STAND TO SPEAK"? WHAT, YOU AND THOSE OTHER GUYS? I HEAR IN FRANCE AND THE USA PROTESTORS GATHER IN THE TENS OF THOUSANDS...
AND WHAT GOOD IS IT TO PROTEST AFTER THE WAR STARTS? KIND OF POINTLESS, ISN'T IT?
WHY DO YOU GUYS ALWAYS HAVE TO BE SO NEGATIVE?
I'M KEEPING AN OPEN MIND, MYSELF.
I'M WITH NUMATA. IF YOU'RE GOING TO SPEND THE TIME AND EFFORT TO SAY SOMETHING'S POINTLESS, SPEND IT IN DOING SOMETHING MORE PRODUCTIVE INSTEAD.
THEN WHAT DOES THAT SAY ABOUT ALL OF US, JUST SITTING HERE AND WATCHING THE PROTEST?

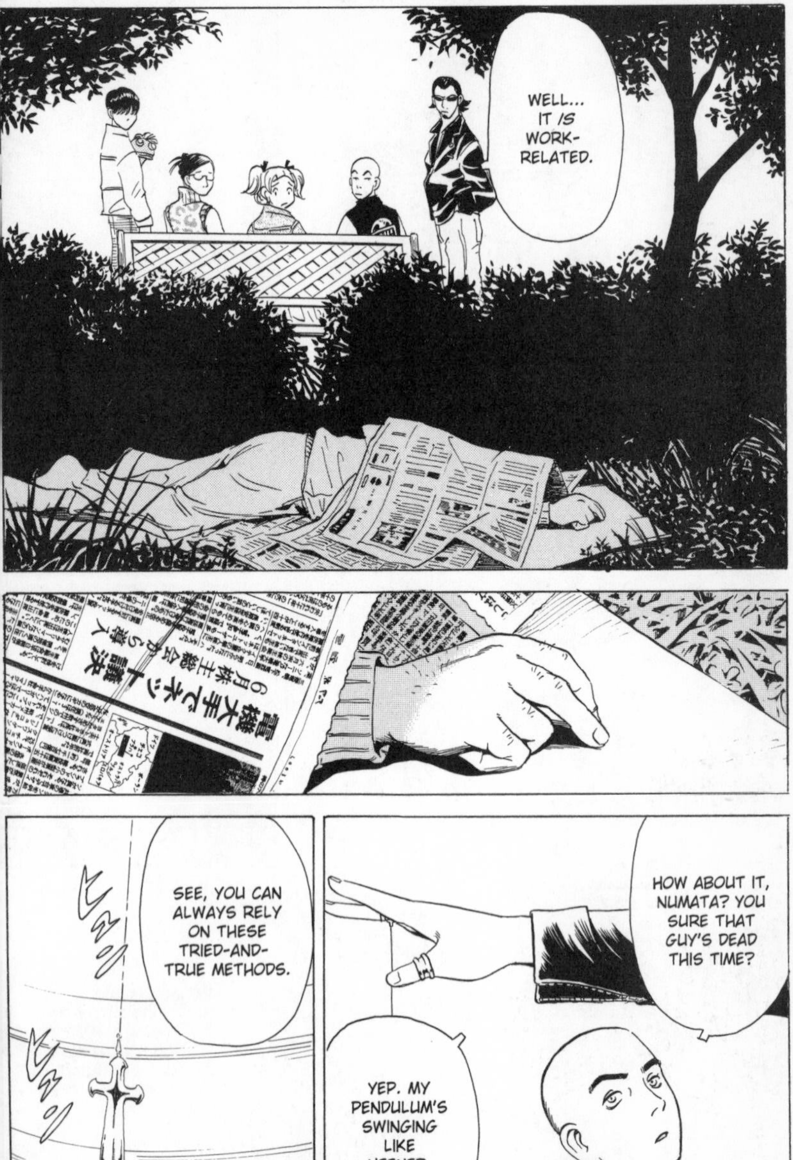
WELL... IT IS WORK-RELATED.
HOW ABOUT IT, NUMATA? YOU SURE THAT GUY'S DEAD THIS TIME?
YEP. MY PENDULUM'S SWINGING LIKE HEFNER.
SEE, YOU CAN ALWAYS RELY ON THESE TRIED-AND-TRUE METHODS.

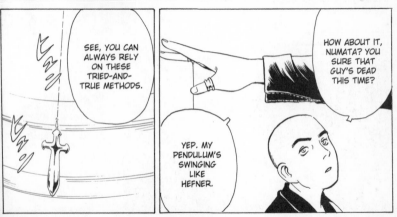

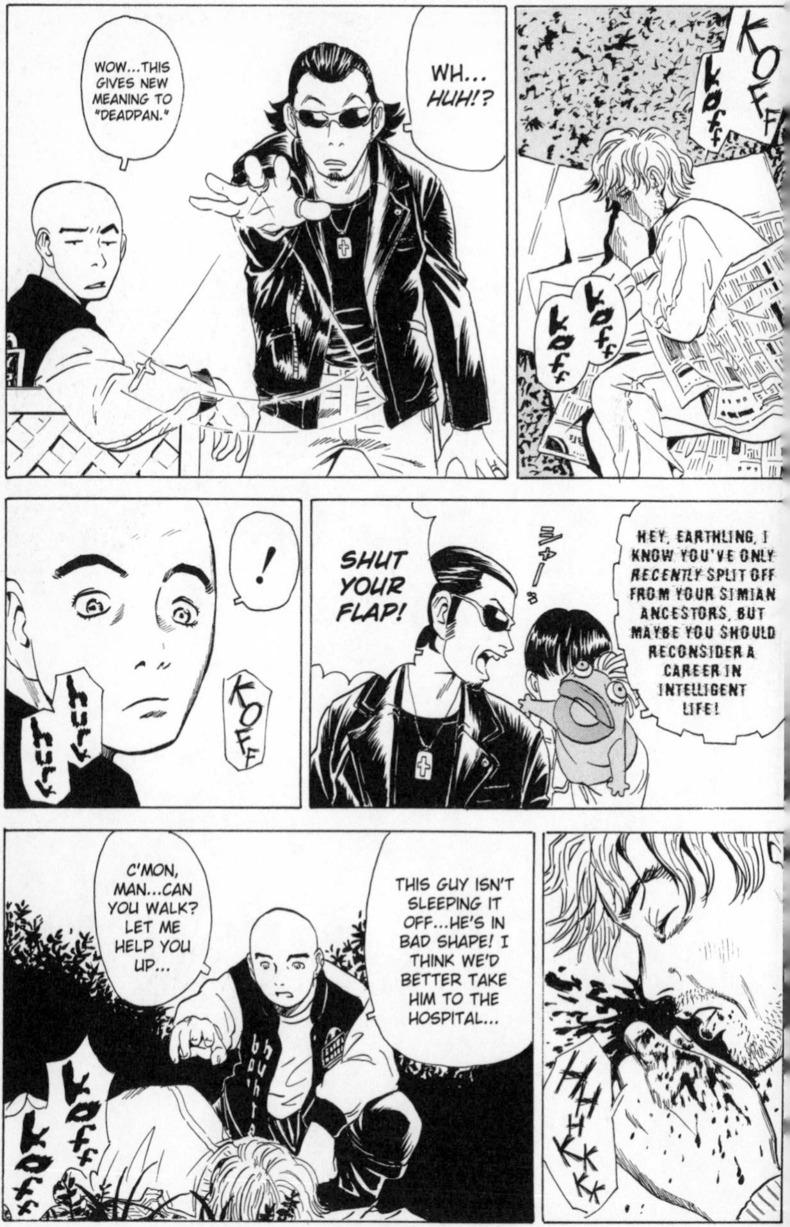
KOFF
koff
koff koff
WH... HUH!?
WOW...THIS GIVES NEW MEANING TO "DEADPAN."
HEY, EARTHLING, I KNOW YOU'VE ONLY RECENTLY SPLIT OFF FROM YOUR SIMIAN ANCESTORS, BUT MAYBE YOU SHOULD RECONSIDER A CAREER IN INTELLIGENT LIFE!
SHUT YOUR FLAP!
!
KOFF
hurk hurk
HHHKKK
THIS GUY ISN'T SLEEPING IT OFF...HE'S IN BAD SHAPE! I THINK WE'D BETTER TAKE HIM TO THE HOSPITAL...
C'MON, MAN...CAN YOU WALK? LET ME HELP YOU UP...
koff koff

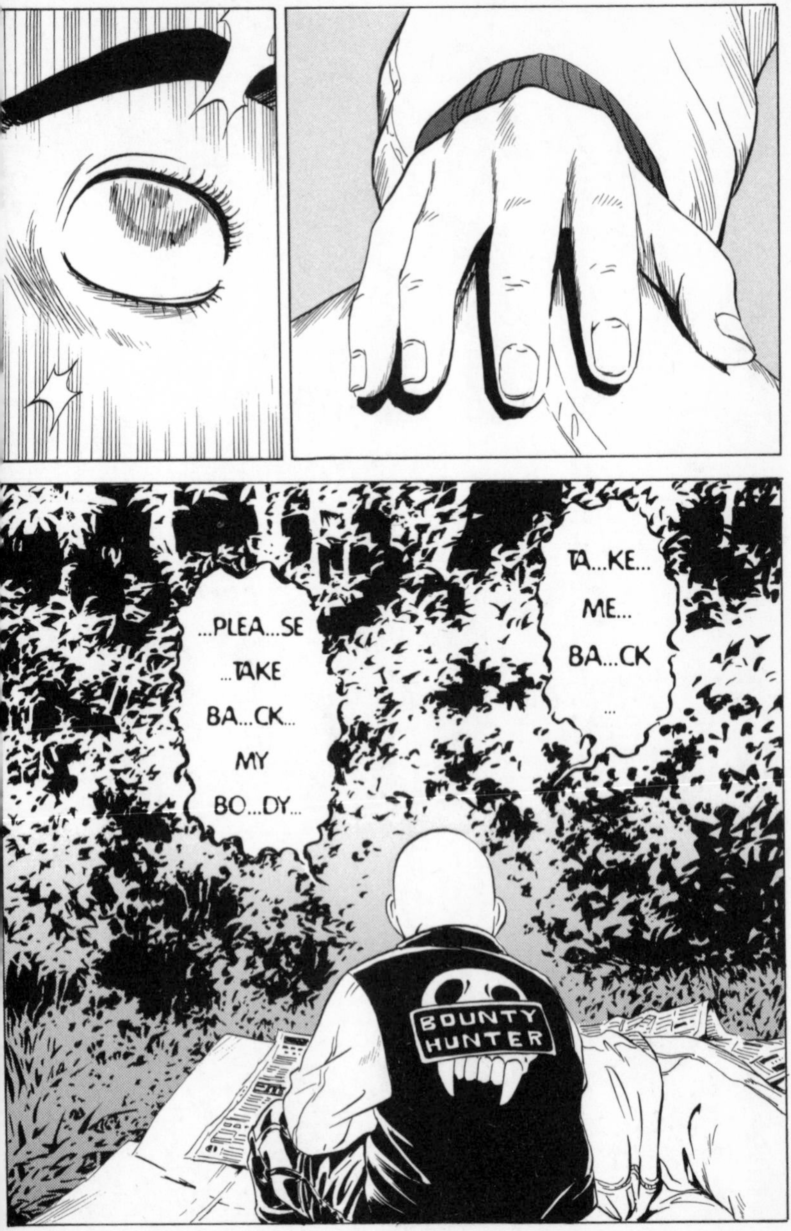
TA...KE... ME... BA...CK ...
...PLEA...SE ...TAKE BA...CK... MY BO...DY...
BOUNTY HUNTER

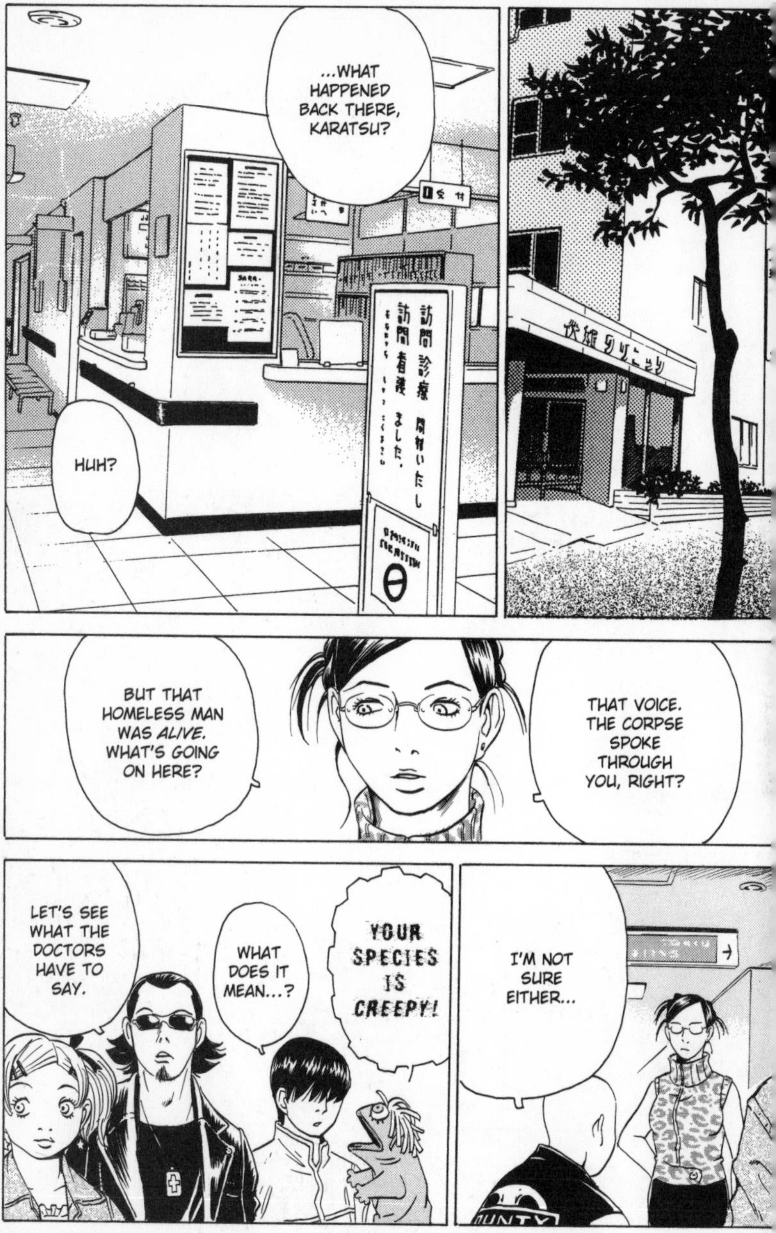
...WHAT HAPPENED BACK THERE, KARATSU?
HUH?
THAT VOICE. THE CORPSE SPOKE THROUGH YOU, RIGHT?
BUT THAT HOMELESS MAN WAS *ALIVE.* WHAT'S GOING ON HERE?
I'M NOT SURE EITHER...
YOUR SPECIES IS CREEPY!
WHAT DOES IT MEAN...?
LET'S SEE WHAT THE DOCTORS HAVE TO SAY.

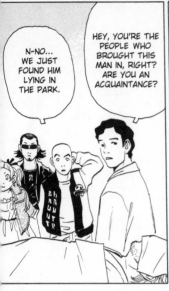

ガコォン
キュッ
キュッ
HEY, YOU'RE THE PEOPLE WHO BROUGHT THIS MAN IN, RIGHT? ARE YOU AN ACQUAINTANCE?
N-NO... WE JUST FOUND HIM LYING IN THE PARK.
DID HE, *uh*, PASS AWAY?
YES, JUST NOW.
HOW... DID HE DIE?
ORGAN FAILURE. HIS BODY SEEMS TO HAVE REJECTED A TRANSPLANT. WE TRIED TO REMOVE IT, BUT WE WERE TOO LATE.

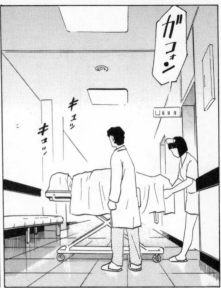

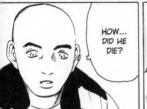

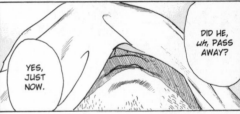

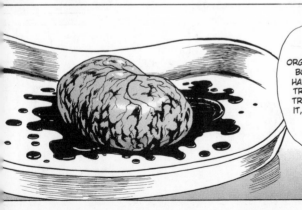

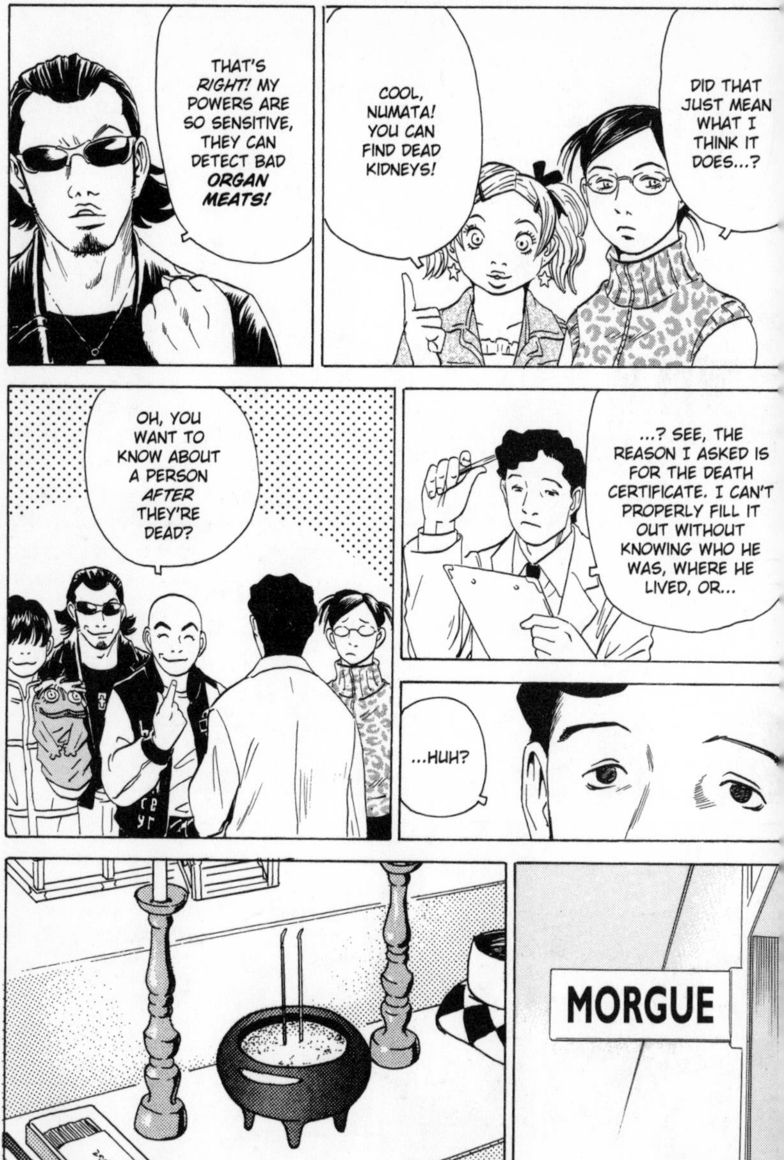
DID THAT JUST MEAN WHAT I THINK IT DOES...?
COOL, NUMATA! YOU CAN FIND DEAD KIDNEYS!
THAT'S *RIGHT!* MY POWERS ARE SO SENSITIVE, THEY CAN DETECT BAD ***ORGAN MEATS!***
...? SEE, THE REASON I ASKED IS FOR THE DEATH CERTIFICATE. I CAN'T PROPERLY FILL IT OUT WITHOUT KNOWING WHO HE WAS, WHERE HE LIVED, OR...
...HUH?
OH, YOU WANT TO KNOW ABOUT A PERSON *AFTER* THEY'RE DEAD?
MORGUE

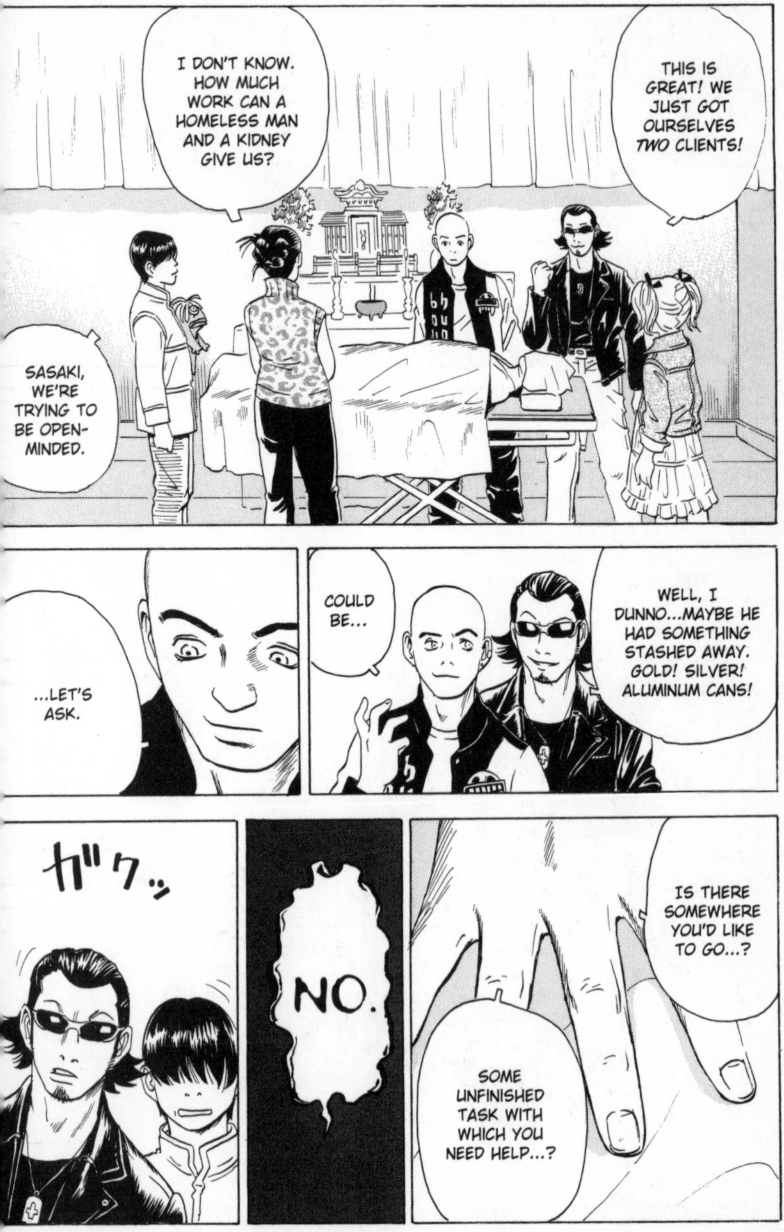
THIS IS GREAT! WE JUST GOT OURSELVES *TWO* CLIENTS!
I DON'T KNOW. HOW MUCH WORK CAN A HOMELESS MAN AND A KIDNEY GIVE US?
SASAKI, WE'RE TRYING TO BE OPEN-MINDED.
WELL, I DUNNO...MAYBE HE HAD SOMETHING STASHED AWAY. GOLD! SILVER! ALUMINUM CANS!
COULD BE...
...LET'S ASK.
IS THERE SOMEWHERE YOU'D LIKE TO GO...?
SOME UNFINISHED TASK WITH WHICH YOU NEED HELP...?
NO.
ガクッ

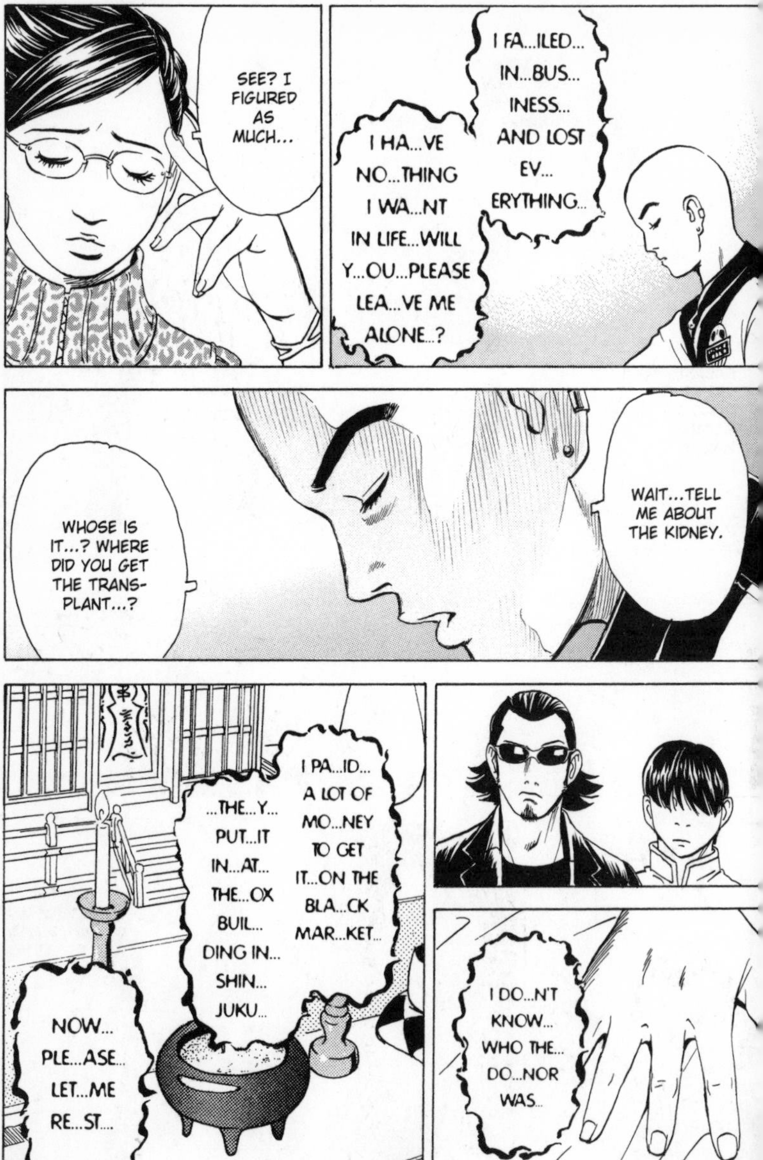
I FA...ILED... IN...BUS... INESS... AND LOST EV... ERYTHING...
I HA...VE NO...THING I WA...NT IN LIFE...WILL Y...OU...PLEASE LEA...VE ME ALONE..?
SEE? I FIGURED AS MUCH...
WAIT...TELL ME ABOUT THE KIDNEY.
WHOSE IS IT...? WHERE DID YOU GET THE TRANS-PLANT...?
I DO...N'T KNOW... WHO THE... DO...NOR WAS...
I PA...ID... A LOT OF MO...NEY TO GET IT...ON THE BLA...CK MAR...KET...
...THE...Y... PUT...IT IN...AT... THE...OX BUIL... DING IN... SHIN... JUKU...
NOW... PLE...ASE... LET...ME RE...ST...

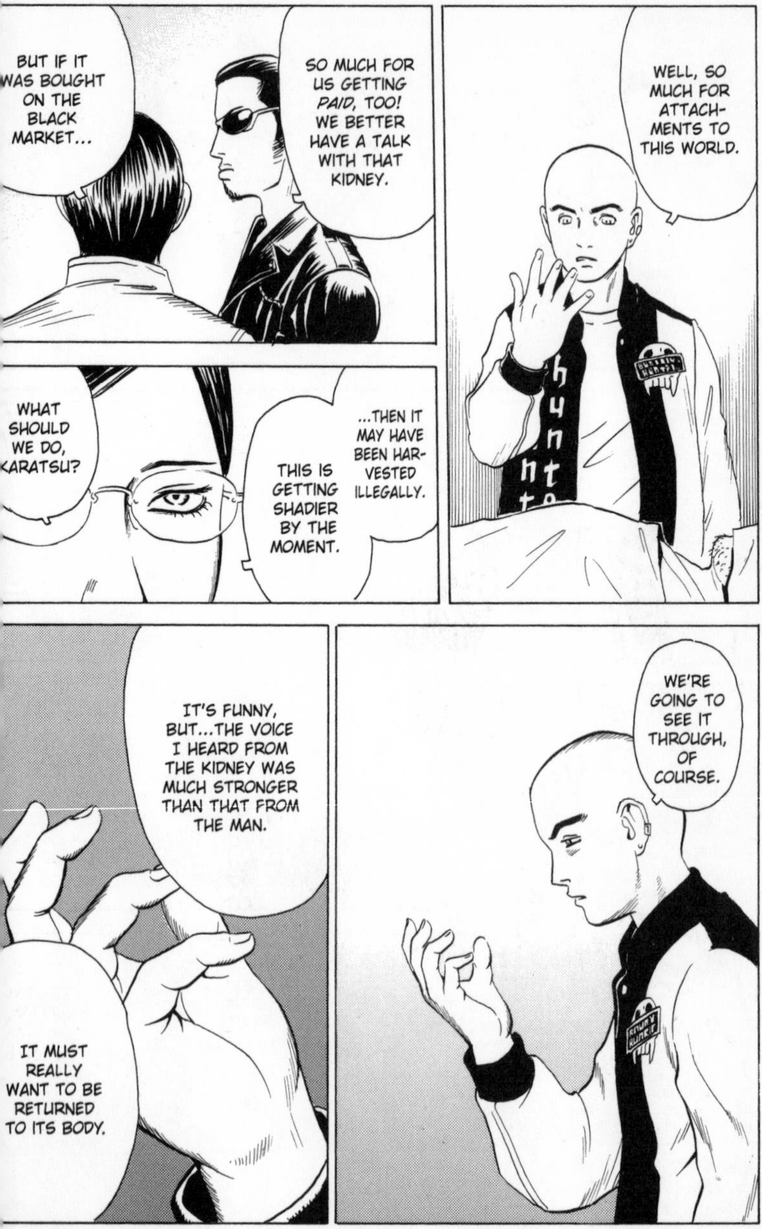
WELL, SO MUCH FOR ATTACH-MENTS TO THIS WORLD.
SO MUCH FOR US GETTING *PAID*, TOO! WE BETTER HAVE A TALK WITH THAT KIDNEY.
BUT IF IT WAS BOUGHT ON THE BLACK MARKET...
...THEN IT MAY HAVE BEEN HAR-VESTED ILLEGALLY.
THIS IS GETTING SHADIER BY THE MOMENT.
WHAT SHOULD WE DO, KARATSU?
WE'RE GOING TO SEE IT THROUGH, OF COURSE.
IT'S FUNNY, BUT...THE VOICE I HEARD FROM THE KIDNEY WAS MUCH STRONGER THAN THAT FROM THE MAN.
IT MUST REALLY WANT TO BE RETURNED TO ITS BODY.

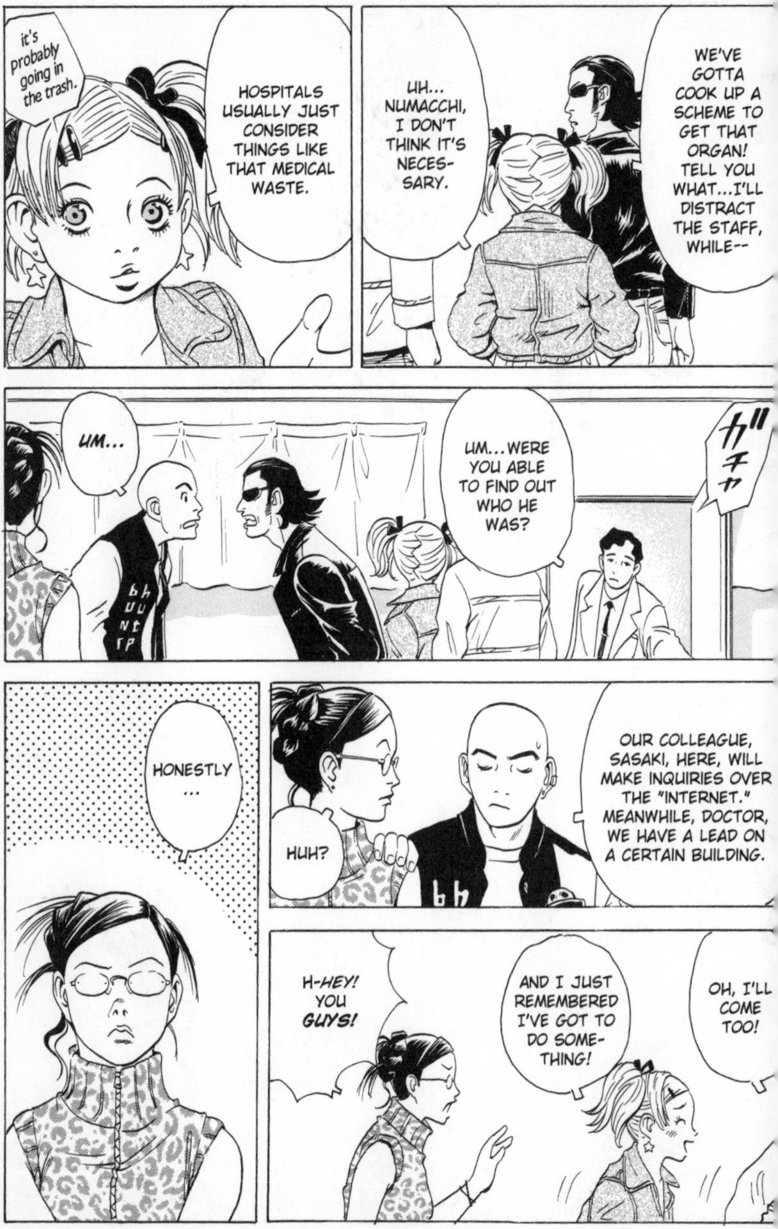
WE'VE GOTTA COOK UP A SCHEME TO GET THAT ORGAN! TELL YOU WHAT...I'LL DISTRACT THE STAFF, WHILE--
UH... NUMACCHI, I DON'T THINK IT'S NECES-SARY.
HOSPITALS USUALLY JUST CONSIDER THINGS LIKE THAT MEDICAL WASTE.
it's probably going in the trash.
ガチャ
UM...WERE YOU ABLE TO FIND OUT WHO HE WAS?
UM...
OUR COLLEAGUE, SASAKI, HERE, WILL MAKE INQUIRIES OVER THE "INTERNET." MEANWHILE, DOCTOR, WE HAVE A LEAD ON A CERTAIN BUILDING.
HUH?
OH, I'LL COME TOO!
AND I JUST REMEMBERED I'VE GOT TO DO SOME-THING!
H-HEY! YOU GUYS!
HONESTLY ...

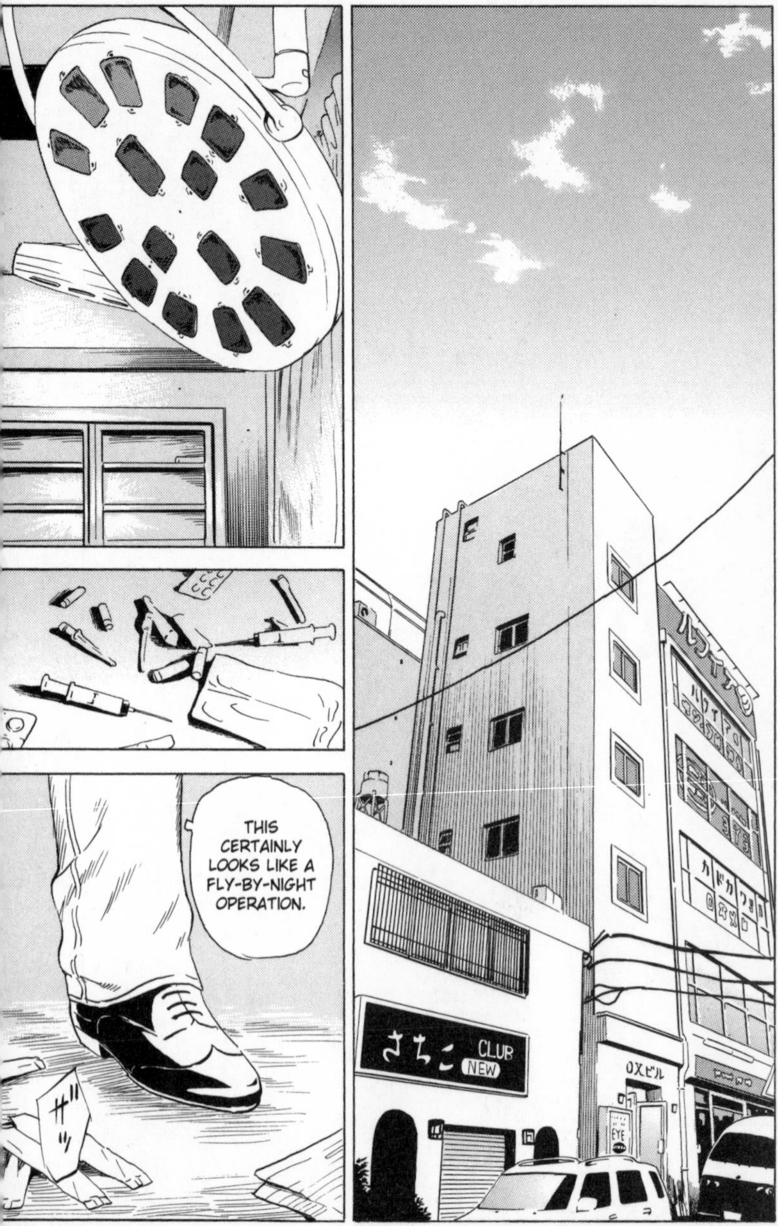
さちこ
CLUB
NEW
EYE
THIS CERTAINLY LOOKS LIKE A FLY-BY-NIGHT OPERATION.
ザッ

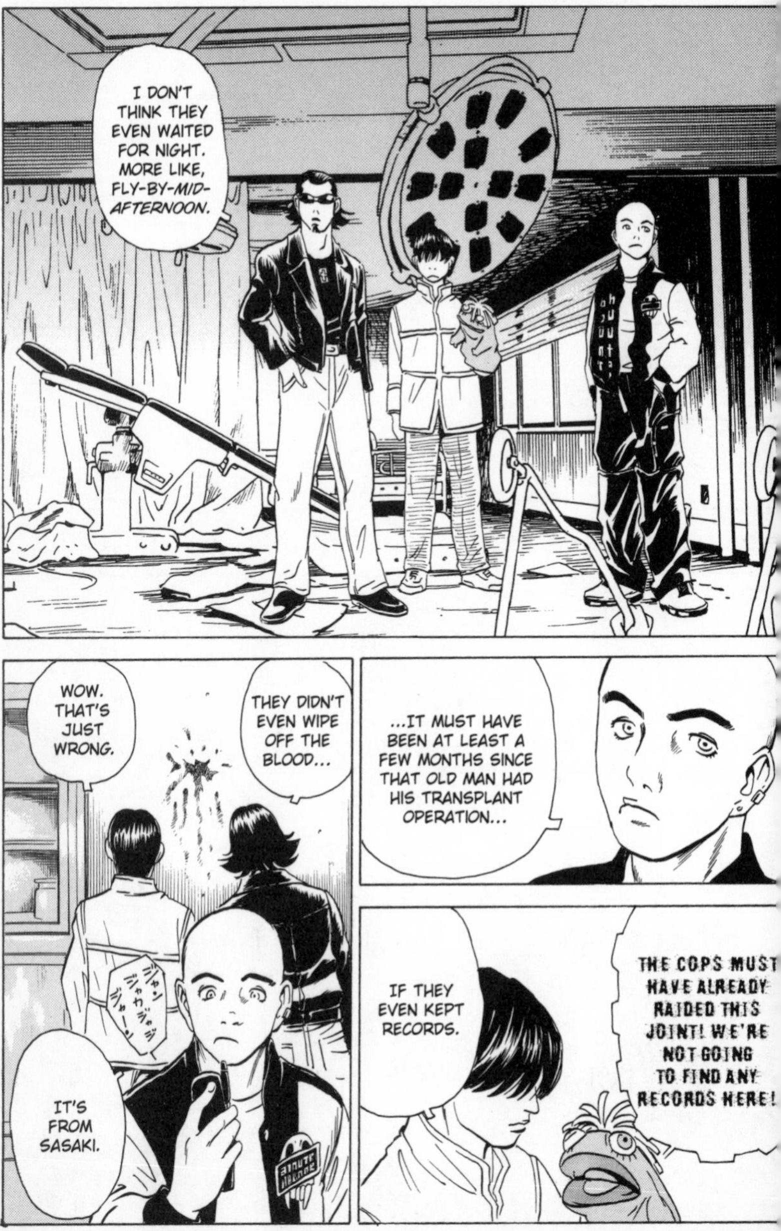
I DON'T THINK THEY EVEN WAITED FOR NIGHT. MORE LIKE, FLY-BY-*MID-AFTERNOON.*
...IT MUST HAVE BEEN AT LEAST A FEW MONTHS SINCE THAT OLD MAN HAD HIS TRANSPLANT OPERATION...
THE COPS MUST HAVE ALREADY RAIDED THIS JOINT! WE'RE NOT GOING TO FIND ANY RECORDS HERE!
IF THEY EVEN KEPT RECORDS.
THEY DIDN'T EVEN WIPE OFF THE BLOOD...
WOW. THAT'S JUST WRONG.
IT'S FROM SASAKI.

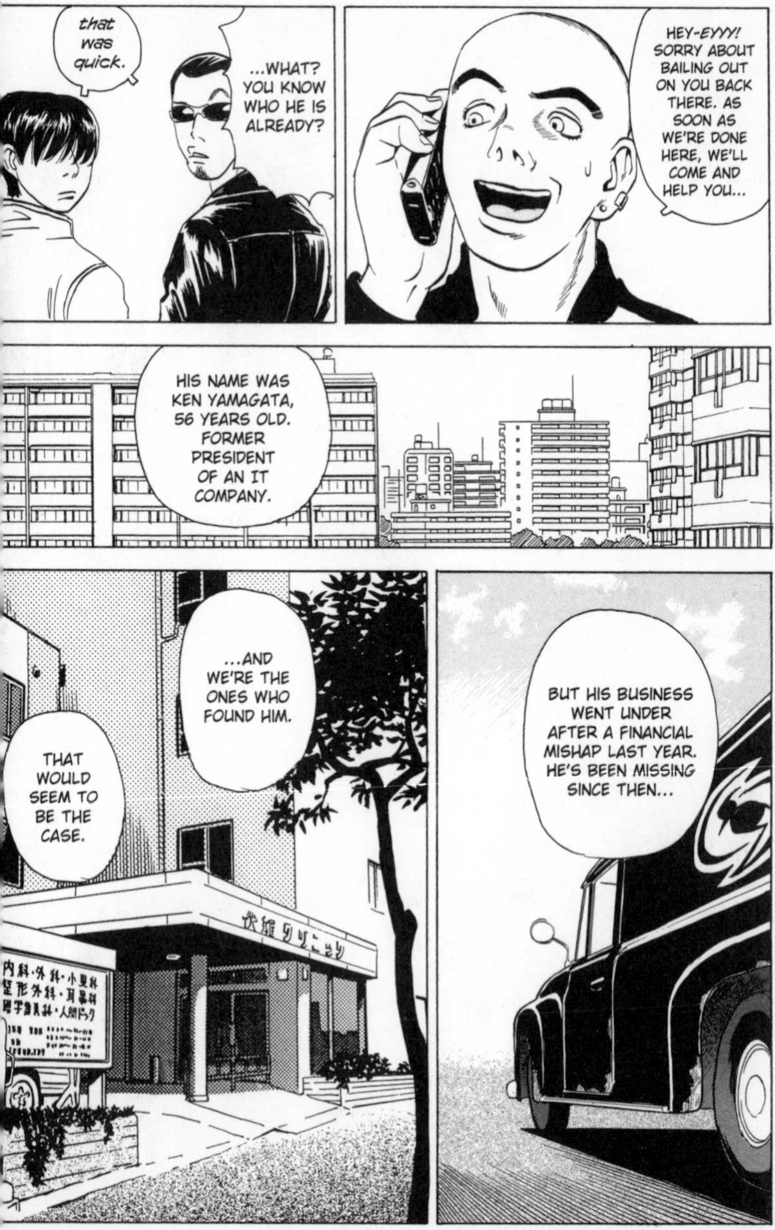
HEY-EYYY! SORRY ABOUT BAILING OUT ON YOU BACK THERE. AS SOON AS WE'RE DONE HERE, WE'LL COME AND HELP YOU...
...WHAT? YOU KNOW WHO HE IS ALREADY?
that was quick.
HIS NAME WAS KEN YAMAGATA, 56 YEARS OLD. FORMER PRESIDENT OF AN IT COMPANY.
BUT HIS BUSINESS WENT UNDER AFTER A FINANCIAL MISHAP LAST YEAR. HE'S BEEN MISSING SINCE THEN...
...AND WE'RE THE ONES WHO FOUND HIM.
THAT WOULD SEEM TO BE THE CASE.

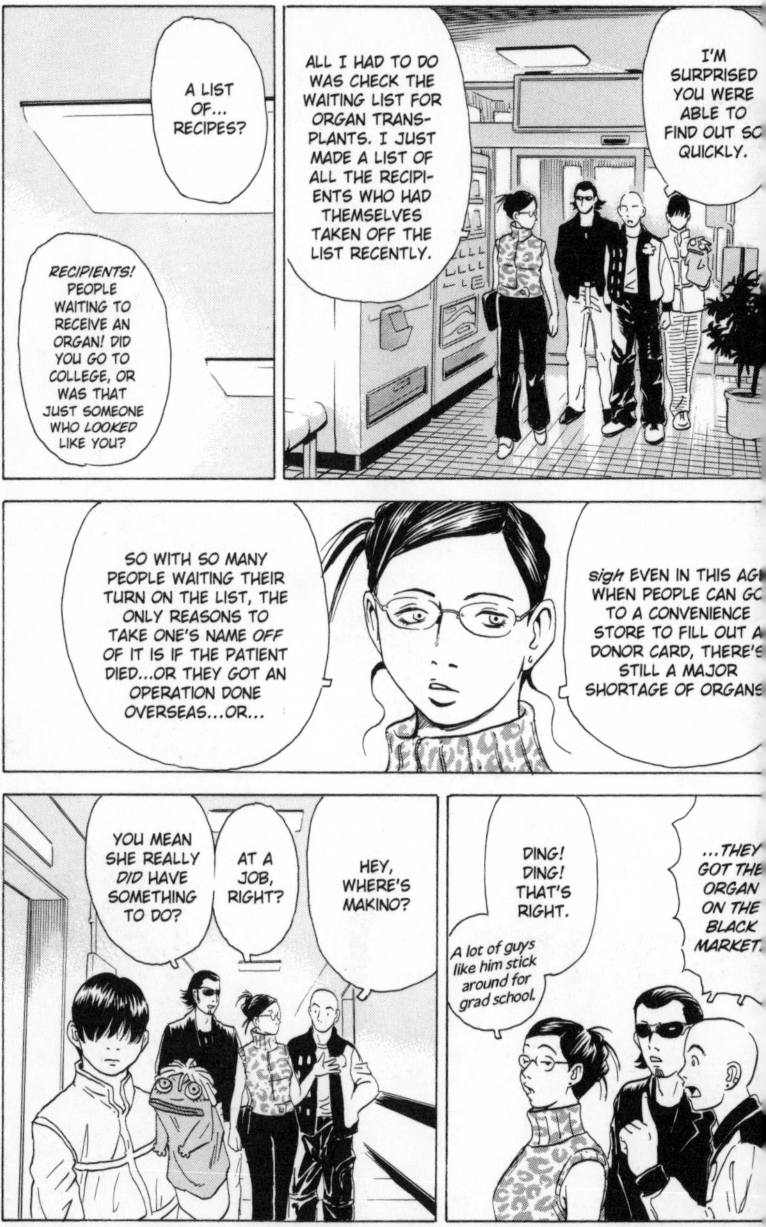
I'M SURPRISED YOU WERE ABLE TO FIND OUT SO QUICKLY.
ALL I HAD TO DO WAS CHECK THE WAITING LIST FOR ORGAN TRANS-PLANTS. I JUST MADE A LIST OF ALL THE RECIPI-ENTS WHO HAD THEMSELVES TAKEN OFF THE LIST RECENTLY.
A LIST OF... RECIPES?
RECIPIENTS! PEOPLE WAITING TO RECEIVE AN ORGAN! DID YOU GO TO COLLEGE, OR WAS THAT JUST SOMEONE WHO *LOOKED* LIKE YOU?
sigh EVEN IN THIS AGE WHEN PEOPLE CAN GO TO A CONVENIENCE STORE TO FILL OUT A DONOR CARD, THERE'S STILL A MAJOR SHORTAGE OF ORGANS
SO WITH SO MANY PEOPLE WAITING THEIR TURN ON THE LIST, THE ONLY REASONS TO TAKE ONE'S NAME *OFF* OF IT IS IF THE PATIENT DIED...OR THEY GOT AN OPERATION DONE OVERSEAS...OR...
...THEY GOT THE ORGAN ON THE BLACK MARKET.
DING! DING! THAT'S RIGHT.
A lot of guys like him stick around for grad school.
HEY, WHERE'S MAKINO?
AT A JOB, RIGHT?
YOU MEAN SHE REALLY *DID* HAVE SOMETHING TO DO?

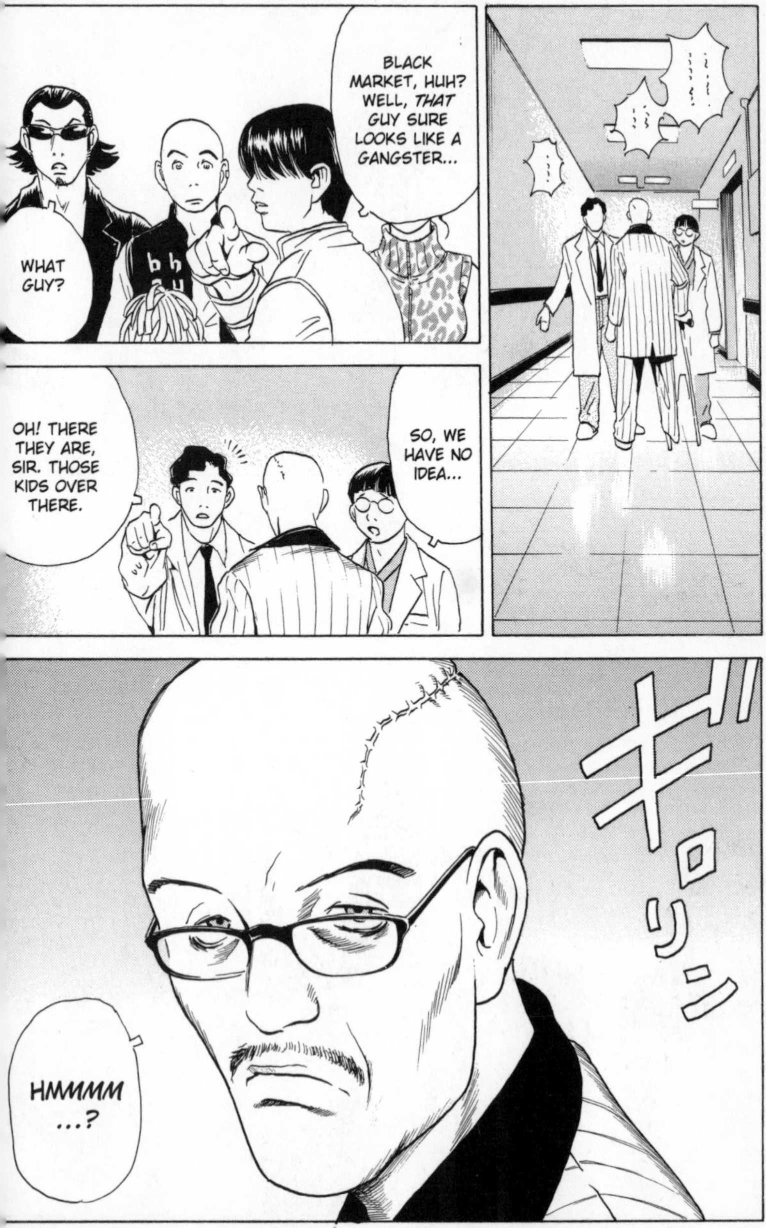
BLACK MARKET, HUH? WELL, *THAT* GUY SURE LOOKS LIKE A GANGSTER...
WHAT GUY?
SO, WE HAVE NO IDEA...
OH! THERE THEY ARE, SIR. THOSE KIDS OVER THERE.
ギロリン
HMMMM ...?

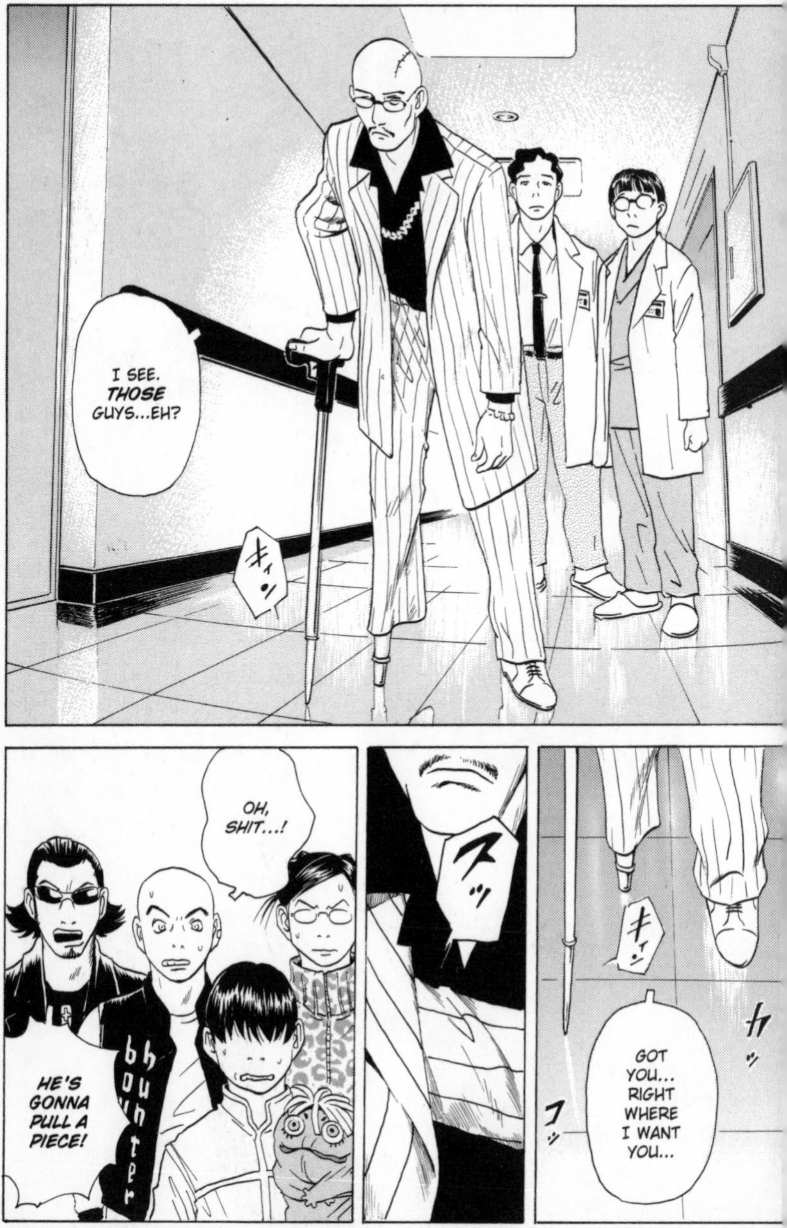
I SEE. *THOSE* GUYS...EH?
キィン
キィン
カッ
GOT YOU... RIGHT WHERE I WANT YOU...
コッ
スッ
OH, SHIT...!
HE'S GONNA PULL A PIECE!

SASAYAMA, FROM THE SHINJUKU CITY HALL SOCIAL WELFARE OFFICE! ARE YOU THE ONES WHO BROUGHT THAT BODY HERE?!

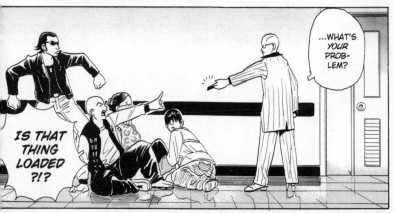

...WHAT'S YOUR PROBLEM?

IS THAT THING LOADED ?!?

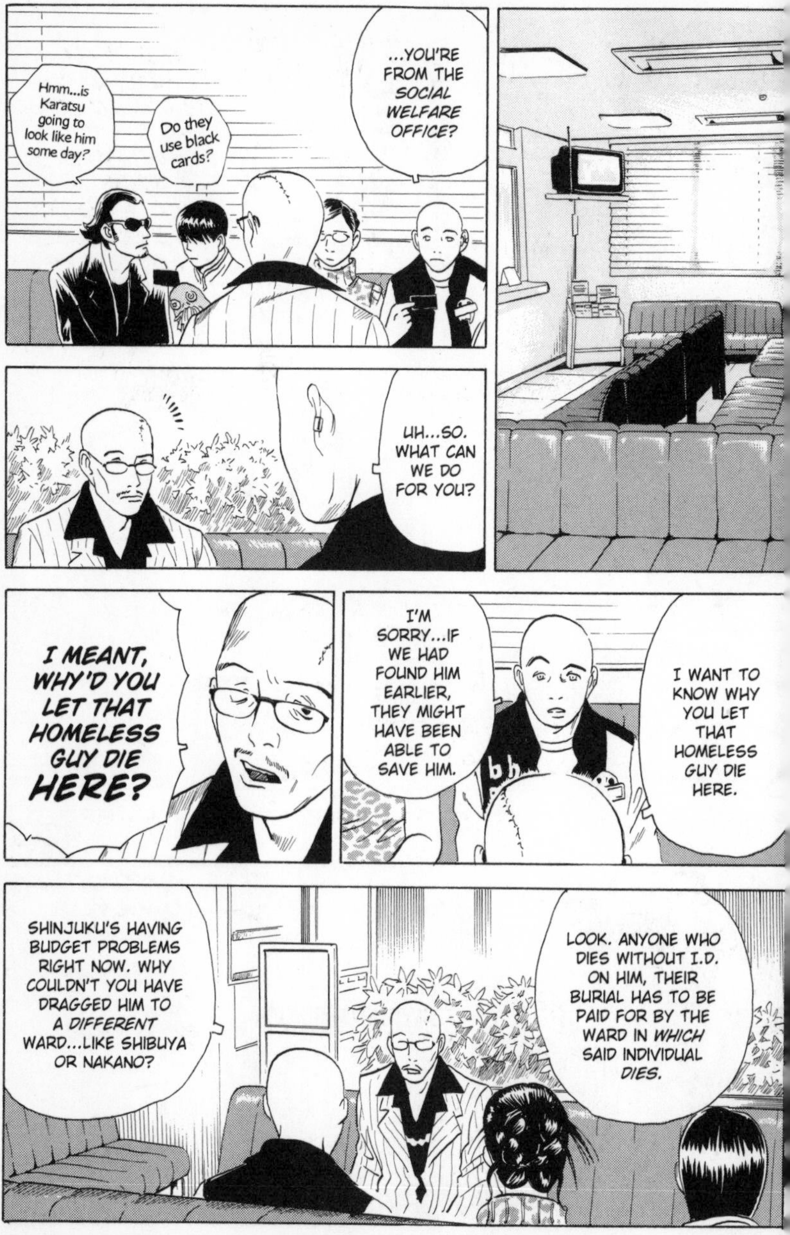
...YOU'RE FROM THE *SOCIAL WELFARE OFFICE?*
Do they use black cards?
Hmm...is Karatsu going to look like him some day?
UH...SO. WHAT CAN WE DO FOR YOU?
I WANT TO KNOW WHY YOU LET THAT HOMELESS GUY DIE HERE.
I'M SORRY...IF WE HAD FOUND HIM EARLIER, THEY MIGHT HAVE BEEN ABLE TO SAVE HIM.
I MEANT, WHY'D YOU LET THAT HOMELESS GUY DIE HERE?
LOOK. ANYONE WHO DIES WITHOUT I.D. ON HIM, THEIR BURIAL HAS TO BE PAID FOR BY THE WARD IN *WHICH* SAID INDIVIDUAL *DIES.*
SHINJUKU'S HAVING BUDGET PROBLEMS RIGHT NOW. WHY COULDN'T YOU HAVE DRAGGED HIM TO A *DIFFERENT* WARD...LIKE SHIBUYA OR NAKANO?

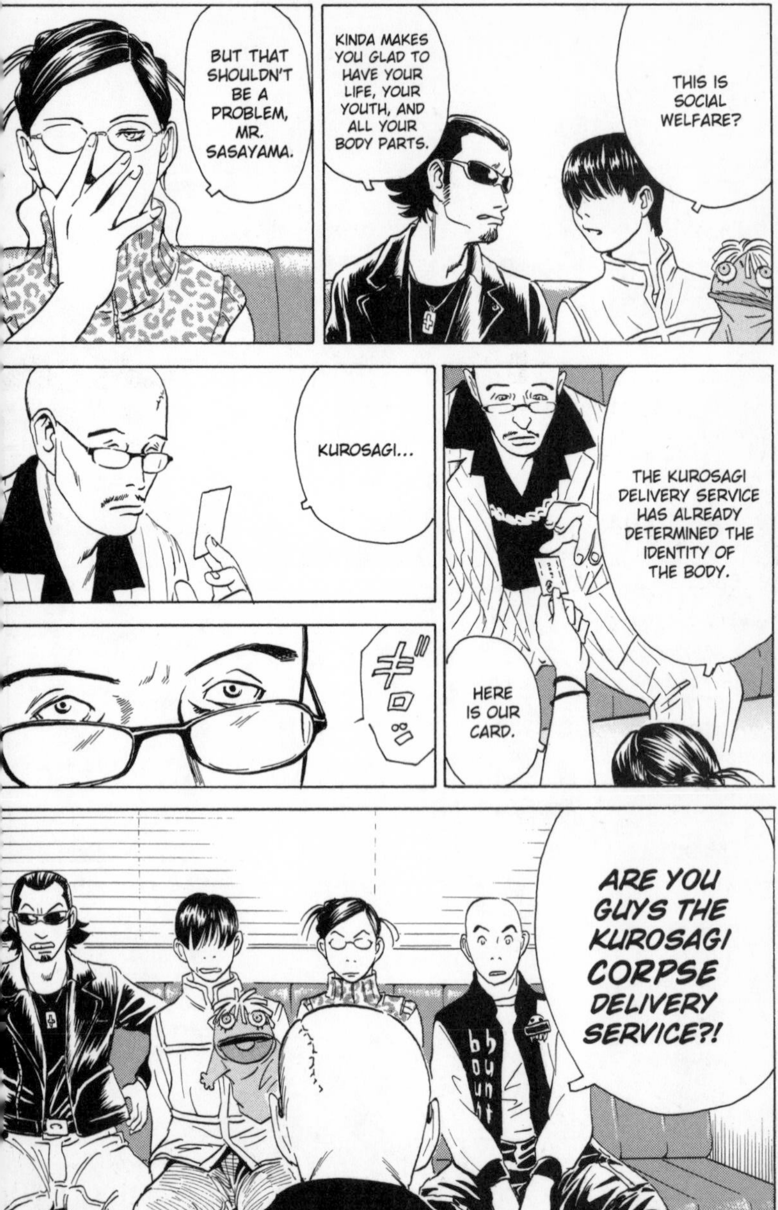
THIS IS SOCIAL WELFARE?
KINDA MAKES YOU GLAD TO HAVE YOUR LIFE, YOUR YOUTH, AND ALL YOUR BODY PARTS.
BUT THAT SHOULDN'T BE A PROBLEM, MR. SASAYAMA.
THE KUROSAGI DELIVERY SERVICE HAS ALREADY DETERMINED THE IDENTITY OF THE BODY.
HERE IS OUR CARD.
KUROSAGI...
ギロッ
ARE YOU GUYS THE KUROSAGI CORPSE DELIVERY SERVICE?!

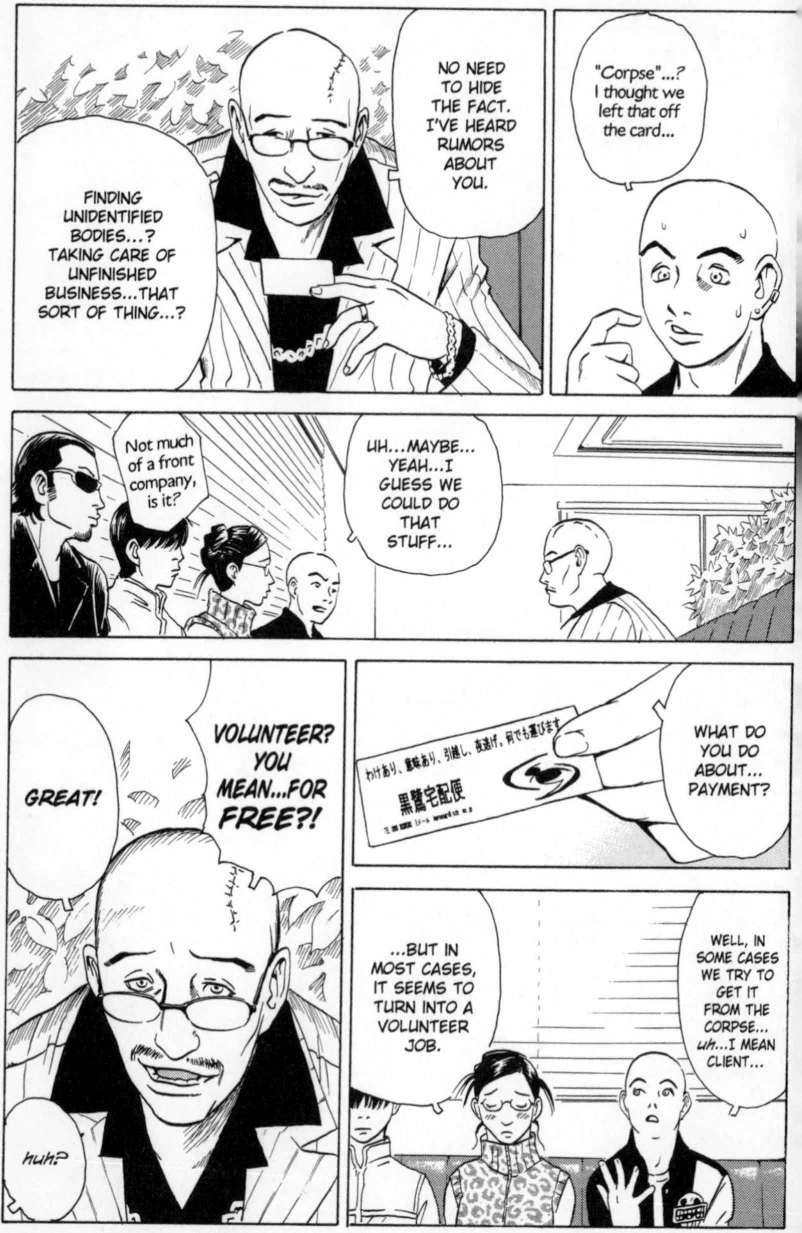
"Corpse"...? I thought we left that off the card...
NO NEED TO HIDE THE FACT. I'VE HEARD RUMORS ABOUT YOU.
FINDING UNIDENTIFIED BODIES...? TAKING CARE OF UNFINISHED BUSINESS...THAT SORT OF THING...?
UH...MAYBE... YEAH...I GUESS WE COULD DO THAT STUFF...
Not much of a front company, is it?
WHAT DO YOU DO ABOUT... PAYMENT?
わけあり、意味あり、引越し、夜逃げ、何でも運びます
黒鷺宅配便
WELL, IN SOME CASES WE TRY TO GET IT FROM THE CORPSE... *uh*...I MEAN CLIENT...
...BUT IN MOST CASES, IT SEEMS TO TURN INTO A VOLUNTEER JOB.
VOLUNTEER? YOU MEAN...FOR FREE?!
GREAT!
huh?

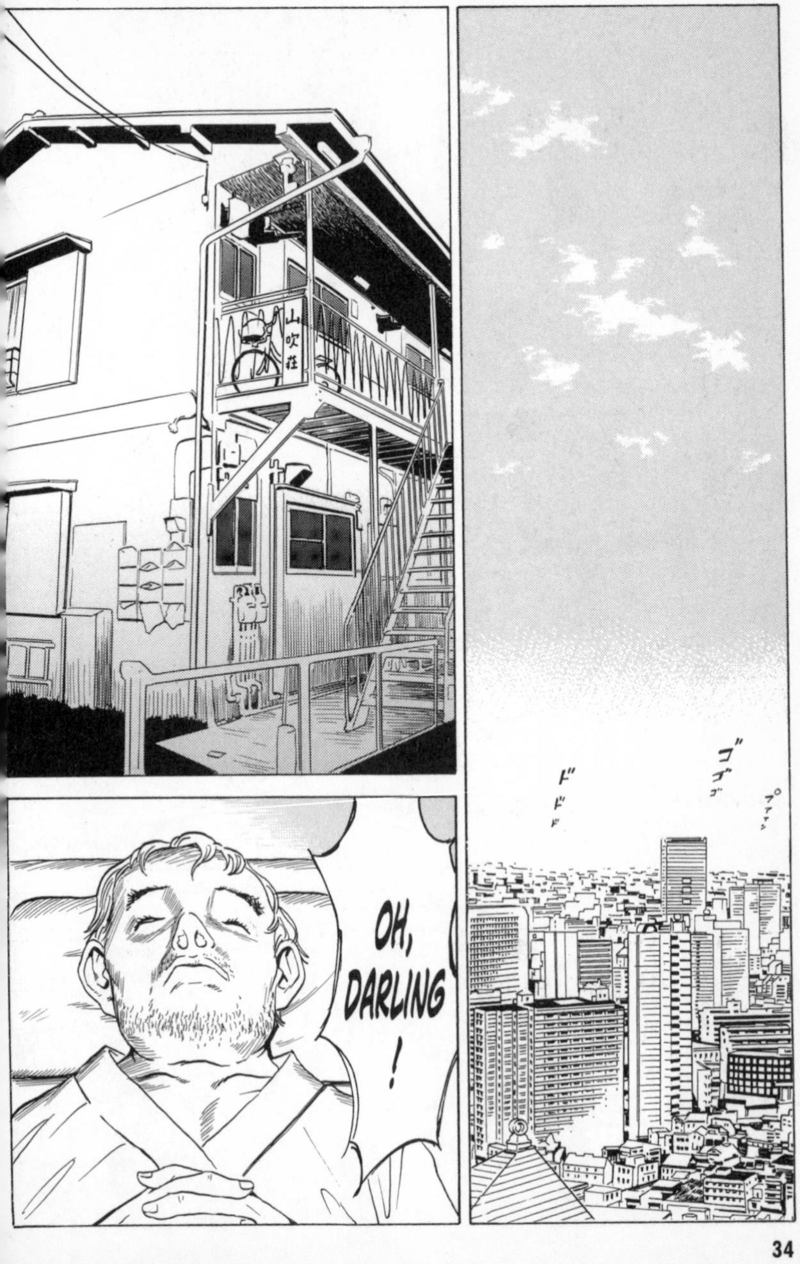
プァァン
ゴゴゴ
ドドド
山吹荘
OH, DARLING!

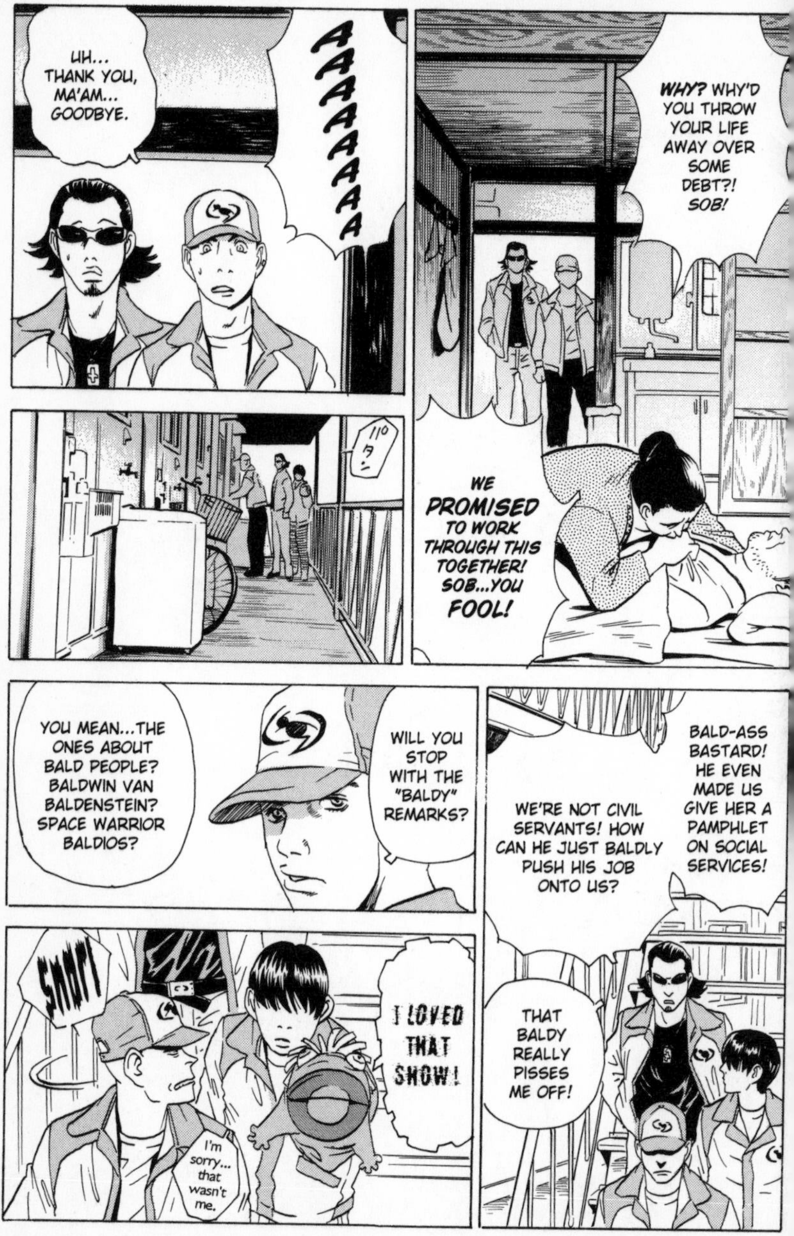
WHY? WHY'D YOU THROW YOUR LIFE AWAY OVER SOME DEBT?! SOB!
WE PROMISED TO WORK THROUGH THIS TOGETHER! SOB...YOU FOOL!
AAAAAAAAA
UH... THANK YOU, MA'AM... GOODBYE.
パタン
BALD-ASS BASTARD! HE EVEN MADE US GIVE HER A PAMPHLET ON SOCIAL SERVICES!
WE'RE NOT CIVIL SERVANTS! HOW CAN HE JUST BALDLY PUSH HIS JOB ONTO US?
THAT BALDY REALLY PISSES ME OFF!
WILL YOU STOP WITH THE "BALDY" REMARKS?
YOU MEAN...THE ONES ABOUT BALD PEOPLE? BALDWIN VAN BALDENSTEIN? SPACE WARRIOR BALDIOS?
I LOVED THAT SHOW!
Snort
I'm sorry... that wasn't me.

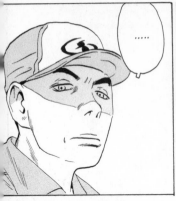

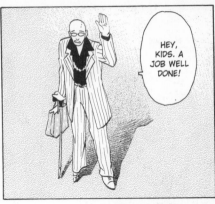

HEY, KIDS. A JOB WELL DONE!
.....
WHAT DO YOU WANT *NOW*, ER... BALDY?
DON'T BE SO CONFRONTA-TIONAL, SON.
I BROUGHT YOU A PRESENT. IT'S NOT A GIFT OF THE *HEART*...
...IT'S A LITTLE BIT LOWER DOWN.
ドサッ

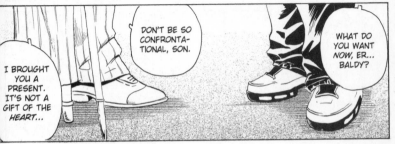

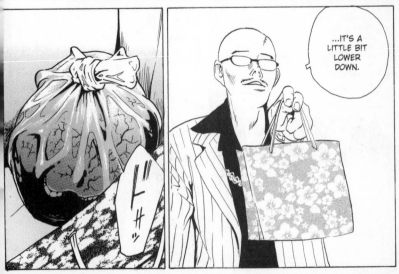

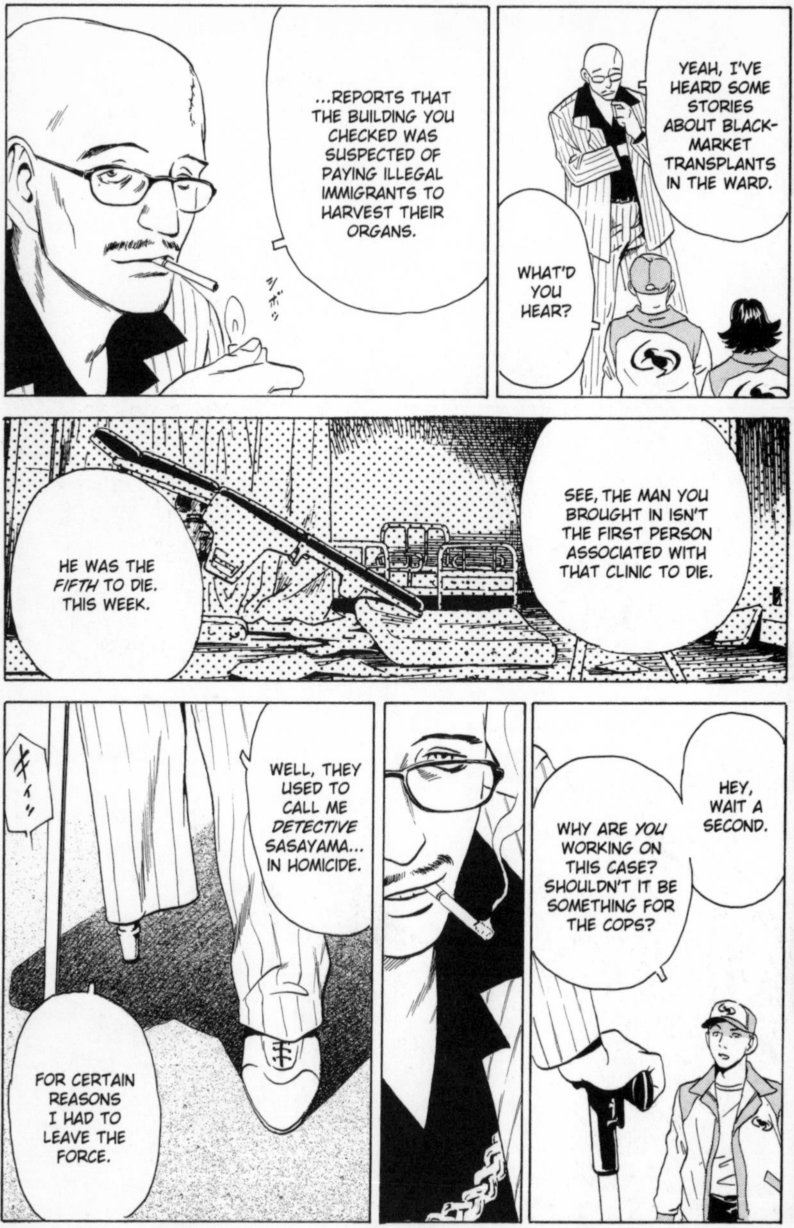
YEAH, I'VE HEARD SOME STORIES ABOUT BLACK-MARKET TRANSPLANTS IN THE WARD.
WHAT'D YOU HEAR?
...REPORTS THAT THE BUILDING YOU CHECKED WAS SUSPECTED OF PAYING ILLEGAL IMMIGRANTS TO HARVEST THEIR ORGANS.
シボッ
SEE, THE MAN YOU BROUGHT IN ISN'T THE FIRST PERSON ASSOCIATED WITH THAT CLINIC TO DIE.
HE WAS THE *FIFTH* TO DIE. THIS WEEK.
HEY, WAIT A SECOND.
WHY ARE *YOU* WORKING ON THIS CASE? SHOULDN'T IT BE SOMETHING FOR THE COPS?
WELL, THEY USED TO CALL ME *DETECTIVE* SASAYAMA... IN HOMICIDE.
キィッ
FOR CERTAIN REASONS I HAD TO LEAVE THE FORCE.

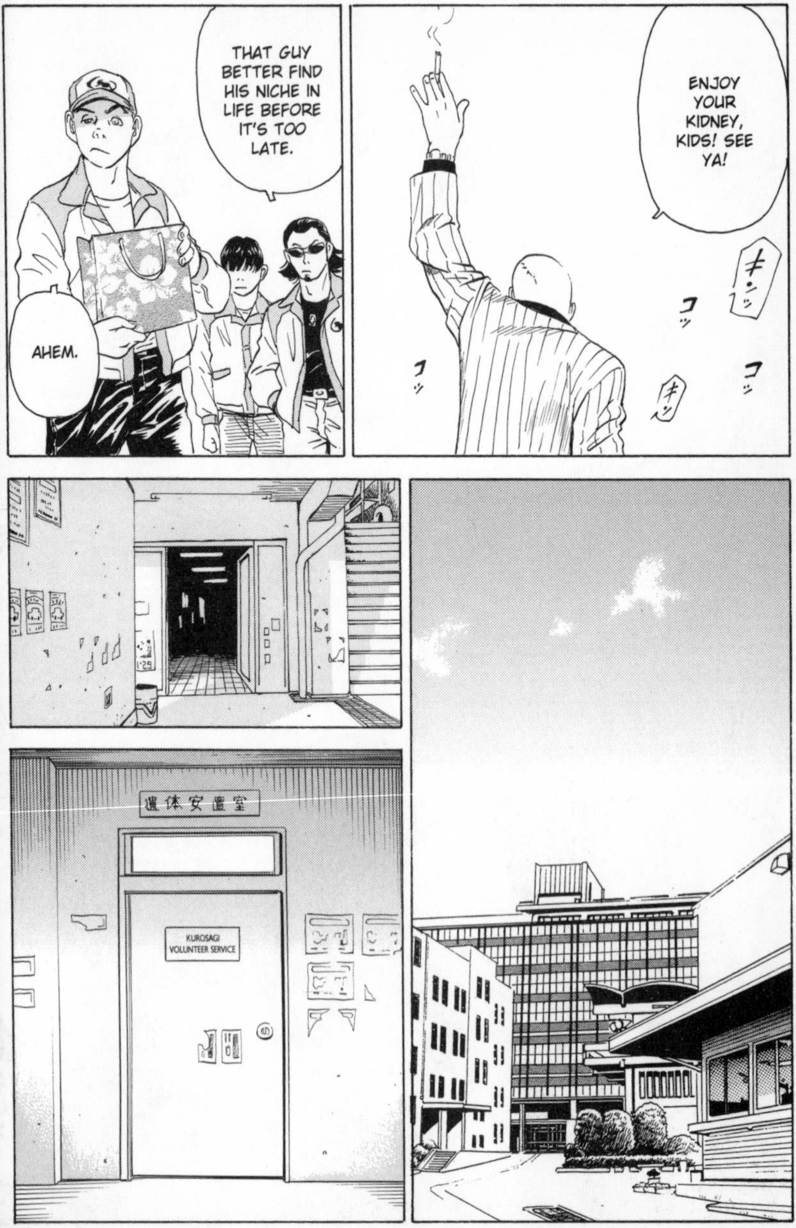
ENJOY YOUR KIDNEY, KIDS! SEE YA!
コッ
コッ
コッ
THAT GUY BETTER FIND HIS NICHE IN LIFE BEFORE IT'S TOO LATE.
AHEM.
遺体安置室
KUROSAGI VOLUNTEER SERVICE

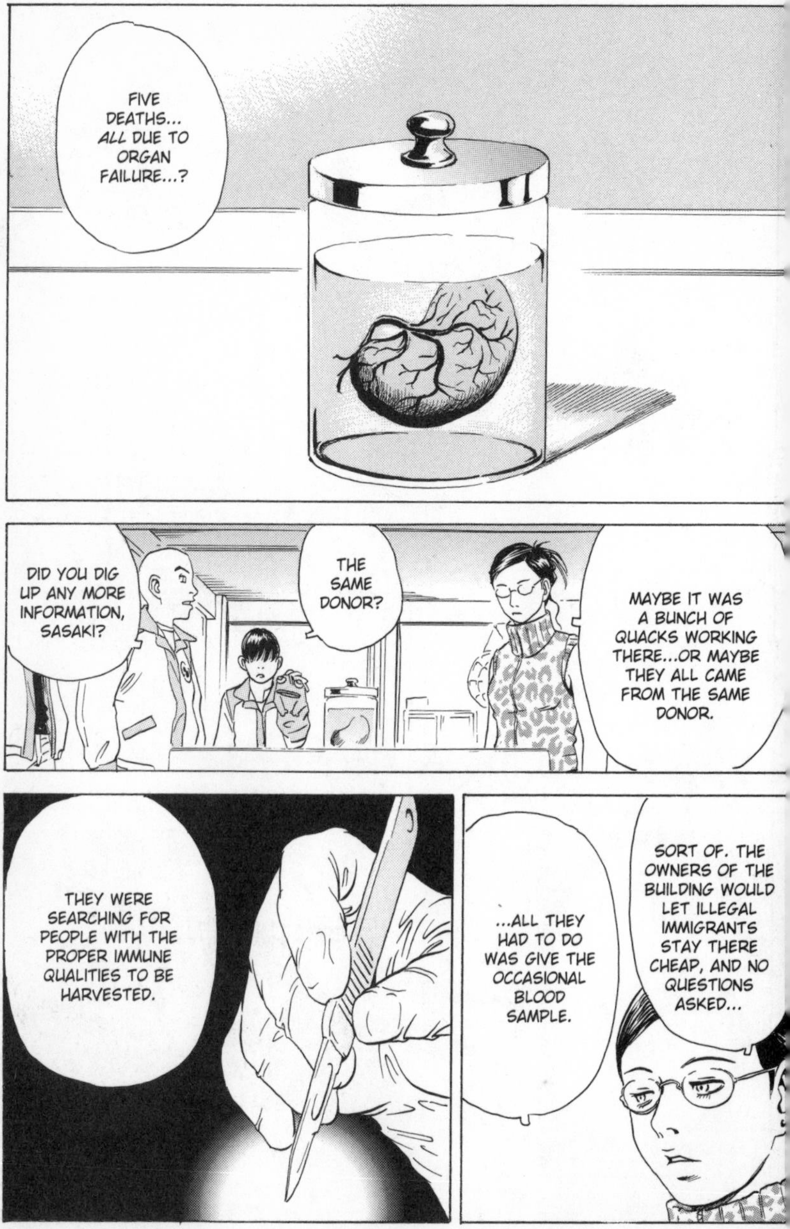
FIVE DEATHS... ALL DUE TO ORGAN FAILURE...?
MAYBE IT WAS A BUNCH OF QUACKS WORKING THERE...OR MAYBE THEY ALL CAME FROM THE SAME DONOR.
THE SAME DONOR?
DID YOU DIG UP ANY MORE INFORMATION, SASAKI?
SORT OF. THE OWNERS OF THE BUILDING WOULD LET ILLEGAL IMMIGRANTS STAY THERE CHEAP, AND NO QUESTIONS ASKED...
...ALL THEY HAD TO DO WAS GIVE THE OCCASIONAL BLOOD SAMPLE.
THEY WERE SEARCHING FOR PEOPLE WITH THE PROPER IMMUNE QUALITIES TO BE HARVESTED.

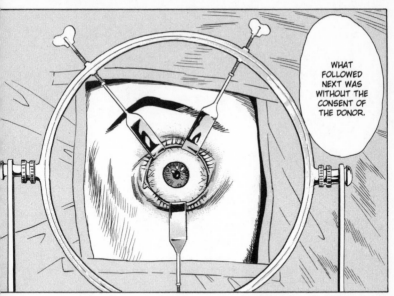

WHAT FOLLOWED NEXT WAS WITHOUT THE CONSENT OF THE DONOR.

IT'S AMAZING HOW MANY THINGS CAN BE REMOVED FROM A BODY BEFORE IT DIES.

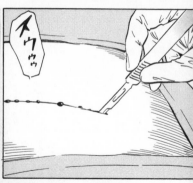

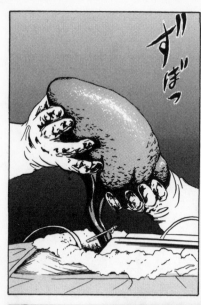

スウゥゥ
ガパッ
ずずぼっ
TO KEEP THEM AS FRESH AS POSSIBLE, THEY BEGAN WITH THE ORGANS UNNECESSARY FOR SURVIVAL.
TWO EYES... A LENGTH OF INTESTINE...ONE LUNG...AND ONE KIDNEY.
ブスウゥ
ズブリ
グチュ

SOMEHOW HE NOT ONLY MANAGED TO LIVE...

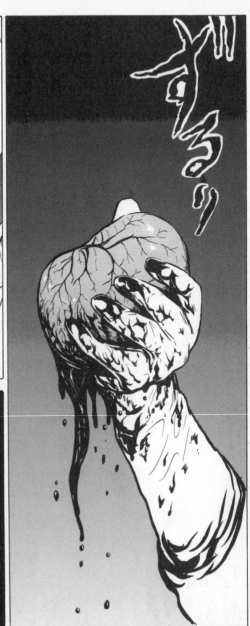

...BUT BLIND AND SUTURED, HE ESCAPED THEM.

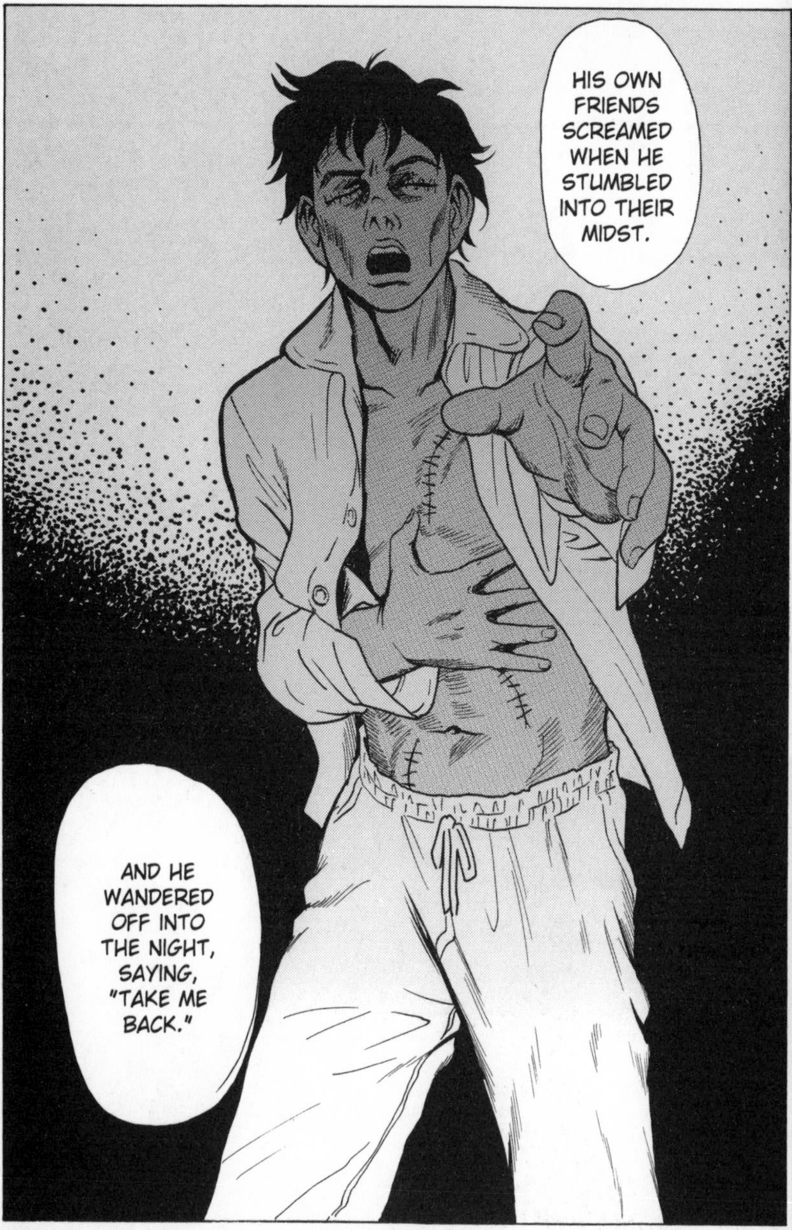
HIS OWN FRIENDS SCREAMED WHEN HE STUMBLED INTO THEIR MIDST.
AND HE WANDERED OFF INTO THE NIGHT, SAYING, "TAKE ME BACK."

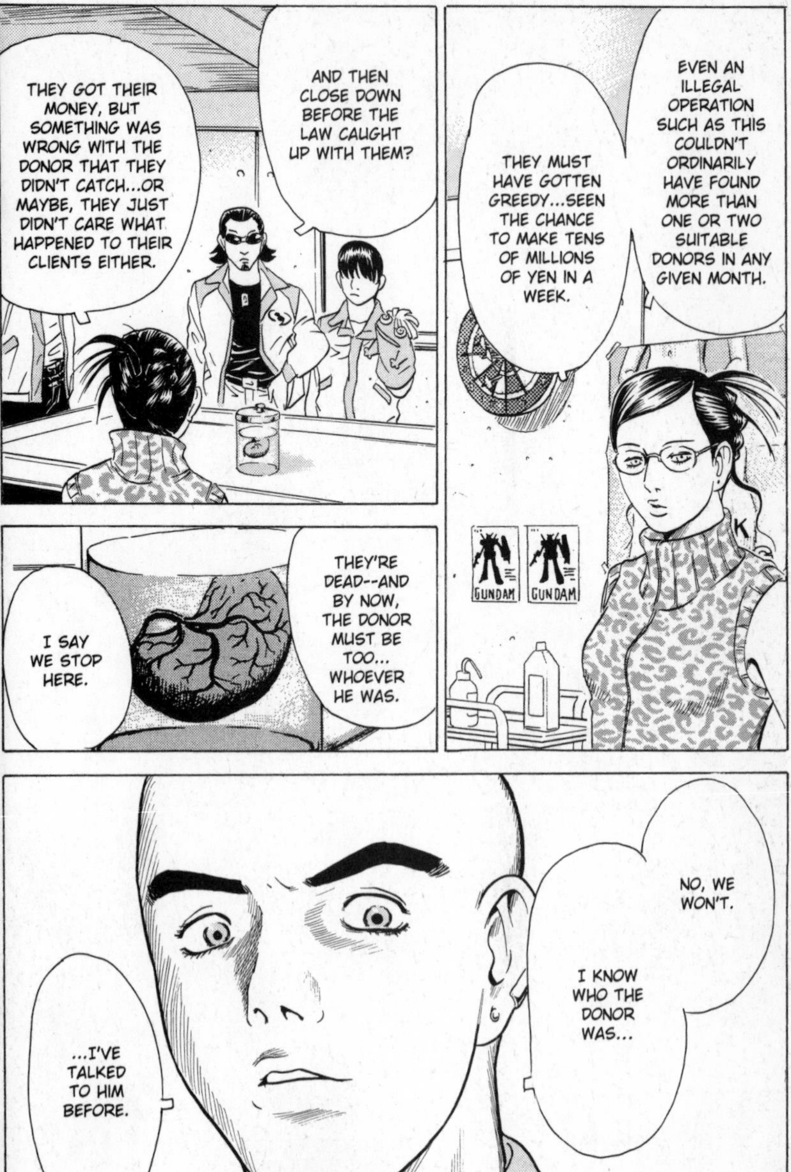
EVEN AN ILLEGAL OPERATION SUCH AS THIS COULDN'T ORDINARILY HAVE FOUND MORE THAN ONE OR TWO SUITABLE DONORS IN ANY GIVEN MONTH.
THEY MUST HAVE GOTTEN GREEDY...SEEN THE CHANCE TO MAKE TENS OF MILLIONS OF YEN IN A WEEK.
GUNDAM
GUNDAM
AND THEN CLOSE DOWN BEFORE THE LAW CAUGHT UP WITH THEM?
THEY GOT THEIR MONEY, BUT SOMETHING WAS WRONG WITH THE DONOR THAT THEY DIDN'T CATCH...OR MAYBE, THEY JUST DIDN'T CARE WHAT HAPPENED TO THEIR CLIENTS EITHER.
THEY'RE DEAD--AND BY NOW, THE DONOR MUST BE TOO... WHOEVER HE WAS.
I SAY WE STOP HERE.
NO, WE WON'T.
I KNOW WHO THE DONOR WAS...
...I'VE TALKED TO HIM BEFORE.

1st delivery: crossing the river—the end

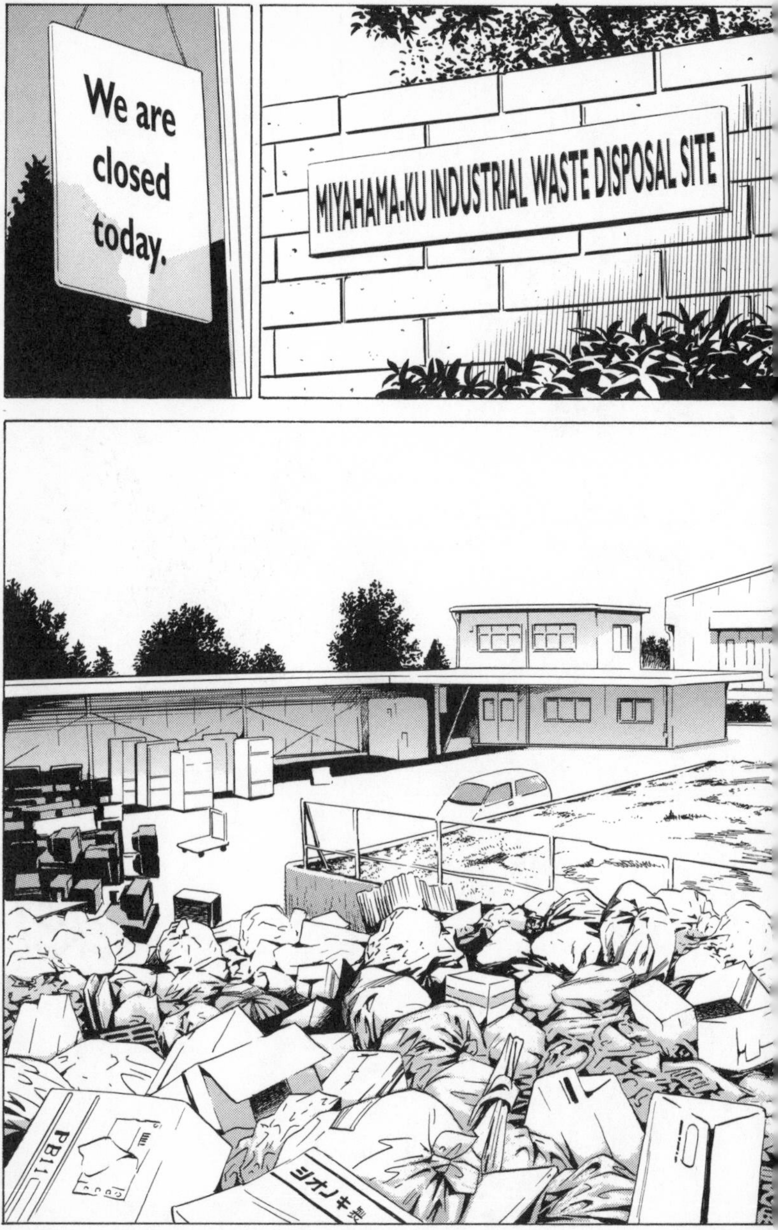
MIYAHAMA-KU INDUSTRIAL WASTE DISPOSAL SITE
We are closed today.
PB11
シオノキ

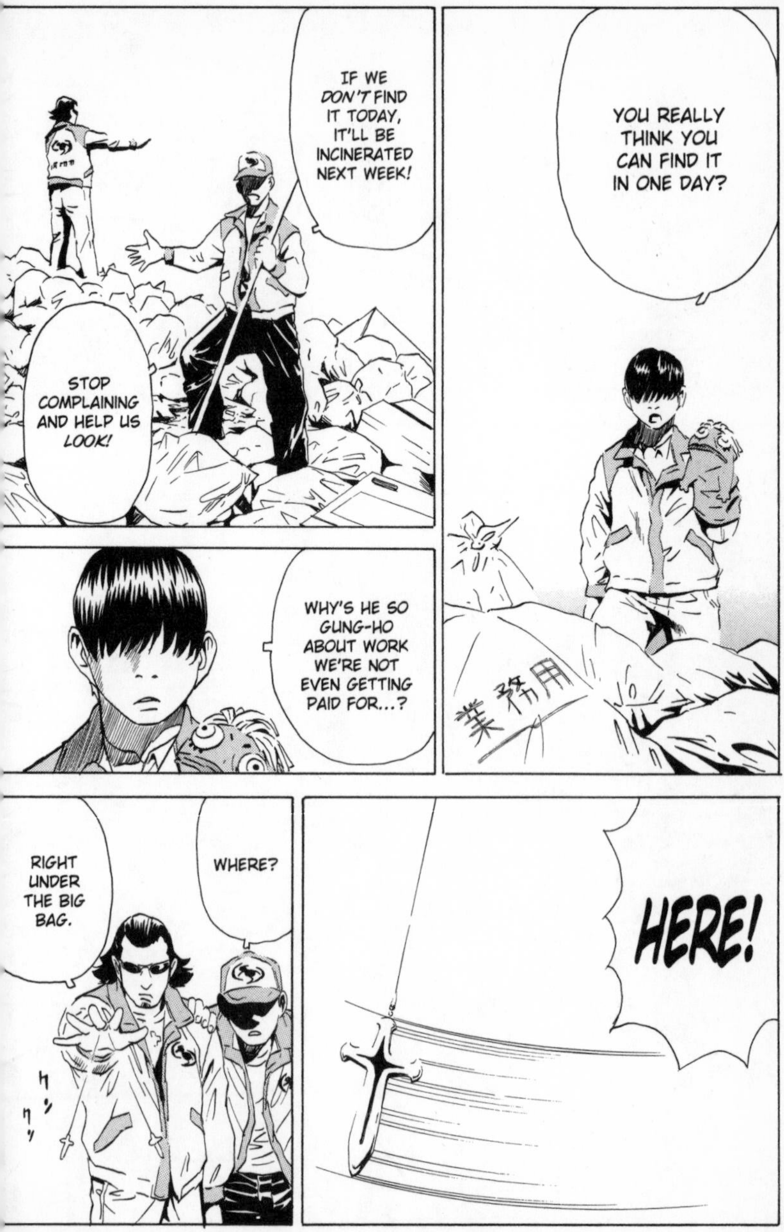
IF WE DON'T FIND IT TODAY, IT'LL BE INCINERATED NEXT WEEK!
STOP COMPLAINING AND HELP US LOOK!
YOU REALLY THINK YOU CAN FIND IT IN ONE DAY?
業務用
WHY'S HE SO GUNG-HO ABOUT WORK WE'RE NOT EVEN GETTING PAID FOR...?
WHERE?
RIGHT UNDER THE BIG BAG.
HERE!

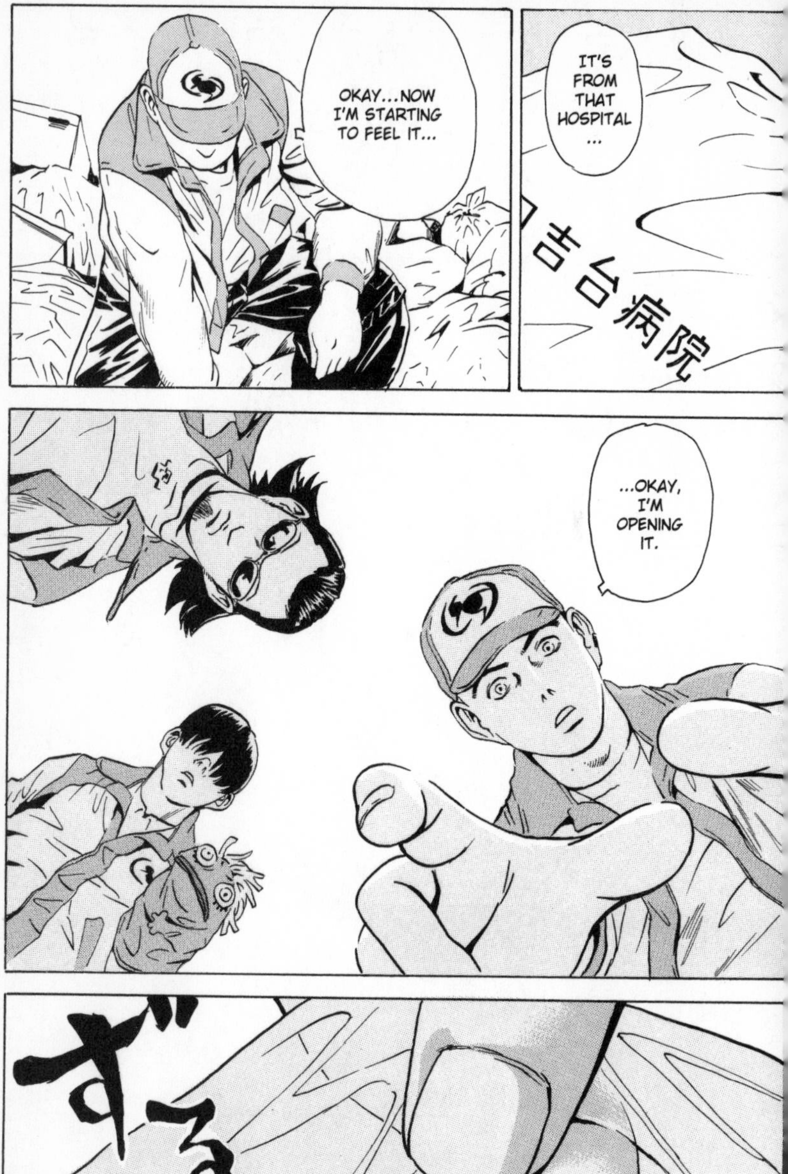
IT'S FROM THAT HOSPITAL ...
吉台病院
OKAY...NOW I'M STARTING TO FEEL IT...
...OKAY, I'M OPENING IT.
ずるっ

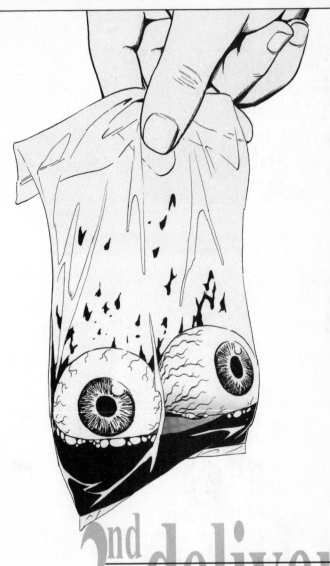

2nd delivery
applause 喝采

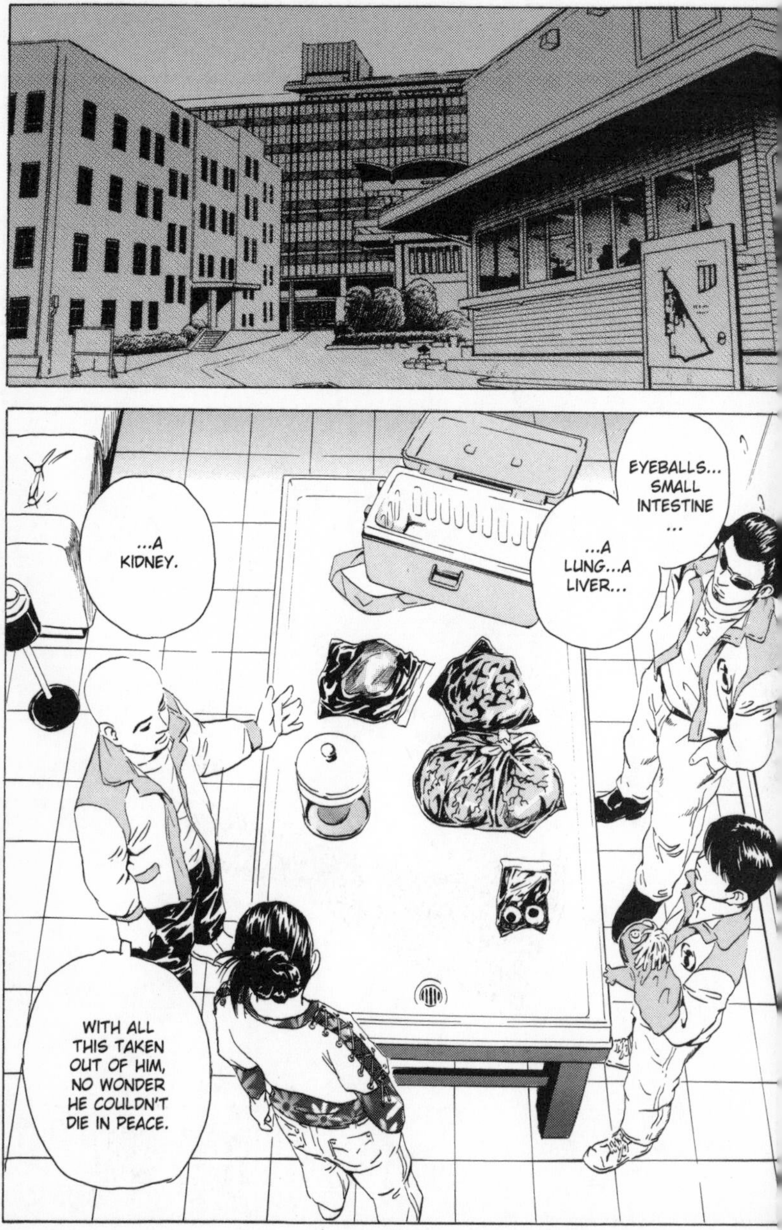
EYEBALLS... SMALL INTESTINE ...
...A LUNG...A LIVER...
...A KIDNEY.
WITH ALL THIS TAKEN OUT OF HIM, NO WONDER HE COULDN'T DIE IN PEACE.

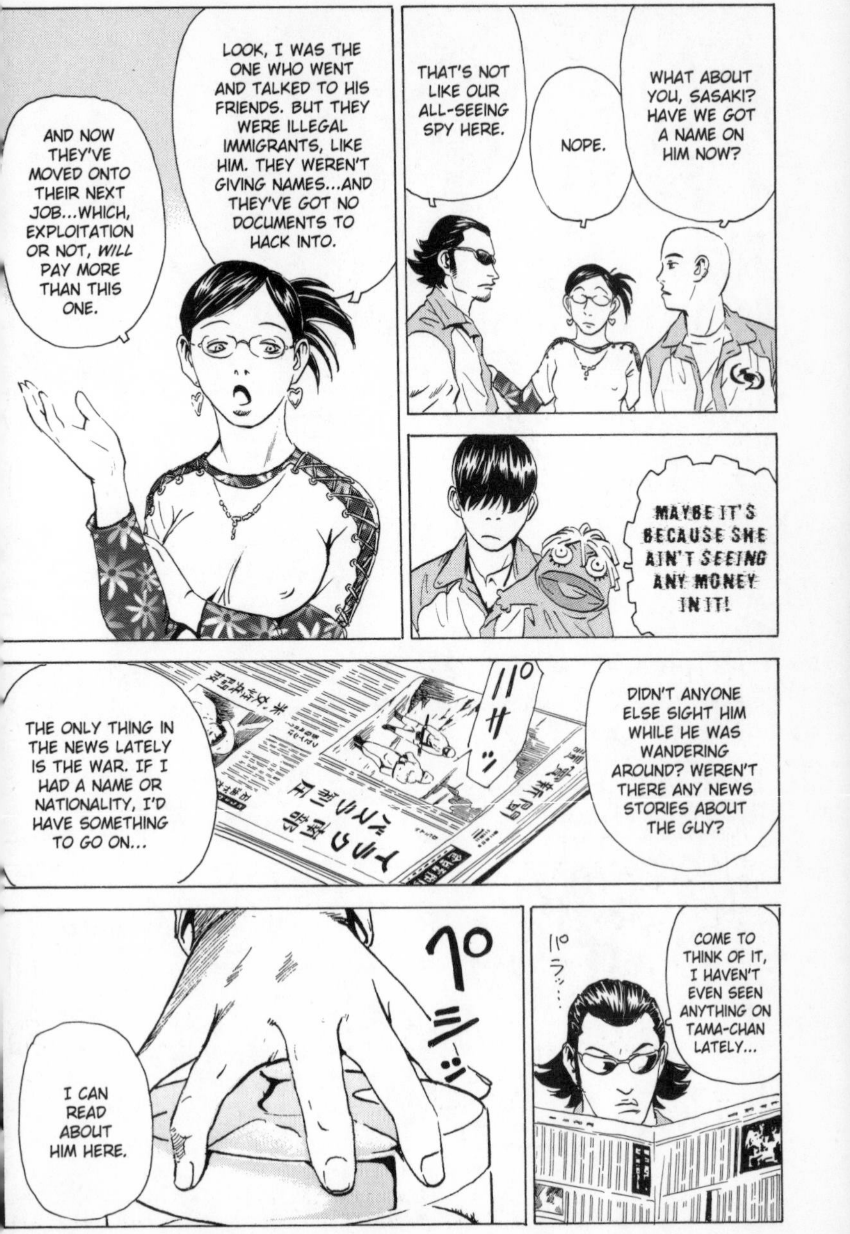

WHAT ABOUT YOU, SASAKI? HAVE WE GOT A NAME ON HIM NOW?
NOPE.
THAT'S NOT LIKE OUR ALL-SEEING SPY HERE.
MAYBE IT'S BECAUSE SHE AIN'T *SEEING* ANY MONEY IN IT!
LOOK, I WAS THE ONE WHO WENT AND TALKED TO HIS FRIENDS. BUT THEY WERE ILLEGAL IMMIGRANTS, LIKE HIM. THEY WEREN'T GIVING NAMES...AND THEY'VE GOT NO DOCUMENTS TO HACK INTO.
AND NOW THEY'VE MOVED ONTO THEIR NEXT JOB...WHICH, EXPLOITATION OR NOT, *WILL* PAY MORE THAN THIS ONE.
DIDN'T ANYONE ELSE SIGHT HIM WHILE HE WAS WANDERING AROUND? WEREN'T THERE ANY NEWS STORIES ABOUT THE GUY?
パサッ
THE ONLY THING IN THE NEWS LATELY IS THE WAR. IF I HAD A NAME OR NATIONALITY, I'D HAVE SOMETHING TO GO ON...
パラッ…
COME TO THINK OF IT, I HAVEN'T EVEN SEEN ANYTHING ON TAMA-CHAN LATELY...
ペシッ
I CAN READ ABOUT HIM HERE.

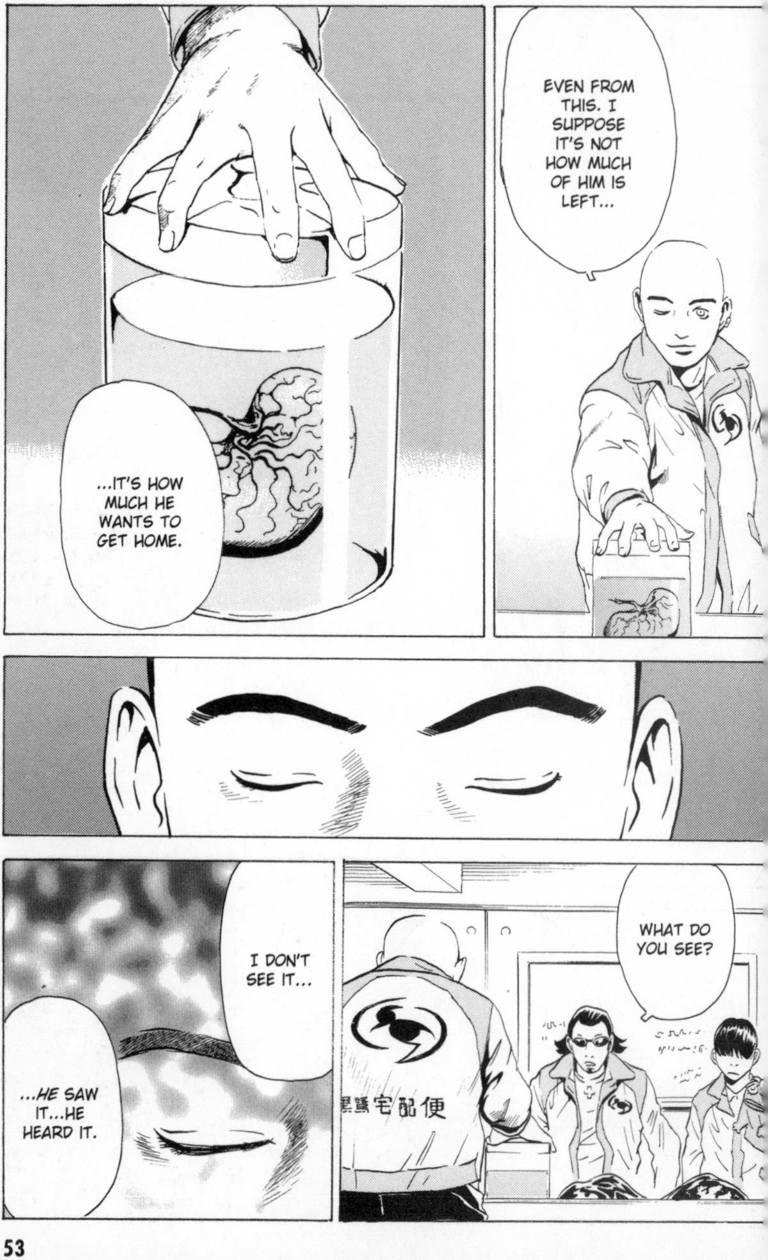
EVEN FROM THIS. I SUPPOSE IT'S NOT HOW MUCH OF HIM IS LEFT...
...IT'S HOW MUCH HE WANTS TO GET HOME.
WHAT DO YOU SEE?
黒鷺宅配便
I DON'T SEE IT...
...*HE* SAW IT...HE HEARD IT.

...SMOKE...
THE SOUND
OF
THUNDER...
FIRE...

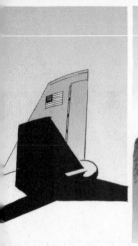

...NO.

...WAS
IT AN
ACCIDENT
...?

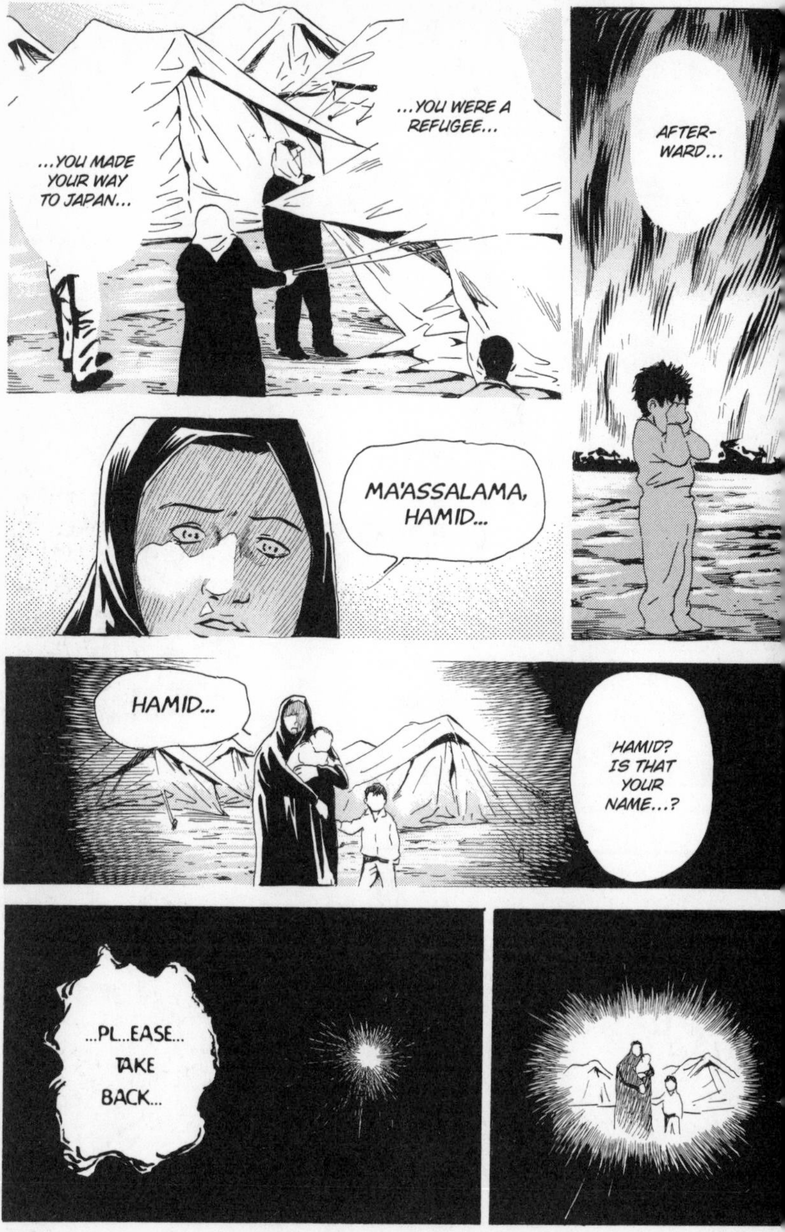
AFTER-WARD...
...YOU WERE A REFUGEE...
...YOU MADE YOUR WAY TO JAPAN...
MA'ASSALAMA, HAMID...
HAMID? IS THAT YOUR NAME...?
HAMID...
...PL...EASE... TAKE BACK...

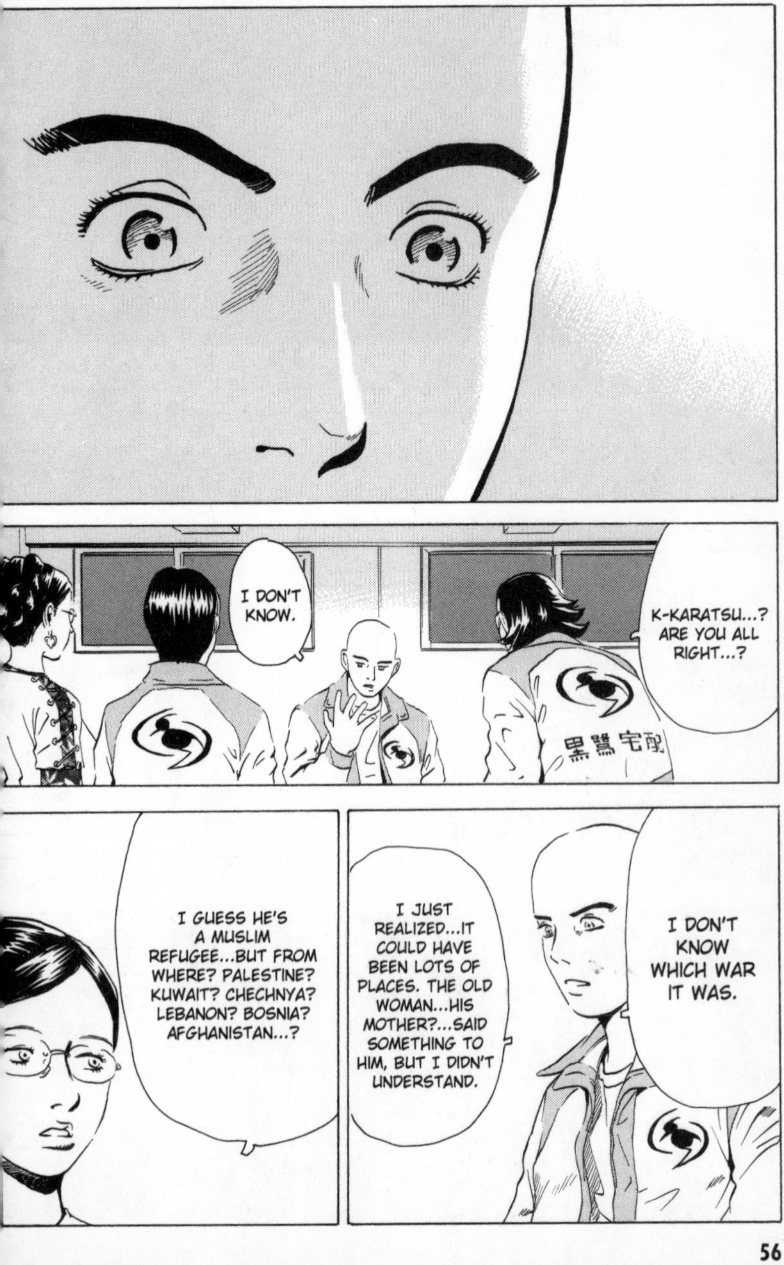
K-KARATSU...? ARE YOU ALL RIGHT...?
I DON'T KNOW.
黒鷺宅配
I DON'T KNOW WHICH WAR IT WAS.
I JUST REALIZED...IT COULD HAVE BEEN LOTS OF PLACES. THE OLD WOMAN...HIS MOTHER?...SAID SOMETHING TO HIM, BUT I DIDN'T UNDERSTAND.
I GUESS HE'S A MUSLIM REFUGEE...BUT FROM WHERE? PALESTINE? KUWAIT? CHECHNYA? LEBANON? BOSNIA? AFGHANISTAN...?

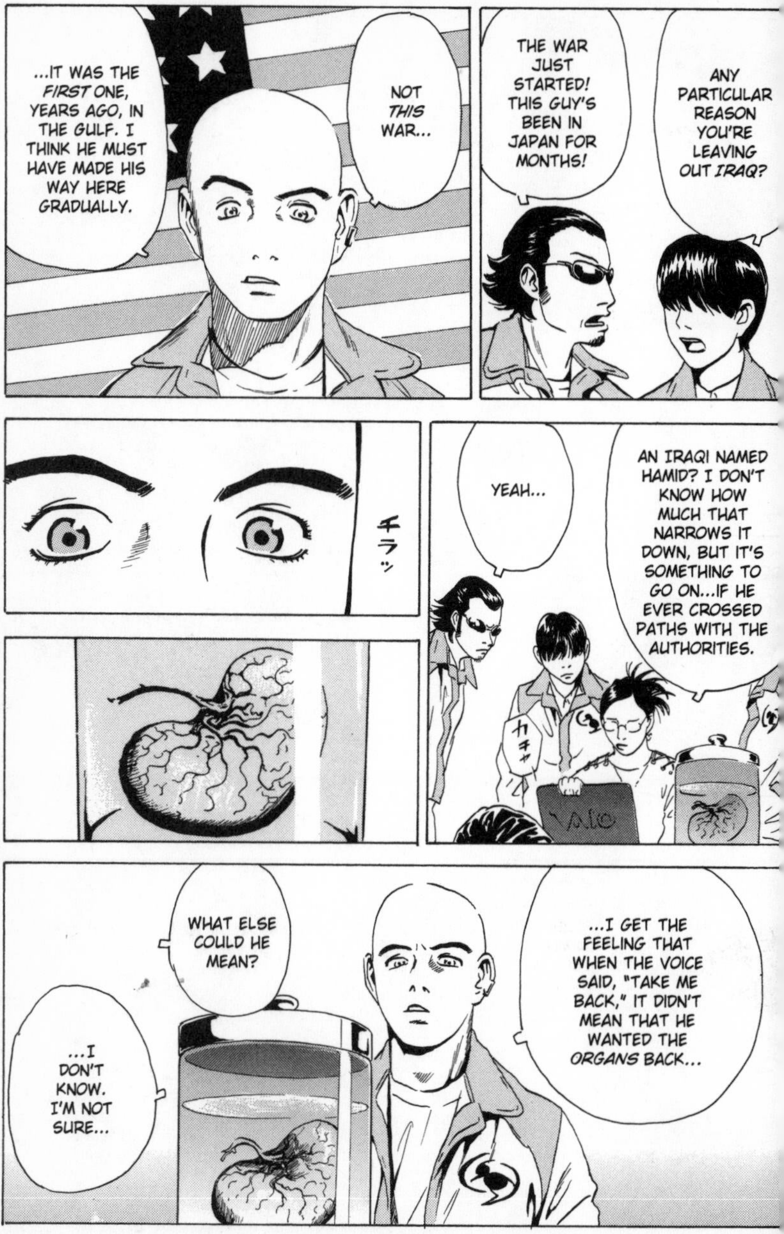
ANY PARTICULAR REASON YOU'RE LEAVING OUT *IRAQ?*
THE WAR JUST STARTED! THIS GUY'S BEEN IN JAPAN FOR MONTHS!
NOT *THIS* WAR...
...IT WAS THE *FIRST* ONE, YEARS AGO, IN THE GULF. I THINK HE MUST HAVE MADE HIS WAY HERE GRADUALLY.
AN IRAQI NAMED HAMID? I DON'T KNOW HOW MUCH THAT NARROWS IT DOWN, BUT IT'S SOMETHING TO GO ON...IF HE EVER CROSSED PATHS WITH THE AUTHORITIES.
YEAH...
カチャ
チラッ
...I GET THE FEELING THAT WHEN THE VOICE SAID, "TAKE ME BACK," IT DIDN'T MEAN THAT HE WANTED THE *ORGANS* BACK...
WHAT ELSE COULD HE MEAN?
...I DON'T KNOW. I'M NOT SURE...

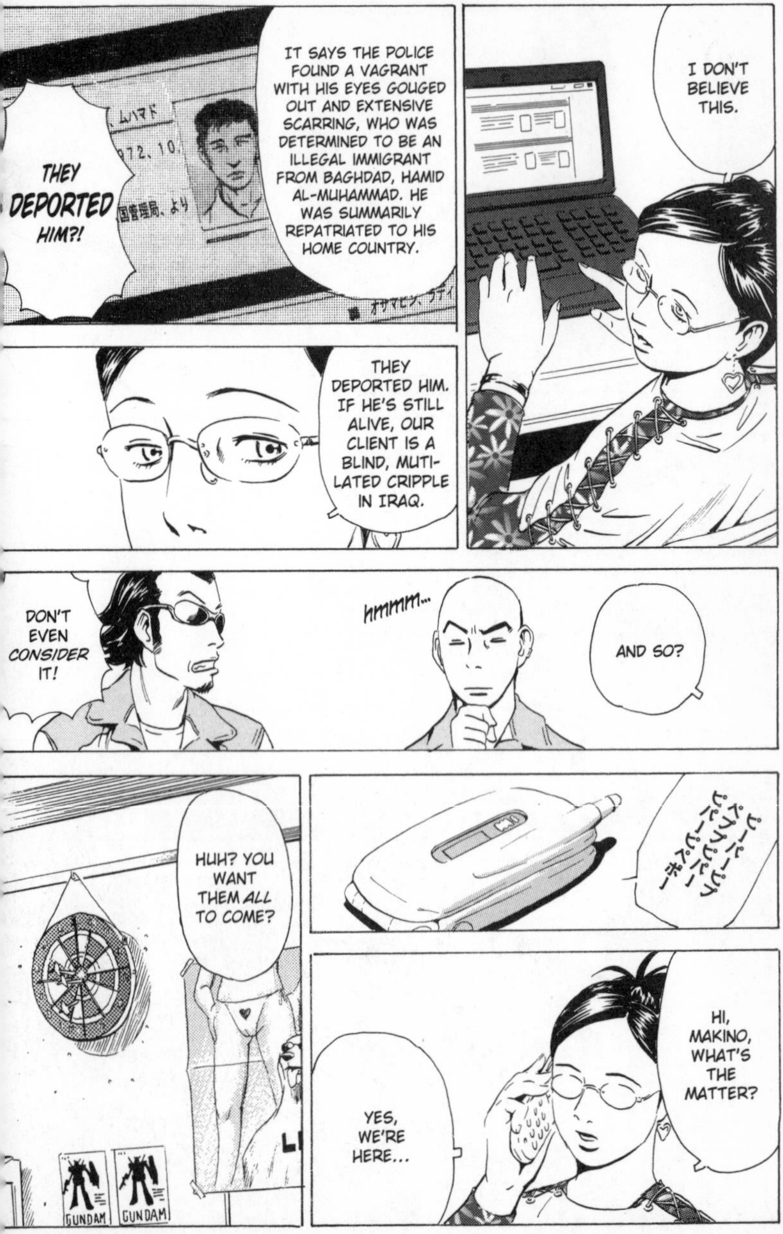
I DON'T BELIEVE THIS.
IT SAYS THE POLICE FOUND A VAGRANT WITH HIS EYES GOUGED OUT AND EXTENSIVE SCARRING, WHO WAS DETERMINED TO BE AN ILLEGAL IMMIGRANT FROM BAGHDAD, HAMID AL-MUHAMMAD. HE WAS SUMMARILY REPATRIATED TO HIS HOME COUNTRY.
THEY *DEPORTED* HIM?!
THEY DEPORTED HIM. IF HE'S STILL ALIVE, OUR CLIENT IS A BLIND, MUTI-LATED CRIPPLE IN IRAQ.
AND SO?
hmmmm...
DON'T EVEN *CONSIDER* IT!
ピーパーピプ ペプピパー ピーピペポー
HI, MAKINO, WHAT'S THE MATTER?
YES, WE'RE HERE...
HUH? YOU WANT THEM *ALL* TO COME?
GUNDAM
GUNDAM

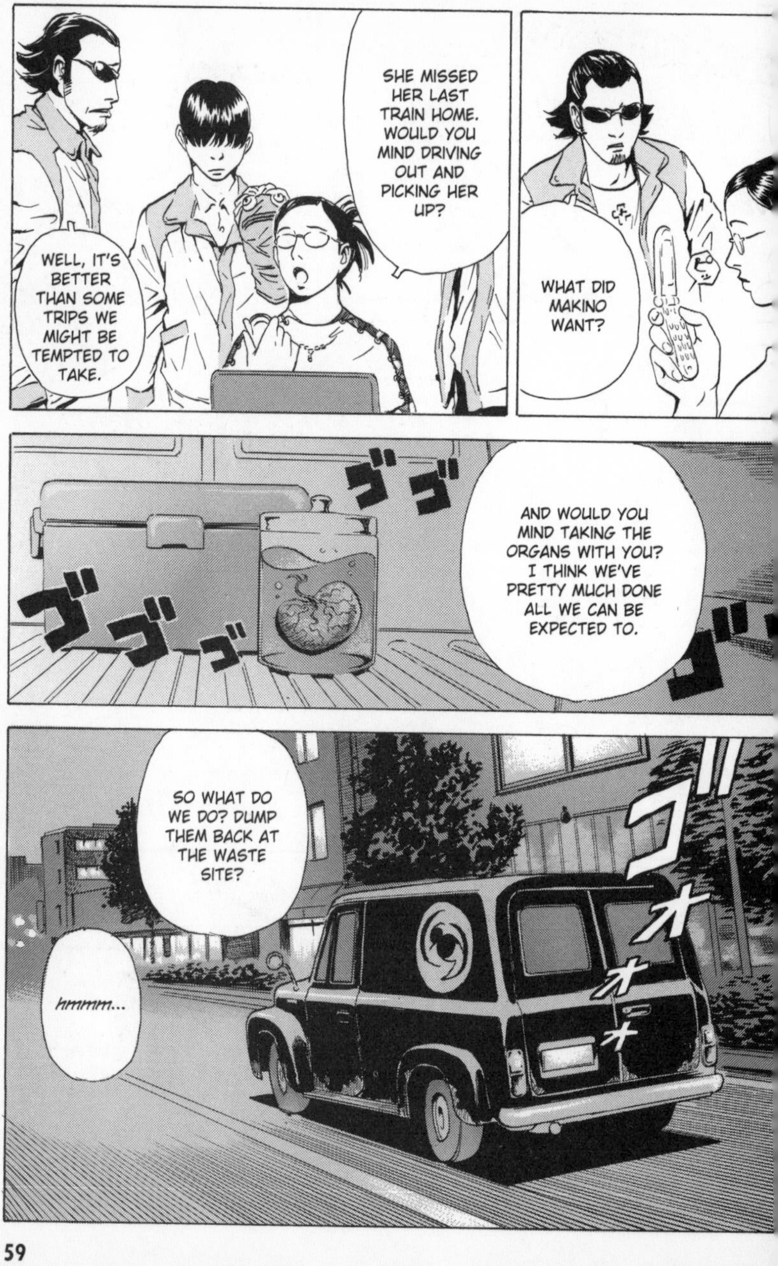
WHAT DID MAKINO WANT?
SHE MISSED HER LAST TRAIN HOME. WOULD YOU MIND DRIVING OUT AND PICKING HER UP?
WELL, IT'S BETTER THAN SOME TRIPS WE MIGHT BE TEMPTED TO TAKE.
AND WOULD YOU MIND TAKING THE ORGANS WITH YOU? I THINK WE'VE PRETTY MUCH DONE ALL WE CAN BE EXPECTED TO.
ゴゴ
ゴゴゴ
SO WHAT DO WE DO? DUMP THEM BACK AT THE WASTE SITE?
hmmm...
ゴォォォ

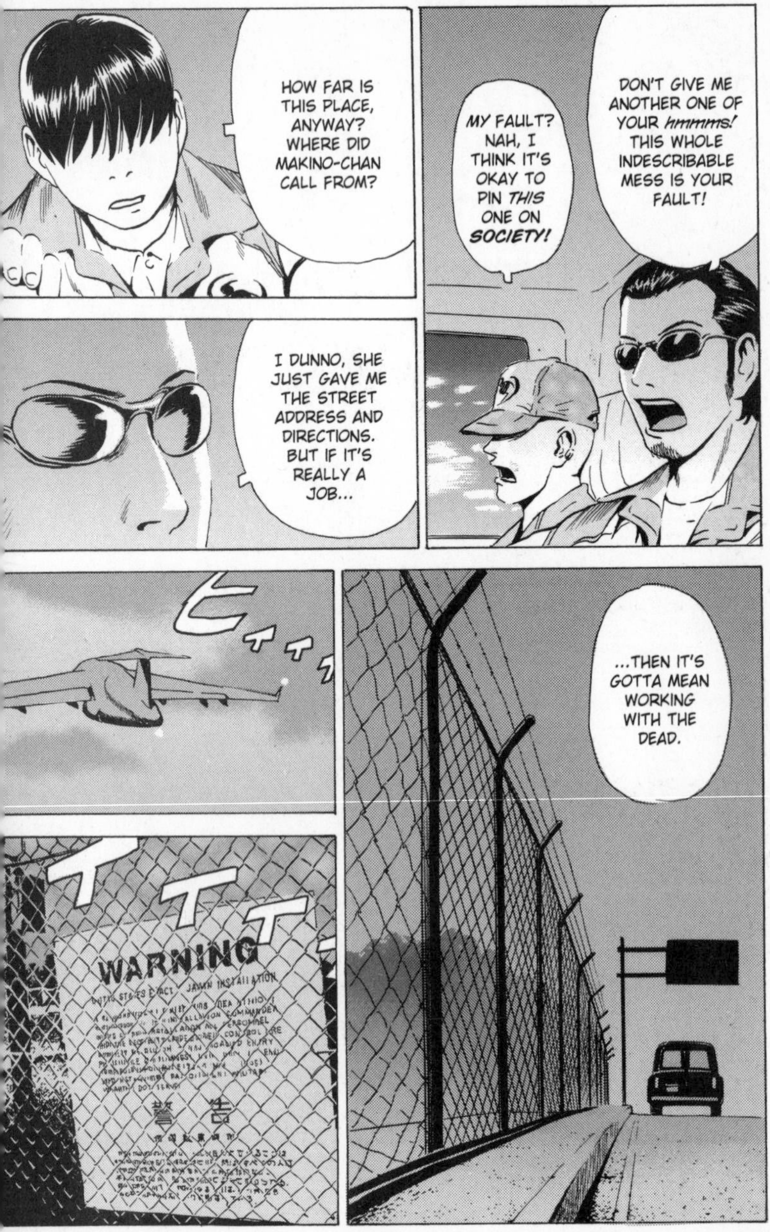
DON'T GIVE ME ANOTHER ONE OF YOUR *hmmmms!* THIS WHOLE INDESCRIBABLE MESS IS YOUR FAULT!
MY FAULT? NAH, I THINK IT'S OKAY TO PIN *THIS* ONE ON ***SOCIETY!***
HOW FAR IS THIS PLACE, ANYWAY? WHERE DID MAKINO-CHAN CALL FROM?
I DUNNO, SHE JUST GAVE ME THE STREET ADDRESS AND DIRECTIONS. BUT IF IT'S REALLY A JOB...
...THEN IT'S GOTTA MEAN WORKING WITH THE DEAD.
WARNING
警告

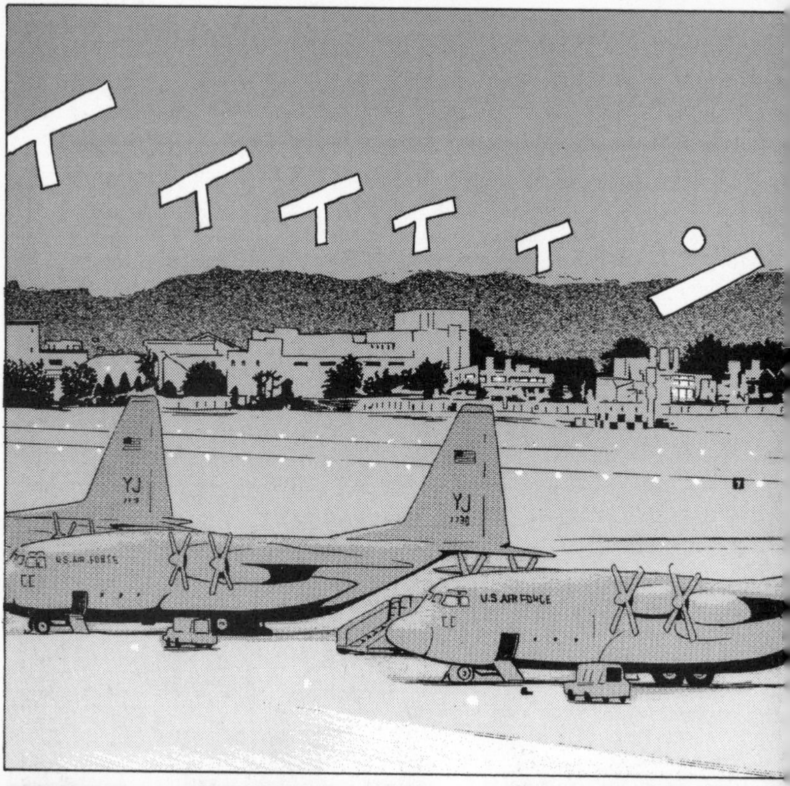
イイイイイン
YJ
YJ
U.S. AIR FORCE
U.S. AIR FORCE

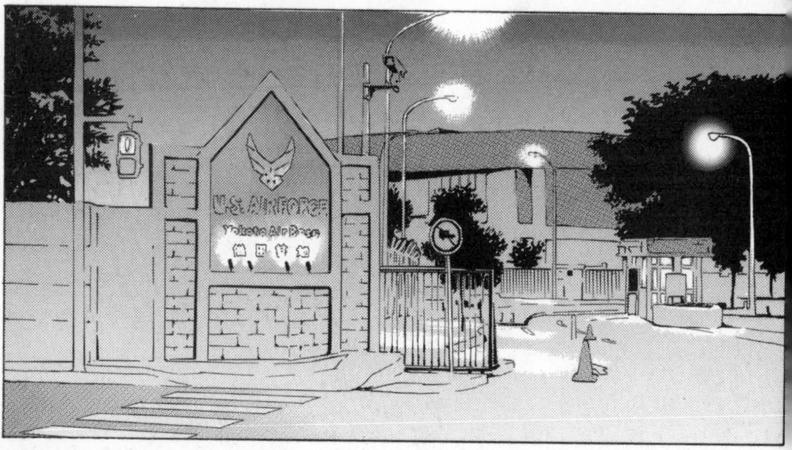
U.S. AIR FORCE

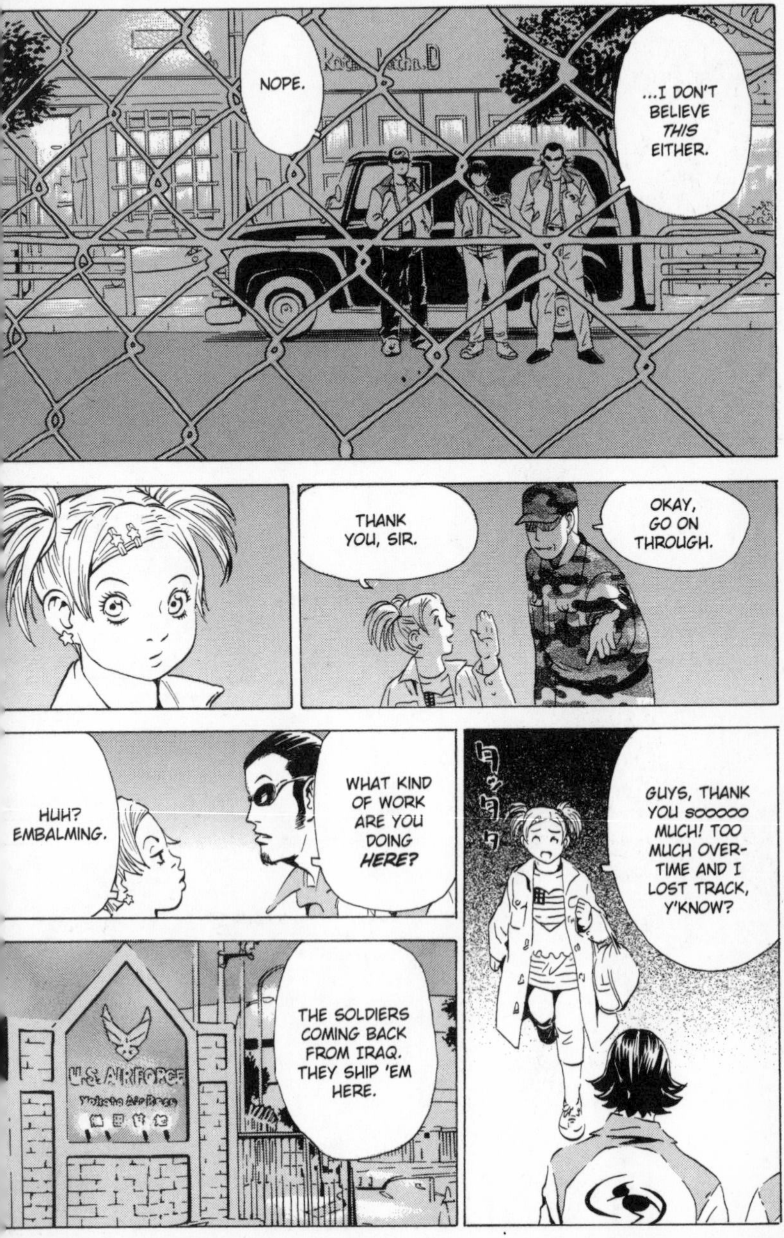
...I DON'T BELIEVE *THIS* EITHER.
NOPE.
OKAY, GO ON THROUGH.
THANK YOU, SIR.
GUYS, THANK YOU SOOOOO MUCH! TOO MUCH OVER-TIME AND I LOST TRACK, Y'KNOW?
WHAT KIND OF WORK ARE YOU DOING *HERE?*
HUH? EMBALMING.
THE SOLDIERS COMING BACK FROM IRAQ. THEY SHIP 'EM HERE.
U.S. AIR FORCE

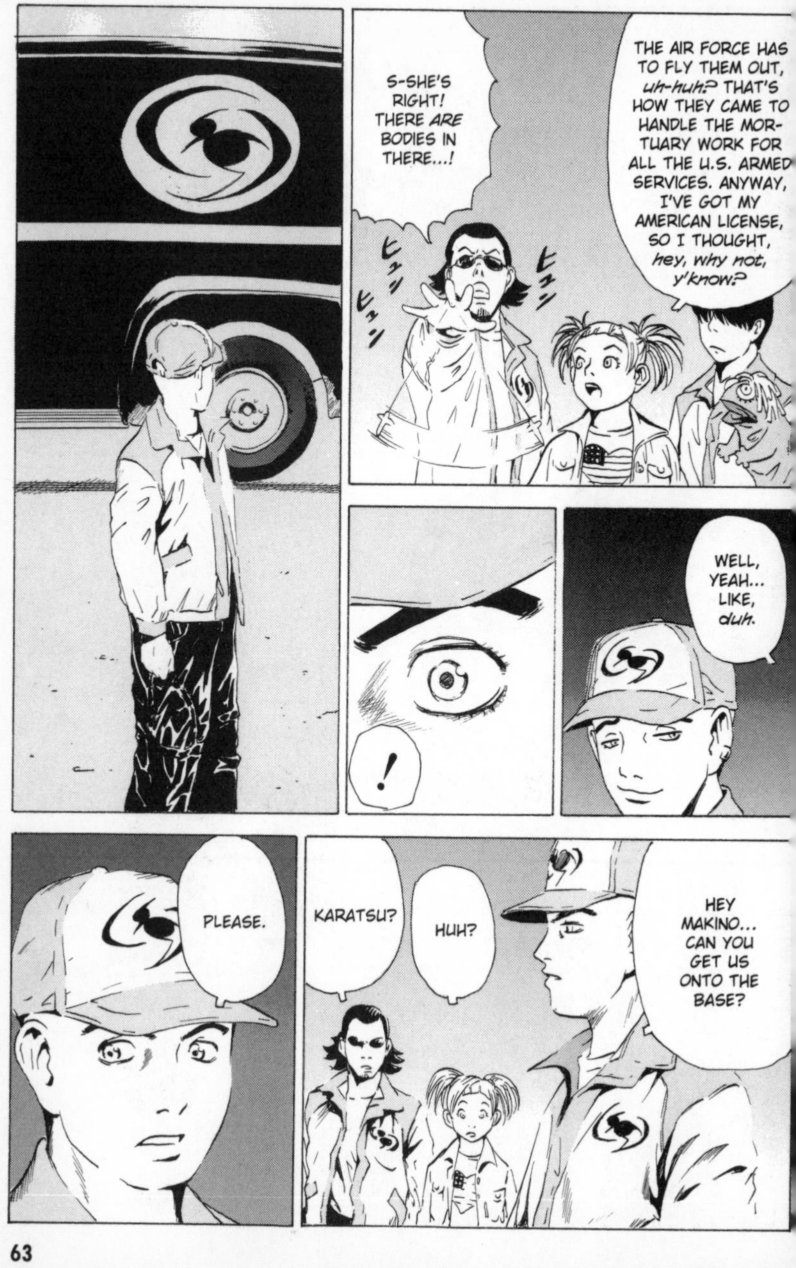
THE AIR FORCE HAS TO FLY THEM OUT, *uh-huh?* THAT'S HOW THEY CAME TO HANDLE THE MOR-TUARY WORK FOR ALL THE U.S. ARMED SERVICES. ANYWAY, I'VE GOT MY AMERICAN LICENSE, SO I THOUGHT, *hey, why not, y'know?*
S-SHE'S RIGHT! THERE *ARE* BODIES IN THERE...!
WELL, YEAH... LIKE, *duh.*
!
HEY MAKINO... CAN YOU GET US ONTO THE BASE?
HUH?
KARATSU?
PLEASE.

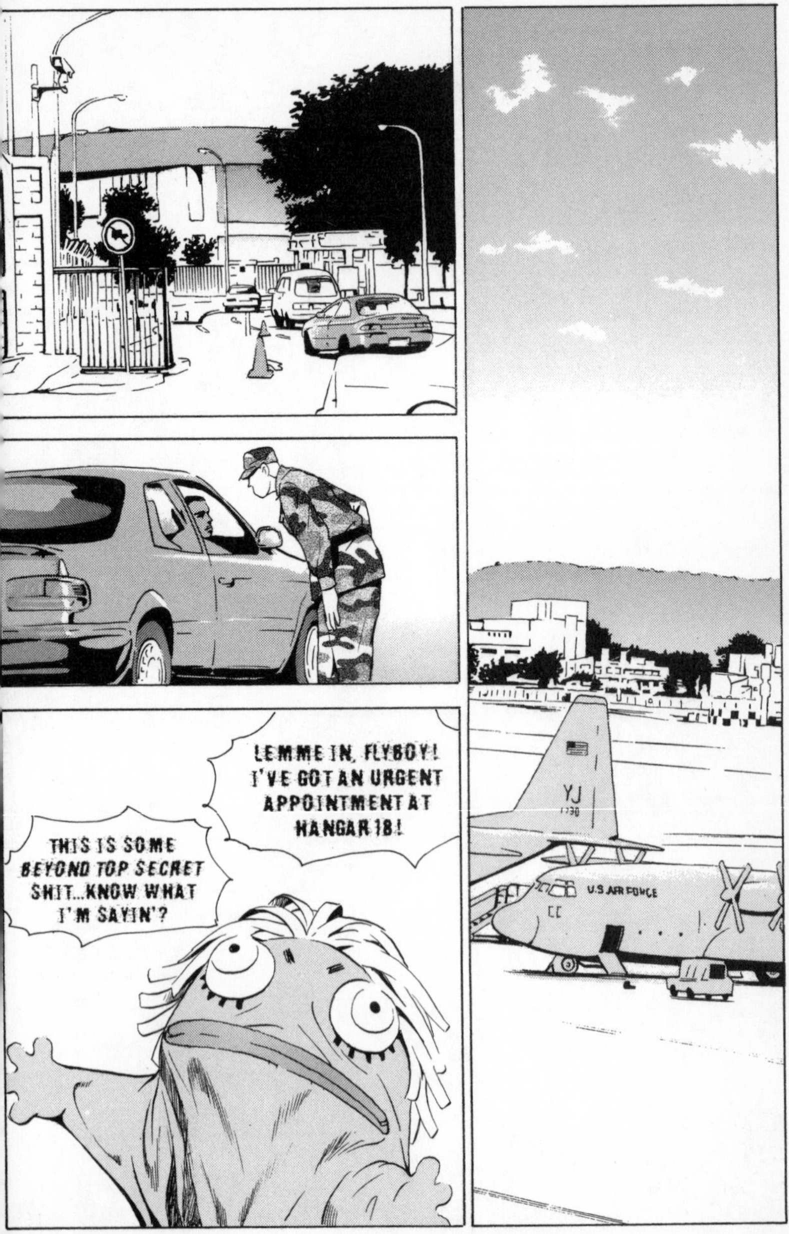
YJ
U.S AIR FORCE
LEMME IN, FLYBOY! I'VE GOT AN URGENT APPOINTMENT AT HANGAR 18!
THIS IS SOME BEYOND TOP SECRET SHIT...KNOW WHAT I'M SAYIN'?

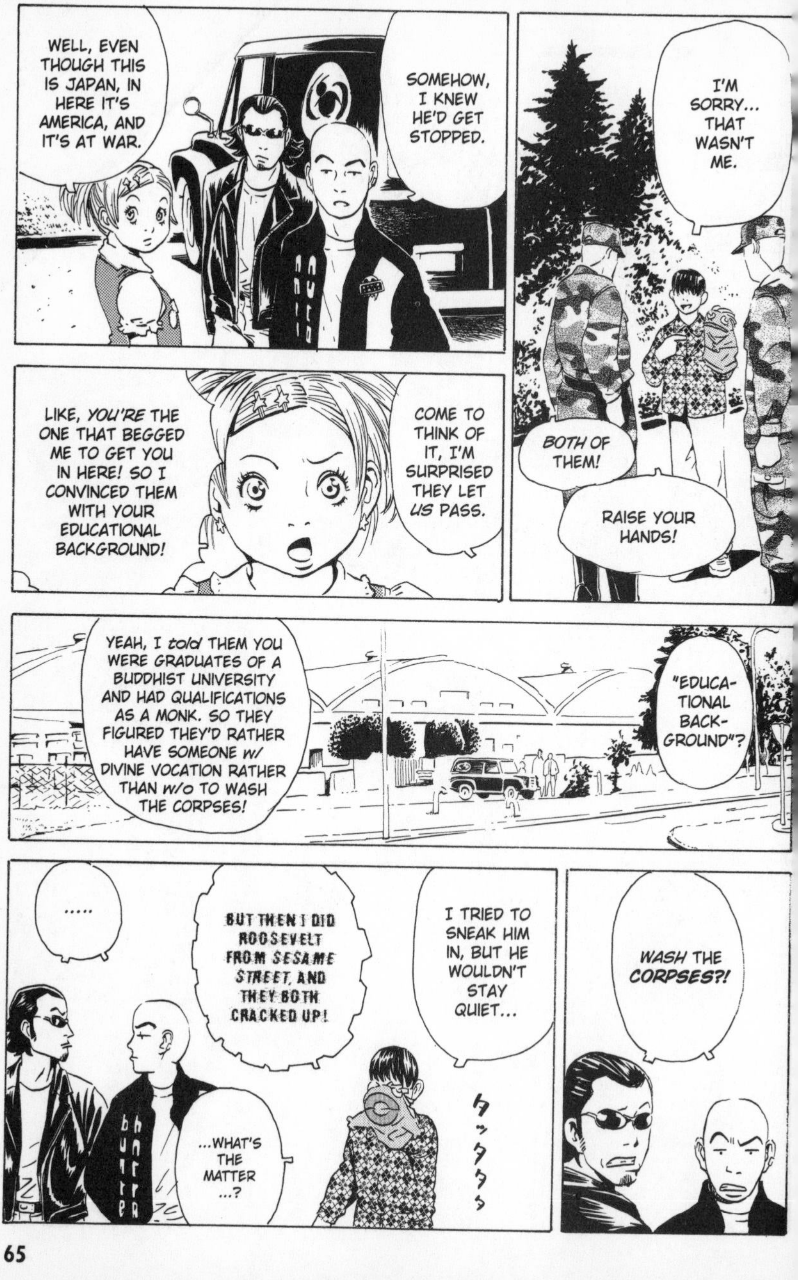
I'M SORRY... THAT WASN'T ME.
BOTH OF THEM!
RAISE YOUR HANDS!
SOMEHOW, I KNEW HE'D GET STOPPED.
WELL, EVEN THOUGH THIS IS JAPAN, IN HERE IT'S AMERICA, AND IT'S AT WAR.
COME TO THINK OF IT, I'M SURPRISED THEY LET *US* PASS.
LIKE, *YOU'RE* THE ONE THAT BEGGED ME TO GET YOU IN HERE! SO I CONVINCED THEM WITH YOUR EDUCATIONAL BACKGROUND!
"EDUCA-TIONAL BACK-GROUND"?
YEAH, I *told* THEM YOU WERE GRADUATES OF A BUDDHIST UNIVERSITY AND HAD QUALIFICATIONS AS A MONK. SO THEY FIGURED THEY'D RATHER HAVE SOMEONE *w/* DIVINE VOCATION RATHER THAN *w/o* TO WASH THE CORPSES!
WASH THE *CORPSES?!*
I TRIED TO SNEAK HIM IN, BUT HE WOULDN'T STAY QUIET...
BUT THEN I DID ROOSEVELT FROM *SESAME STREET*, AND THEY BOTH CRACKED UP!
......
...WHAT'S THE MATTER ...?
タッタッタ

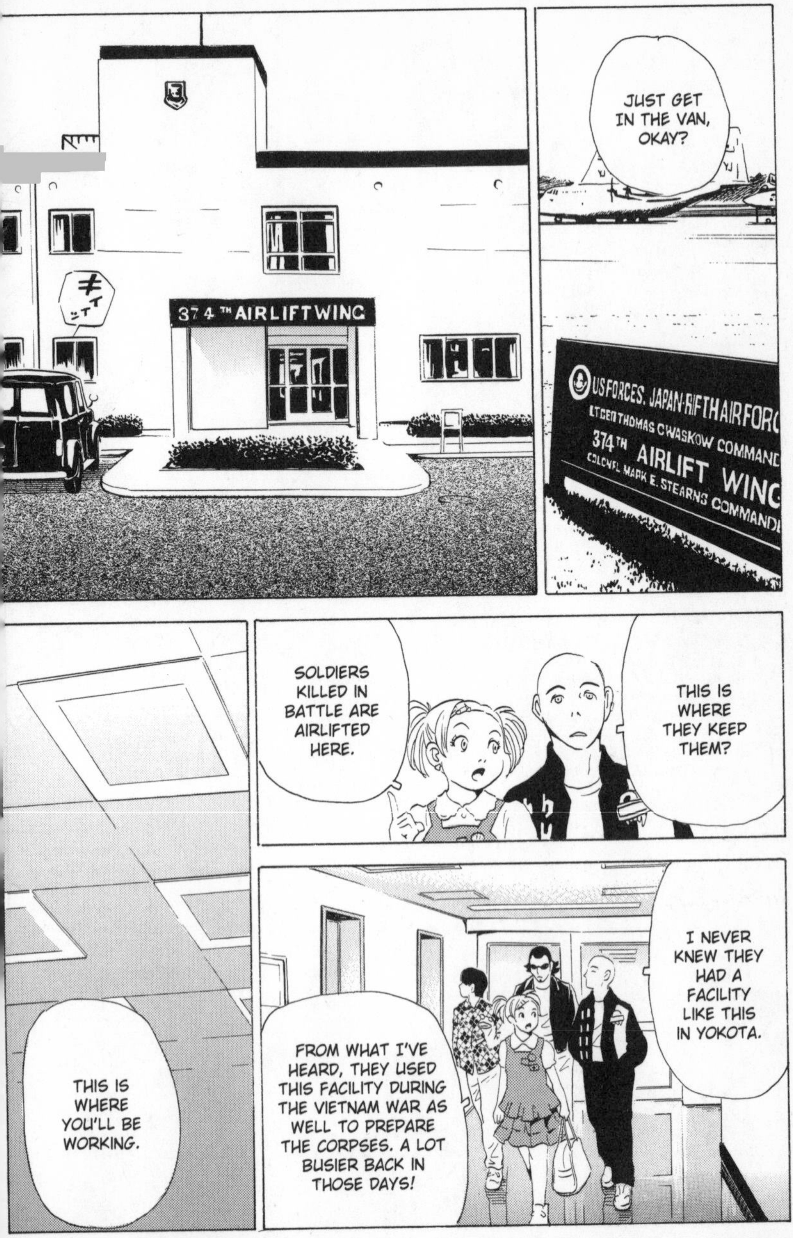
JUST GET IN THE VAN, OKAY?
US FORCES, JAPAN-FIFTH AIR FORC
LT.GEN THOMAS C WASKOW COMMAND
374TH AIRLIFT WING
COLONEL MARK E. STEARNS COMMAND
374TH AIRLIFT WING
キイッ
THIS IS WHERE THEY KEEP THEM?
SOLDIERS KILLED IN BATTLE ARE AIRLIFTED HERE.
I NEVER KNEW THEY HAD A FACILITY LIKE THIS IN YOKOTA.
FROM WHAT I'VE HEARD, THEY USED THIS FACILITY DURING THE VIETNAM WAR AS WELL TO PREPARE THE CORPSES. A LOT BUSIER BACK IN THOSE DAYS!
THIS IS WHERE YOU'LL BE WORKING.

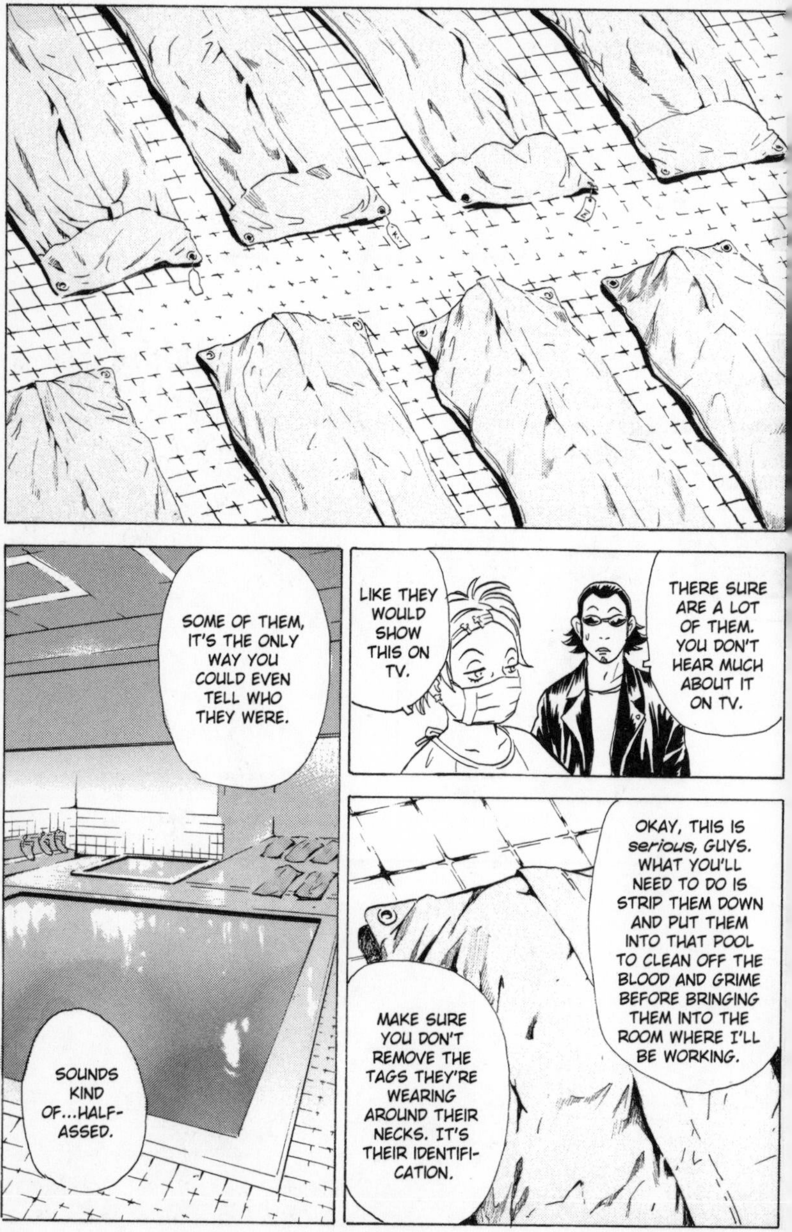
THERE SURE ARE A LOT OF THEM. YOU DON'T HEAR MUCH ABOUT IT ON TV.
LIKE THEY WOULD SHOW THIS ON TV.
OKAY, THIS IS *serious*, GUYS. WHAT YOU'LL NEED TO DO IS STRIP THEM DOWN AND PUT THEM INTO THAT POOL TO CLEAN OFF THE BLOOD AND GRIME BEFORE BRINGING THEM INTO THE ROOM WHERE I'LL BE WORKING.
MAKE SURE YOU DON'T REMOVE THE TAGS THEY'RE WEARING AROUND THEIR NECKS. IT'S THEIR IDENTIFI-CATION.
SOME OF THEM, IT'S THE ONLY WAY YOU COULD EVEN TELL WHO THEY WERE.
SOUNDS KIND OF...HALF-ASSED.

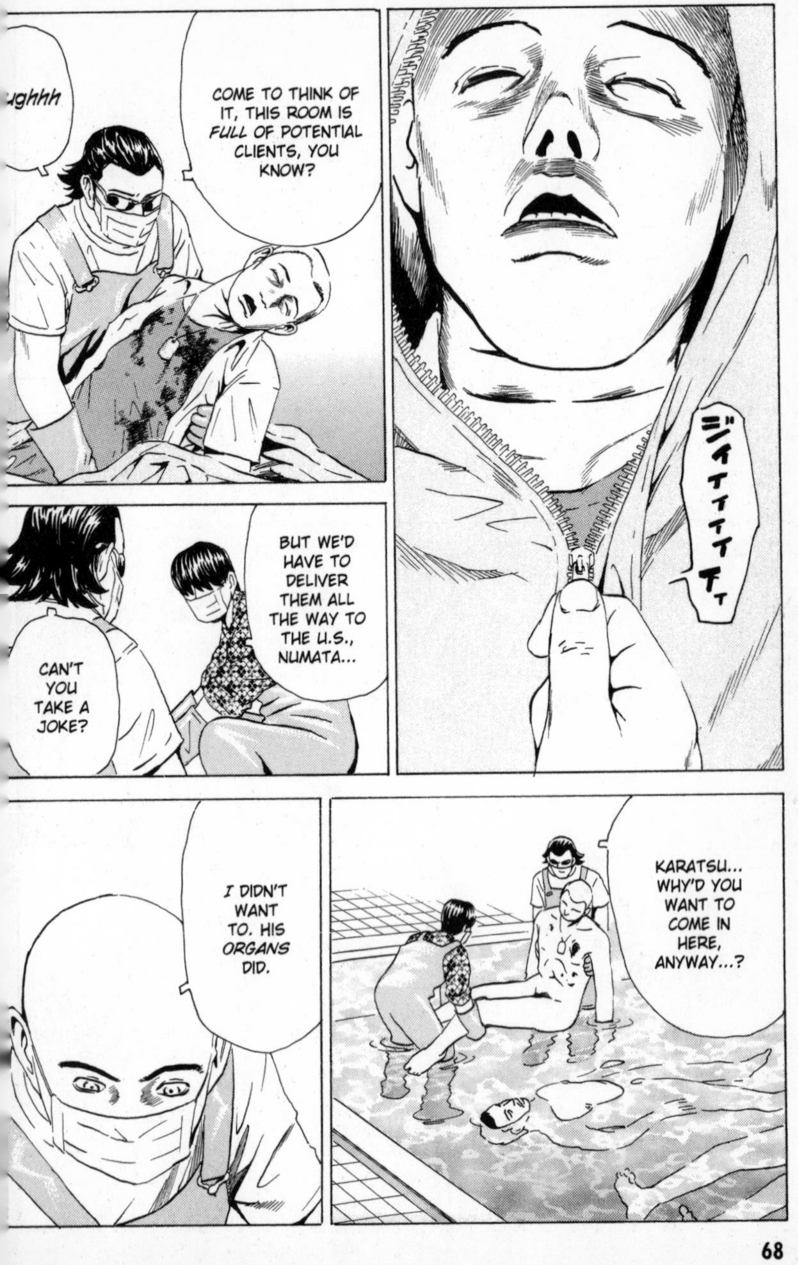
ジイイイイイィ
COME TO THINK OF IT, THIS ROOM IS *FULL* OF POTENTIAL CLIENTS, YOU KNOW?
ughhh
BUT WE'D HAVE TO DELIVER THEM ALL THE WAY TO THE U.S., NUMATA...
CAN'T YOU TAKE A JOKE?
KARATSU... WHY'D YOU WANT TO COME IN HERE, ANYWAY...?
I DIDN'T WANT TO. HIS *ORGANS* DID.

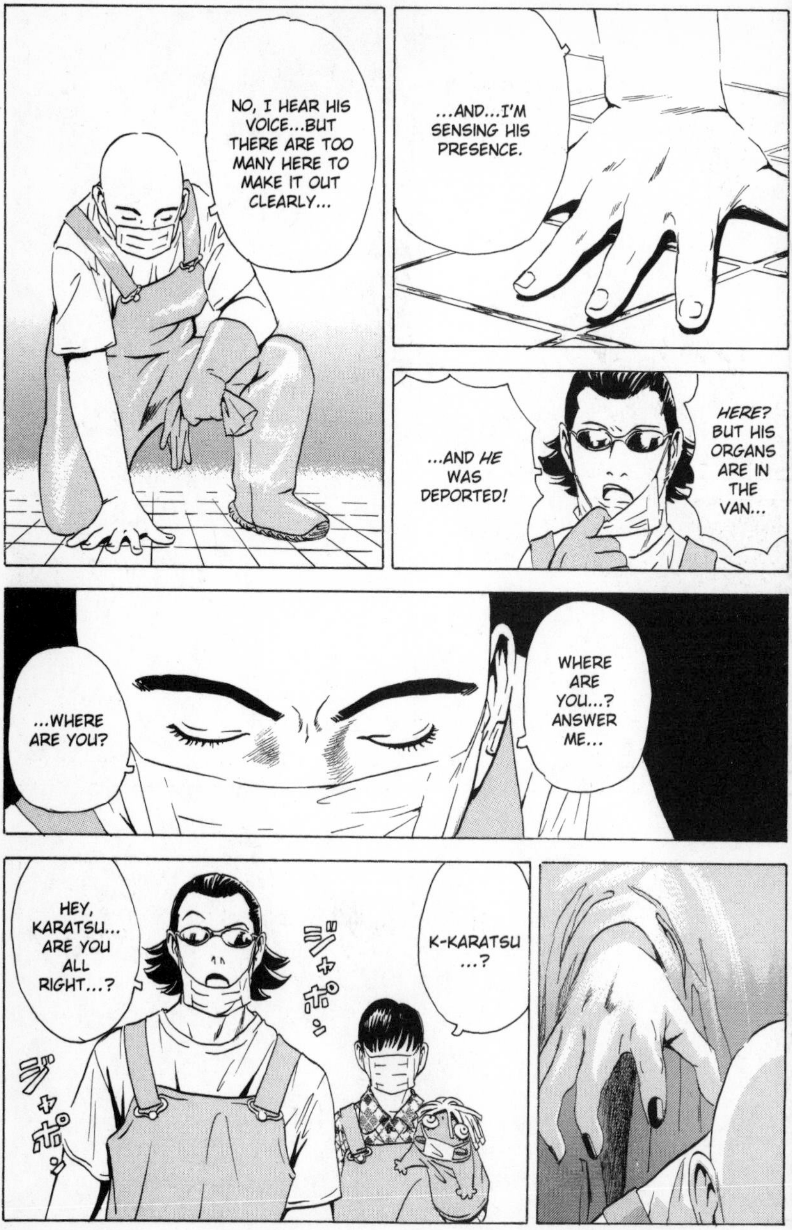
...AND...I'M SENSING HIS PRESENCE.
HERE? BUT HIS ORGANS ARE IN THE VAN...
...AND HE WAS DEPORTED!
NO, I HEAR HIS VOICE...BUT THERE ARE TOO MANY HERE TO MAKE IT OUT CLEARLY...
WHERE ARE YOU...? ANSWER ME...
...WHERE ARE YOU?
K-KARATSU ...?
ジャポン
HEY, KARATSU... ARE YOU ALL RIGHT...?
ジャポン

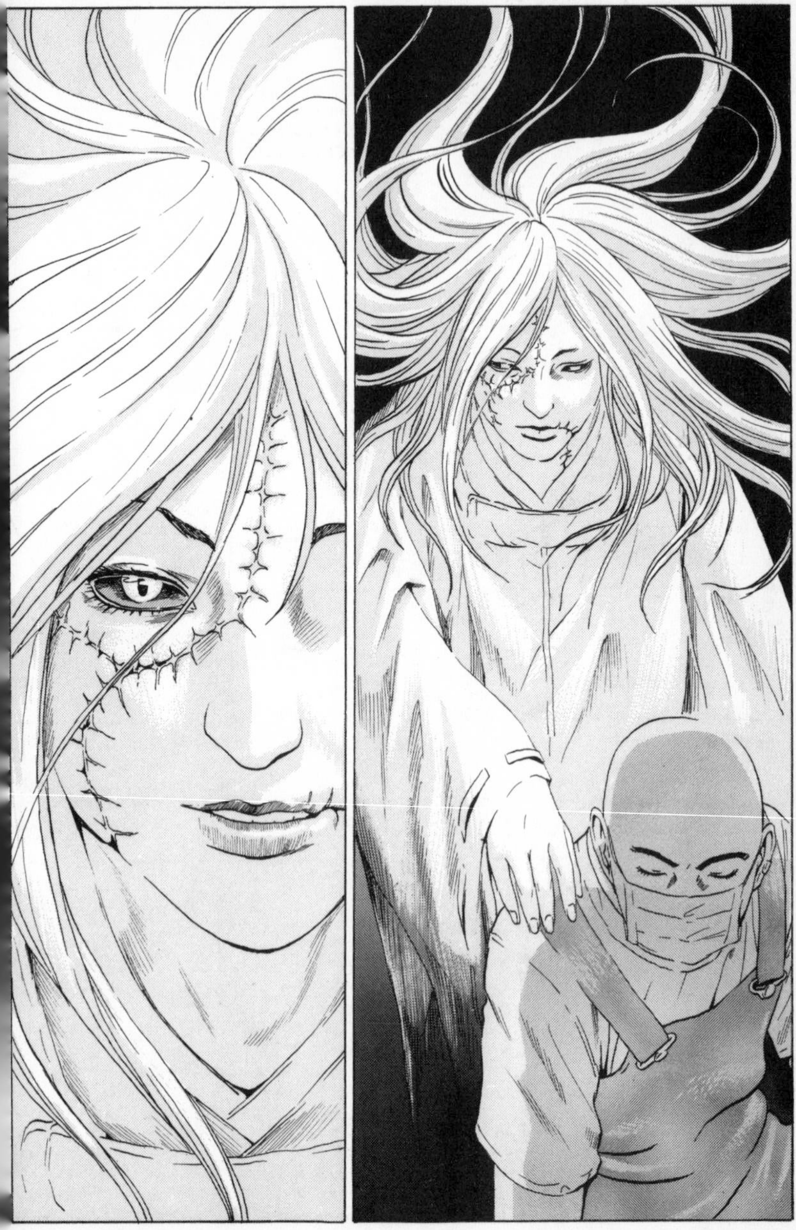

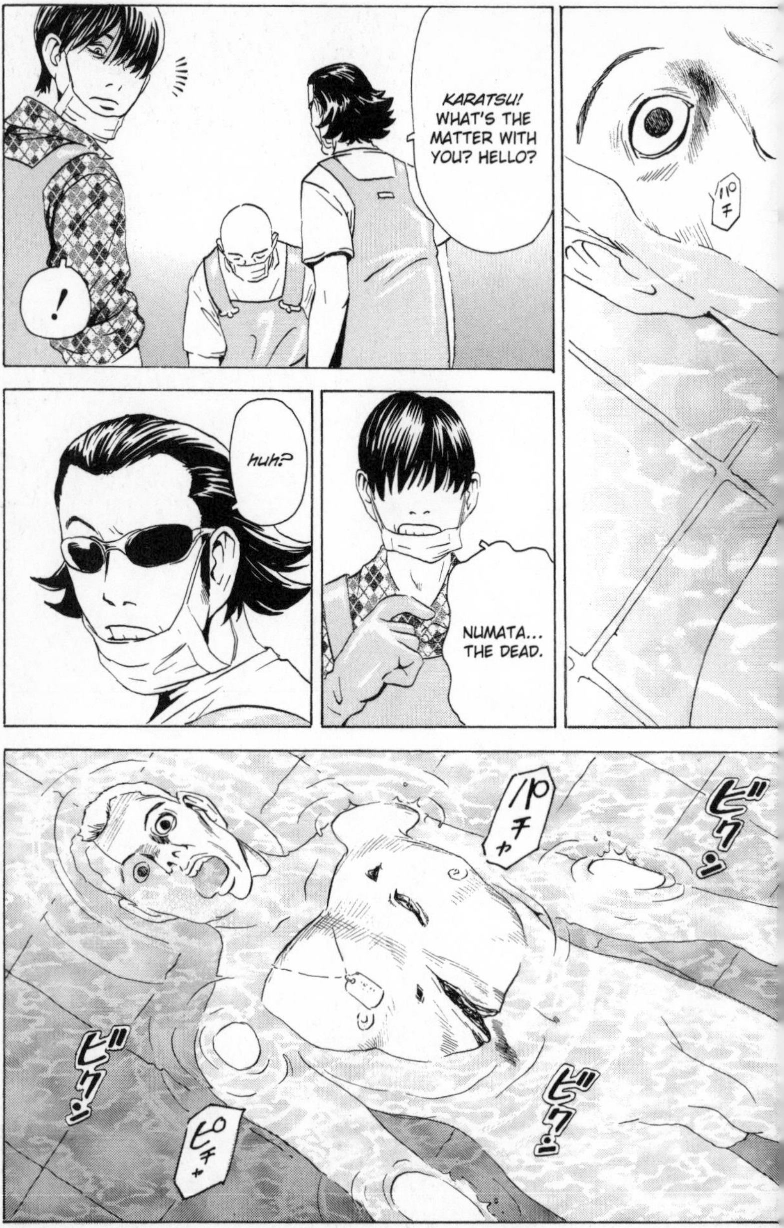

パチ
KARATSU! WHAT'S THE MATTER WITH YOU? HELLO?
!
NUMATA... THE DEAD.
huh?
ビクッ
パチャ
ビクッ
ビクッ
ピチャ

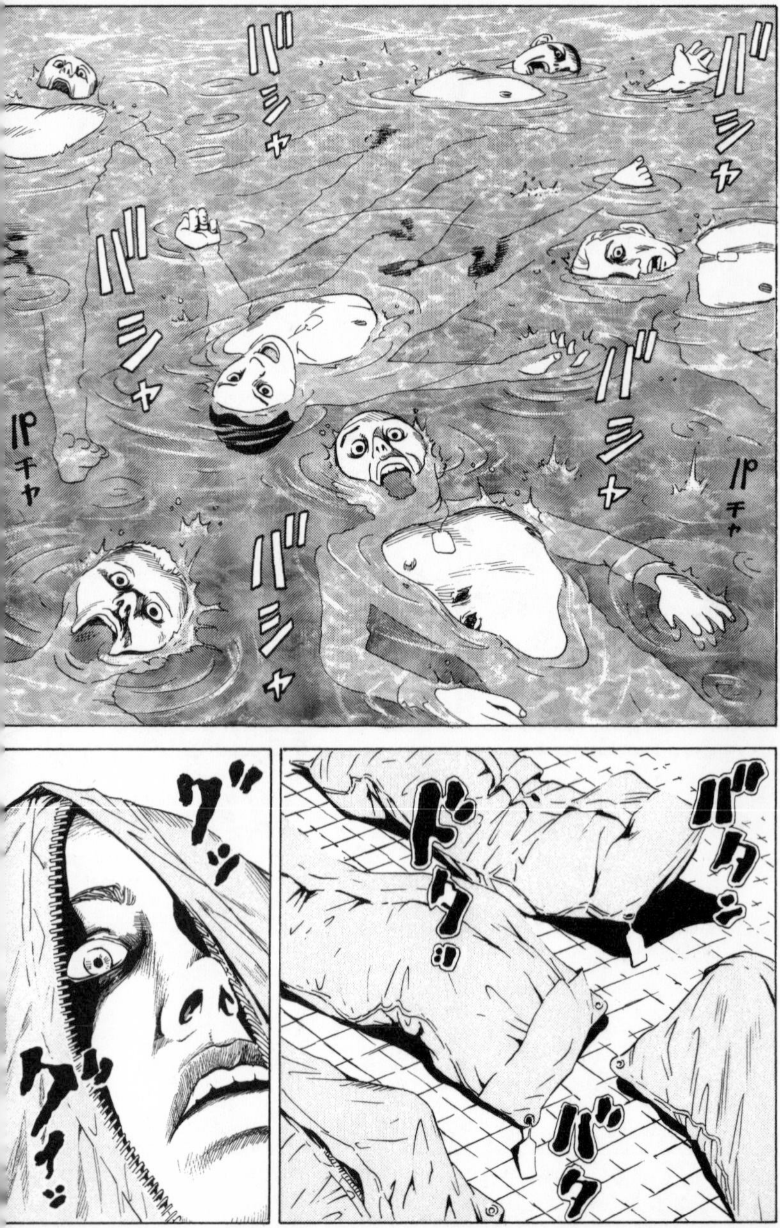
バシャ
パチャ
バシャ
バシャ
バシャ
バシャ
パチャ
バタン
ドタッ!!
バタ
グッ
ウィィ…

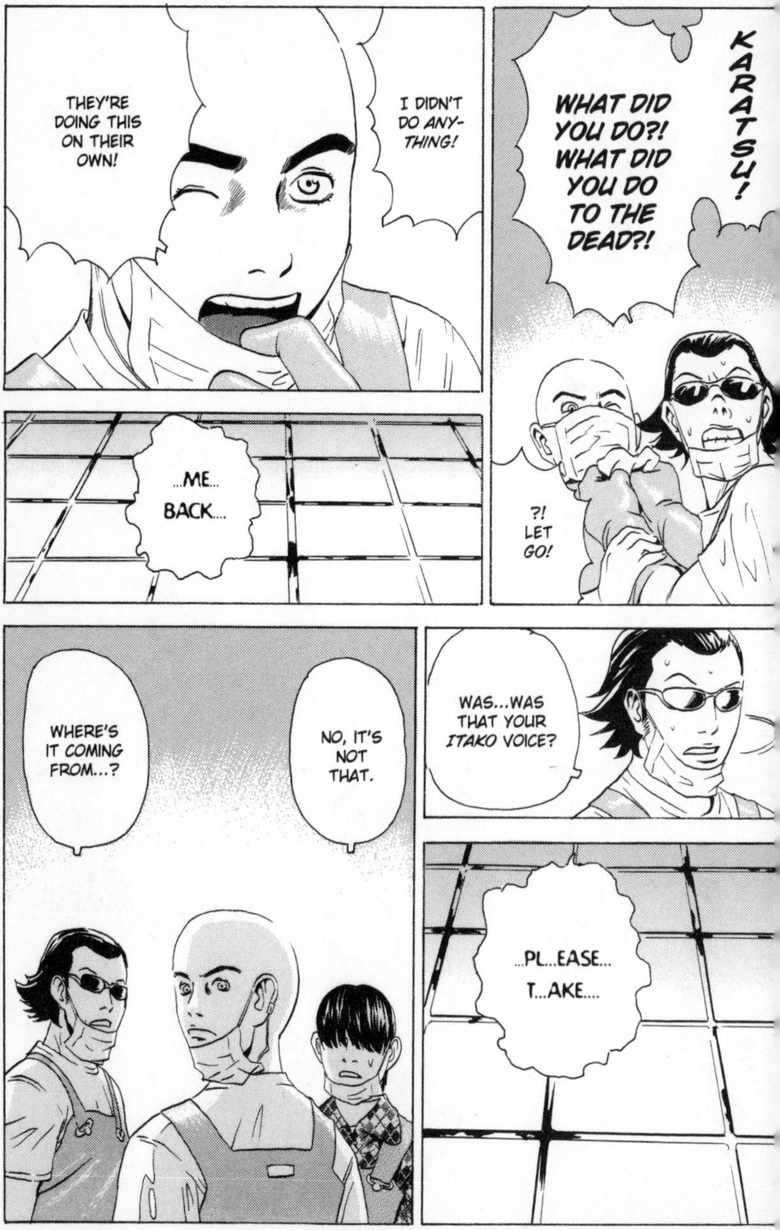
KARATSU!
WHAT DID YOU DO?! WHAT DID YOU DO TO THE DEAD?!
?! LET GO!
I DIDN'T DO *ANY*-*THING!*
THEY'RE DOING THIS ON THEIR OWN!
...ME... BACK....
WAS...WAS THAT YOUR *ITAKO* VOICE?
...PL...EASE... T...AKE....
NO, IT'S NOT THAT.
WHERE'S IT COMING FROM...?

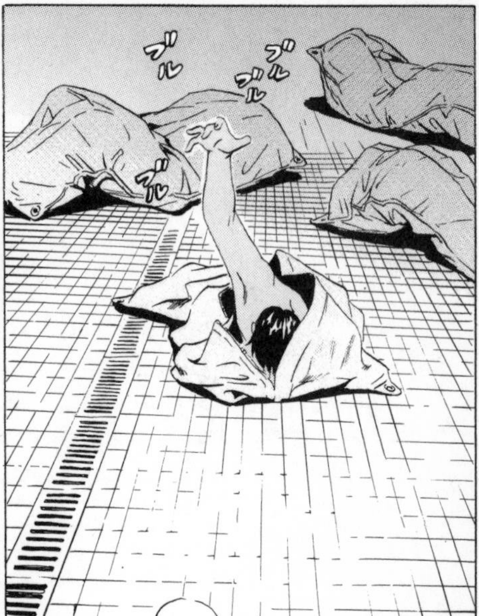
ブル
ブルブル
ブル
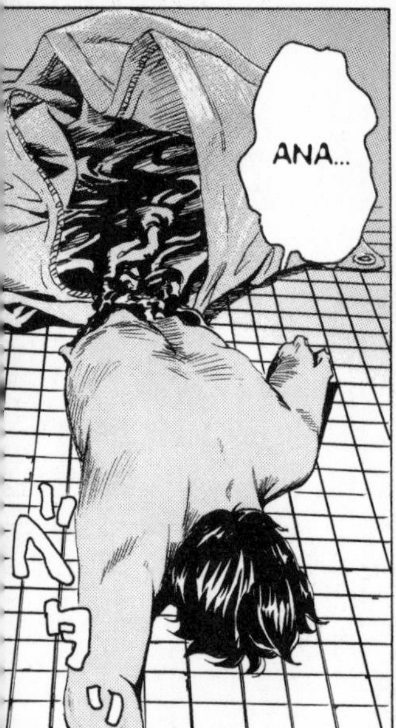
ANA...
...MA... REED...
...I... F...EEL... SI...CK...

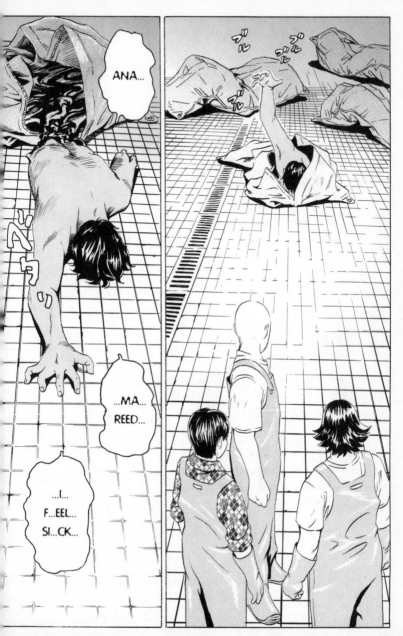

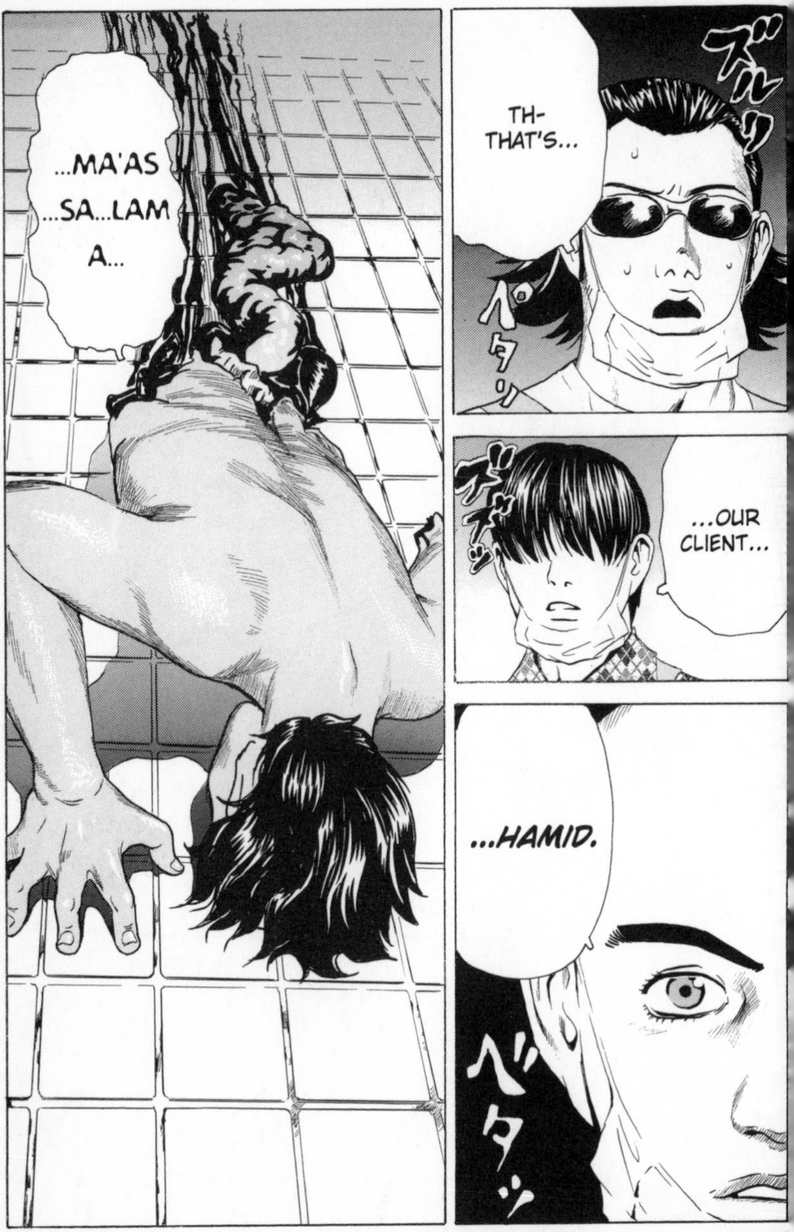
ズルッ
TH-
THAT'S...
...OUR
CLIENT...
...HAMID.
...MA'AS
...SA...LAM
A...

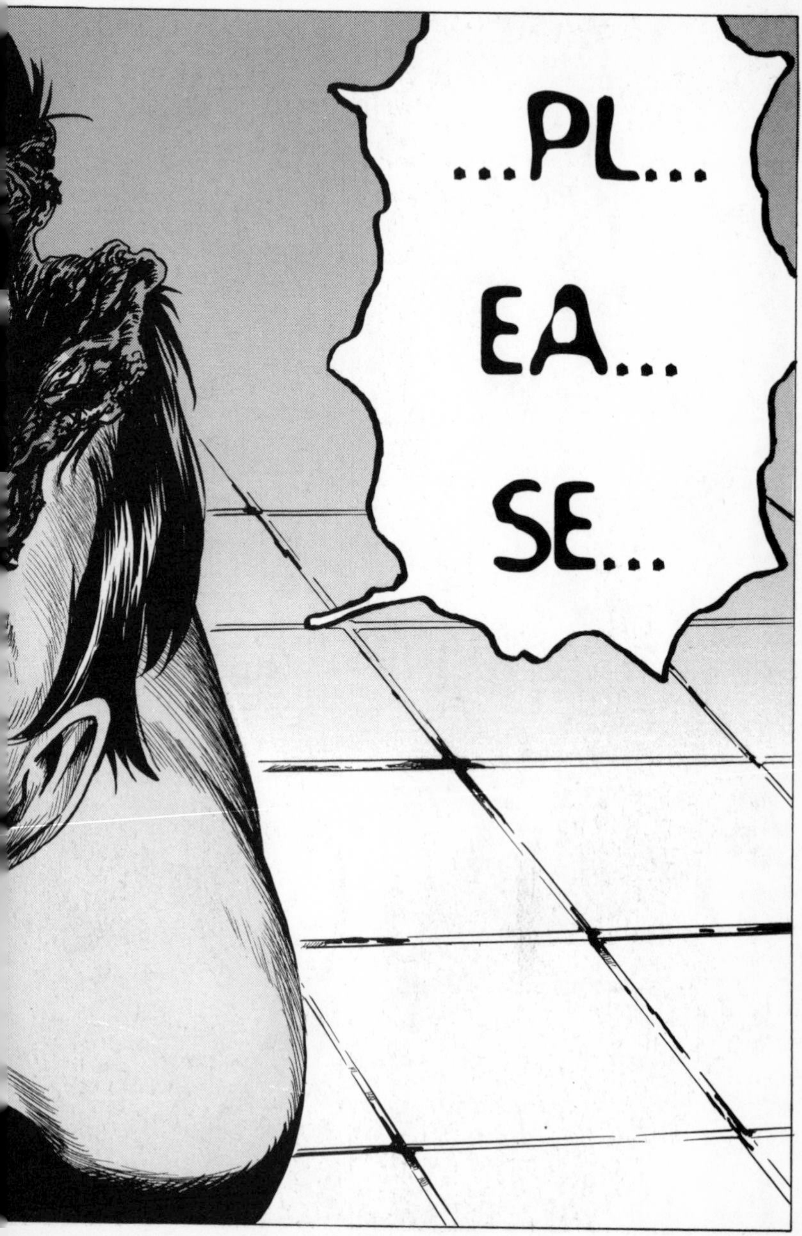
...PL...
EA...
SE...

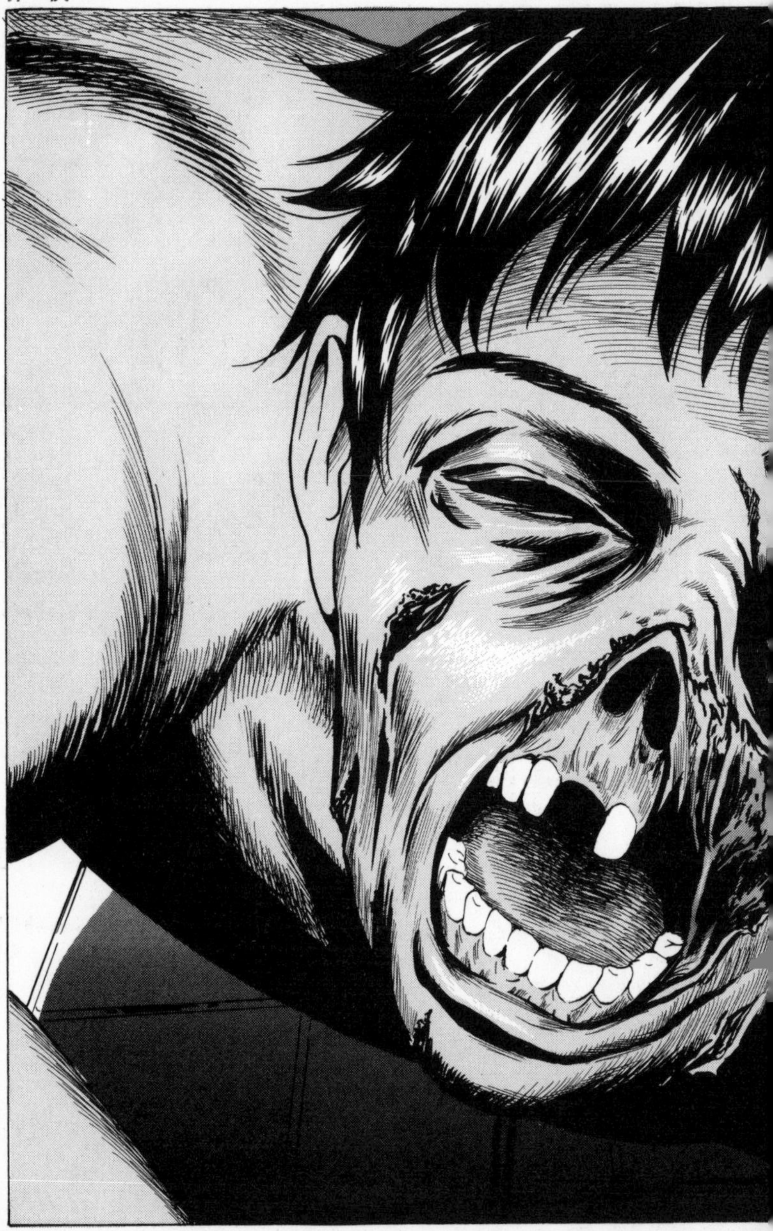

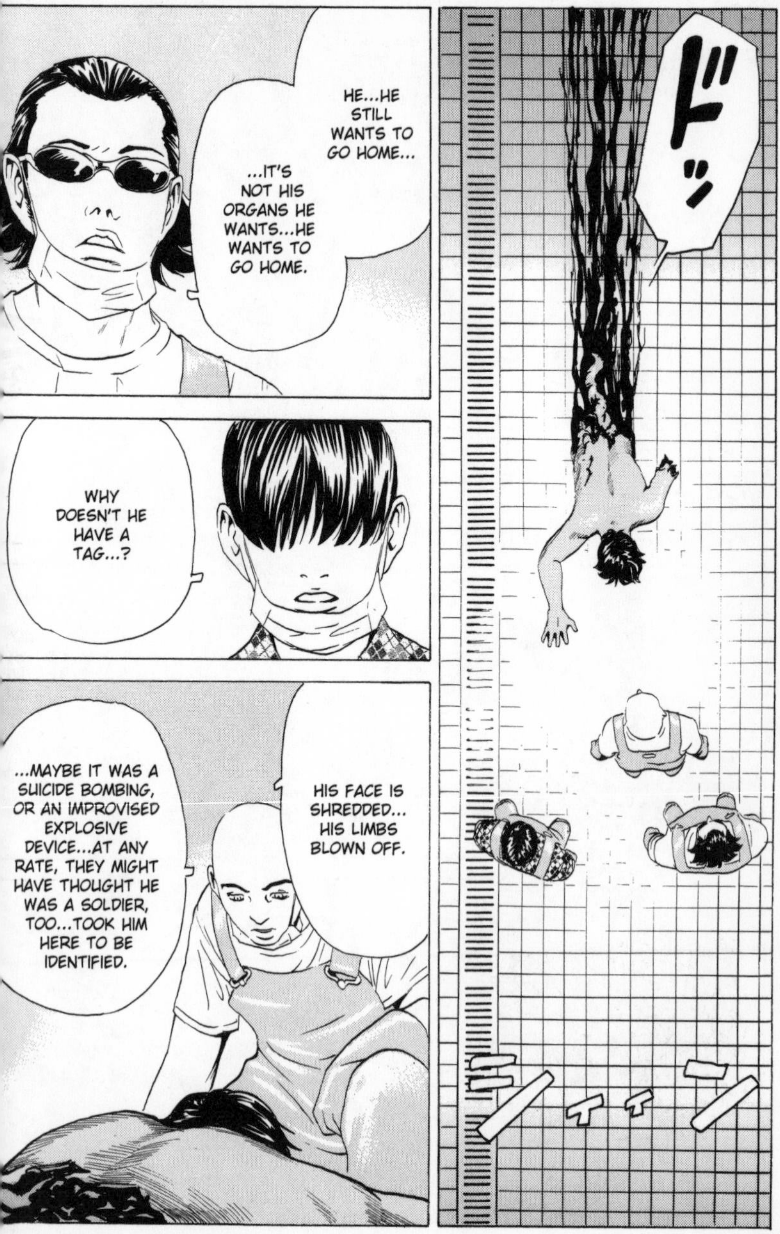
ドッ
HE...HE STILL WANTS TO GO HOME...
...IT'S NOT HIS ORGANS HE WANTS...HE WANTS TO GO HOME.
WHY DOESN'T HE HAVE A TAG...?
HIS FACE IS SHREDDED... HIS LIMBS BLOWN OFF.
...MAYBE IT WAS A SUICIDE BOMBING, OR AN IMPROVISED EXPLOSIVE DEVICE...AT ANY RATE, THEY MIGHT HAVE THOUGHT HE WAS A SOLDIER, TOO...TOOK HIM HERE TO BE IDENTIFIED.

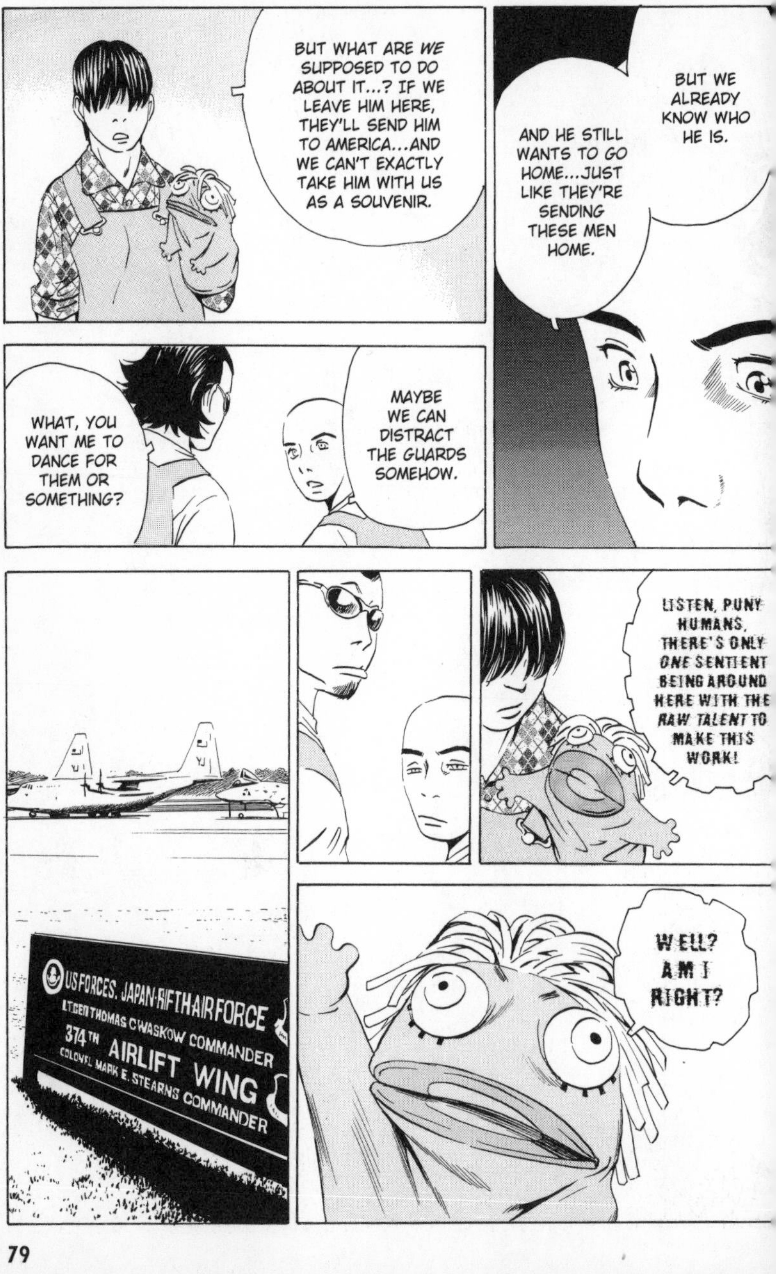
BUT WE ALREADY KNOW WHO HE IS.
AND HE STILL WANTS TO GO HOME...JUST LIKE THEY'RE SENDING THESE MEN HOME.
BUT WHAT ARE *WE* SUPPOSED TO DO ABOUT IT...? IF WE LEAVE HIM HERE, THEY'LL SEND HIM TO AMERICA...AND WE CAN'T EXACTLY TAKE HIM WITH US AS A SOUVENIR.
MAYBE WE CAN DISTRACT THE GUARDS SOMEHOW.
WHAT, YOU WANT ME TO DANCE FOR THEM OR SOMETHING?
LISTEN, PUNY HUMANS, THERE'S ONLY *ONE* SENTIENT BEING AROUND HERE WITH THE *RAW TALENT* TO MAKE THIS WORK!
WELL? AM I RIGHT?
US FORCES. JAPAN·FIFTH AIR FORCE
LT.GEN THOMAS C.WASKOW COMMANDER
374TH AIRLIFT WING
COLONEL MARK E. STEARNS COMMANDER

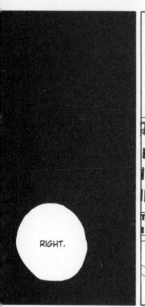

RIGHT.

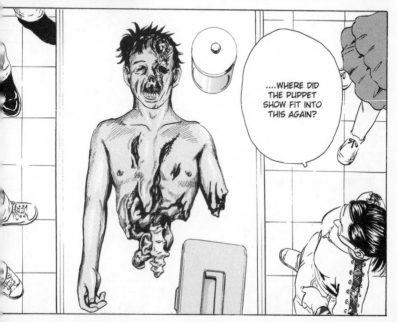

....WHERE DID THE PUPPET SHOW FIT INTO THIS AGAIN?

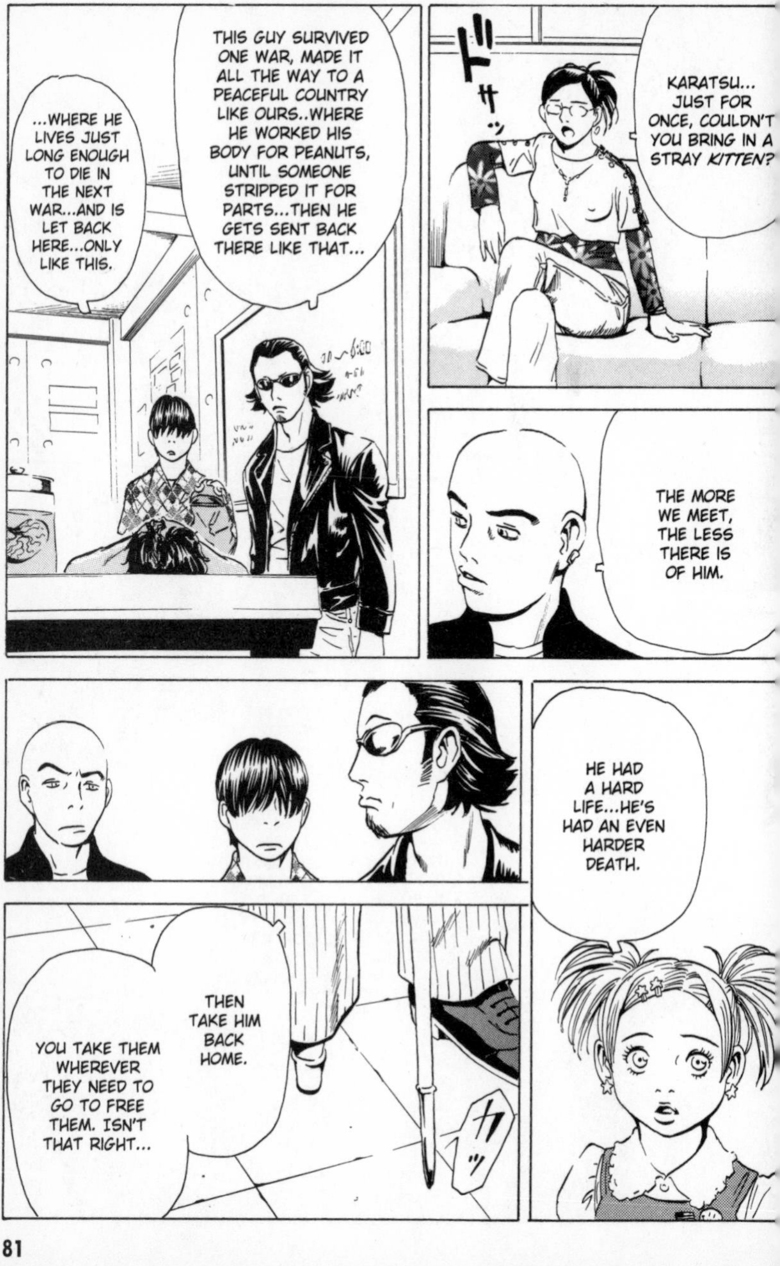
ドサッ
KARATSU... JUST FOR ONCE, COULDN'T YOU BRING IN A STRAY *KITTEN?*
THE MORE WE MEET, THE LESS THERE IS OF HIM.
THIS GUY SURVIVED ONE WAR, MADE IT ALL THE WAY TO A PEACEFUL COUNTRY LIKE OURS..WHERE HE WORKED HIS BODY FOR PEANUTS, UNTIL SOMEONE STRIPPED IT FOR PARTS...THEN HE GETS SENT BACK THERE LIKE THAT...
...WHERE HE LIVES JUST LONG ENOUGH TO DIE IN THE NEXT WAR...AND IS LET BACK HERE...ONLY LIKE THIS.
HE HAD A HARD LIFE...HE'S HAD AN EVEN HARDER DEATH.
THEN TAKE HIM BACK HOME.
YOU TAKE THEM WHEREVER THEY NEED TO GO TO FREE THEM. ISN'T THAT RIGHT...
カッ

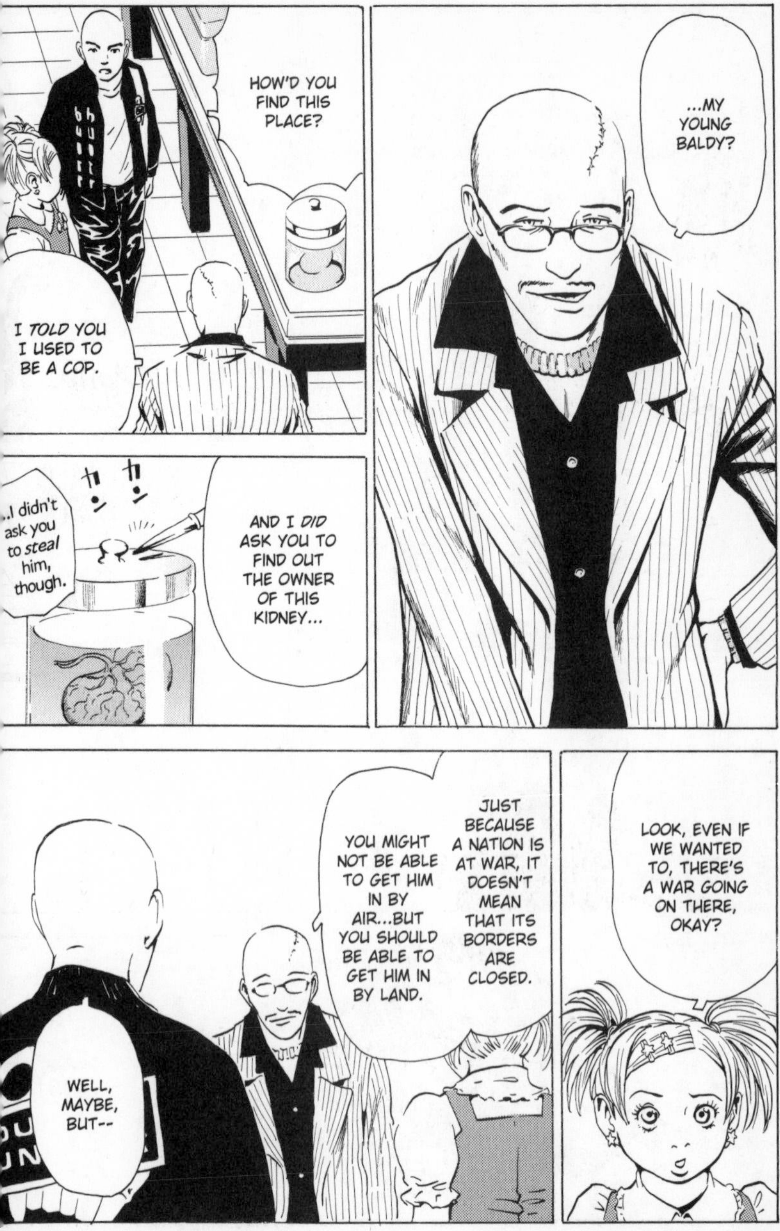
...MY YOUNG BALDY?
HOW'D YOU FIND THIS PLACE?
I *TOLD* YOU I USED TO BE A COP.
カン カン
AND I *DID* ASK YOU TO FIND OUT THE OWNER OF THIS KIDNEY...
..I didn't ask you to *steal* him, though.
LOOK, EVEN IF WE WANTED TO, THERE'S A WAR GOING ON THERE, OKAY?
JUST BECAUSE A NATION IS AT WAR, IT DOESN'T MEAN THAT ITS BORDERS ARE CLOSED.
YOU MIGHT NOT BE ABLE TO GET HIM IN BY AIR...BUT YOU SHOULD BE ABLE TO GET HIM IN BY LAND.
WELL, MAYBE, BUT--

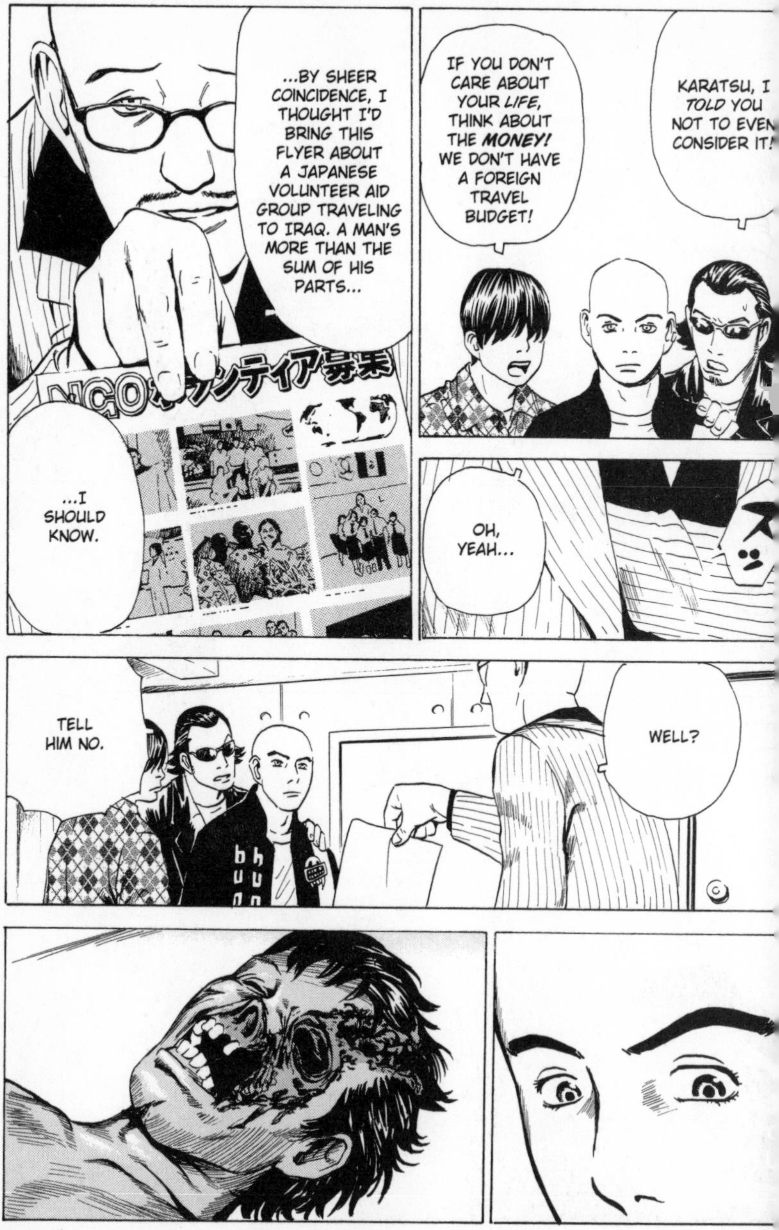
KARATSU, I TOLD YOU NOT TO EVEN CONSIDER IT!
IF YOU DON'T CARE ABOUT YOUR LIFE, THINK ABOUT THE MONEY! WE DON'T HAVE A FOREIGN TRAVEL BUDGET!
OH, YEAH...
...BY SHEER COINCIDENCE, I THOUGHT I'D BRING THIS FLYER ABOUT A JAPANESE VOLUNTEER AID GROUP TRAVELING TO IRAQ. A MAN'S MORE THAN THE SUM OF HIS PARTS...
...I SHOULD KNOW.
WELL?
TELL HIM NO.

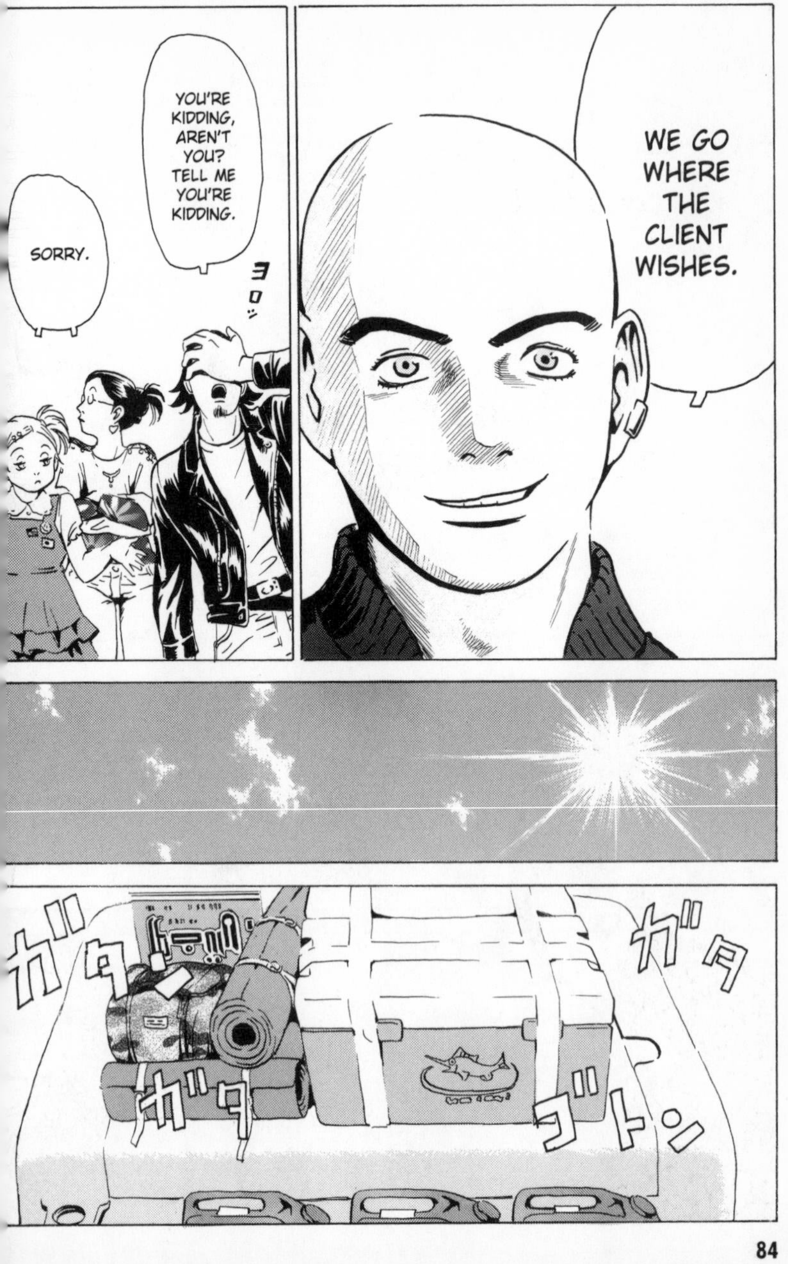
WE GO WHERE THE CLIENT WISHES.
YOU'RE KIDDING, AREN'T YOU? TELL ME YOU'RE KIDDING.
ヨロッ
SORRY.
ガタ
ガタ
ゴトン
ガタ

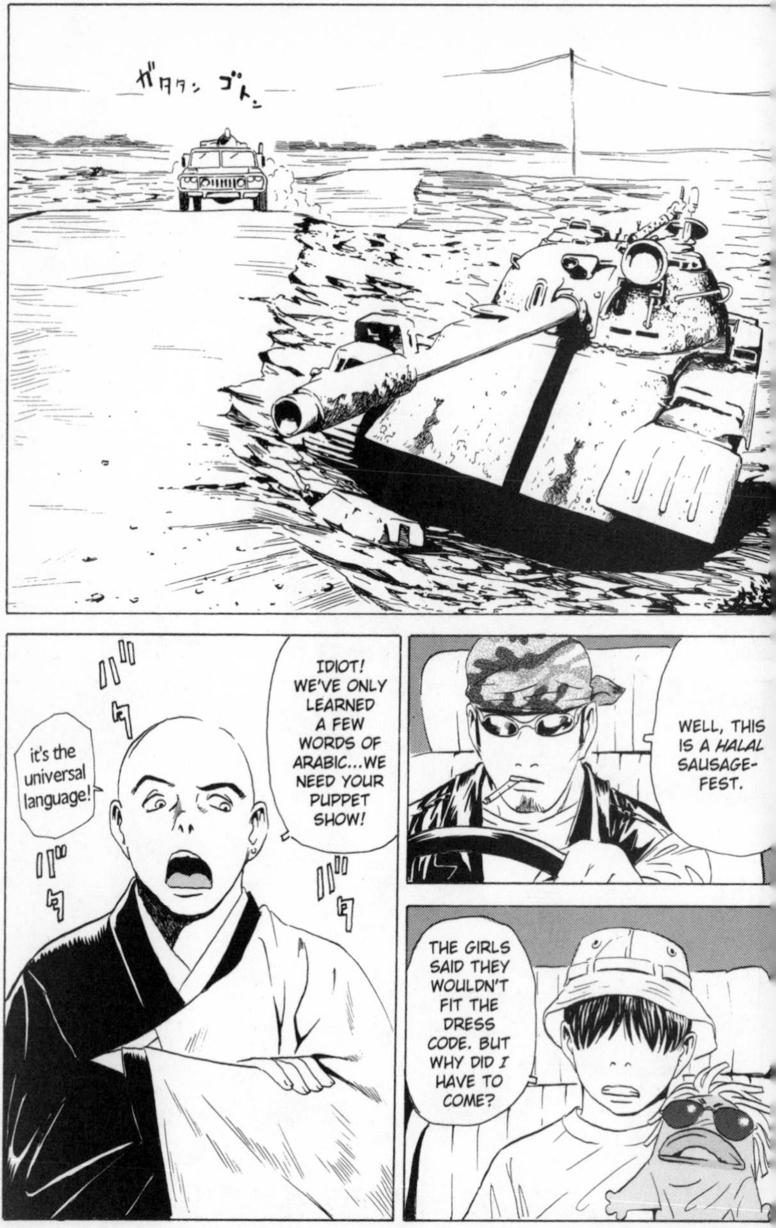
ガタタン ゴトン
WELL, THIS IS A *HALAL* SAUSAGE-FEST.
THE GIRLS SAID THEY WOULDN'T FIT THE DRESS CODE. BUT WHY DID *I* HAVE TO COME?
IDIOT! WE'VE ONLY LEARNED A FEW WORDS OF ARABIC...WE NEED YOUR PUPPET SHOW!
バタ
it's the universal language!
バタ
バタ

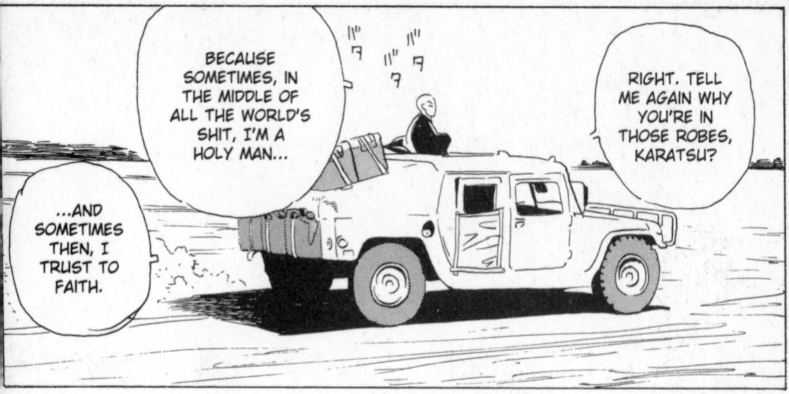
RIGHT. TELL ME AGAIN WHY YOU'RE IN THOSE ROBES, KARATSU?
BECAUSE SOMETIMES, IN THE MIDDLE OF ALL THE WORLD'S SHIT, I'M A HOLY MAN...
...AND SOMETIMES THEN, I TRUST TO FAITH.

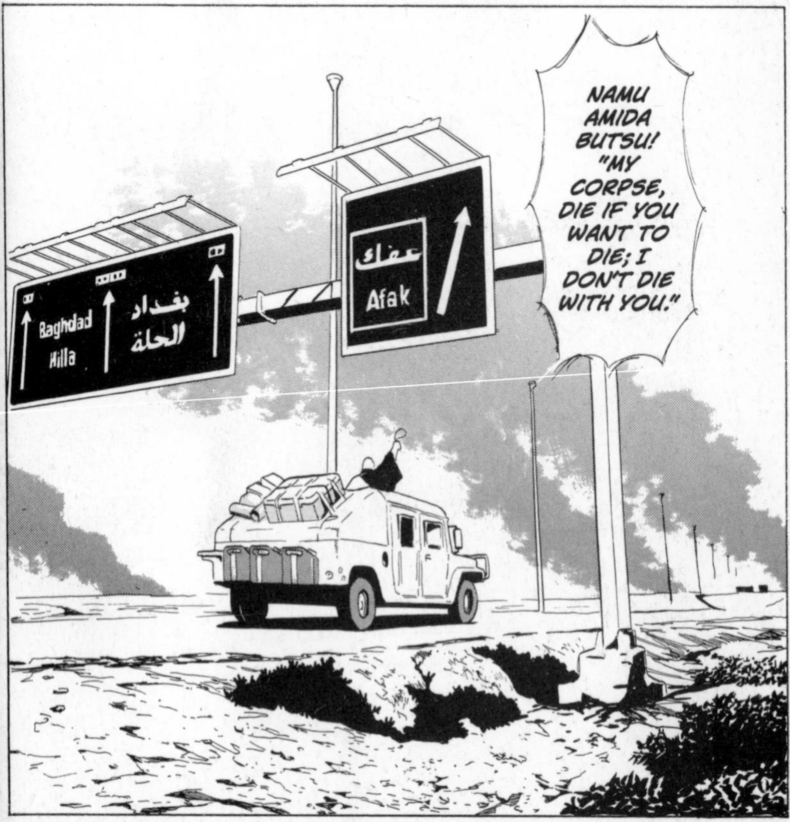
NAMU AMIDA BUTSU! "MY CORPSE, DIE IF YOU WANT TO DIE; I DON'T DIE WITH YOU."
عفك
Afak
بغداد
الحلة
Baghdad
Hilla

2nd delivery: applause—the end

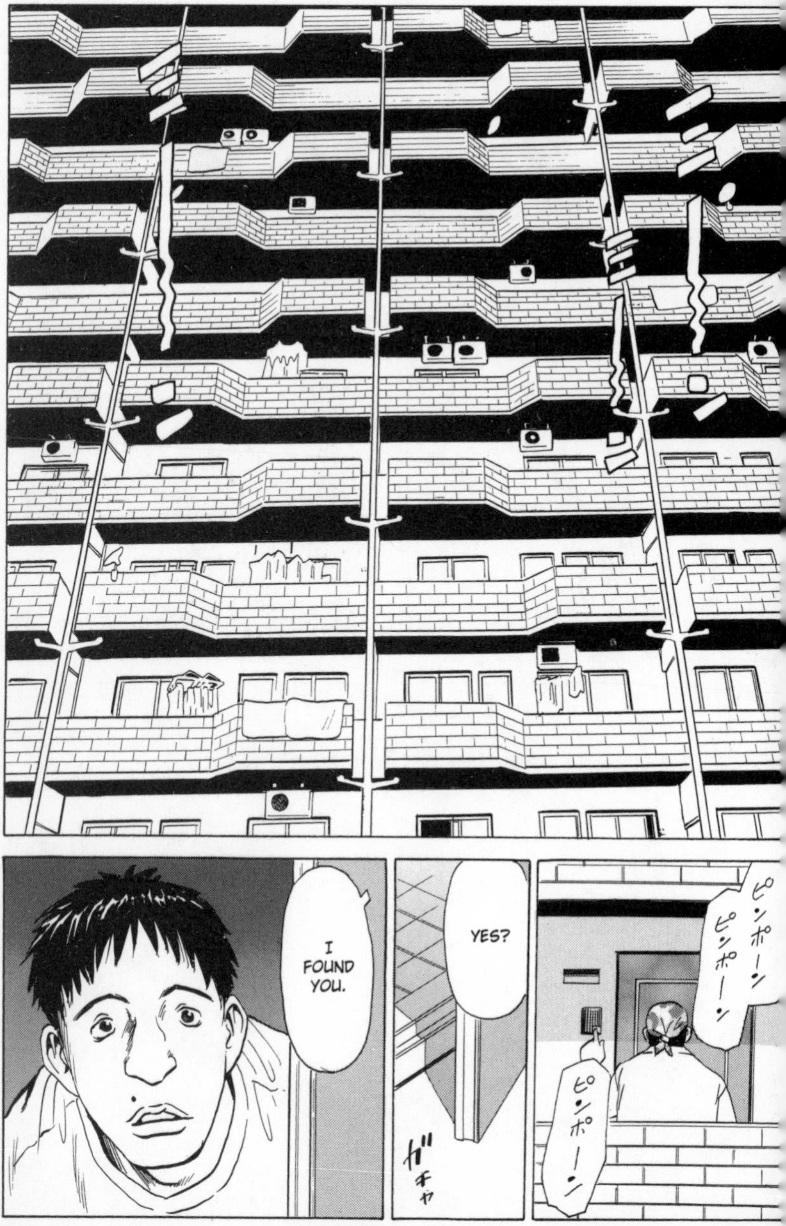
ピンポーン
ピンポーン
ピンポーン
YES?
ガチャ
I FOUND YOU.

ドカ
ドコっ
ビチャ
ズズッ
hahhh
hahhh
hahhh
チキ
チキ
チキ

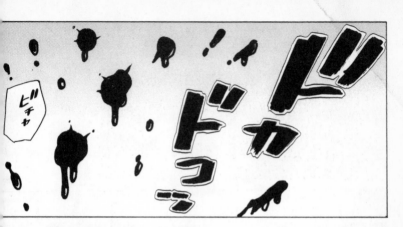

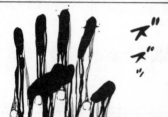

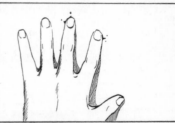

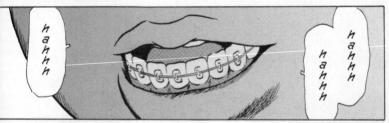

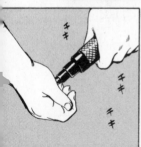

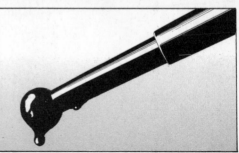

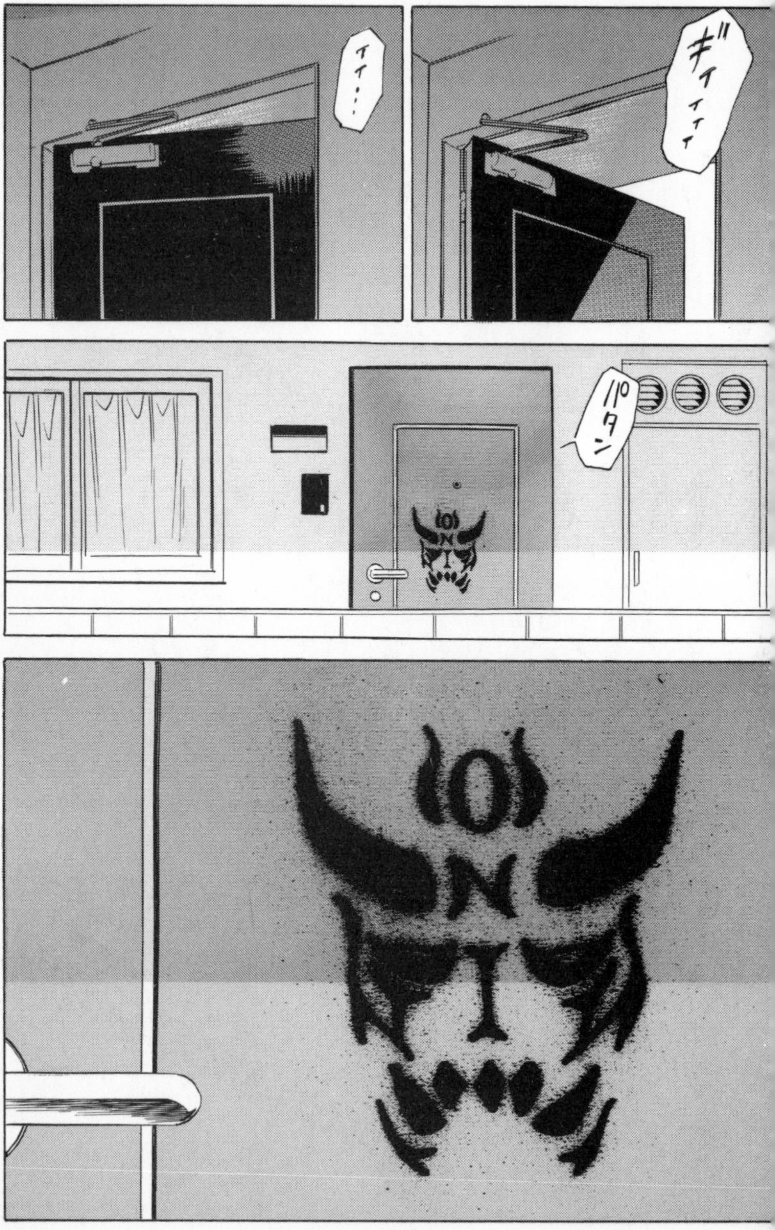
ギィィィィ
ィィ・・・
パタン

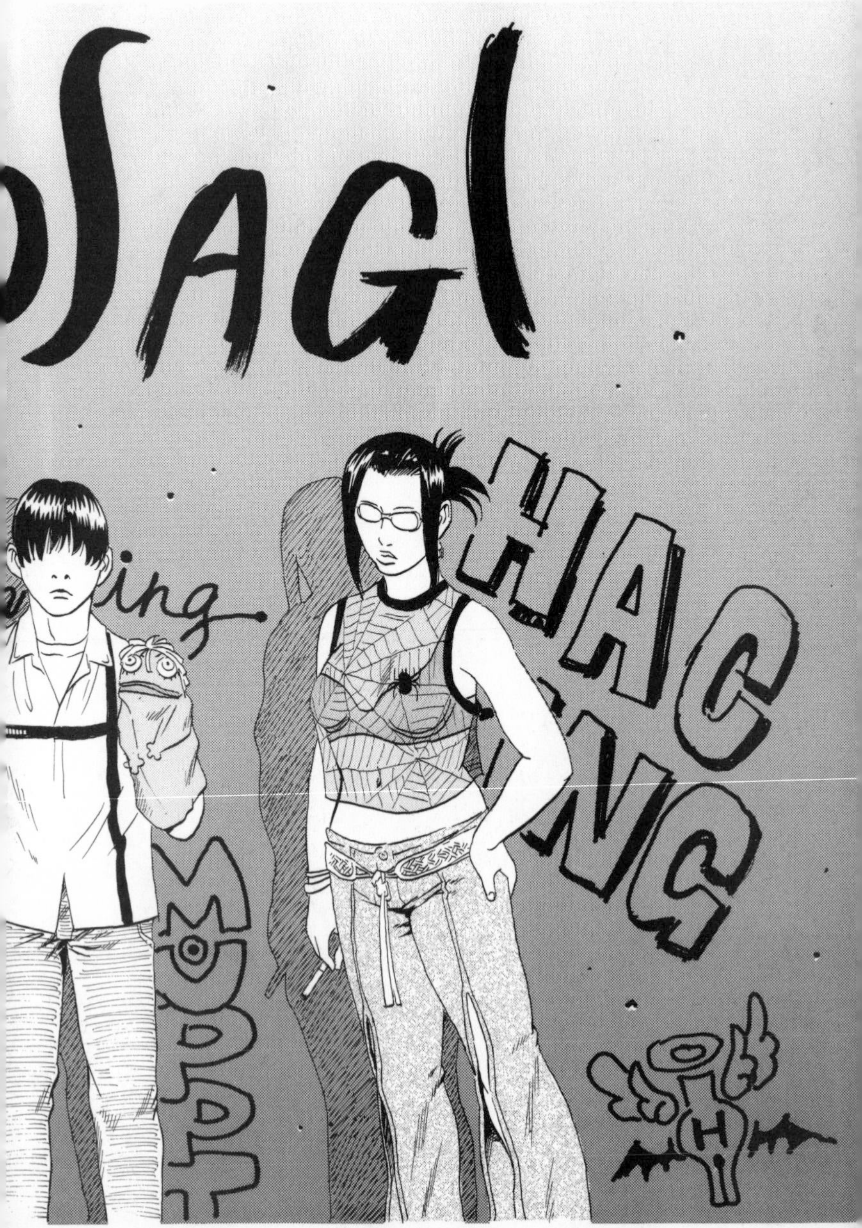

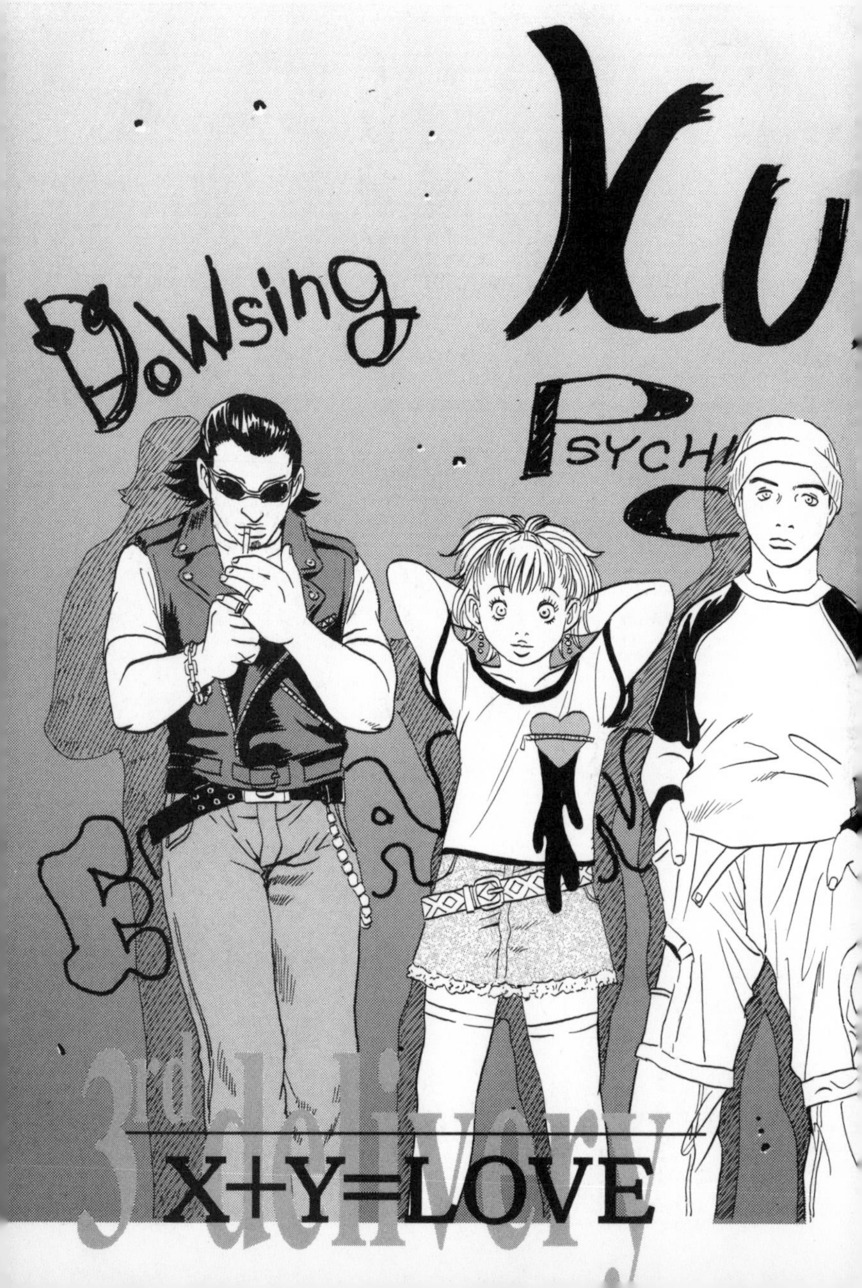
Dowsing
3rd delivery
X+Y=LOVE

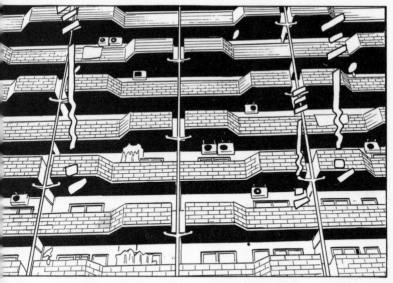

THIS STUFF IS HEAVY...

5 0 3

DON'T ANY OF THESE PEOPLE PUT THEIR NAMES ON THE DOOR?

SHHH! GOTTA BE BUSINESS-LIKE AND PROFES-SIONAL.

...AND IT'S HOT.

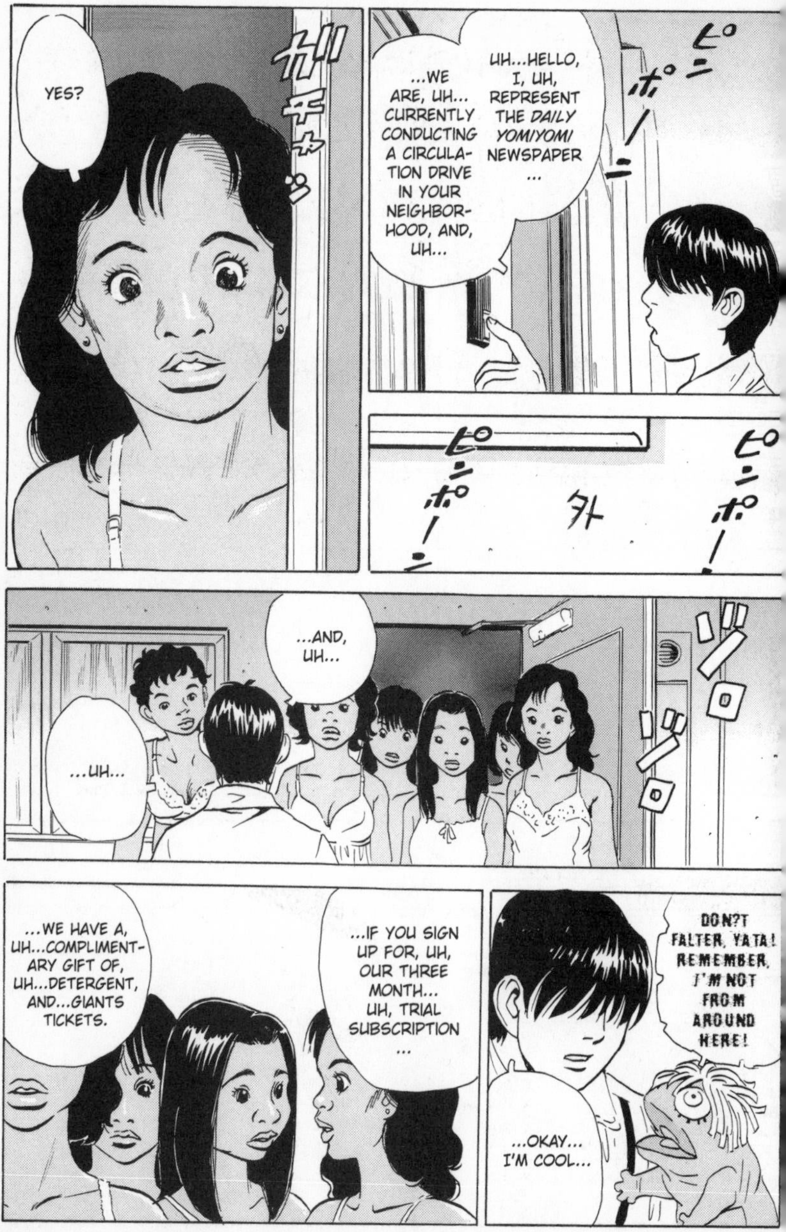
ピンポーン
UH...HELLO, I, UH, REPRESENT THE *DAILY YOMIYOMI* NEWSPAPER ...
...WE ARE, UH... CURRENTLY CONDUCTING A CIRCULATION DRIVE IN YOUR NEIGHBORHOOD, AND, UH...
ピンポーン
外
ピンポーン
YES?
...AND, UH...
...UH...
DON?T FALTER, YATA! REMEMBER, I'M NOT FROM AROUND HERE!
...OKAY... I'M COOL...
...IF YOU SIGN UP FOR, UH, OUR THREE MONTH... UH, TRIAL SUBSCRIPTION ...
...WE HAVE A, UH...COMPLIMENTARY GIFT OF, UH...DETERGENT, AND...GIANTS TICKETS.

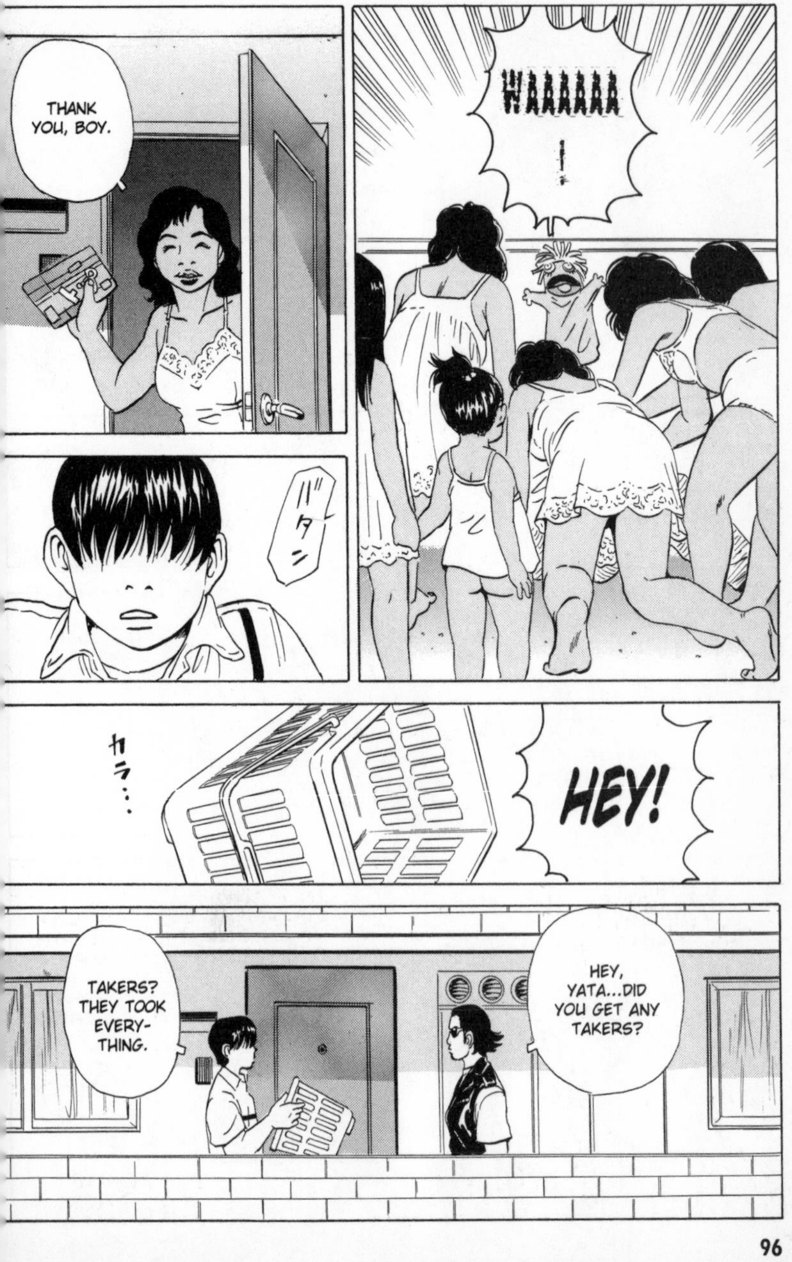
WAAAAAA!
THANK YOU, BOY.
バタン
HEY!
カラ…
HEY, YATA...DID YOU GET ANY TAKERS?
TAKERS? THEY TOOK EVERY-THING.

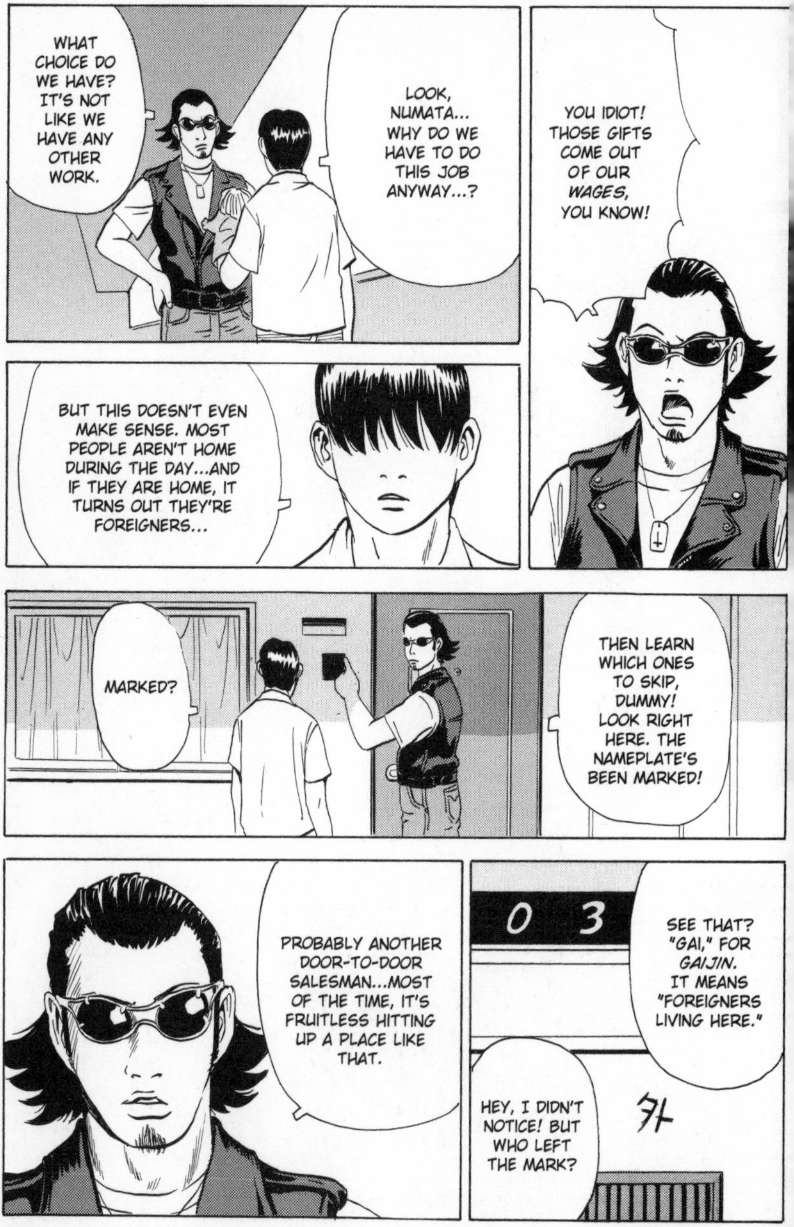
YOU IDIOT! THOSE GIFTS COME OUT OF OUR *WAGES*, YOU KNOW!
LOOK, NUMATA... WHY DO WE HAVE TO DO THIS JOB ANYWAY...?
WHAT CHOICE DO WE HAVE? IT'S NOT LIKE WE HAVE ANY OTHER WORK.
BUT THIS DOESN'T EVEN MAKE SENSE. MOST PEOPLE AREN'T HOME DURING THE DAY...AND IF THEY ARE HOME, IT TURNS OUT THEY'RE FOREIGNERS...
THEN LEARN WHICH ONES TO SKIP, DUMMY! LOOK RIGHT HERE. THE NAMEPLATE'S BEEN MARKED!
MARKED?
0 3
SEE THAT? "GAI," FOR *GAIJIN*. IT MEANS "FOREIGNERS LIVING HERE."
外
HEY, I DIDN'T NOTICE! BUT WHO LEFT THE MARK?
PROBABLY ANOTHER DOOR-TO-DOOR SALESMAN...MOST OF THE TIME, IT'S FRUITLESS HITTING UP A PLACE LIKE THAT.

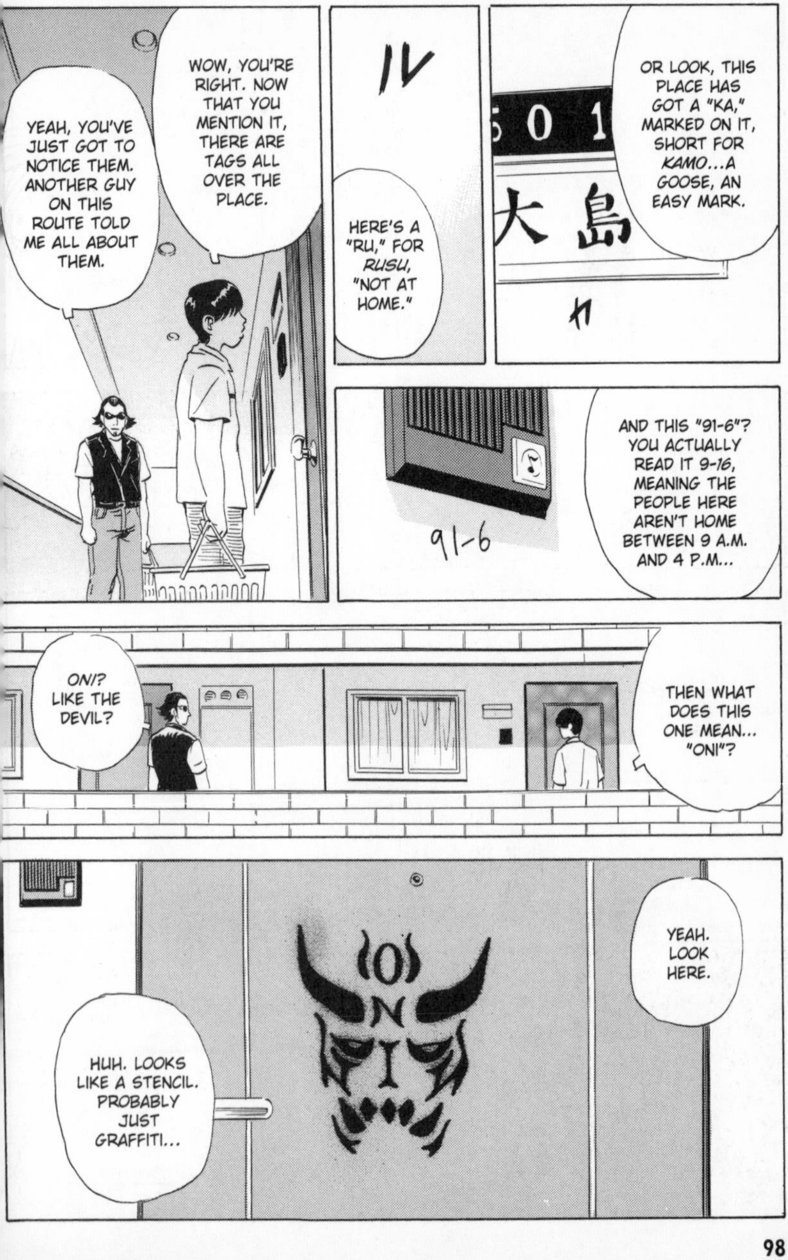
OR LOOK, THIS PLACE HAS GOT A "KA," MARKED ON IT, SHORT FOR *KAMO*...A GOOSE, AN EASY MARK.
HERE'S A "RU," FOR *RUSU*, "NOT AT HOME."
AND THIS "91-6"? YOU ACTUALLY READ IT 9-*16*, MEANING THE PEOPLE HERE AREN'T HOME BETWEEN 9 A.M. AND 4 P.M...
WOW, YOU'RE RIGHT. NOW THAT YOU MENTION IT, THERE ARE TAGS ALL OVER THE PLACE.
YEAH, YOU'VE JUST GOT TO NOTICE THEM. ANOTHER GUY ON THIS ROUTE TOLD ME ALL ABOUT THEM.
THEN WHAT DOES THIS ONE MEAN... "ONI"?
ONI? LIKE THE DEVIL?
YEAH. LOOK HERE.
HUH. LOOKS LIKE A STENCIL. PROBABLY JUST GRAFFITI...

THINK THOSE ARE PAINT DROPS DOWN THERE...OR JUST HUMAN BLOOD?
チャラン
IT'S REACTING, ISN'T IT?
YEP. NOW *THIS* MEANS A CORPSE LIVES HERE.
SH- SHOULD WE...?
ガチャ

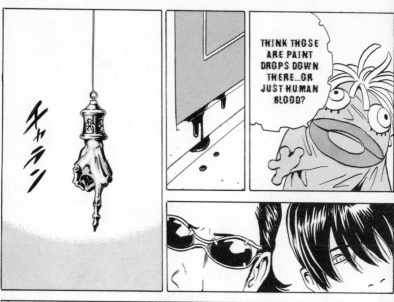

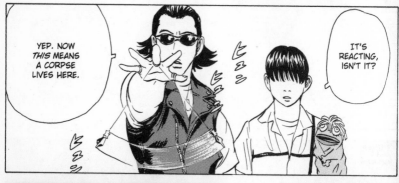

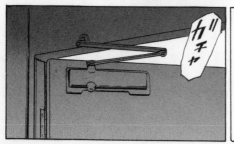

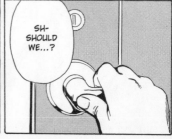

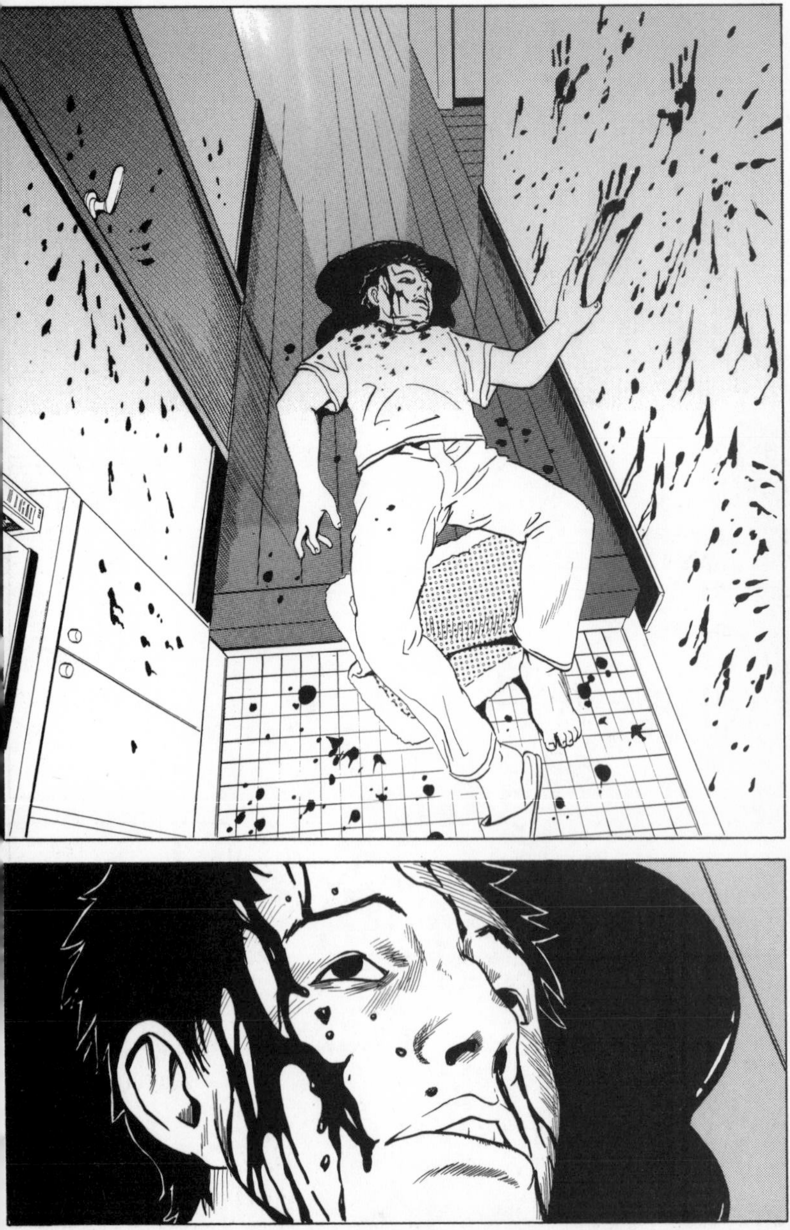

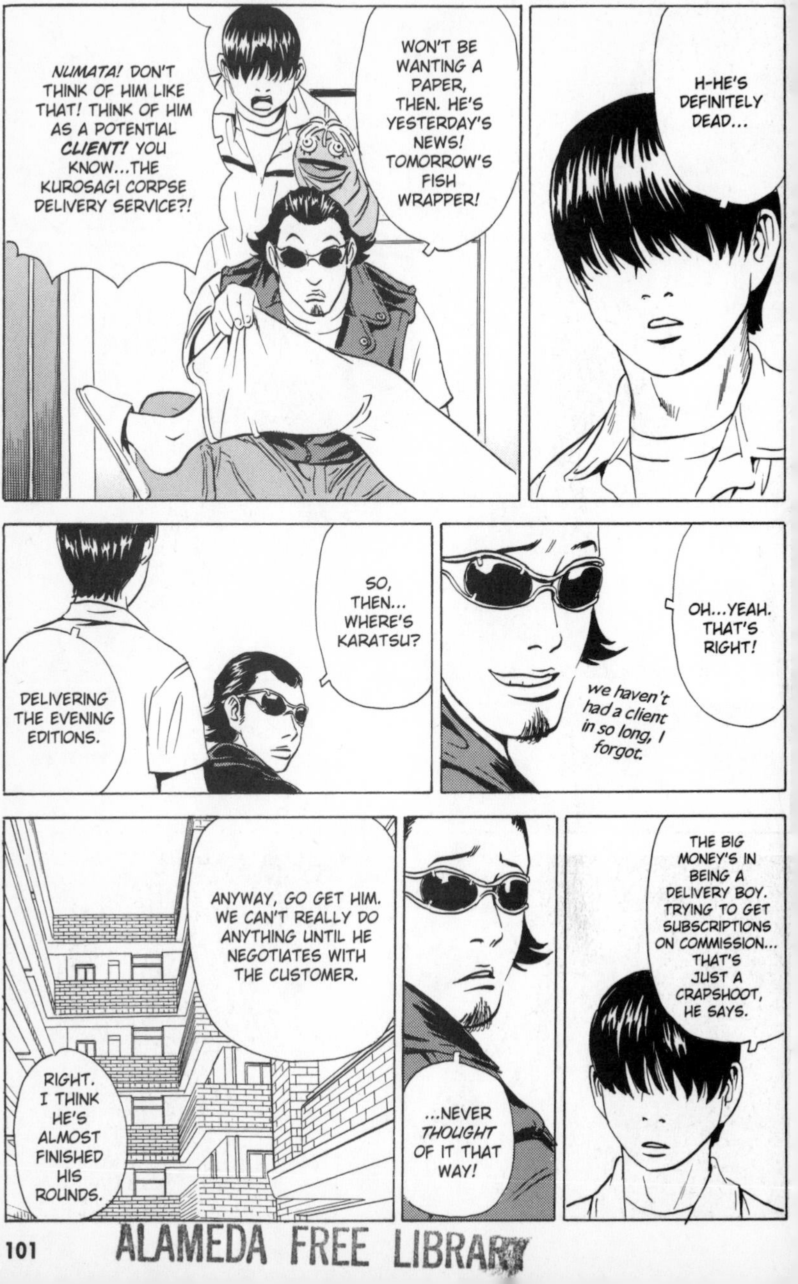
H-HE'S DEFINITELY DEAD...
WON'T BE WANTING A PAPER, THEN. HE'S YESTERDAY'S NEWS! TOMORROW'S FISH WRAPPER!
NUMATA! DON'T THINK OF HIM LIKE THAT! THINK OF HIM AS A POTENTIAL ***CLIENT!*** YOU KNOW...THE KUROSAGI CORPSE DELIVERY SERVICE?!
OH...YEAH. THAT'S RIGHT!
we haven't had a client in so long, I forgot.
SO, THEN... WHERE'S KARATSU?
DELIVERING THE EVENING EDITIONS.
THE BIG MONEY'S IN BEING A DELIVERY BOY. TRYING TO GET SUBSCRIPTIONS ON COMMISSION... THAT'S JUST A CRAPSHOOT, HE SAYS.
...NEVER *THOUGHT* OF IT THAT WAY!
ANYWAY, GO GET HIM. WE CAN'T REALLY DO ANYTHING UNTIL HE NEGOTIATES WITH THE CUSTOMER.
RIGHT. I THINK HE'S ALMOST FINISHED HIS ROUNDS.

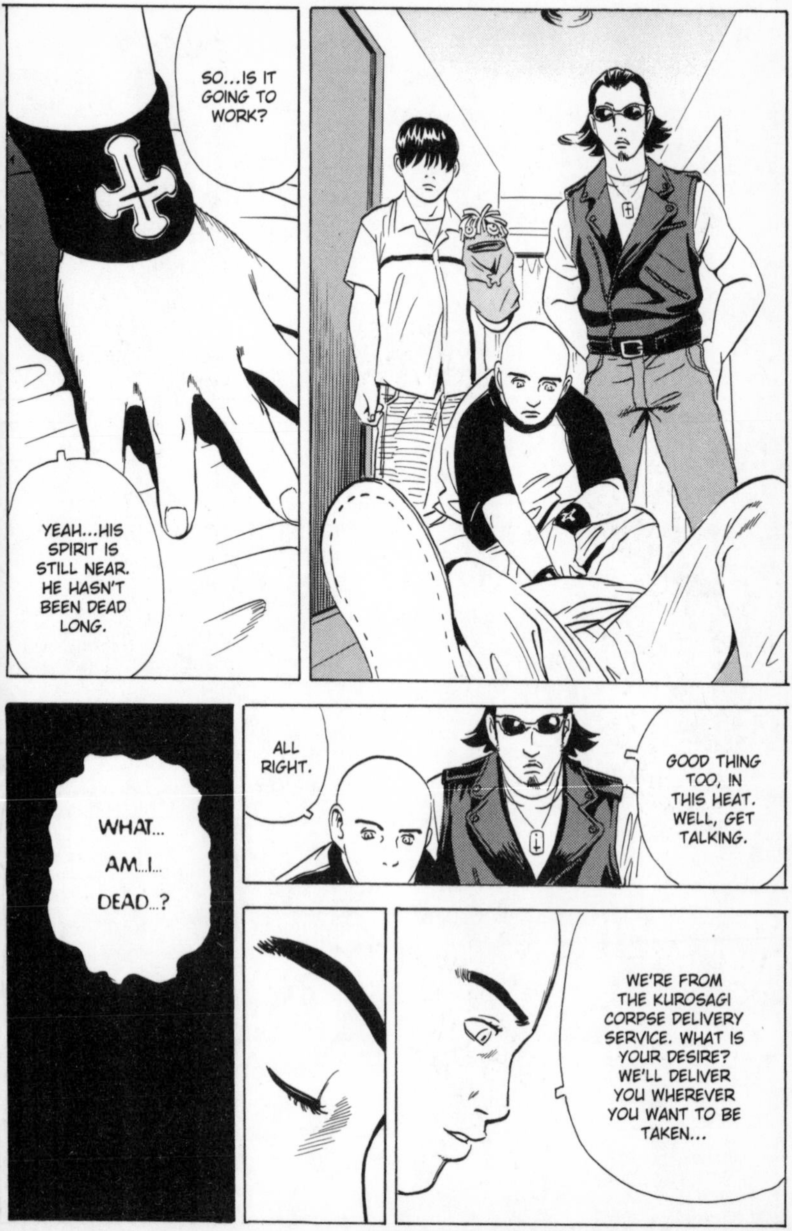
SO...IS IT GOING TO WORK?
YEAH...HIS SPIRIT IS STILL NEAR. HE HASN'T BEEN DEAD LONG.
GOOD THING TOO, IN THIS HEAT. WELL, GET TALKING.
ALL RIGHT.
WE'RE FROM THE KUROSAGI CORPSE DELIVERY SERVICE. WHAT IS YOUR DESIRE? WE'LL DELIVER YOU WHEREVER YOU WANT TO BE TAKEN...
WHAT... AM...I... DEAD...?

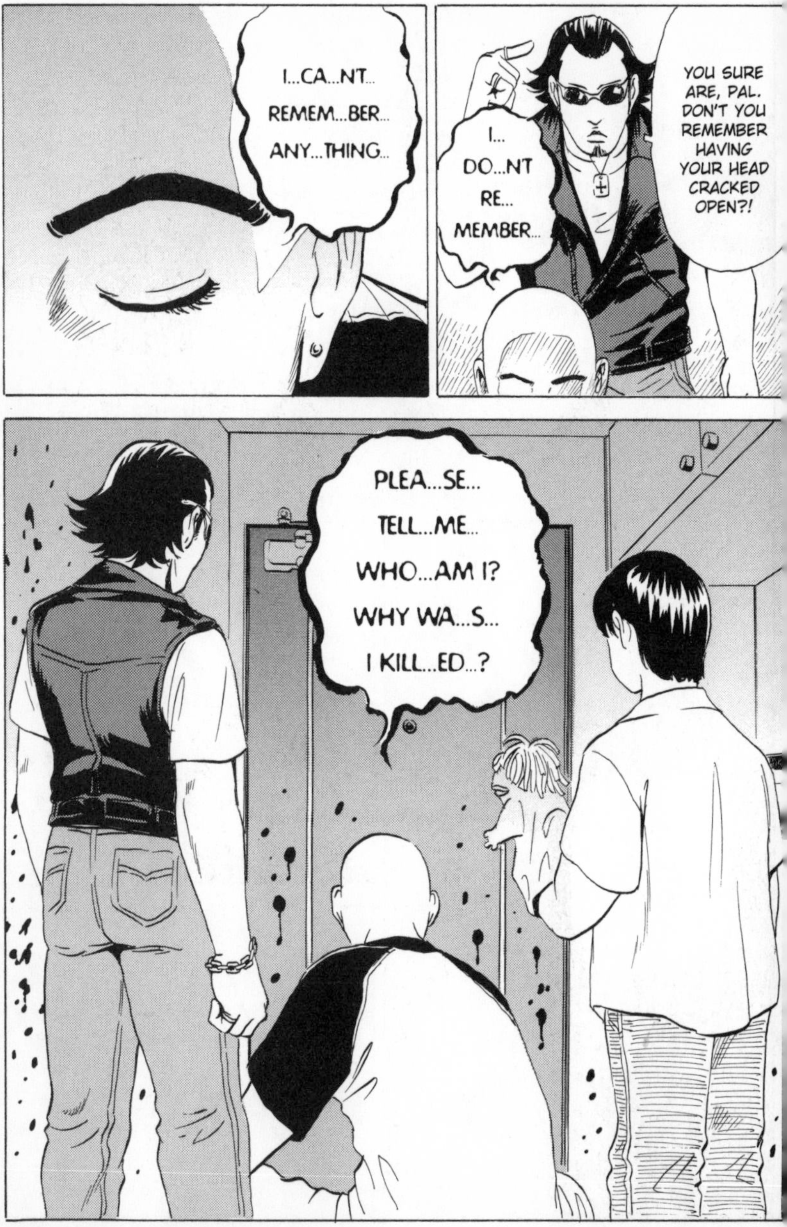
YOU SURE ARE, PAL. DON'T YOU REMEMBER HAVING YOUR HEAD CRACKED OPEN?!
I... DO...NT RE... MEMBER...
I...CA...NT... REMEM...BER... ANY...THING...
PLEA...SE... TELL...ME... WHO...AM I? WHY WA...S... I KILL...ED...?

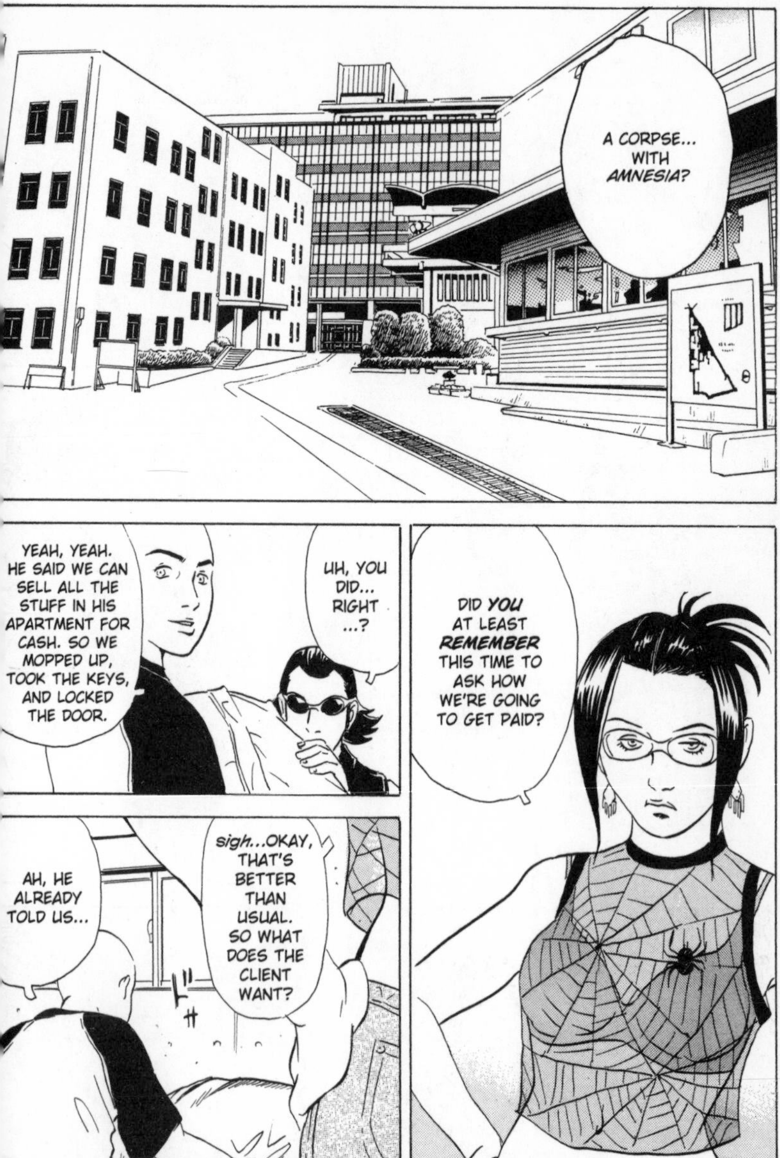
A CORPSE... WITH *AMNESIA?*
DID *YOU* AT LEAST *REMEMBER* THIS TIME TO ASK HOW WE'RE GOING TO GET PAID?
UH, YOU DID... RIGHT ...?
YEAH, YEAH. HE SAID WE CAN SELL ALL THE STUFF IN HIS APARTMENT FOR CASH. SO WE MOPPED UP, TOOK THE KEYS, AND LOCKED THE DOOR.
sigh...OKAY, THAT'S BETTER THAN USUAL. SO WHAT DOES THE CLIENT WANT?
AH, HE ALREADY TOLD US...

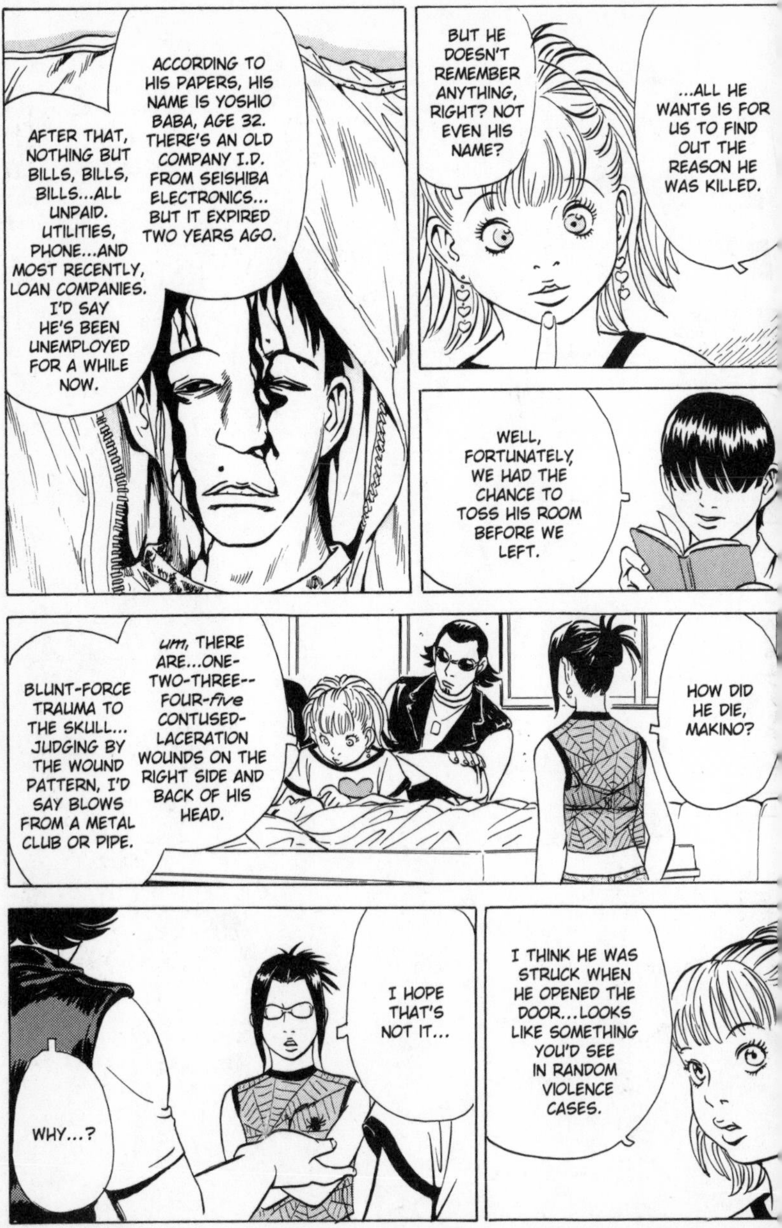
...ALL HE WANTS IS FOR US TO FIND OUT THE REASON HE WAS KILLED.
BUT HE DOESN'T REMEMBER ANYTHING, RIGHT? NOT EVEN HIS NAME?
WELL, FORTUNATELY, WE HAD THE CHANCE TO TOSS HIS ROOM BEFORE WE LEFT.
ACCORDING TO HIS PAPERS, HIS NAME IS YOSHIO BABA, AGE 32. THERE'S AN OLD COMPANY I.D. FROM SEISHIBA ELECTRONICS... BUT IT EXPIRED TWO YEARS AGO.
AFTER THAT, NOTHING BUT BILLS, BILLS, BILLS...ALL UNPAID. UTILITIES, PHONE...AND MOST RECENTLY, LOAN COMPANIES. I'D SAY HE'S BEEN UNEMPLOYED FOR A WHILE NOW.
HOW DID HE DIE, MAKINO?
um, THERE ARE...ONE-TWO-THREE--FOUR-*five* CONTUSED-LACERATION WOUNDS ON THE RIGHT SIDE AND BACK OF HIS HEAD.
BLUNT-FORCE TRAUMA TO THE SKULL... JUDGING BY THE WOUND PATTERN, I'D SAY BLOWS FROM A METAL CLUB OR PIPE.
I THINK HE WAS STRUCK WHEN HE OPENED THE DOOR...LOOKS LIKE SOMETHING YOU'D SEE IN RANDOM VIOLENCE CASES.
I HOPE THAT'S NOT IT...
WHY...?

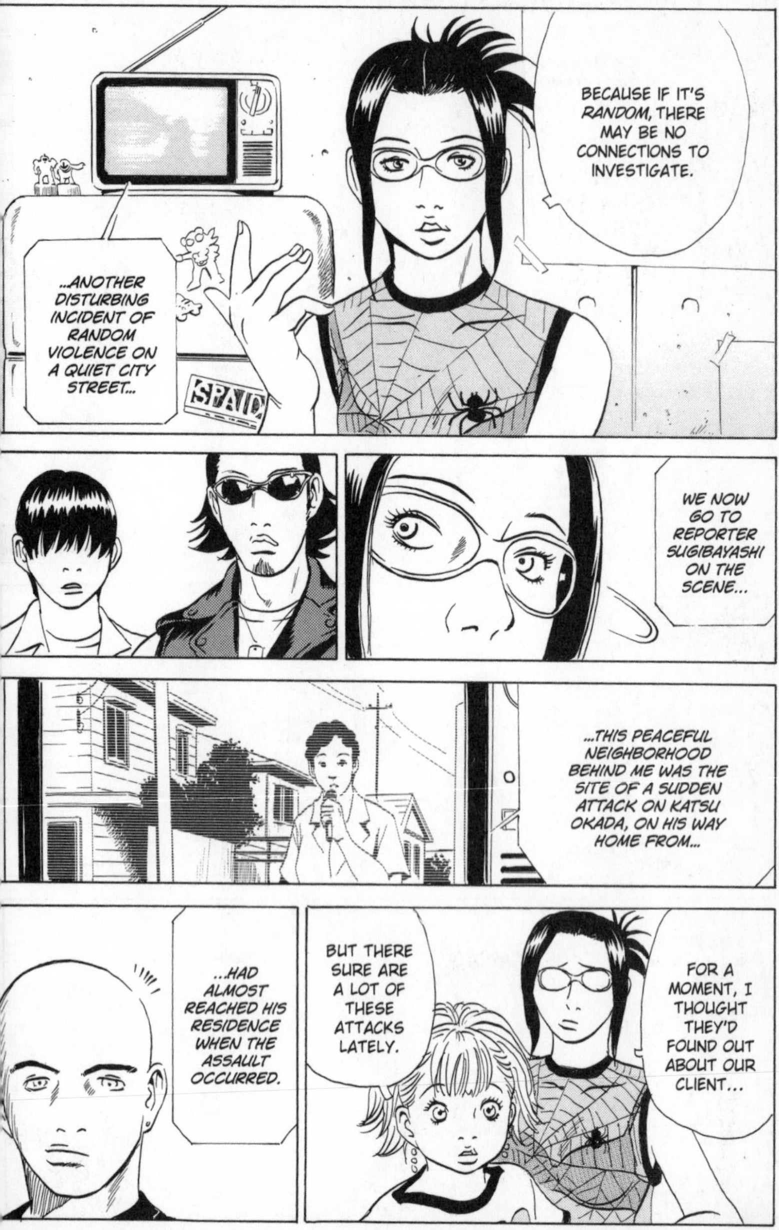

BECAUSE IF IT'S *RANDOM*, THERE MAY BE NO CONNECTIONS TO INVESTIGATE.
...ANOTHER DISTURBING INCIDENT OF RANDOM VIOLENCE ON A QUIET CITY STREET...
WE NOW GO TO REPORTER SUGIBAYASHI ON THE SCENE...
...THIS PEACEFUL NEIGHBORHOOD BEHIND ME WAS THE SITE OF A SUDDEN ATTACK ON KATSU OKADA, ON HIS WAY HOME FROM...
FOR A MOMENT, I THOUGHT THEY'D FOUND OUT ABOUT OUR CLIENT...
BUT THERE SURE ARE A LOT OF THESE ATTACKS LATELY.
...HAD ALMOST REACHED HIS RESIDENCE WHEN THE ASSAULT OCCURRED.

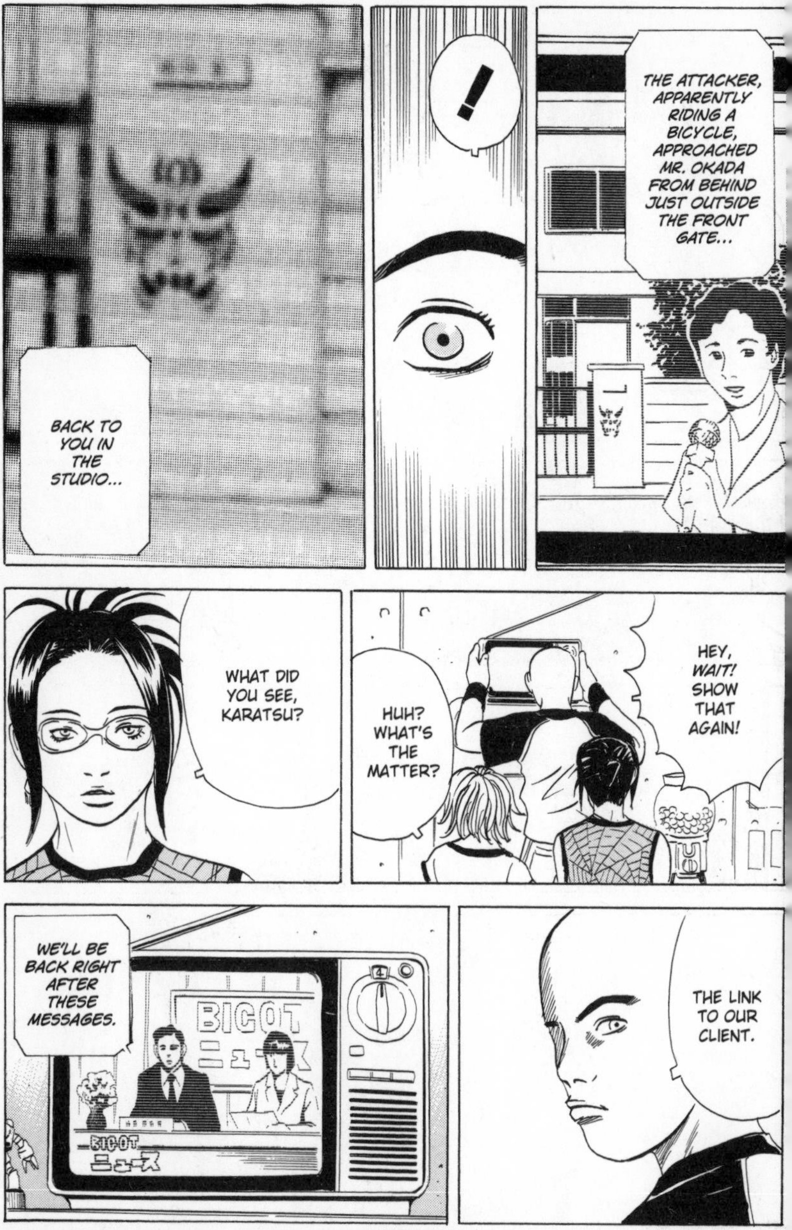
THE ATTACKER, APPARENTLY RIDING A BICYCLE, APPROACHED MR. OKADA FROM BEHIND JUST OUTSIDE THE FRONT GATE...
!
BACK TO YOU IN THE STUDIO...
HEY, WAIT! SHOW THAT AGAIN!
HUH? WHAT'S THE MATTER?
WHAT DID YOU SEE, KARATSU?
THE LINK TO OUR CLIENT.
WE'LL BE BACK RIGHT AFTER THESE MESSAGES.
BIGOT
ニュース

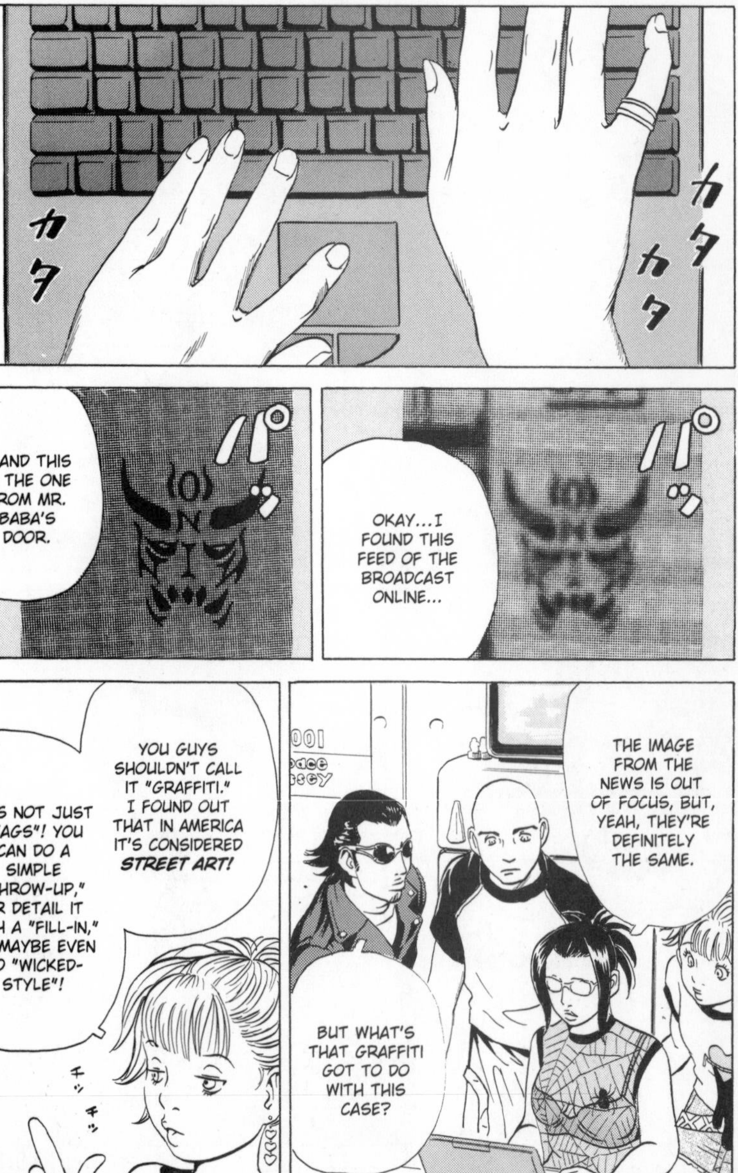
カタ
カタ
カタ
OKAY...I FOUND THIS FEED OF THE BROADCAST ONLINE...
パッ
...AND THIS IS THE ONE FROM MR. BABA'S DOOR.
パッ
THE IMAGE FROM THE NEWS IS OUT OF FOCUS, BUT, YEAH, THEY'RE DEFINITELY THE SAME.
BUT WHAT'S THAT GRAFFITI GOT TO DO WITH THIS CASE?
YOU GUYS SHOULDN'T CALL IT "GRAFFITI." I FOUND OUT THAT IN AMERICA IT'S CONSIDERED ***STREET ART!***
IT'S NOT JUST "TAGS"! YOU CAN DO A SIMPLE "THROW-UP," OR DETAIL IT WITH A "FILL-IN," OR MAYBE EVEN GO "WICKED-STYLE"!
チッ
チッ

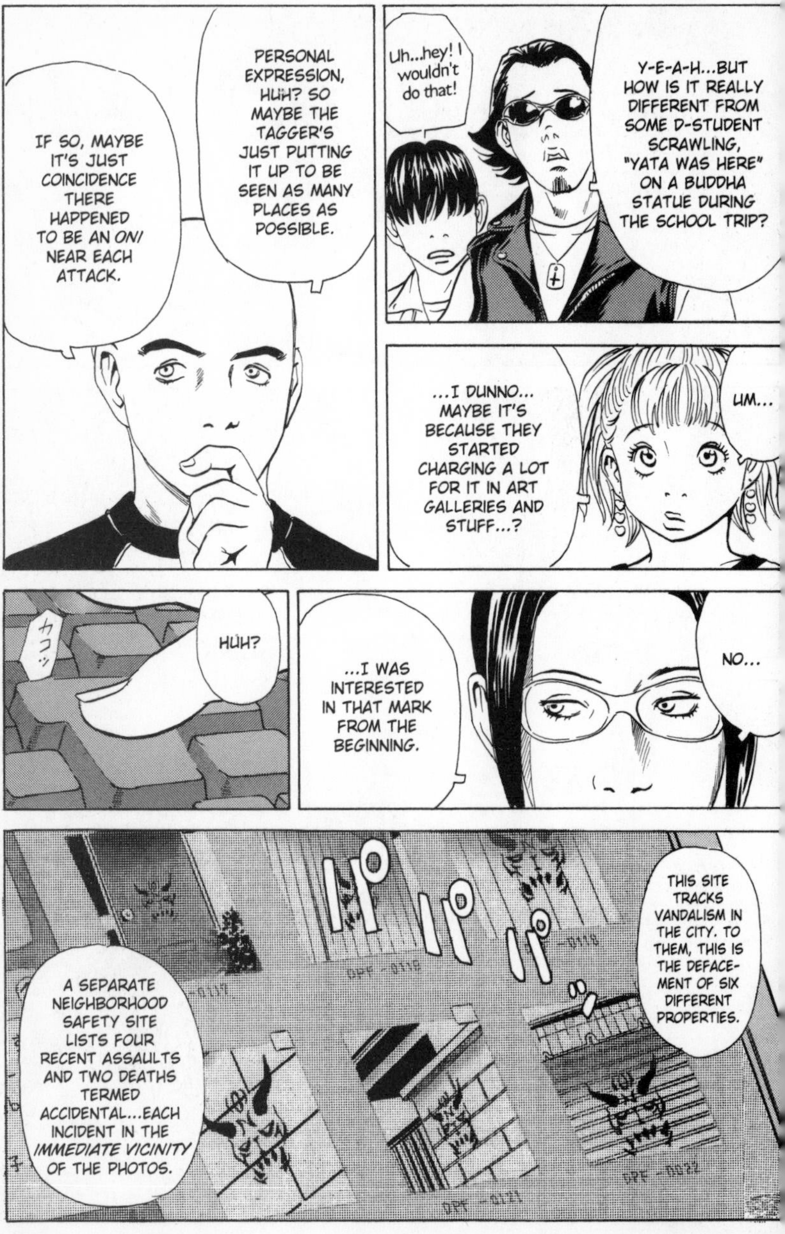
Y-E-A-H...BUT HOW IS IT REALLY DIFFERENT FROM SOME D-STUDENT SCRAWLING, "YATA WAS HERE" ON A BUDDHA STATUE DURING THE SCHOOL TRIP?
Uh...hey! I wouldn't do that!
UM...
...I DUNNO... MAYBE IT'S BECAUSE THEY STARTED CHARGING A LOT FOR IT IN ART GALLERIES AND STUFF...?
PERSONAL EXPRESSION, HUH? SO MAYBE THE TAGGER'S JUST PUTTING IT UP TO BE SEEN AS MANY PLACES AS POSSIBLE.
IF SO, MAYBE IT'S JUST COINCIDENCE THERE HAPPENED TO BE AN *ONI* NEAR EACH ATTACK.
NO...
...I WAS INTERESTED IN THAT MARK FROM THE BEGINNING.
HUH?
カコッ
THIS SITE TRACKS VANDALISM IN THE CITY. TO THEM, THIS IS THE DEFACEMENT OF SIX DIFFERENT PROPERTIES.
A SEPARATE NEIGHBORHOOD SAFETY SITE LISTS FOUR RECENT ASSAULTS AND TWO DEATHS TERMED ACCIDENTAL...EACH INCIDENT IN THE *IMMEDIATE VICINITY* OF THE PHOTOS.

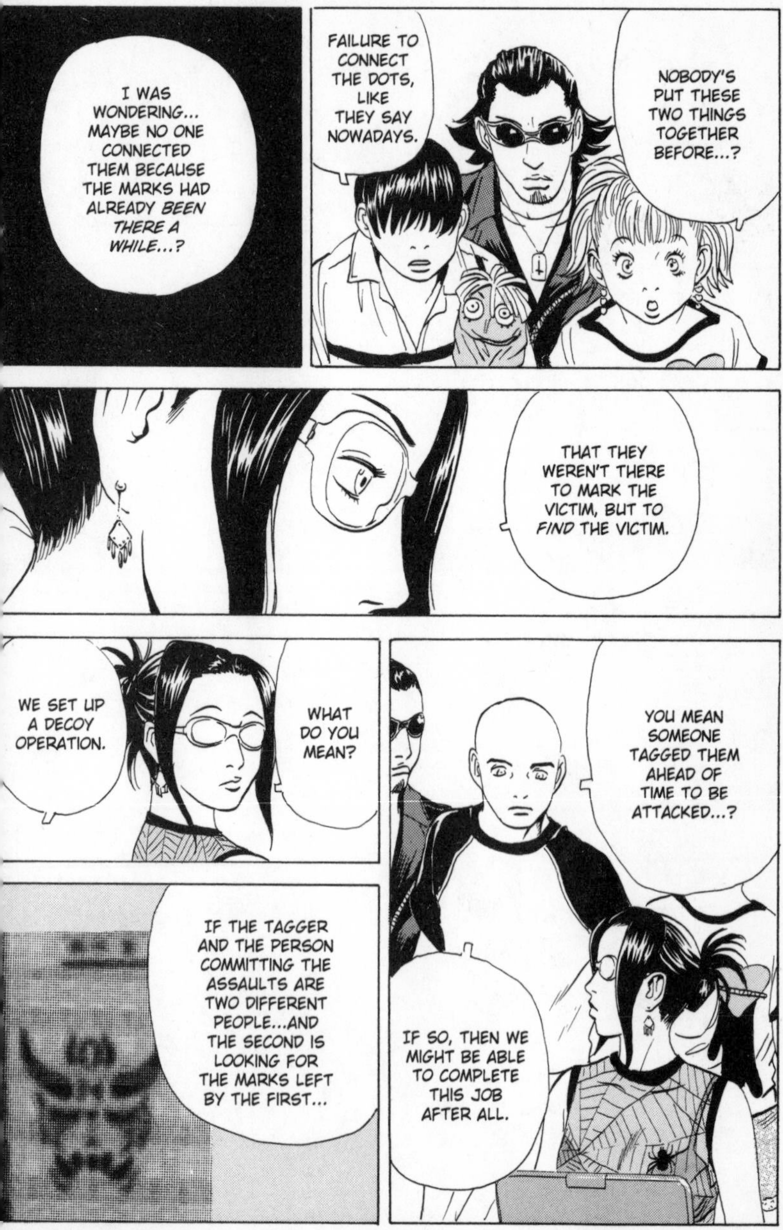
NOBODY'S PUT THESE TWO THINGS TOGETHER BEFORE...?
FAILURE TO CONNECT THE DOTS, LIKE THEY SAY NOWADAYS.
I WAS WONDERING... MAYBE NO ONE CONNECTED THEM BECAUSE THE MARKS HAD ALREADY *BEEN THERE A WHILE...?*
THAT THEY WEREN'T THERE TO MARK THE VICTIM, BUT TO *FIND* THE VICTIM.
YOU MEAN SOMEONE TAGGED THEM AHEAD OF TIME TO BE ATTACKED...?
IF SO, THEN WE MIGHT BE ABLE TO COMPLETE THIS JOB AFTER ALL.
WHAT DO YOU MEAN?
WE SET UP A DECOY OPERATION.
IF THE TAGGER AND THE PERSON COMMITTING THE ASSAULTS ARE TWO DIFFERENT PEOPLE...AND THE SECOND IS LOOKING FOR THE MARKS LEFT BY THE FIRST...

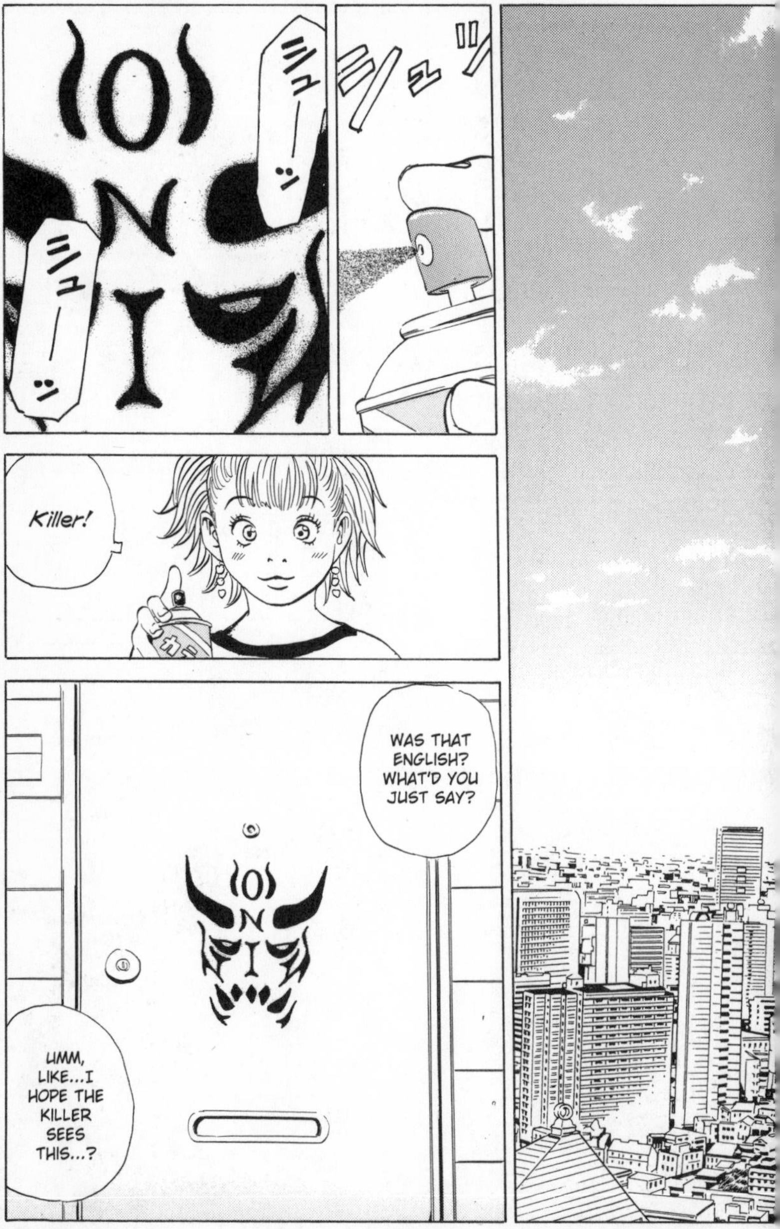
シュッ
シューーッ
シューーッ
Killer!
WAS THAT ENGLISH? WHAT'D YOU JUST SAY?
UMM, LIKE...I HOPE THE KILLER SEES THIS...?

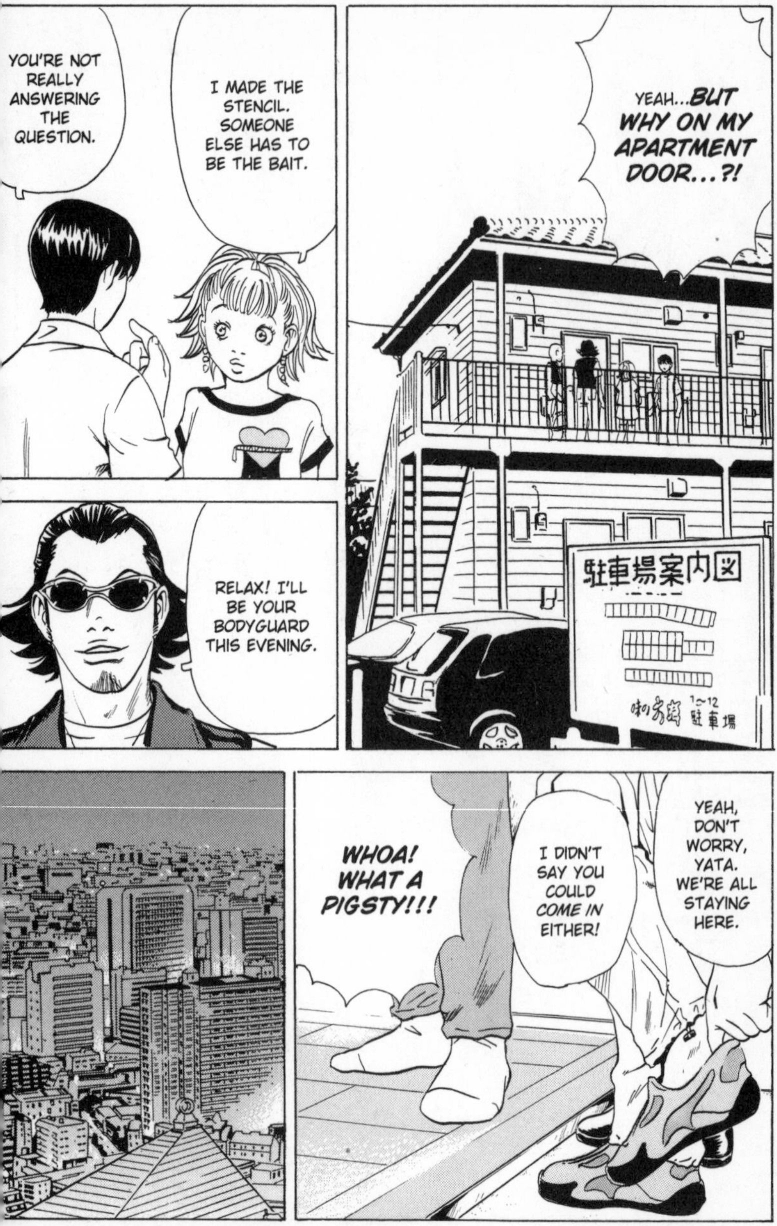
YEAH...BUT WHY ON MY APARTMENT DOOR...?!
駐車場案内図
I MADE THE STENCIL. SOMEONE ELSE HAS TO BE THE BAIT.
YOU'RE NOT REALLY ANSWERING THE QUESTION.
RELAX! I'LL BE YOUR BODYGUARD THIS EVENING.
YEAH, DON'T WORRY, YATA. WE'RE ALL STAYING HERE.
I DIDN'T SAY YOU COULD COME IN EITHER!
WHOA! WHAT A PIGSTY!!!

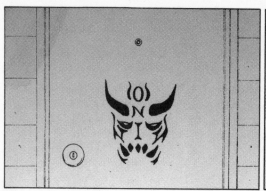

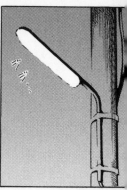

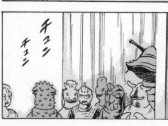

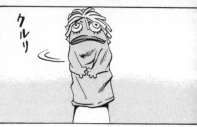

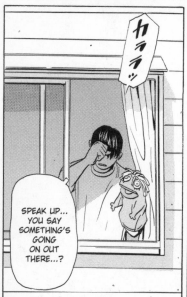

ONI
チュン
チュン
クルリ
HEY, YATA, YOUR PLANET HAS ROTATED ONCE MORE TO FACE ITS PRIMARY! GET UP!
Huh? Whuh is it...?
カラララッ
SPEAK UP... YOU SAY SOMETHING'S GOING ON OUT THERE...?

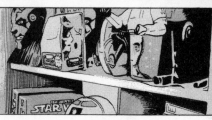

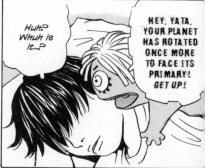

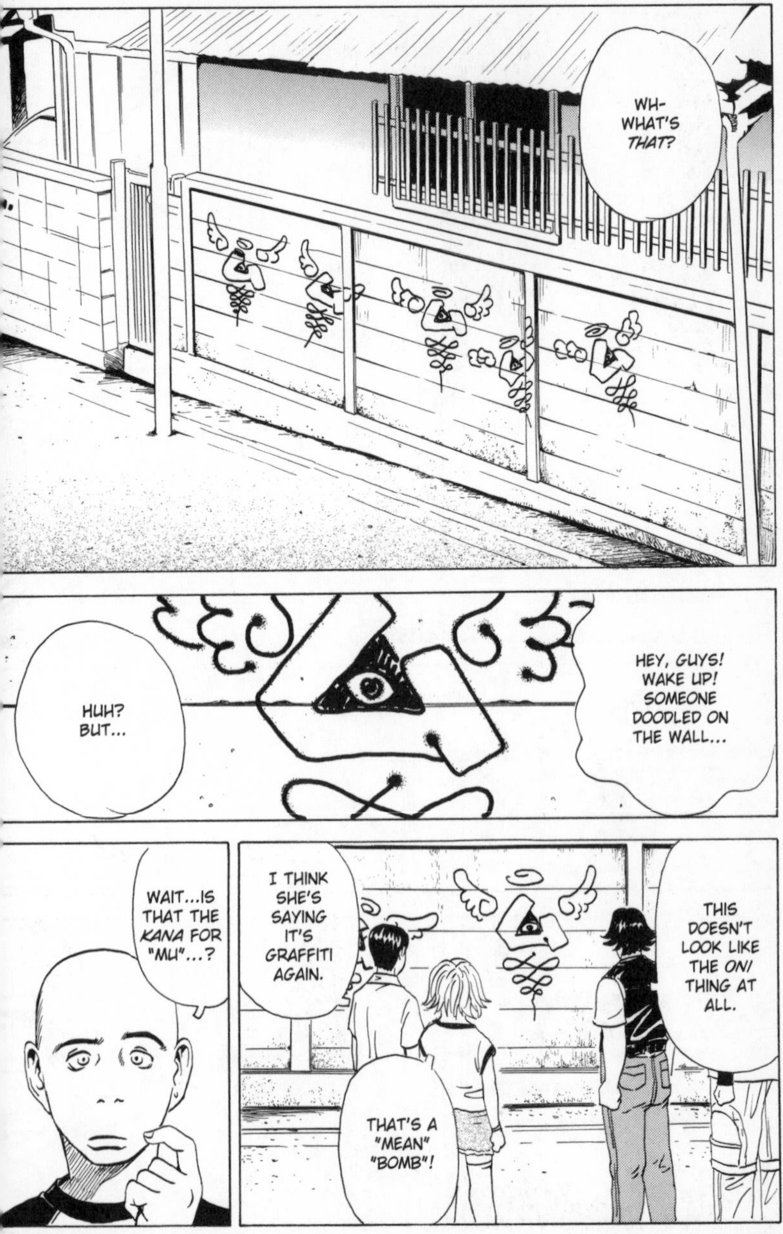
WH-
WHAT'S
THAT?
HEY, GUYS! WAKE UP! SOMEONE DOODLED ON THE WALL...
HUH? BUT...
THIS DOESN'T LOOK LIKE THE *ONI* THING AT ALL.
I THINK SHE'S SAYING IT'S GRAFFITI AGAIN.
THAT'S A "MEAN" "BOMB"!
WAIT...IS THAT THE *KANA* FOR "MU"...?

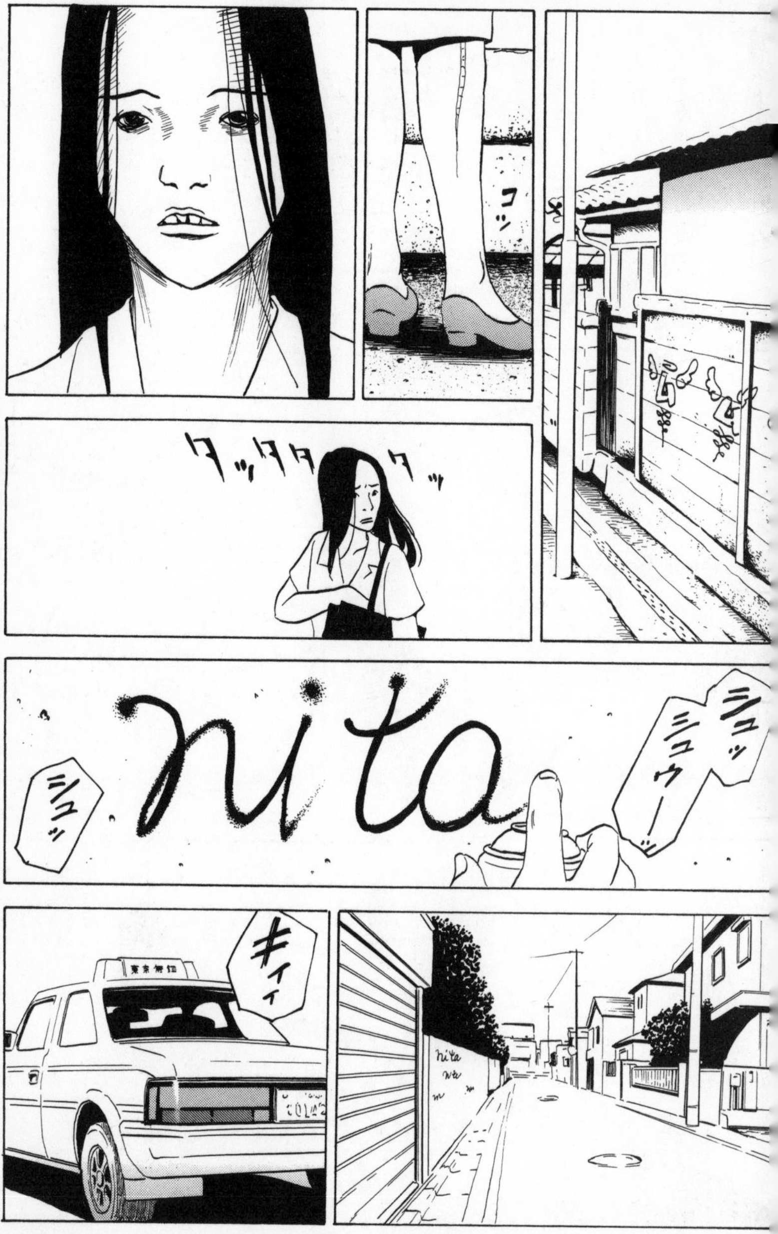
コツ
タッタタ
タッ
シュッシュウー…
nita
シュッ
キイイ
nita
nita

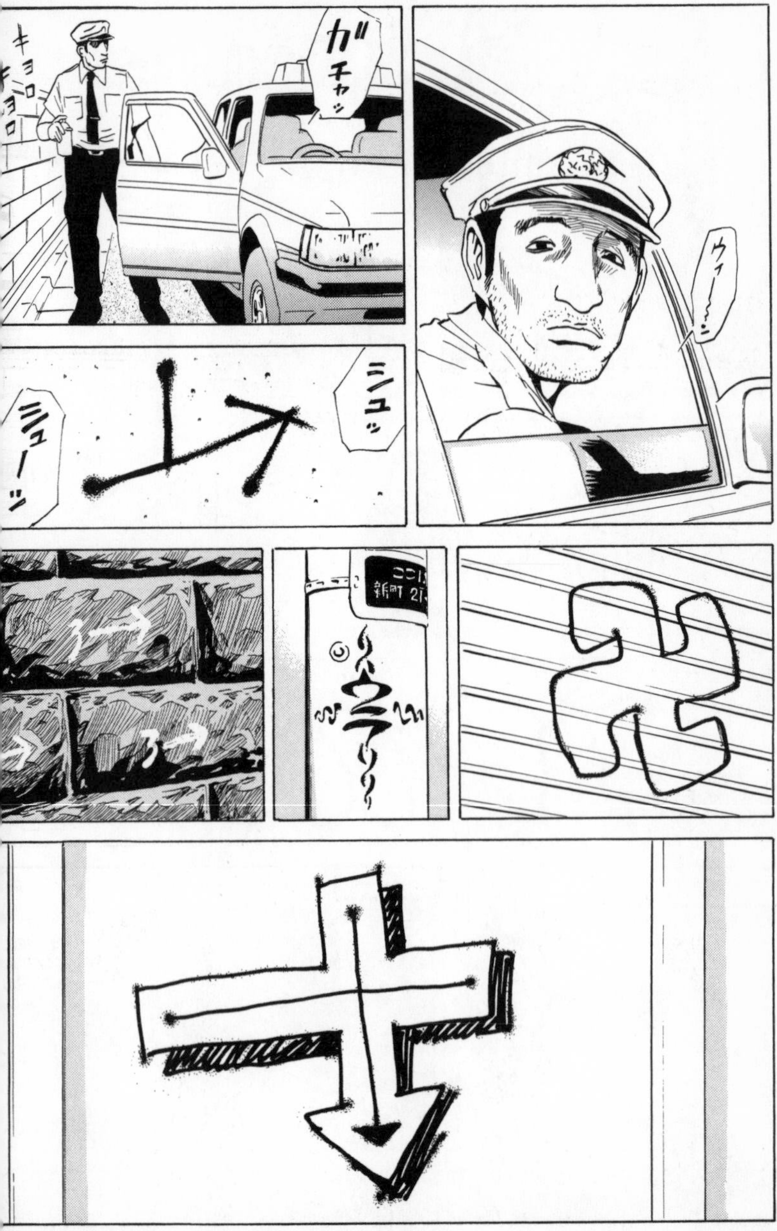
ウァ〜〜ン
ガチャッ
キョロキョロ
シュッ
シューッ
ウラ

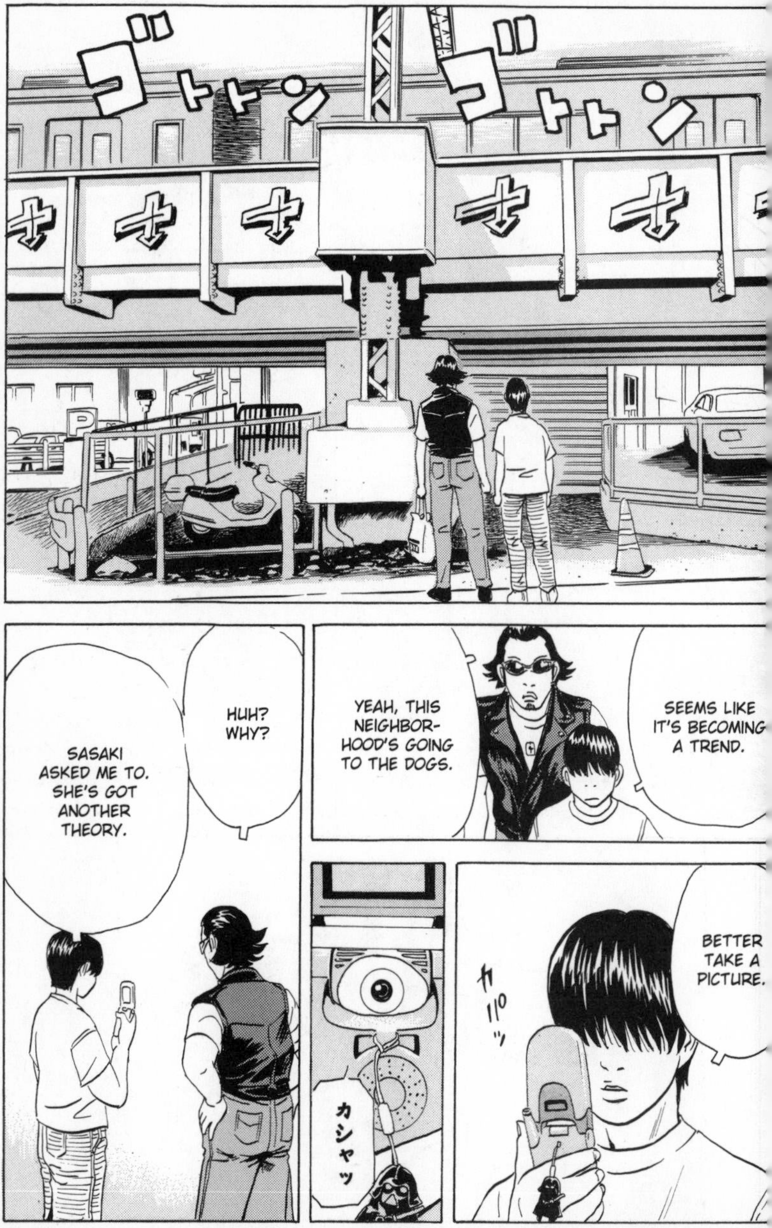
ゴトトン
ゴトトン
SEEMS LIKE IT'S BECOMING A TREND.
YEAH, THIS NEIGHBOR-HOOD'S GOING TO THE DOGS.
BETTER TAKE A PICTURE.
カパッ
カシャッ
HUH? WHY?
SASAKI ASKED ME TO. SHE'S GOT ANOTHER THEORY.

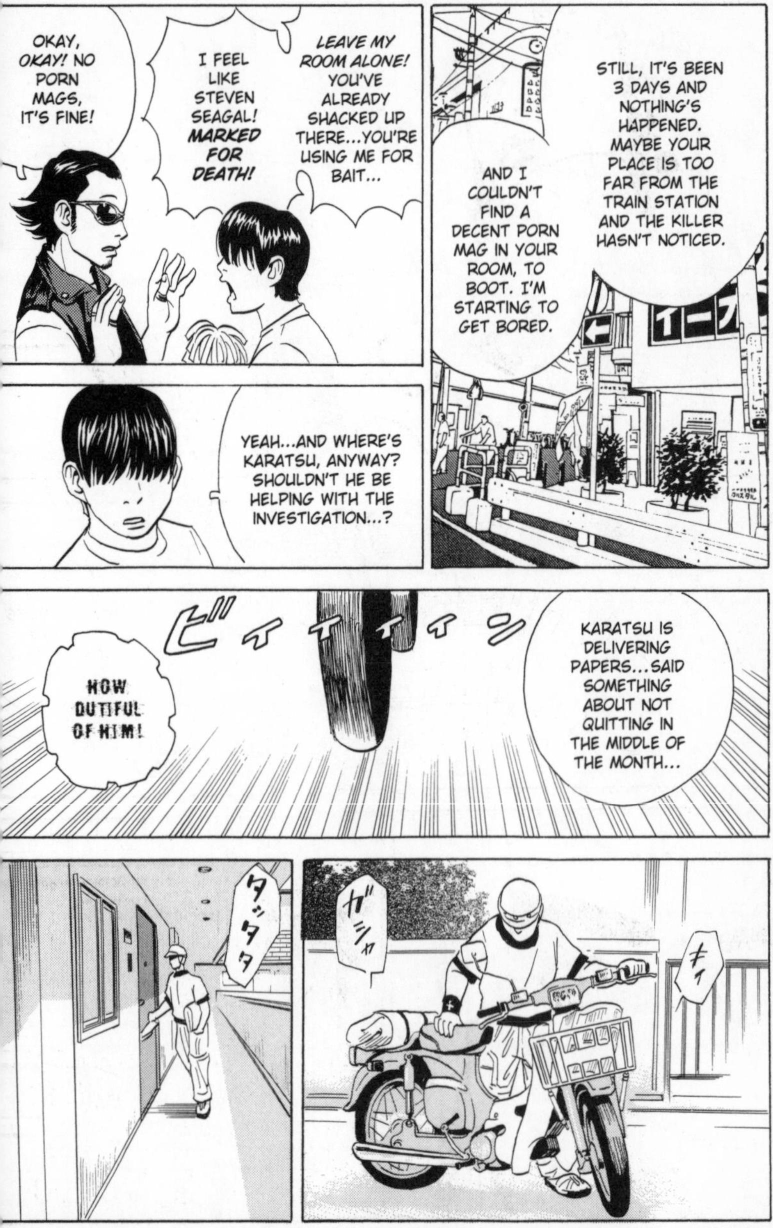
STILL, IT'S BEEN 3 DAYS AND NOTHING'S HAPPENED. MAYBE YOUR PLACE IS TOO FAR FROM THE TRAIN STATION AND THE KILLER HASN'T NOTICED.
AND I COULDN'T FIND A DECENT PORN MAG IN YOUR ROOM, TO BOOT. I'M STARTING TO GET BORED.
LEAVE MY ROOM ALONE! YOU'VE ALREADY SHACKED UP THERE...YOU'RE USING ME FOR BAIT...
I FEEL LIKE STEVEN SEAGAL! ***MARKED FOR DEATH!***
OKAY, *OKAY!* NO PORN MAGS, IT'S FINE!
YEAH...AND WHERE'S KARATSU, ANYWAY? SHOULDN'T HE BE HELPING WITH THE INVESTIGATION...?
KARATSU IS DELIVERING PAPERS...SAID SOMETHING ABOUT NOT QUITTING IN THE MIDDLE OF THE MONTH...
ビィィィィン
HOW DUTIFUL OF HIM!
キィ
ガシャ
タッタタ

IT'S HERE, TOO...?

HUH?

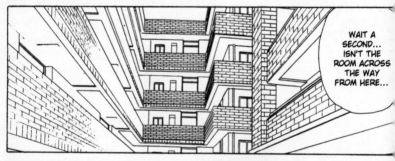

WAIT A SECOND... ISN'T THE ROOM ACROSS THE WAY FROM HERE...

MU... "MUKAI"...

...ACROSS.

YEAH. IT'S WHERE OUR CLIENT LIVED.

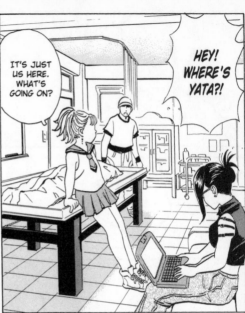

HEY! WHERE'S YATA?!
IT'S JUST US HERE. WHAT'S GOING ON?
I JUST FIGURED IT OUT...
...WHAT'S THAT?
HUH? THIS? THESE ARE ALL THE TAGS THAT HAVE SHOWN UP AROUND YATA'S NEIGH-BORHOOD.
SO MANY ALREADY? THIS IS BAD.
BAD? HOW DO YOU MEAN, BAD...?
THEY AREN'T TAGS.
THEY'RE ROUTE CODES. WITH JUST THE *ONI* MARK, THERE'S NO WAY THE KILLER COULD HAVE SEARCHED EVERY DOOR IN THE AREA.
LOOK. THESE ARE THE CODES DELIVERY PEOPLE ARE GIVEN FOR PAPER ROUTES.
APER ROUTE CODE
Straight at Intersection
Bend
Switchback
Forward
T-Intersection

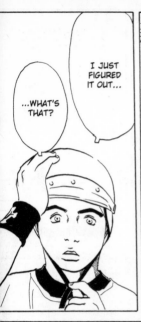

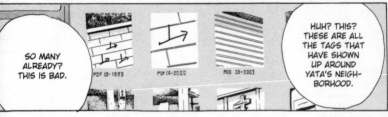

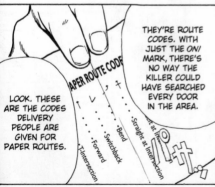

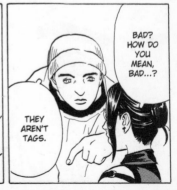

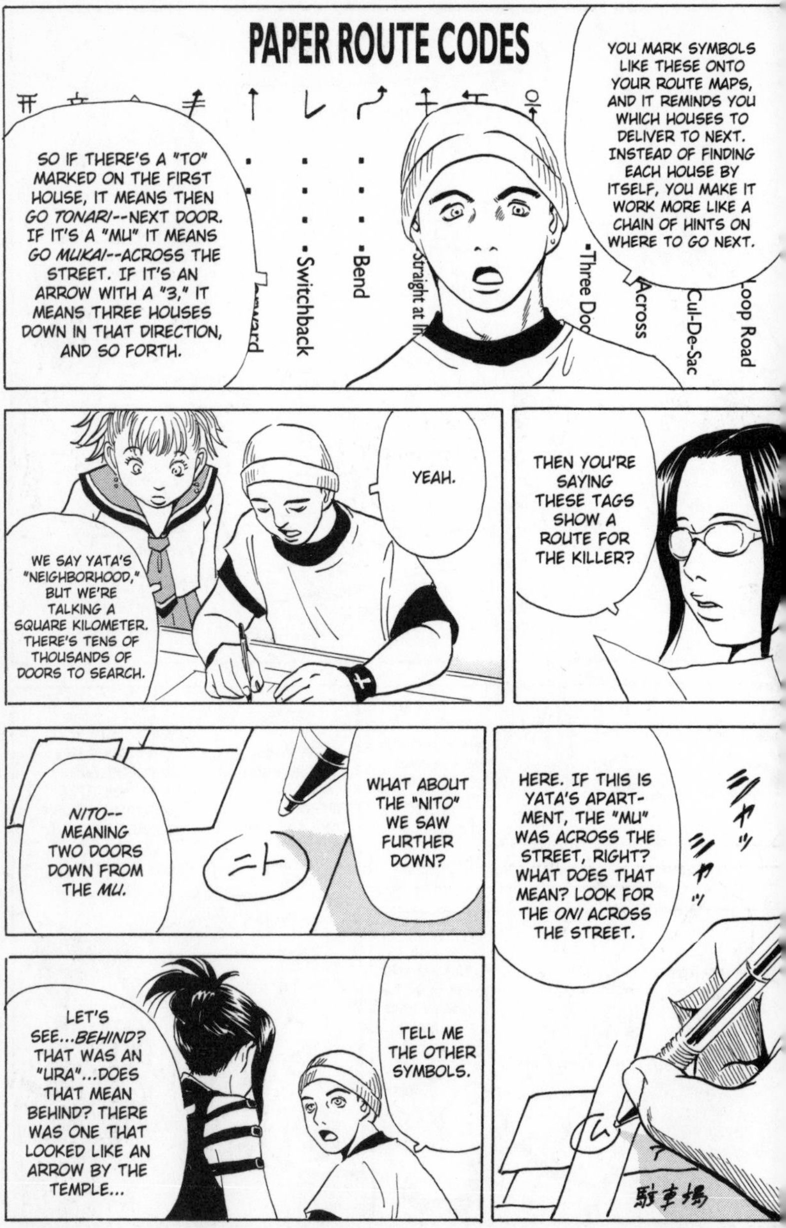

YOU MARK SYMBOLS LIKE THESE ONTO YOUR ROUTE MAPS, AND IT REMINDS YOU WHICH HOUSES TO DELIVER TO NEXT. INSTEAD OF FINDING EACH HOUSE BY ITSELF, YOU MAKE IT WORK MORE LIKE A CHAIN OF HINTS ON WHERE TO GO NEXT.
PAPER ROUTE CODES
Loop Road
Cul-De-Sac
Across
Bend
Switchback
SO IF THERE'S A "TO" MARKED ON THE FIRST HOUSE, IT MEANS THEN GO *TONARI*--NEXT DOOR. IF IT'S A "MU" IT MEANS GO *MUKAI*--ACROSS THE STREET. IF IT'S AN ARROW WITH A "3," IT MEANS THREE HOUSES DOWN IN THAT DIRECTION, AND SO FORTH.
THEN YOU'RE SAYING THESE TAGS SHOW A ROUTE FOR THE KILLER?
YEAH.
WE SAY YATA'S "NEIGHBORHOOD," BUT WE'RE TALKING A SQUARE KILOMETER. THERE'S TENS OF THOUSANDS OF DOORS TO SEARCH.
シャッ
シャッ
HERE. IF THIS IS YATA'S APARTMENT, THE "MU" WAS ACROSS THE STREET, RIGHT? WHAT DOES THAT MEAN? LOOK FOR THE *ONI* ACROSS THE STREET.
ム
駐車場
WHAT ABOUT THE "NITO" WE SAW FURTHER DOWN?
ニト
NITO--MEANING TWO DOORS DOWN FROM THE *MU*.
TELL ME THE OTHER SYMBOLS.
LET'S SEE...*BEHIND*? THAT WAS AN "URA"...DOES THAT MEAN BEHIND? THERE WAS ONE THAT LOOKED LIKE AN ARROW BY THE TEMPLE...

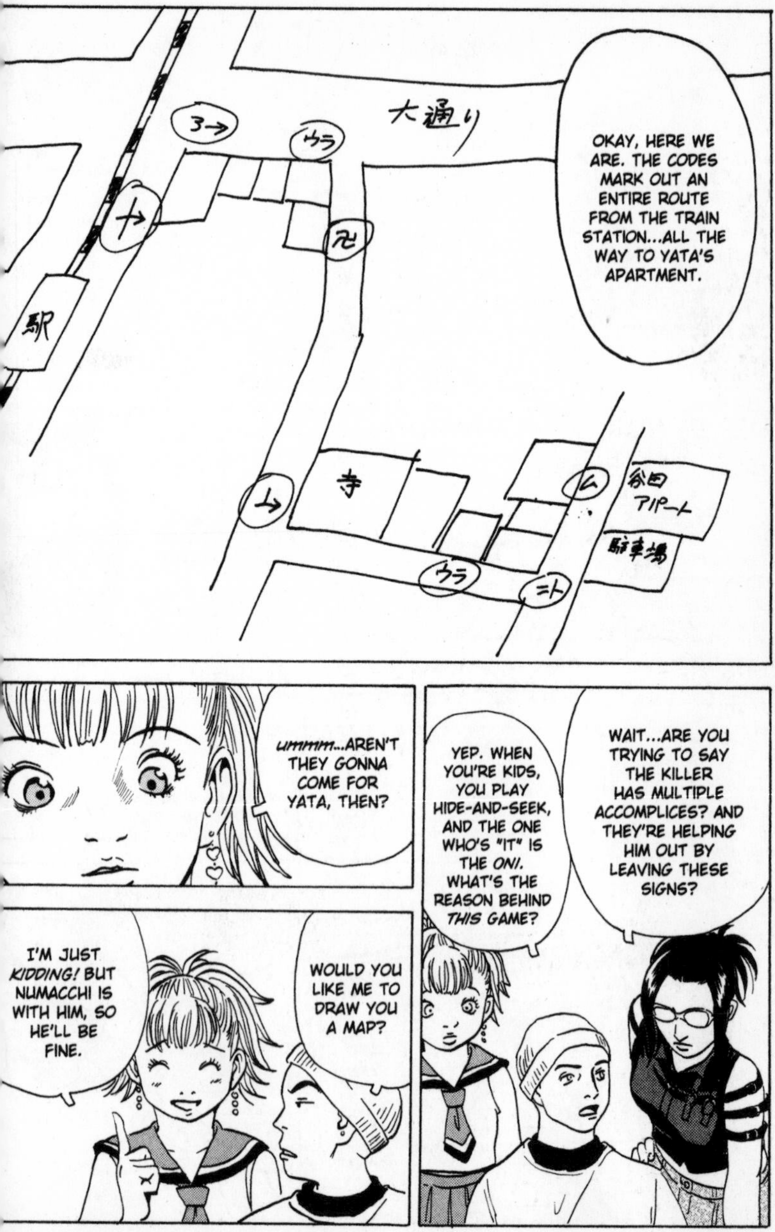
OKAY, HERE WE ARE. THE CODES MARK OUT AN ENTIRE ROUTE FROM THE TRAIN STATION...ALL THE WAY TO YATA'S APARTMENT.
大通り
駅
寺
谷田アパート
駐車場
ウラ
ウラ
卍
WAIT...ARE YOU TRYING TO SAY THE KILLER HAS MULTIPLE ACCOMPLICES? AND THEY'RE HELPING HIM OUT BY LEAVING THESE SIGNS?
YEP. WHEN YOU'RE KIDS, YOU PLAY HIDE-AND-SEEK, AND THE ONE WHO'S "IT" IS THE *ONI*. WHAT'S THE REASON BEHIND *THIS* GAME?
ummmm...AREN'T THEY GONNA COME FOR YATA, THEN?
WOULD YOU LIKE ME TO DRAW YOU A MAP?
I'M JUST *KIDDING!* BUT NUMACCHI IS WITH HIM, SO HE'LL BE FINE.

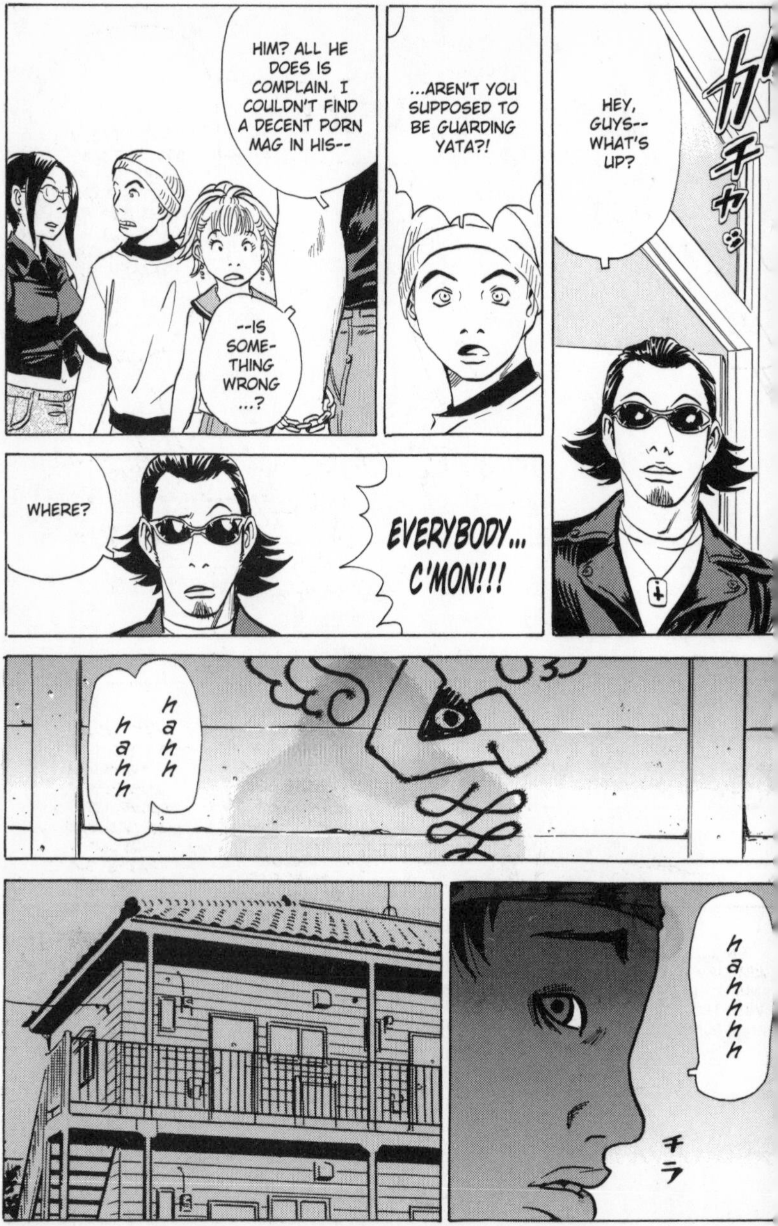
ガチャッ
HEY, GUYS--WHAT'S UP?
...AREN'T YOU SUPPOSED TO BE GUARDING YATA?!
HIM? ALL HE DOES IS COMPLAIN. I COULDN'T FIND A DECENT PORN MAG IN HIS--
--IS SOMETHING WRONG ...?
EVERYBODY... C'MON!!!
WHERE?
hahh hahh
hahhhh
チラ

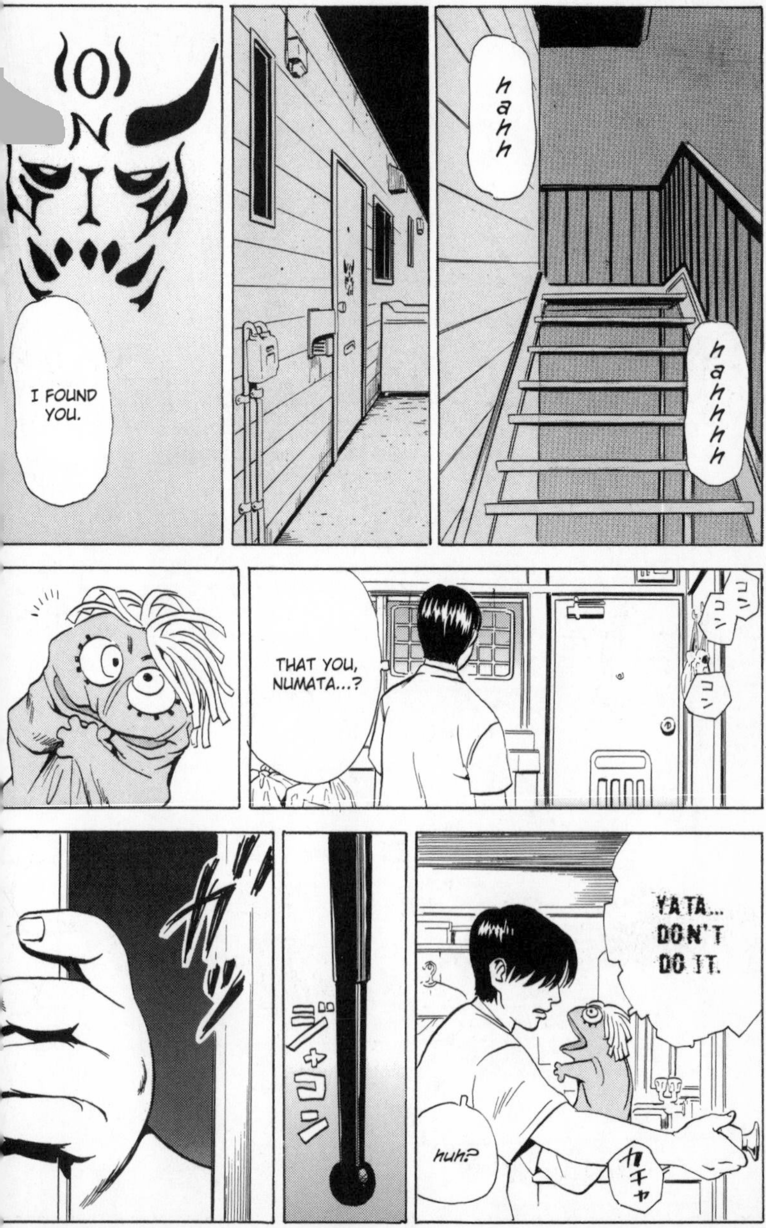
hahh
hahhhh
ONI
I FOUND YOU.
コン コン
コン
THAT YOU, NUMATA...?
YATA... DON'T DO IT.
カチャ
huh?
ジャコン
ガッ

hahhhhh
hahhhhh

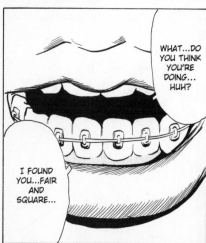

WHAT...DO
YOU THINK
YOU'RE
DOING...
HUH?

I FOUND
YOU...FAIR
AND
SQUARE...

UM...

...HEY!!

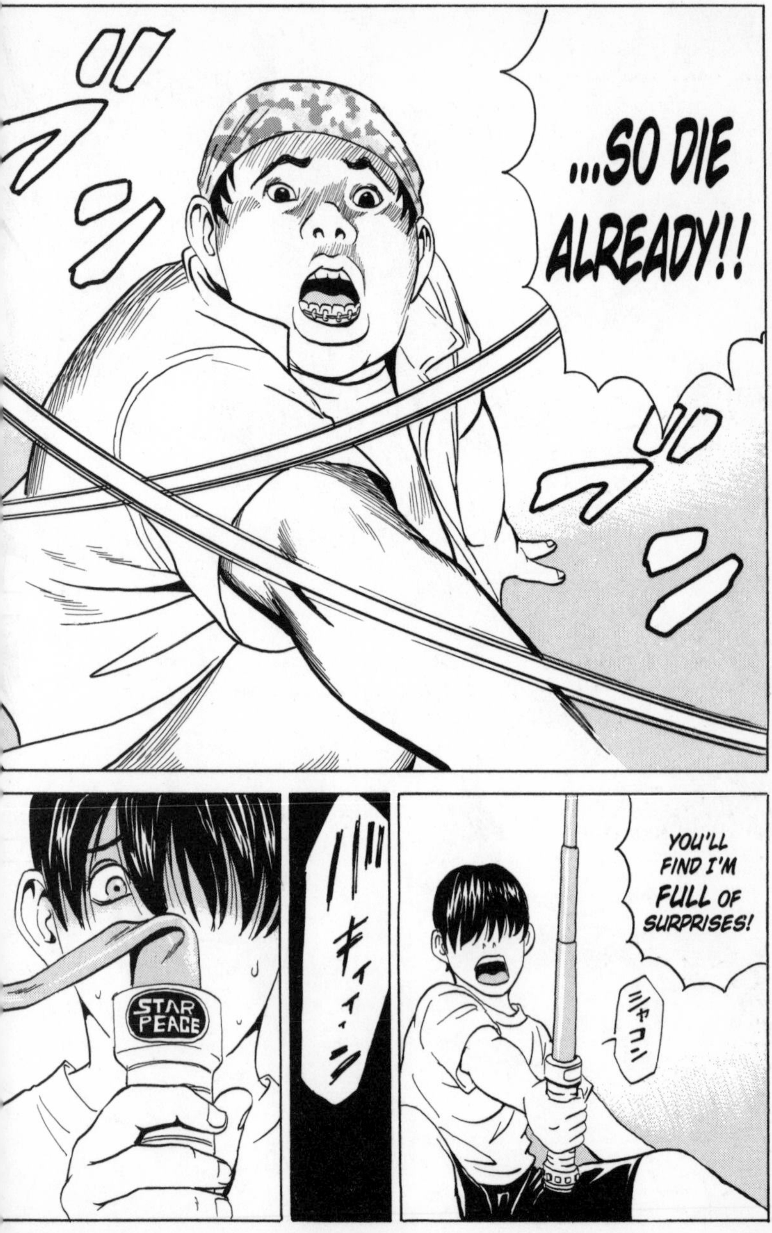
...SO DIE ALREADY!!
YOU'LL FIND I'M FULL OF SURPRISES!
シャコン
キィィン
STAR PEACE

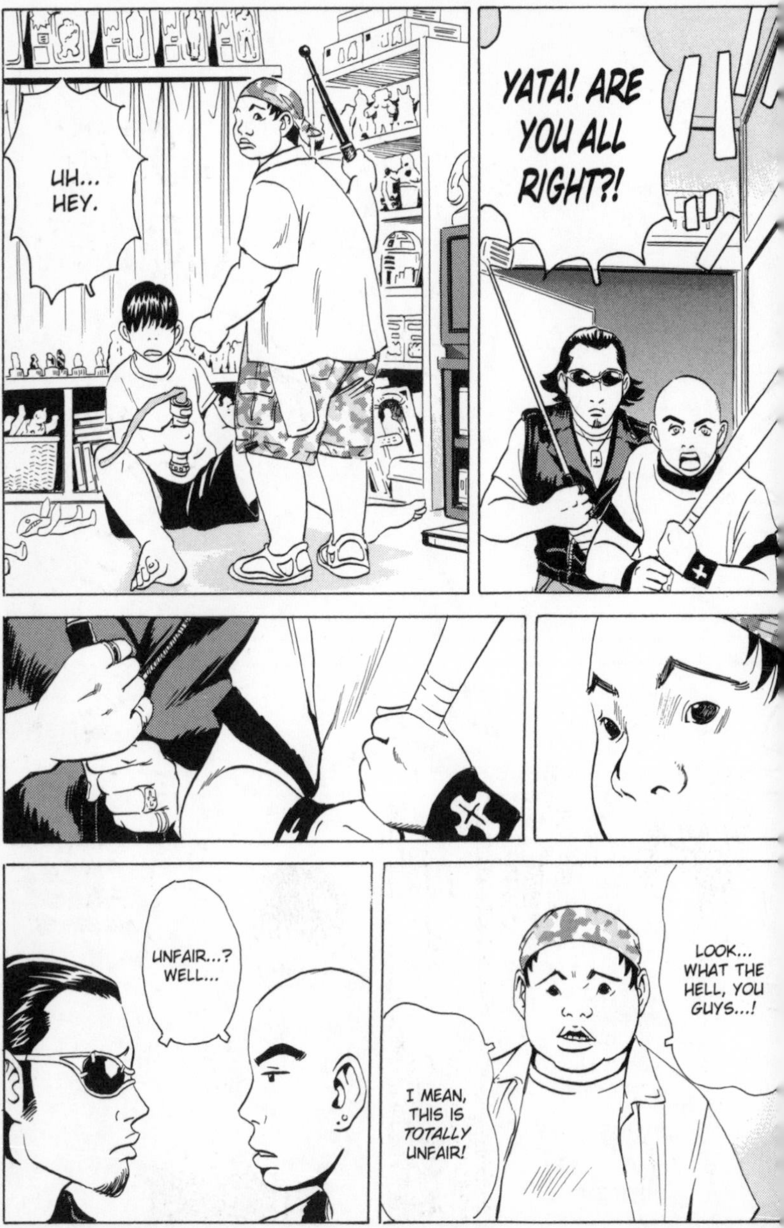
YATA! ARE YOU ALL RIGHT?!
UH... HEY.
LOOK... WHAT THE HELL, YOU GUYS...!
I MEAN, THIS IS *TOTALLY* UNFAIR!
UNFAIR...? WELL...

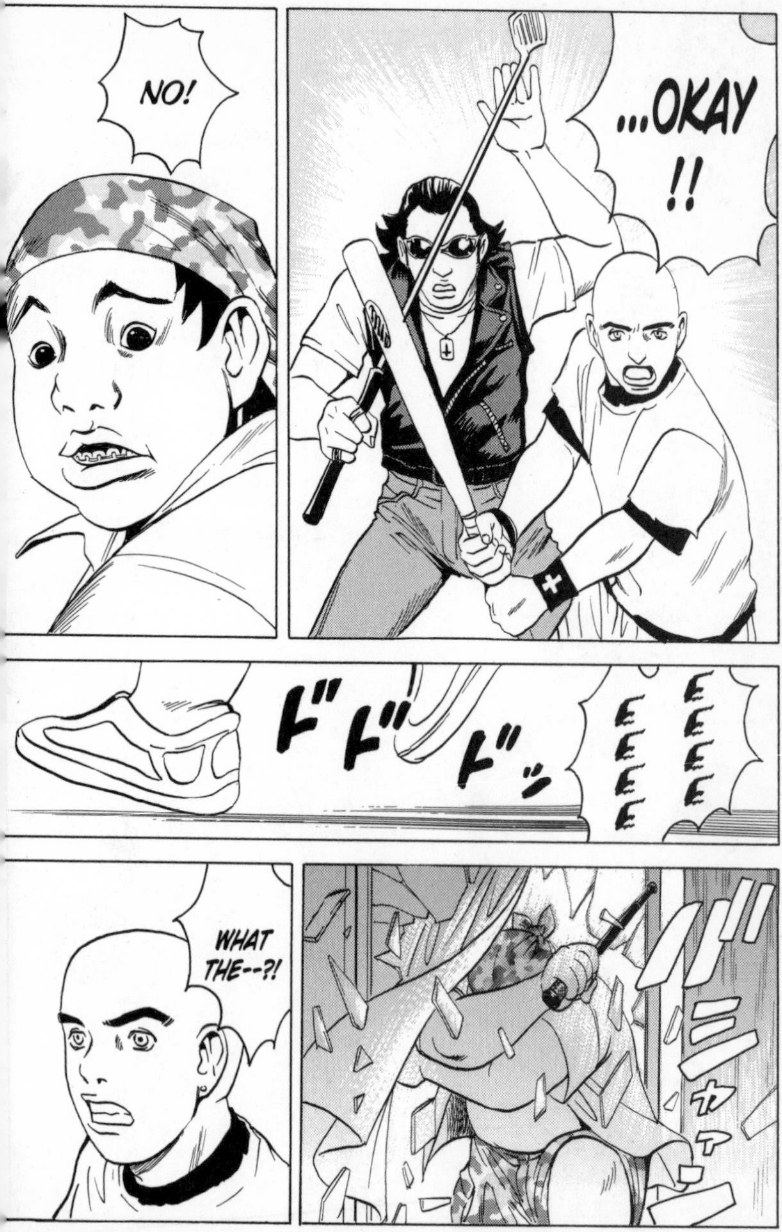
...OKAY !!
NO!
ドドドッ
WHAT THE--?!

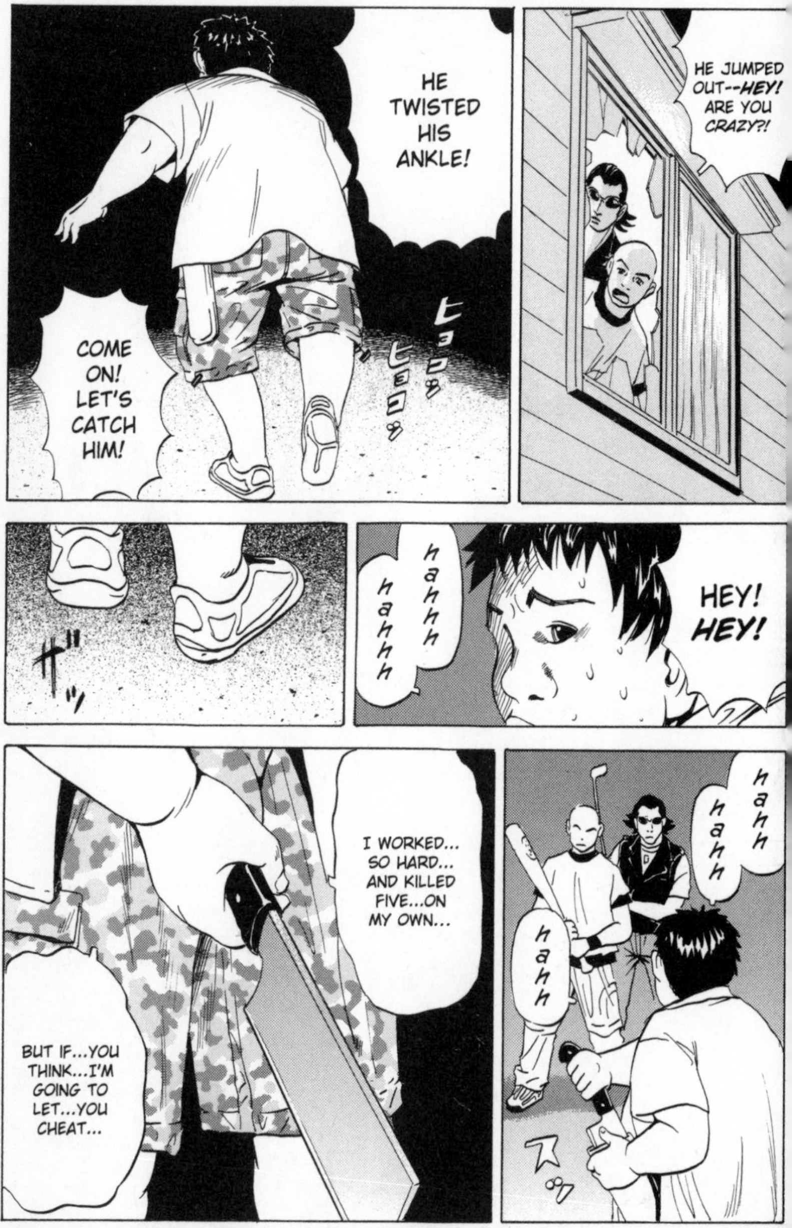
HE JUMPED OUT--*HEY!* ARE YOU *CRAZY?!*
HE TWISTED HIS ANKLE!
COME ON! LET'S CATCH HIM!
HEY! *HEY!*
hahhh hahhh
hahh hahh
hahh
I WORKED... SO HARD... AND KILLED FIVE...ON MY OWN...
BUT IF...YOU THINK...I'M GOING TO LET...YOU CHEAT...

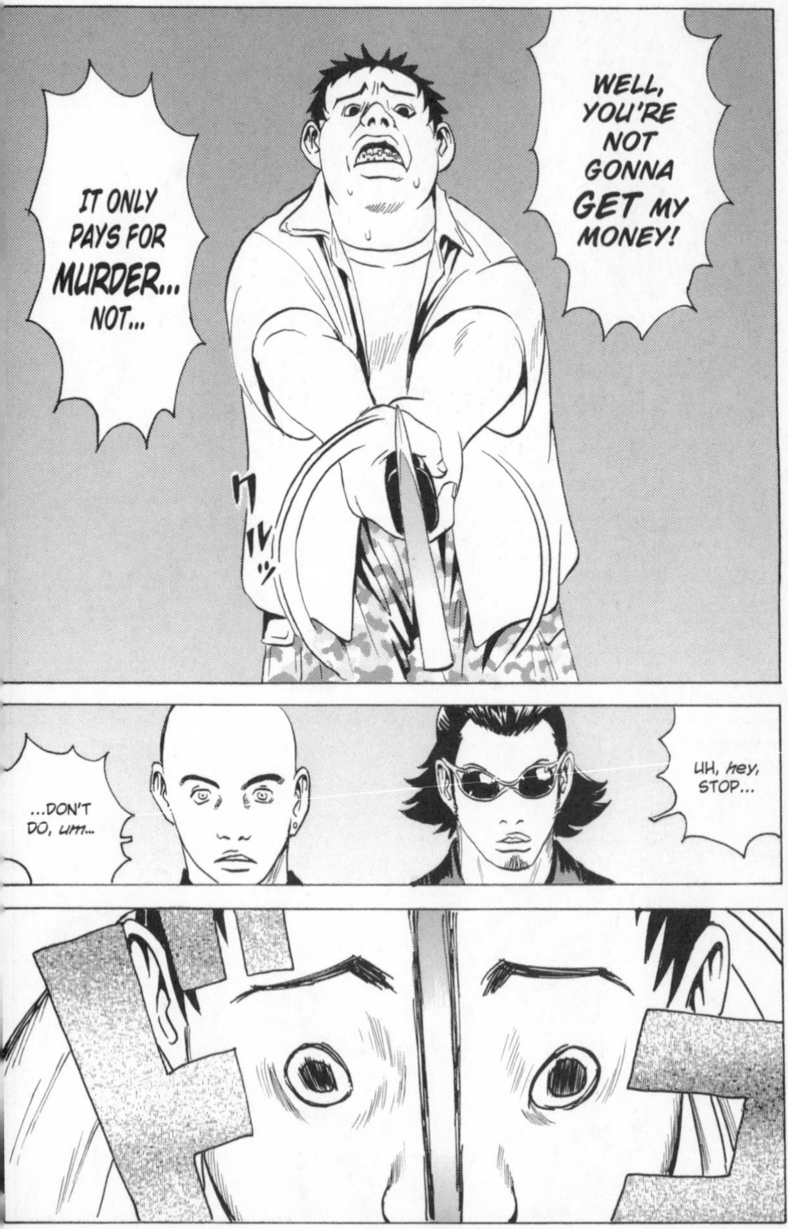
WELL, YOU'RE NOT GONNA GET MY MONEY!
IT ONLY PAYS FOR MURDER... NOT...
UH, hey, STOP...
...DON'T DO, um...

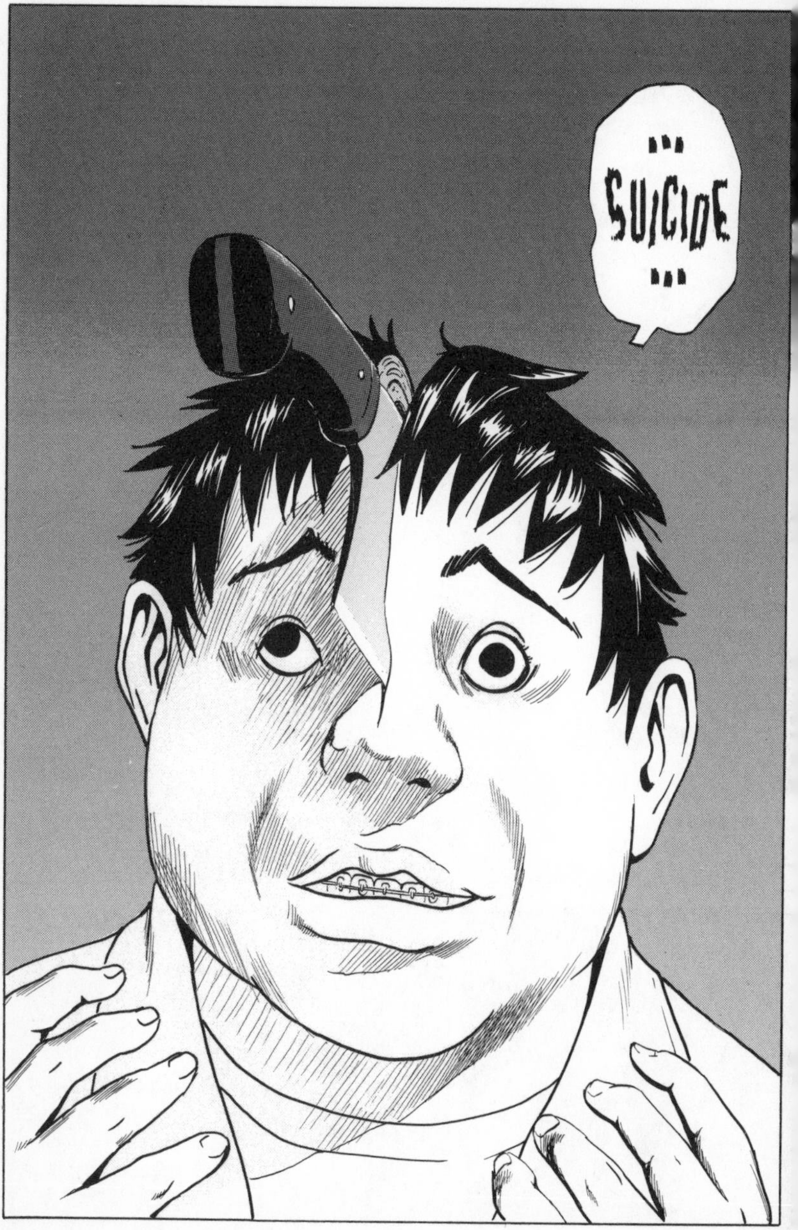
...SUICIDE...

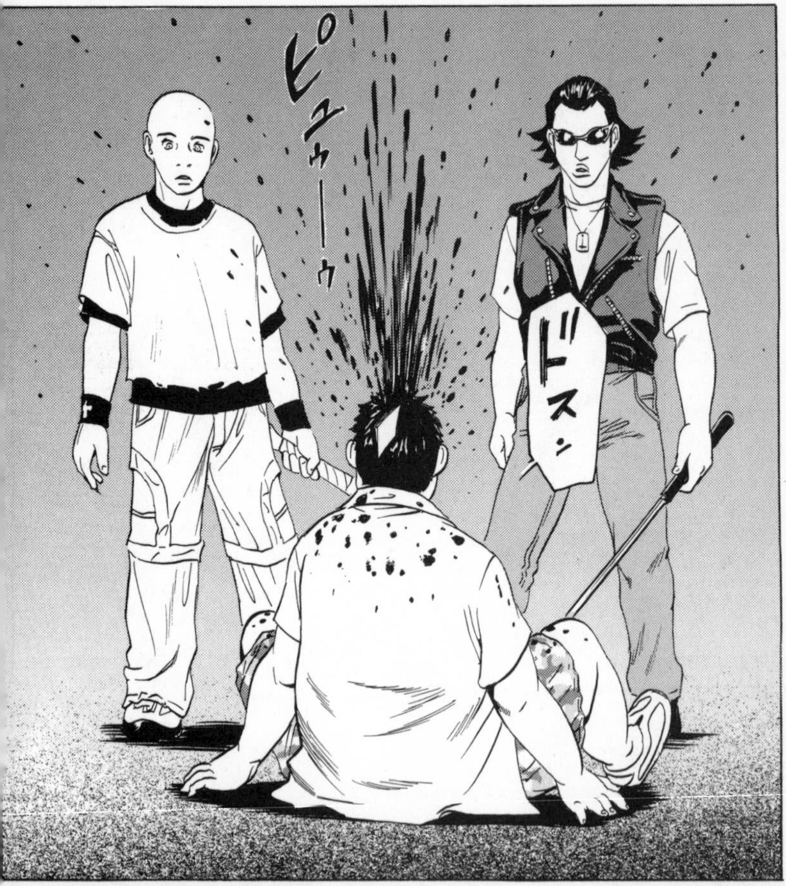
ピュゥーーウ
ドスン
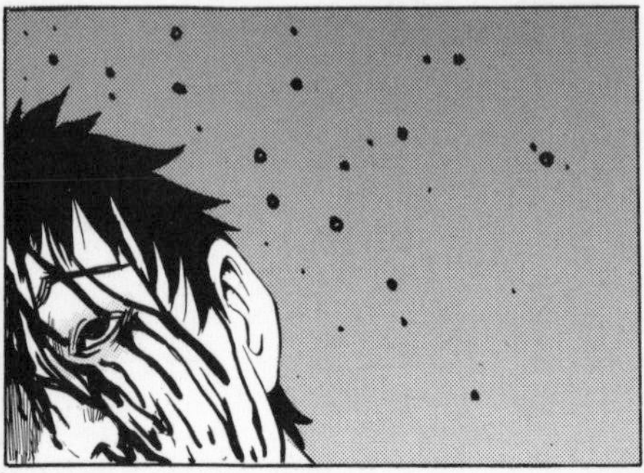
ドッ
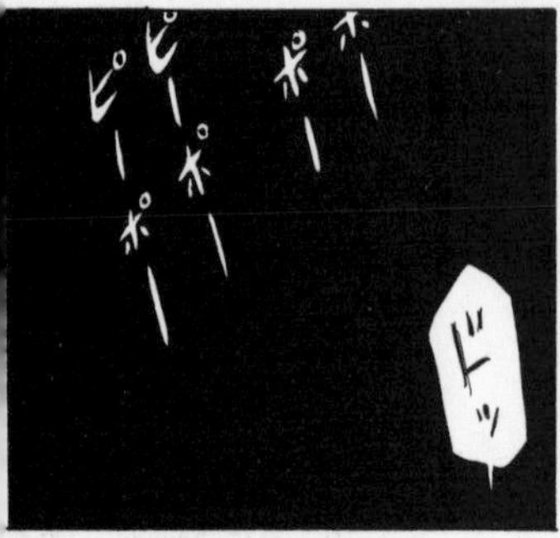
ポー
ポー
ピーポー
ピーポー

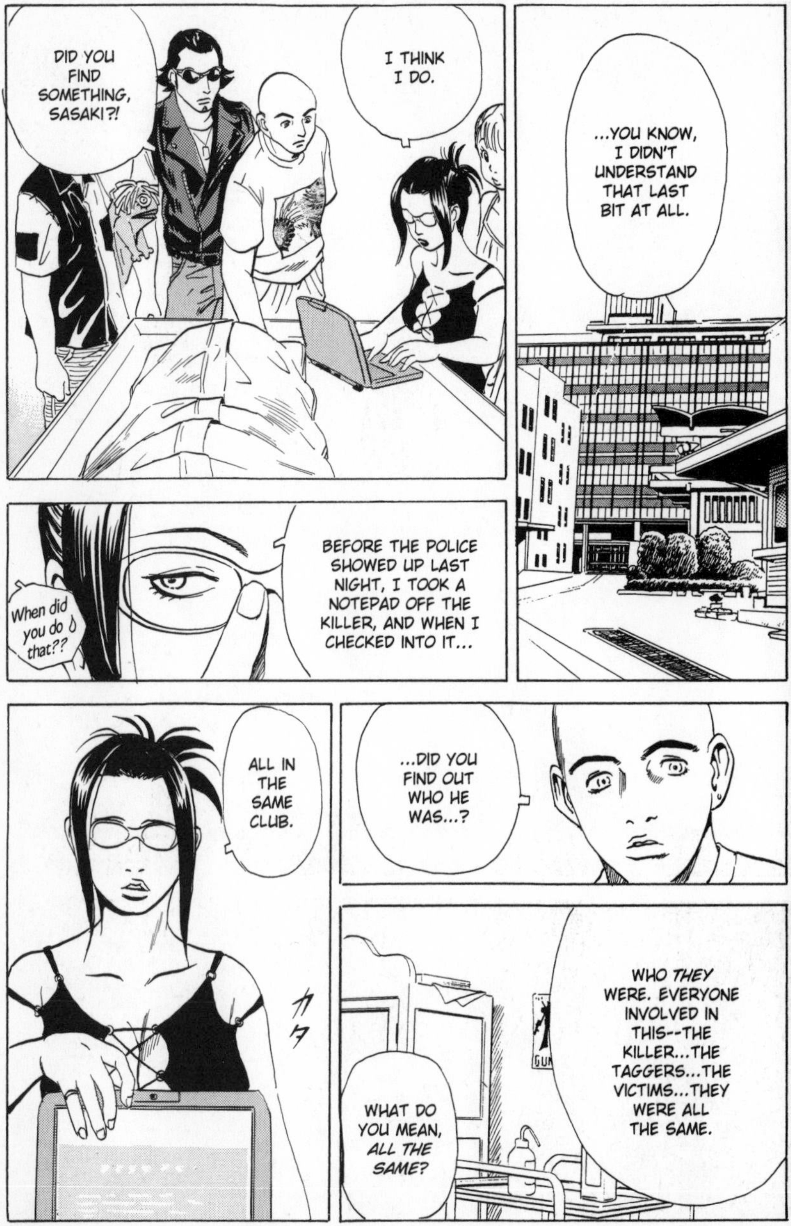
...YOU KNOW, I DIDN'T UNDERSTAND THAT LAST BIT AT ALL.
I THINK I DO.
DID YOU FIND SOMETHING, SASAKI?!
BEFORE THE POLICE SHOWED UP LAST NIGHT, I TOOK A NOTEPAD OFF THE KILLER, AND WHEN I CHECKED INTO IT...
When did you do that??
...DID YOU FIND OUT WHO HE WAS...?
WHO *THEY* WERE. EVERYONE INVOLVED IN THIS--THE KILLER...THE TAGGERS...THE VICTIMS...THEY WERE ALL THE SAME.
WHAT DO YOU MEAN, *ALL THE SAME?*
ALL IN THE SAME CLUB.
カタ

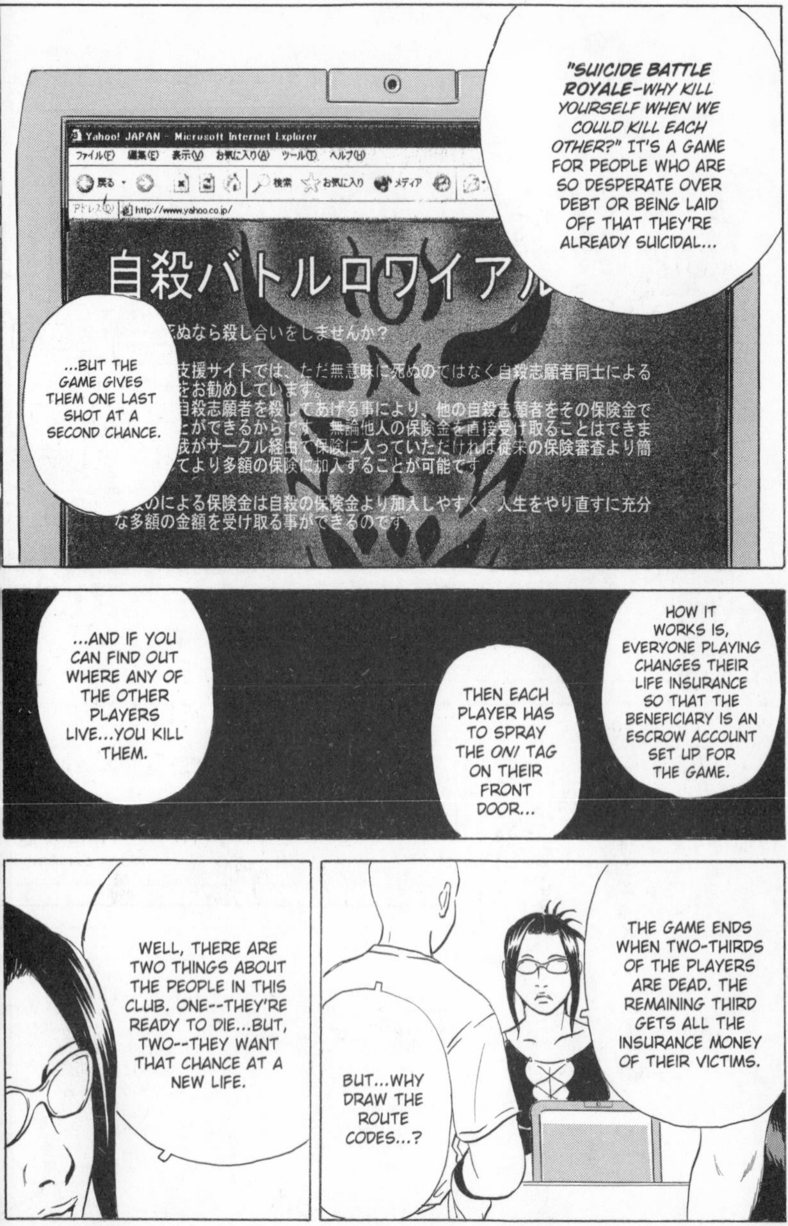
Yahoo! JAPAN - Microsoft Internet Explorer
http://www.yahoo.co.jp/
"SUICIDE BATTLE ROYALE-WHY KILL YOURSELF WHEN WE COULD KILL EACH OTHER?" IT'S A GAME FOR PEOPLE WHO ARE SO DESPERATE OVER DEBT OR BEING LAID OFF THAT THEY'RE ALREADY SUICIDAL...
...BUT THE GAME GIVES THEM ONE LAST SHOT AT A SECOND CHANCE.
HOW IT WORKS IS, EVERYONE PLAYING CHANGES THEIR LIFE INSURANCE SO THAT THE BENEFICIARY IS AN ESCROW ACCOUNT SET UP FOR THE GAME.
THEN EACH PLAYER HAS TO SPRAY THE ONI TAG ON THEIR FRONT DOOR...
...AND IF YOU CAN FIND OUT WHERE ANY OF THE OTHER PLAYERS LIVE...YOU KILL THEM.
THE GAME ENDS WHEN TWO-THIRDS OF THE PLAYERS ARE DEAD. THE REMAINING THIRD GETS ALL THE INSURANCE MONEY OF THEIR VICTIMS.
BUT...WHY DRAW THE ROUTE CODES...?
WELL, THERE ARE TWO THINGS ABOUT THE PEOPLE IN THIS CLUB. ONE--THEY'RE READY TO DIE...BUT, TWO--THEY WANT THAT CHANCE AT A NEW LIFE.

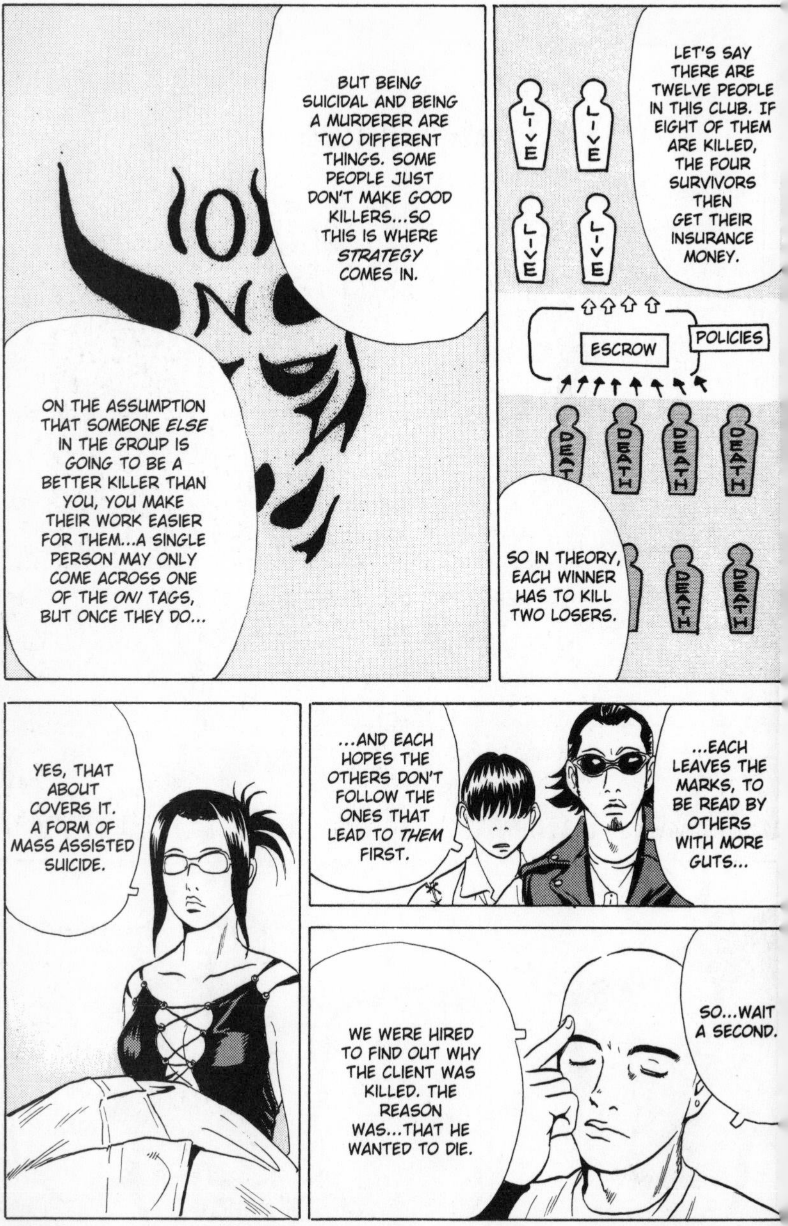
LET'S SAY THERE ARE TWELVE PEOPLE IN THIS CLUB. IF EIGHT OF THEM ARE KILLED, THE FOUR SURVIVORS THEN GET THEIR INSURANCE MONEY.
LIVE
LIVE
LIVE
LIVE
POLICIES
ESCROW
DEATH
DEATH
DEATH
DEATH
DEATH
DEATH
SO IN THEORY, EACH WINNER HAS TO KILL TWO LOSERS.
BUT BEING SUICIDAL AND BEING A MURDERER ARE TWO DIFFERENT THINGS. SOME PEOPLE JUST DON'T MAKE GOOD KILLERS...SO THIS IS WHERE *STRATEGY* COMES IN.
ON THE ASSUMPTION THAT SOMEONE *ELSE* IN THE GROUP IS GOING TO BE A BETTER KILLER THAN YOU, YOU MAKE THEIR WORK EASIER FOR THEM...A SINGLE PERSON MAY ONLY COME ACROSS ONE OF THE *ONI* TAGS, BUT ONCE THEY DO...
...EACH LEAVES THE MARKS, TO BE READ BY OTHERS WITH MORE GUTS...
...AND EACH HOPES THE OTHERS DON'T FOLLOW THE ONES THAT LEAD TO *THEM* FIRST.
SO...WAIT A SECOND.
WE WERE HIRED TO FIND OUT WHY THE CLIENT WAS KILLED. THE REASON WAS...THAT HE WANTED TO DIE.
YES, THAT ABOUT COVERS IT. A FORM OF MASS ASSISTED SUICIDE.

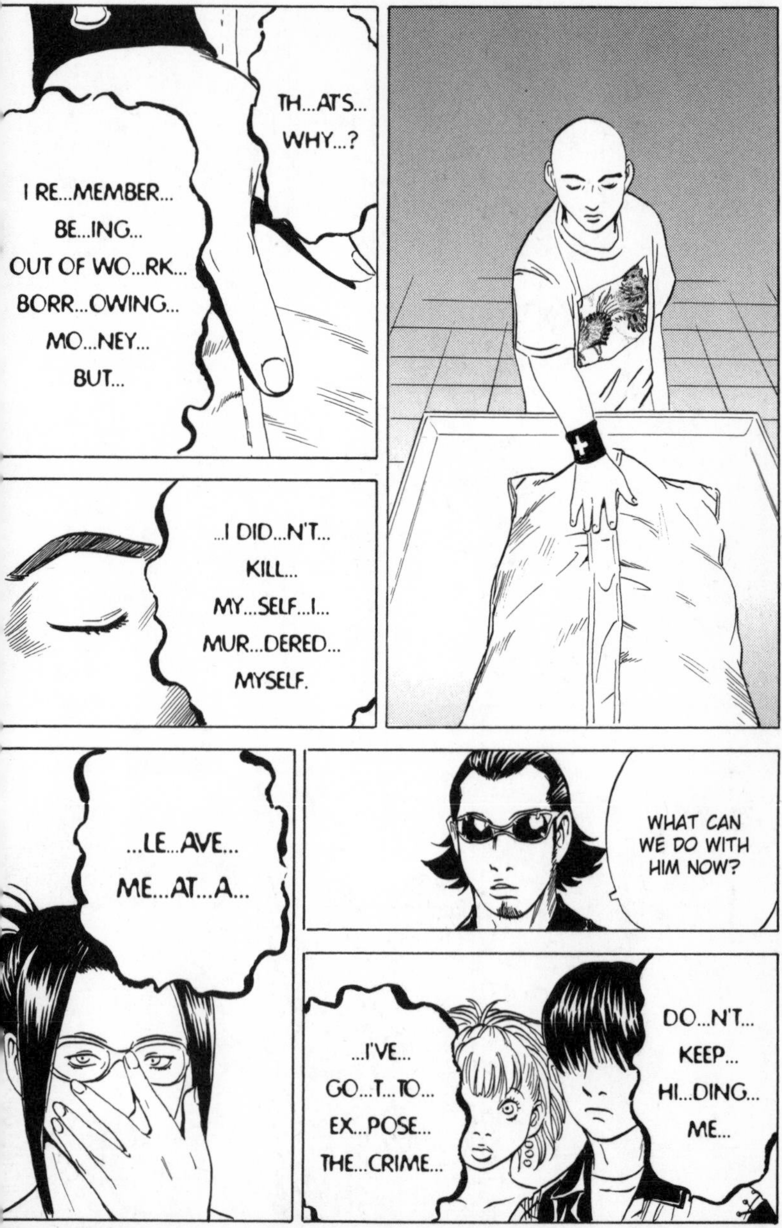
TH...AT'S... WHY...?
I RE...MEMBER... BE...ING... OUT OF WO...RK... BORR...OWING... MO...NEY... BUT...
...I DID...N'T... KILL... MY...SELF...I... MUR...DERED... MYSELF.
WHAT CAN WE DO WITH HIM NOW?
DO...N'T... KEEP... HI...DING... ME...
...I'VE... GO...T...TO... EX...POSE... THE...CRIME...
...LE...AVE... ME...AT...A...

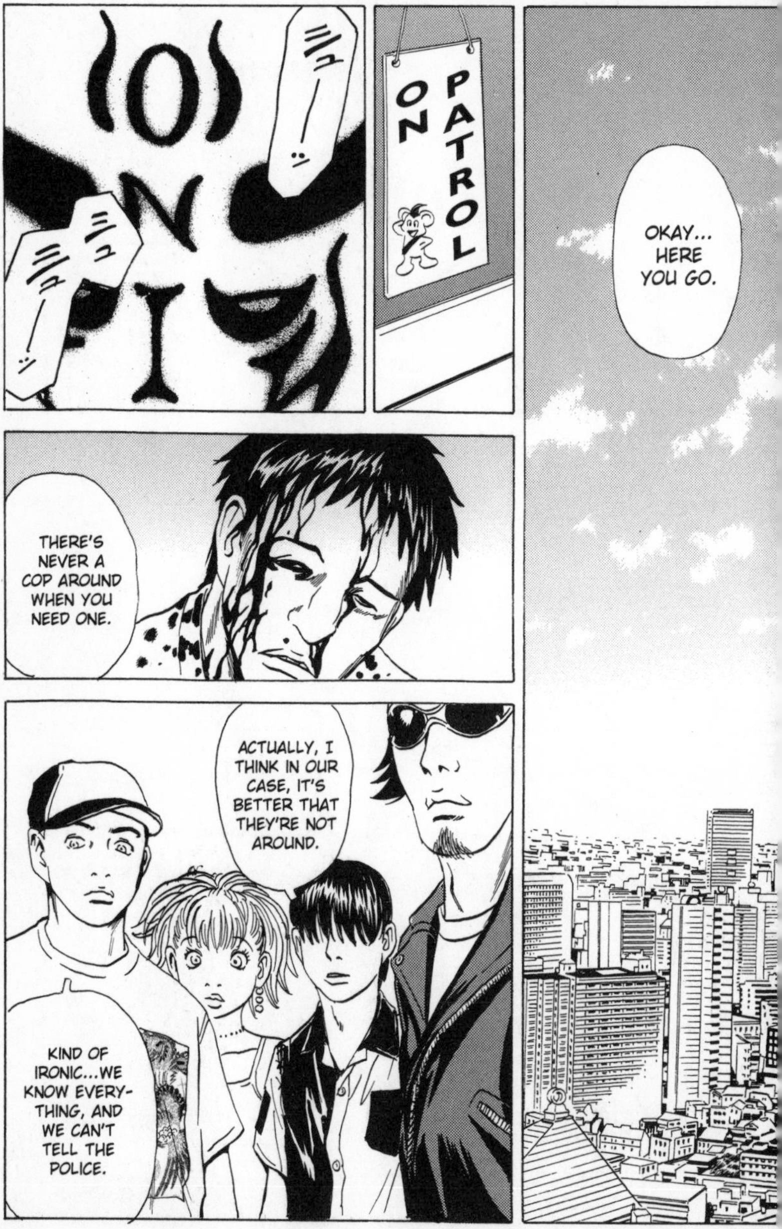
OKAY... HERE YOU GO.
ON PATROL
ミュー
ミュミュー
THERE'S NEVER A COP AROUND WHEN YOU NEED ONE.
ACTUALLY, I THINK IN OUR CASE, IT'S BETTER THAT THEY'RE NOT AROUND.
KIND OF IRONIC...WE KNOW EVERY-THING, AND WE CAN'T TELL THE POLICE.

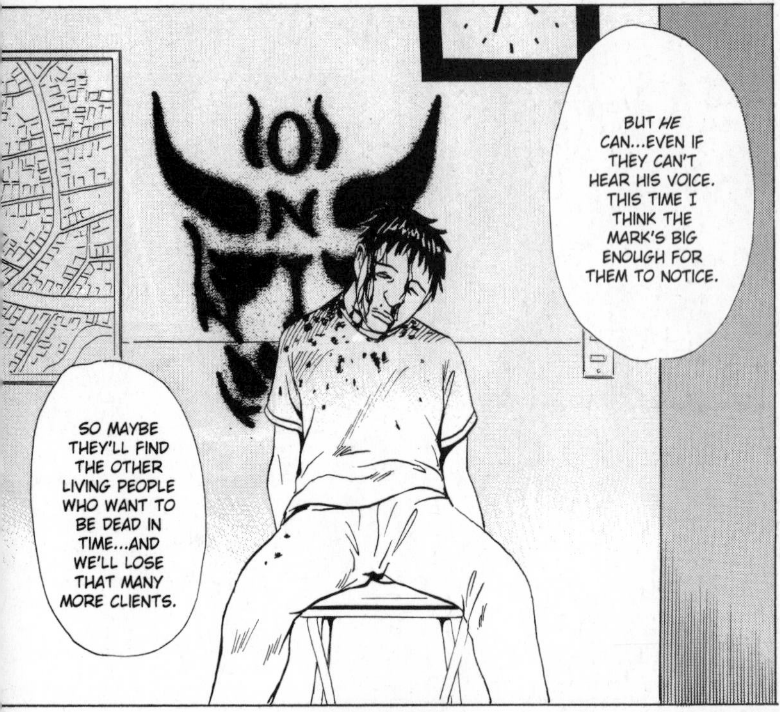
BUT *HE* CAN...EVEN IF THEY CAN'T HEAR HIS VOICE. THIS TIME I THINK THE MARK'S BIG ENOUGH FOR THEM TO NOTICE.
SO MAYBE THEY'LL FIND THE OTHER LIVING PEOPLE WHO WANT TO BE DEAD IN TIME...AND WE'LL LOSE THAT MANY MORE CLIENTS.
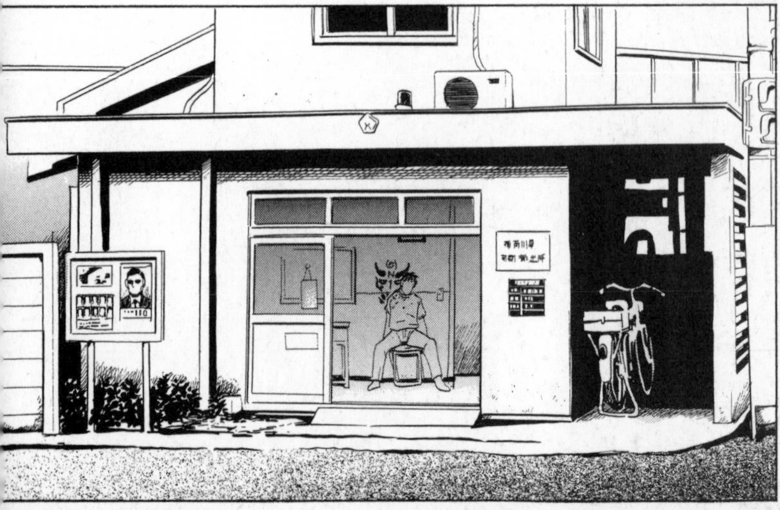

3rd delivery: x+y=love—the end

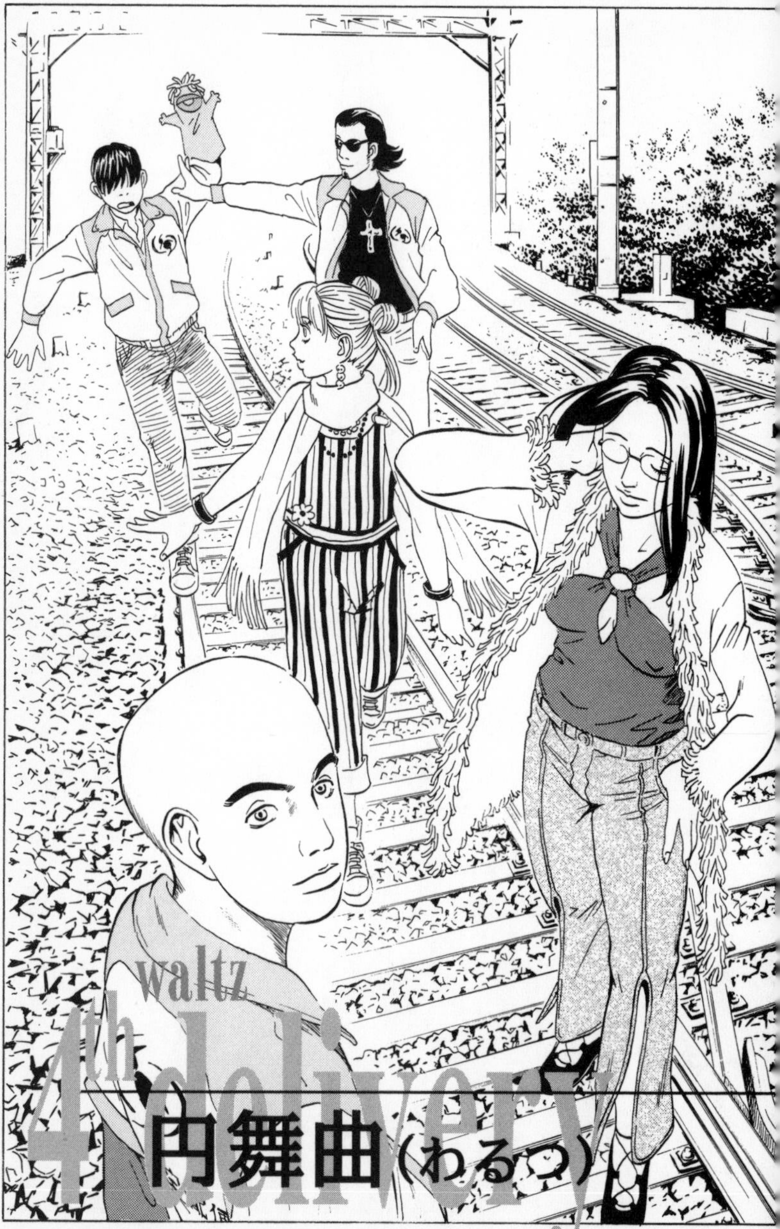
waltz
4th delivery
円舞曲(わるつ)

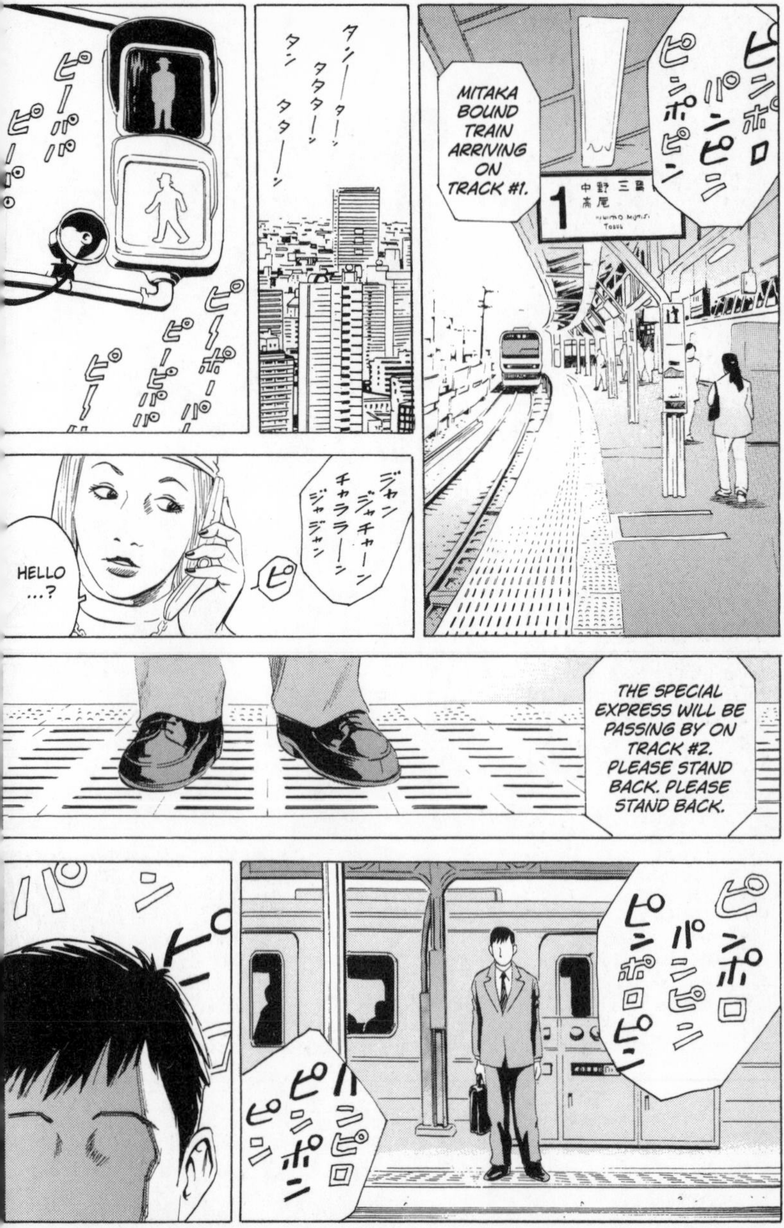
ピンポロパンピンピンポピン
MITAKA BOUND TRAIN ARRIVING ON TRACK #1.
1 中野 三鷹 高尾
タンーターン タタターン タン タターン
ピーパパ ピーポ。
ピーポーパ ピーピポパ ピー
ジャン ジャチャーン チャララーン ジャジャン
ピ
HELLO ...?
THE SPECIAL EXPRESS WILL BE PASSING BY ON TRACK #2. PLEASE STAND BACK. PLEASE STAND BACK.
ピンポロパンピンピンポロピン
パンピロピンポンピン
パン
ピー

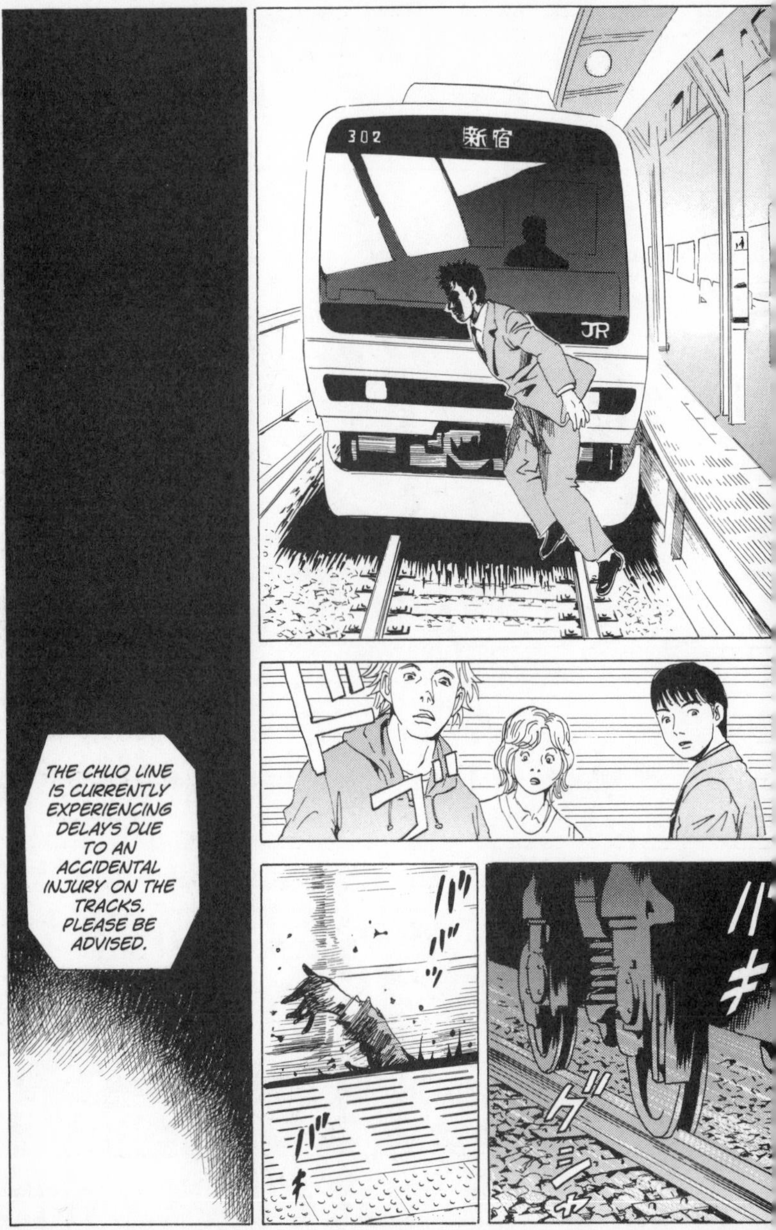
302
新宿
JR
THE CHUO LINE IS CURRENTLY EXPERIENCING DELAYS DUE TO AN ACCIDENTAL INJURY ON THE TRACKS. PLEASE BE ADVISED.

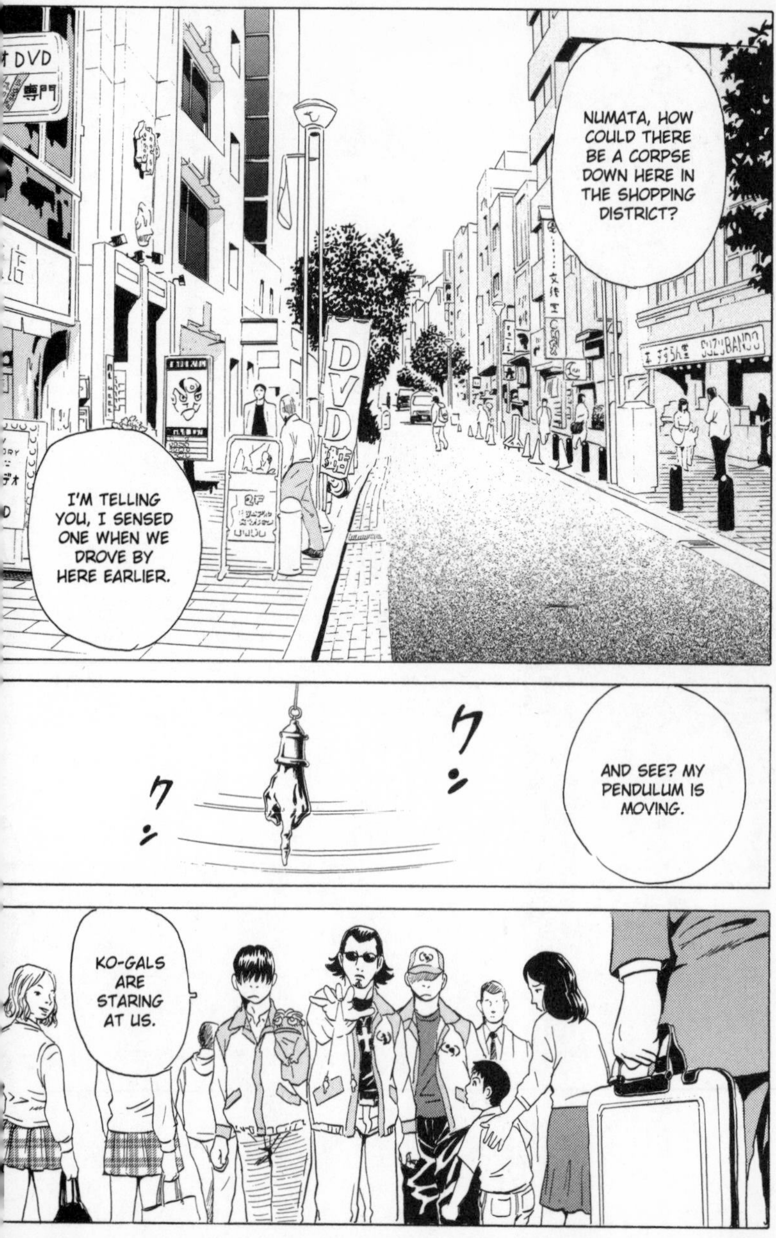
NUMATA, HOW COULD THERE BE A CORPSE DOWN HERE IN THE SHOPPING DISTRICT?
I'M TELLING YOU, I SENSED ONE WHEN WE DROVE BY HERE EARLIER.
AND SEE? MY PENDULUM IS MOVING.
クン
クン
KO-GALS ARE STARING AT US.

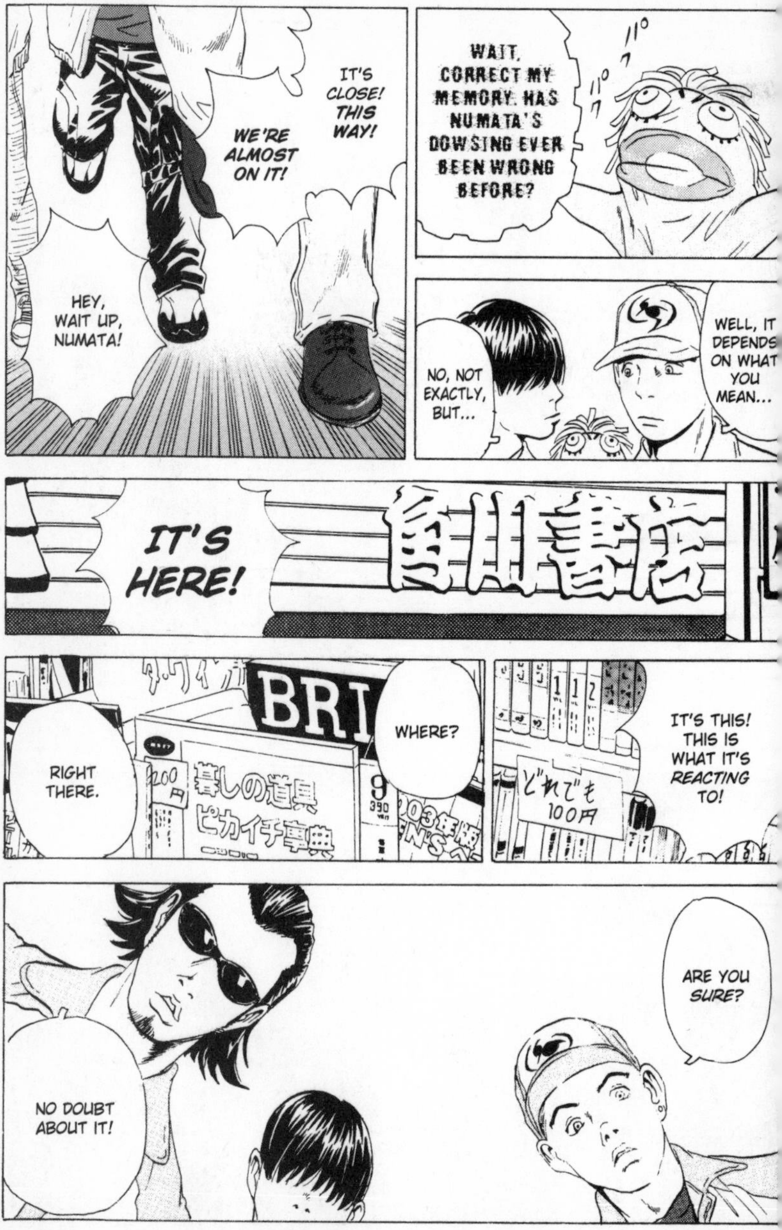
WAIT, CORRECT MY MEMORY. HAS NUMATA'S DOWSING EVER BEEN WRONG BEFORE?
WELL, IT DEPENDS ON WHAT YOU MEAN...
NO, NOT EXACTLY, BUT...
IT'S CLOSE! THIS WAY!
WE'RE ALMOST ON IT!
HEY, WAIT UP, NUMATA!
IT'S HERE!
角川書店
IT'S THIS! THIS IS WHAT IT'S REACTING TO!
どれでも 100円
WHERE?
BRI
RIGHT THERE.
200円
暮しの道具 ピカイチ事典
ARE YOU SURE?
NO DOUBT ABOUT IT!

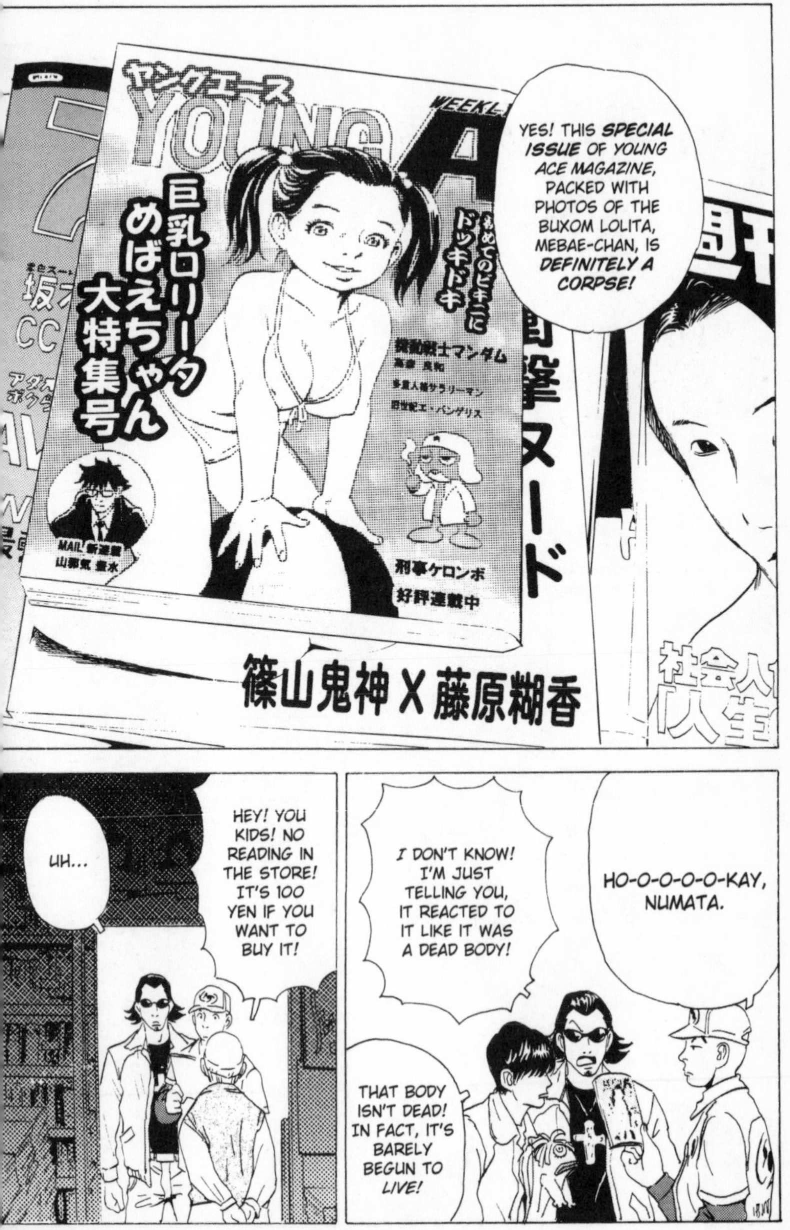
YES! THIS SPECIAL ISSUE OF YOUNG ACE MAGAZINE, PACKED WITH PHOTOS OF THE BUXOM LOLITA, MEBAE-CHAN, IS DEFINITELY A CORPSE!
ヤングエース
YOUNG A
巨乳ロリータめばえちゃん大特集号
初めてのビキニにドッキドキ
刑事ケロンボ
好評連載中
篠山鬼神X藤原糊香
HO-O-O-O-O-KAY, NUMATA.
I DON'T KNOW! I'M JUST TELLING YOU, IT REACTED TO IT LIKE IT WAS A DEAD BODY!
THAT BODY ISN'T DEAD! IN FACT, IT'S BARELY BEGUN TO LIVE!
HEY! YOU KIDS! NO READING IN THE STORE! IT'S 100 YEN IF YOU WANT TO BUY IT!
UH...

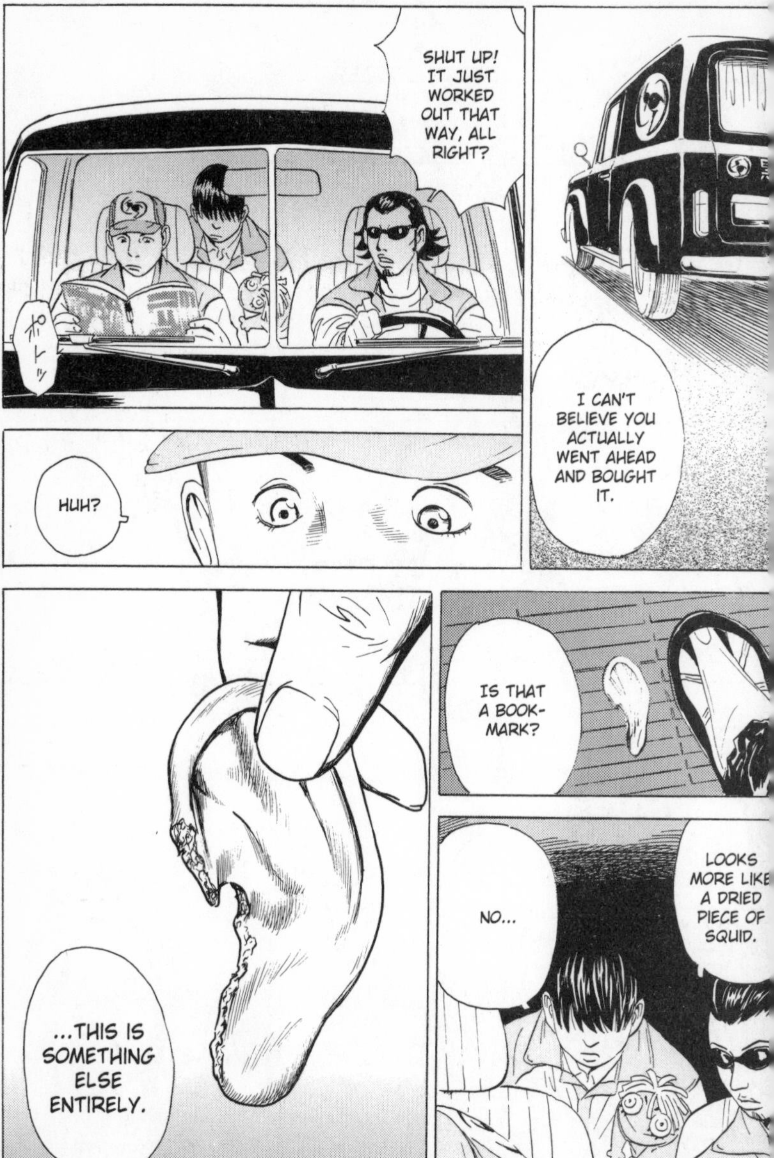
I CAN'T BELIEVE YOU ACTUALLY WENT AHEAD AND BOUGHT IT.
SHUT UP! IT JUST WORKED OUT THAT WAY, ALL RIGHT?
ポトッ
HUH?
IS THAT A BOOK-MARK?
LOOKS MORE LIKE A DRIED PIECE OF SQUID.
NO...
...THIS IS SOMETHING ELSE ENTIRELY.

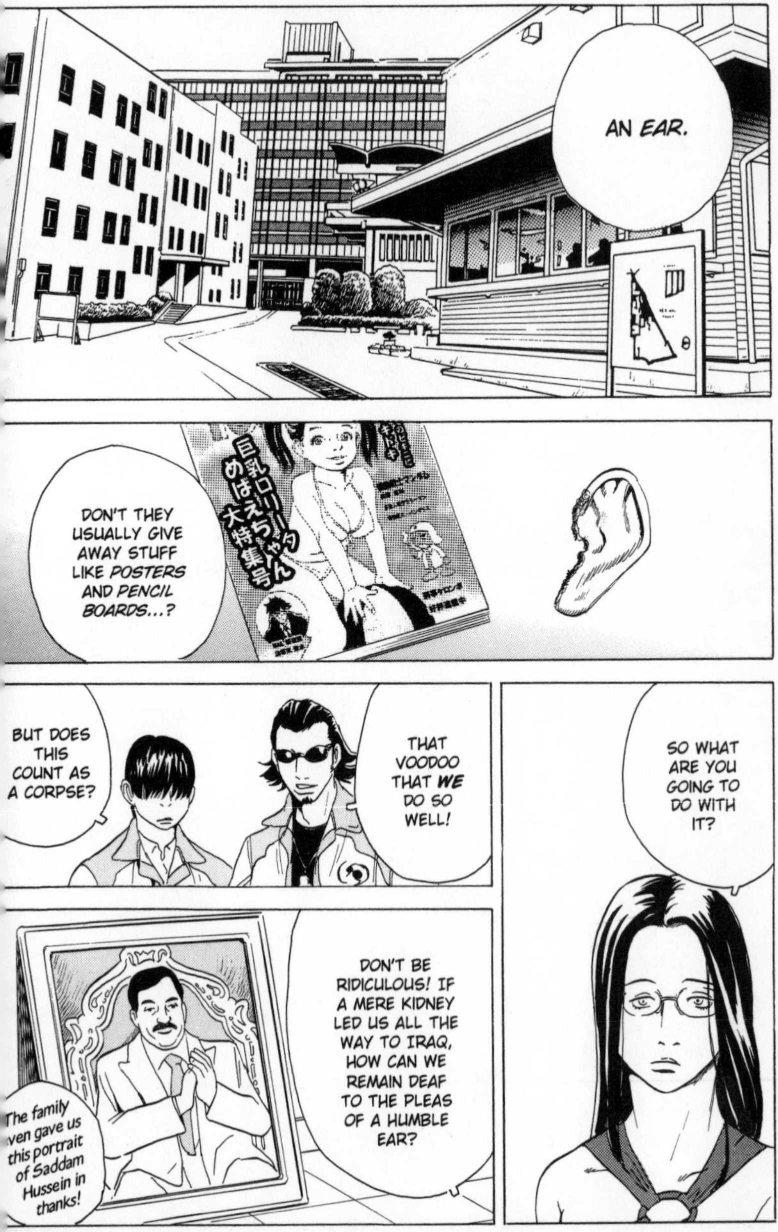
AN EAR.
巨乳ロリータめばえちゃん大特集号
DON'T THEY USUALLY GIVE AWAY STUFF LIKE POSTERS AND PENCIL BOARDS...?
SO WHAT ARE YOU GOING TO DO WITH IT?
THAT VOODOO THAT WE DO SO WELL!
BUT DOES THIS COUNT AS A CORPSE?
DON'T BE RIDICULOUS! IF A MERE KIDNEY LED US ALL THE WAY TO IRAQ, HOW CAN WE REMAIN DEAF TO THE PLEAS OF A HUMBLE EAR?
The family ven gave us this portrait of Saddam Hussein in thanks!

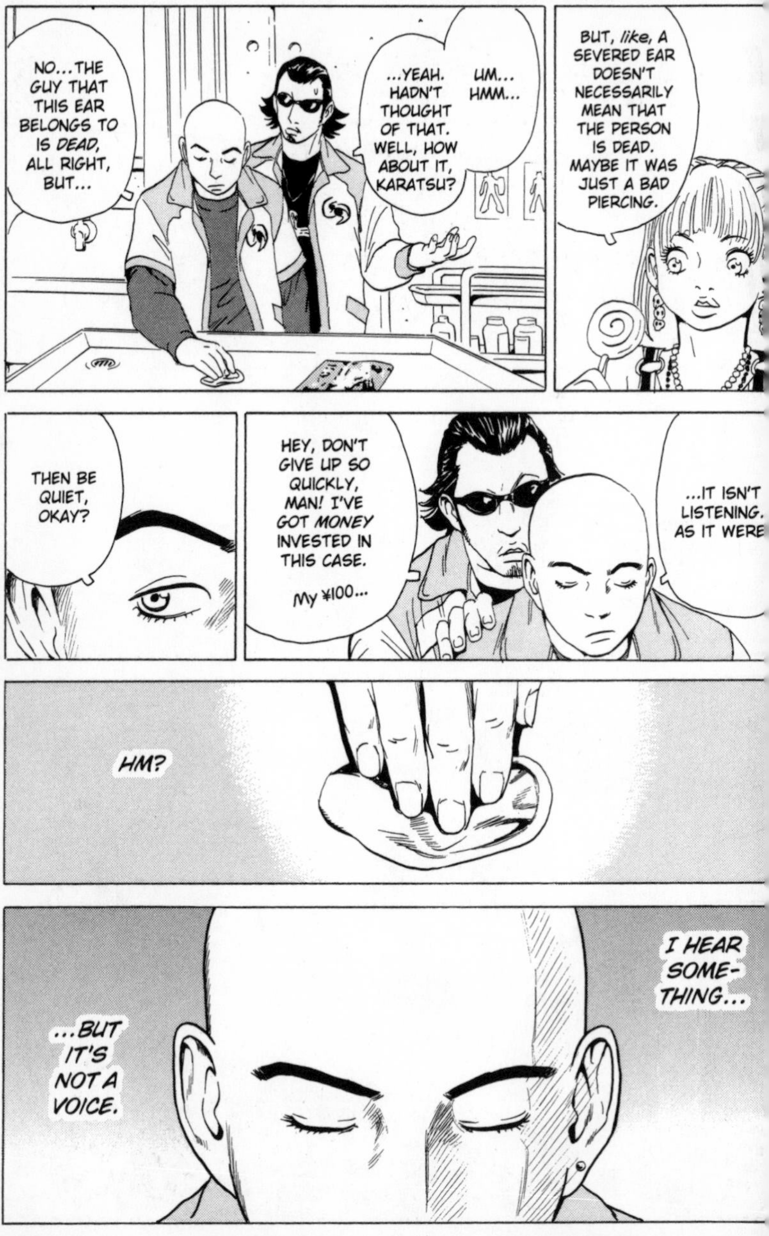
BUT, *like*, A SEVERED EAR DOESN'T NECESSARILY MEAN THAT THE PERSON IS DEAD. MAYBE IT WAS JUST A BAD PIERCING.
UM... HMM...
...YEAH. HADN'T THOUGHT OF THAT. WELL, HOW ABOUT IT, KARATSU?
NO...THE GUY THAT THIS EAR BELONGS TO IS *DEAD*, ALL RIGHT, BUT...
...IT ISN'T LISTENING. AS IT WERE
HEY, DON'T GIVE UP SO QUICKLY, MAN! I'VE GOT *MONEY* INVESTED IN THIS CASE.
My ¥100...
THEN BE QUIET, OKAY?
HM?
I HEAR SOME-THING...
...BUT IT'S NOT A VOICE.

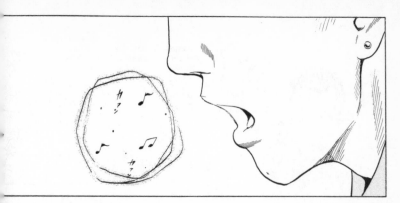

HE'S...
SINGING.

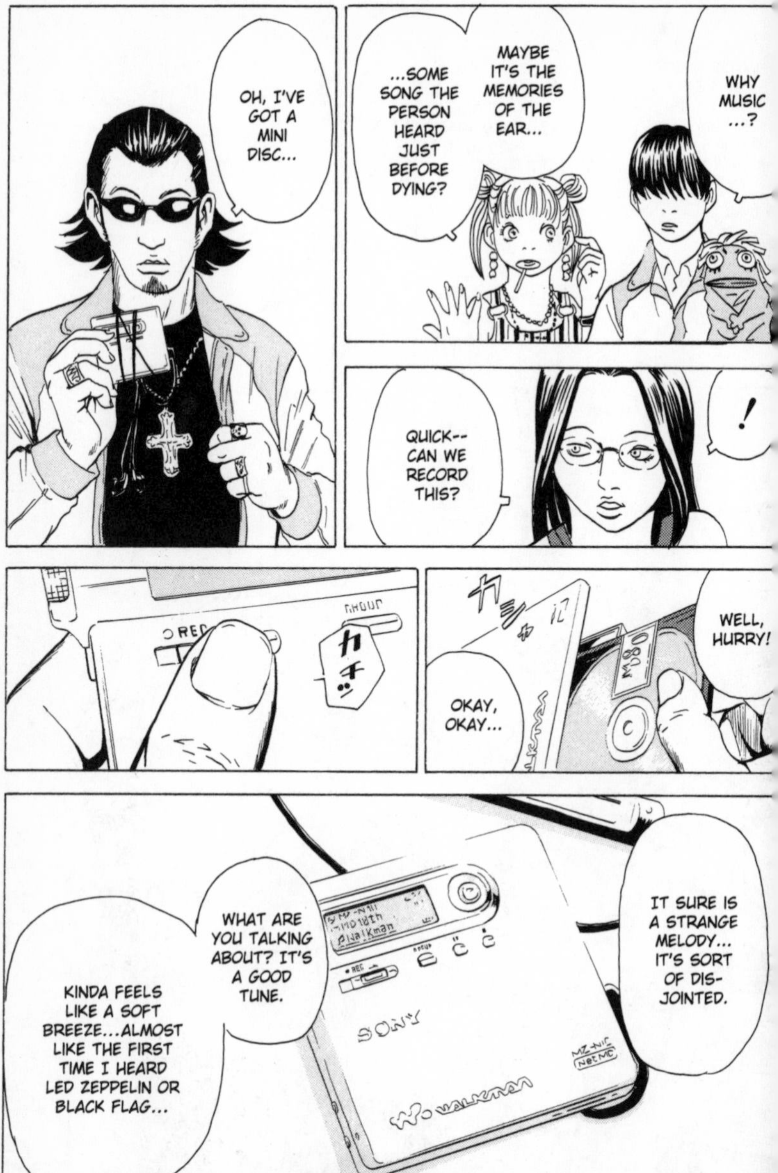
WHY MUSIC ...?
MAYBE IT'S THE MEMORIES OF THE EAR...
...SOME SONG THE PERSON HEARD JUST BEFORE DYING?
!
QUICK-- CAN WE RECORD THIS?
OH, I'VE GOT A MINI DISC...
WELL, HURRY!
OKAY, OKAY...
カチッ
IT SURE IS A STRANGE MELODY... IT'S SORT OF DIS-JOINTED.
WHAT ARE YOU TALKING ABOUT? IT'S A GOOD TUNE.
KINDA FEELS LIKE A SOFT BREEZE...ALMOST LIKE THE FIRST TIME I HEARD LED ZEPPELIN OR BLACK FLAG...
SONY

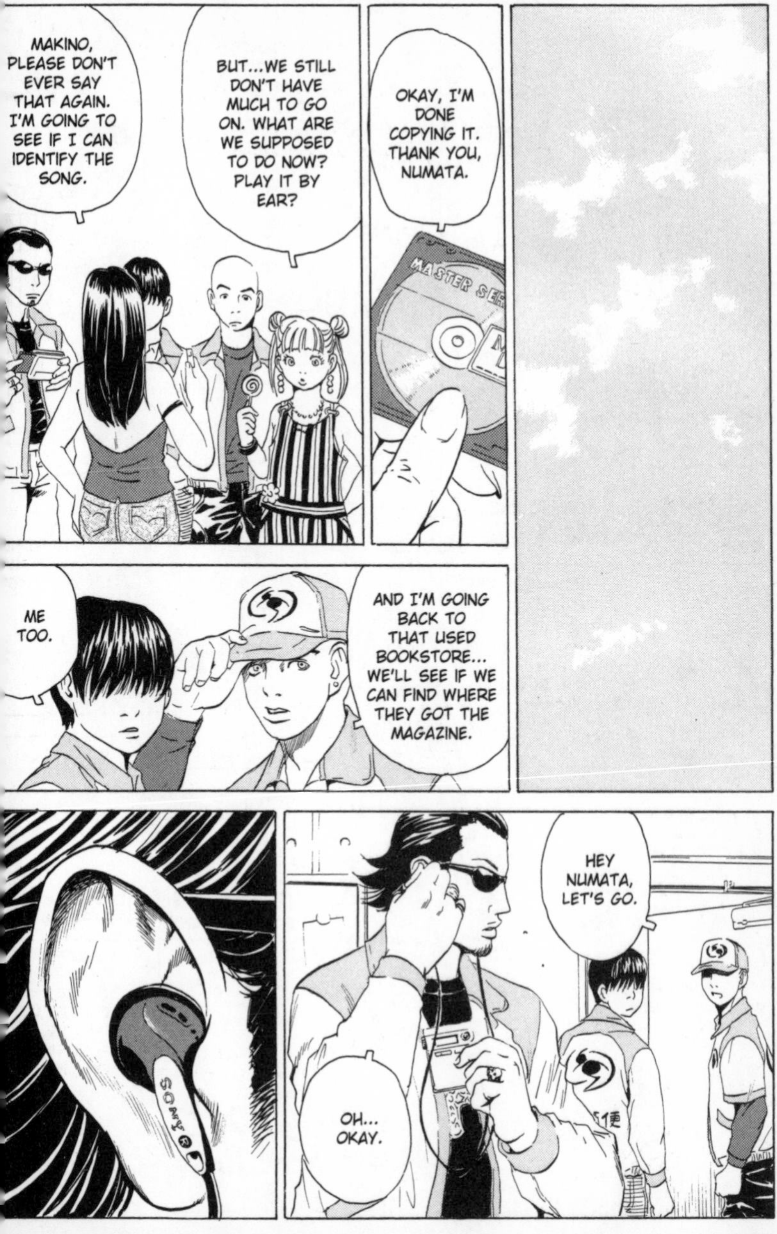
OKAY, I'M DONE COPYING IT. THANK YOU, NUMATA.
BUT...WE STILL DON'T HAVE MUCH TO GO ON. WHAT ARE WE SUPPOSED TO DO NOW? PLAY IT BY EAR?
MAKINO, PLEASE DON'T EVER SAY THAT AGAIN. I'M GOING TO SEE IF I CAN IDENTIFY THE SONG.
AND I'M GOING BACK TO THAT USED BOOKSTORE... WE'LL SEE IF WE CAN FIND WHERE THEY GOT THE MAGAZINE.
ME TOO.
HEY NUMATA, LET'S GO.
OH... OKAY.
SONY

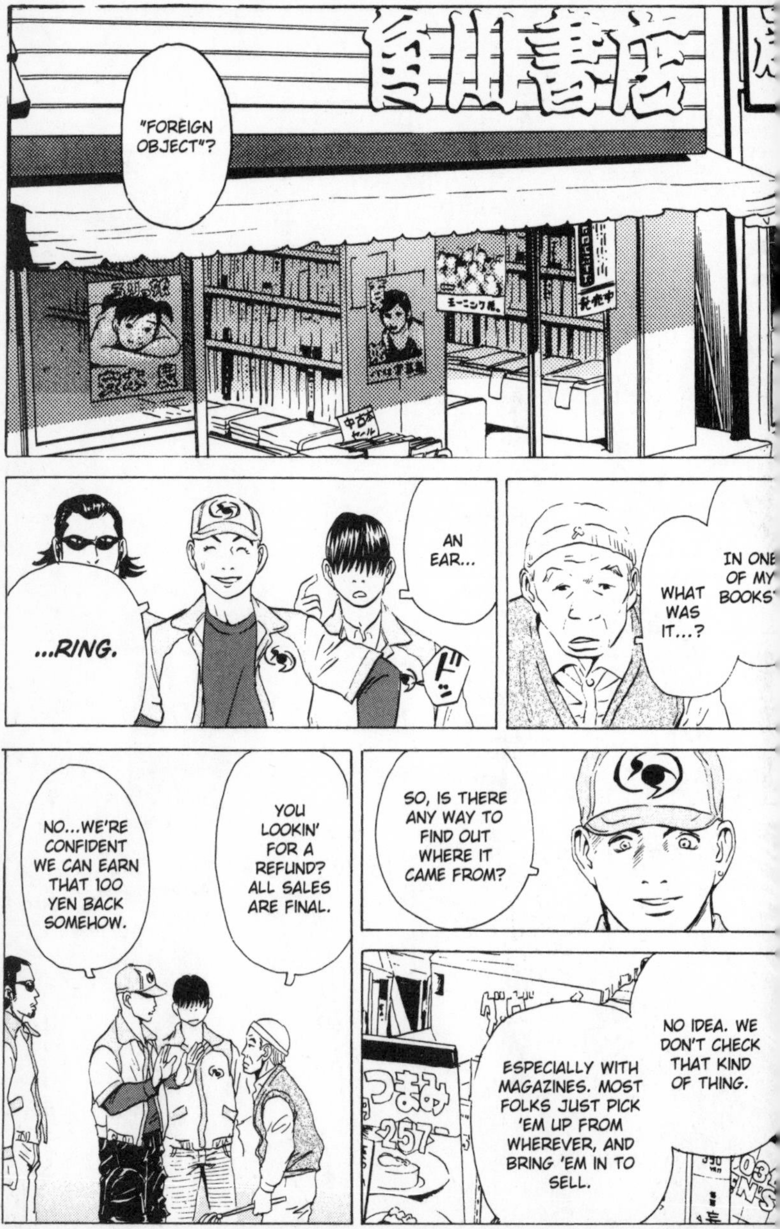
"FOREIGN OBJECT"?
IN ONE OF MY BOOKS
WHAT WAS IT...?
AN EAR...
...RING.
SO, IS THERE ANY WAY TO FIND OUT WHERE IT CAME FROM?
NO IDEA. WE DON'T CHECK THAT KIND OF THING.
ESPECIALLY WITH MAGAZINES. MOST FOLKS JUST PICK 'EM UP FROM WHEREVER, AND BRING 'EM IN TO SELL.
YOU LOOKIN' FOR A REFUND? ALL SALES ARE FINAL.
NO...WE'RE CONFIDENT WE CAN EARN THAT 100 YEN BACK SOMEHOW.

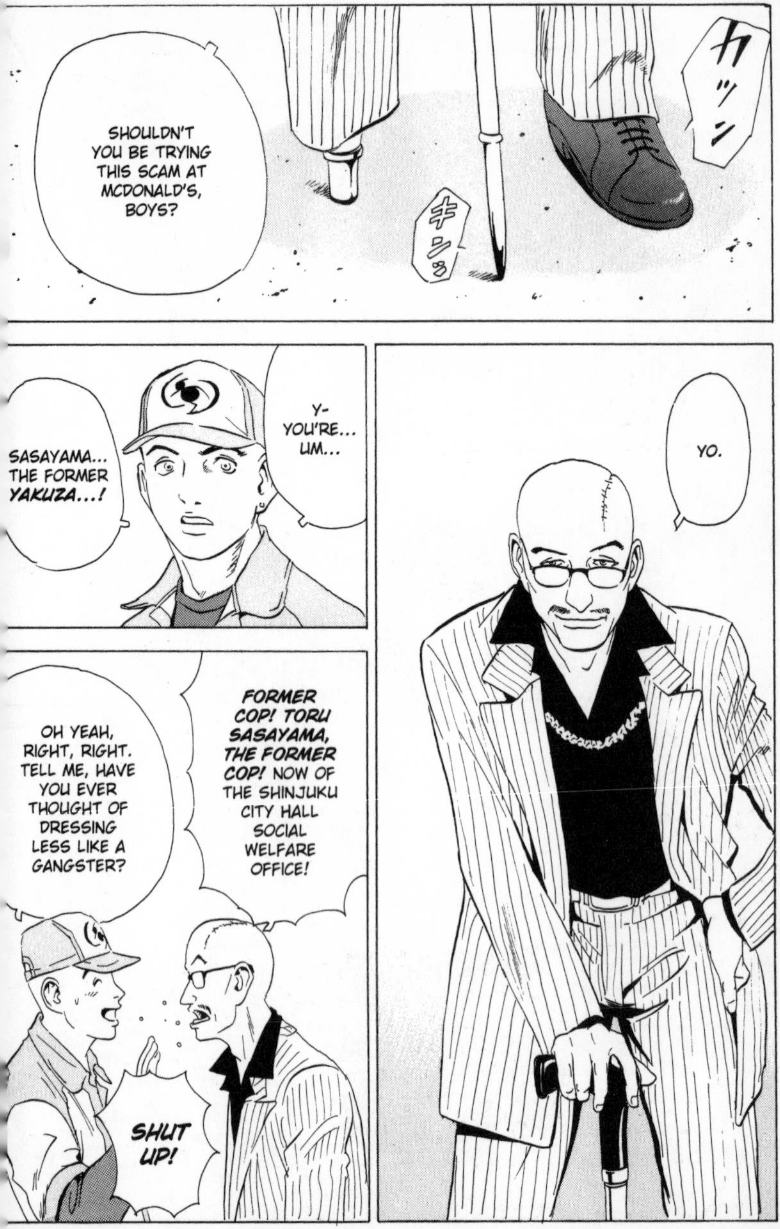
カッン
キン
SHOULDN'T YOU BE TRYING THIS SCAM AT MCDONALD'S, BOYS?
YO.
Y-YOU'RE... UM...
SASAYAMA... THE FORMER *YAKUZA*...!
FORMER COP! TORU SASAYAMA, THE FORMER COP! NOW OF THE SHINJUKU CITY HALL SOCIAL WELFARE OFFICE!
OH YEAH, RIGHT, RIGHT. TELL ME, HAVE YOU EVER THOUGHT OF DRESSING LESS LIKE A GANGSTER?
SHUT UP!

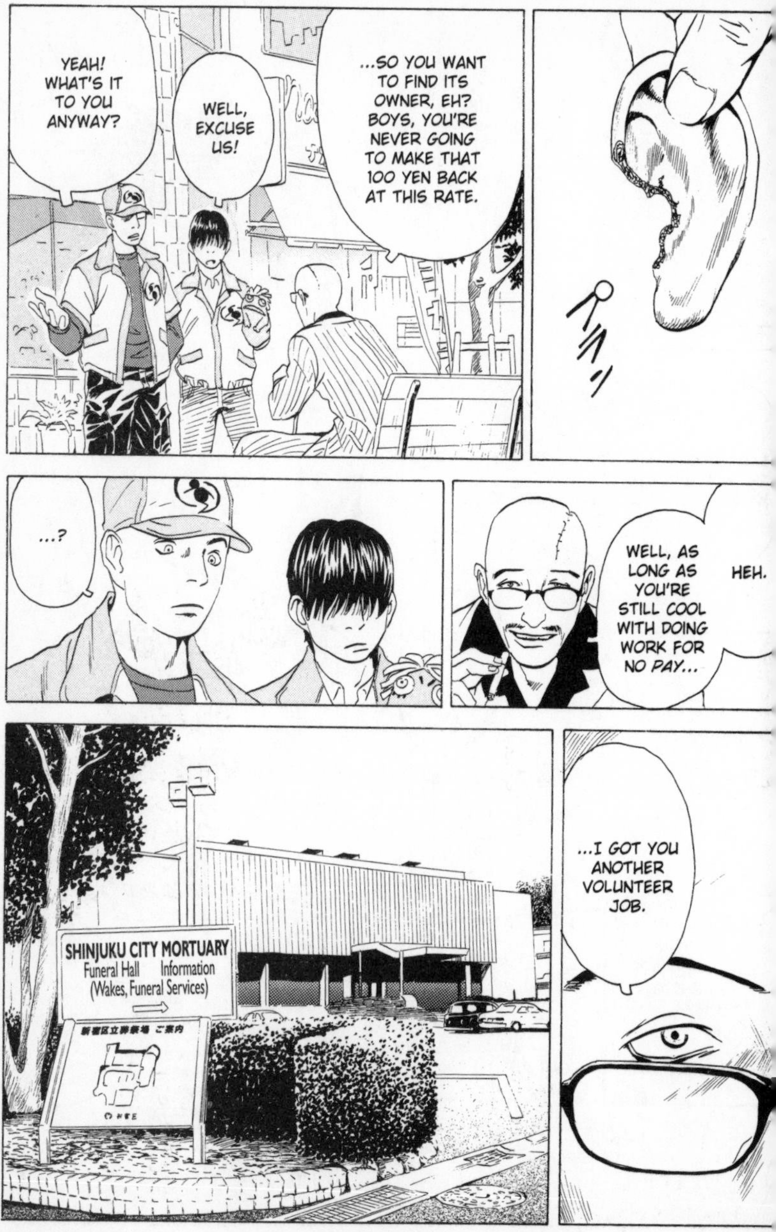
...SO YOU WANT TO FIND ITS OWNER, EH? BOYS, YOU'RE NEVER GOING TO MAKE THAT 100 YEN BACK AT THIS RATE.
WELL, EXCUSE US!
YEAH! WHAT'S IT TO YOU ANYWAY?
HEH.
WELL, AS LONG AS YOU'RE STILL COOL WITH DOING WORK FOR NO PAY...
...?
...I GOT YOU ANOTHER VOLUNTEER JOB.
SHINJUKU CITY MORTUARY
Funeral Hall Information
(Wakes, Funeral Services)
新宿区立葬祭場 ご案内

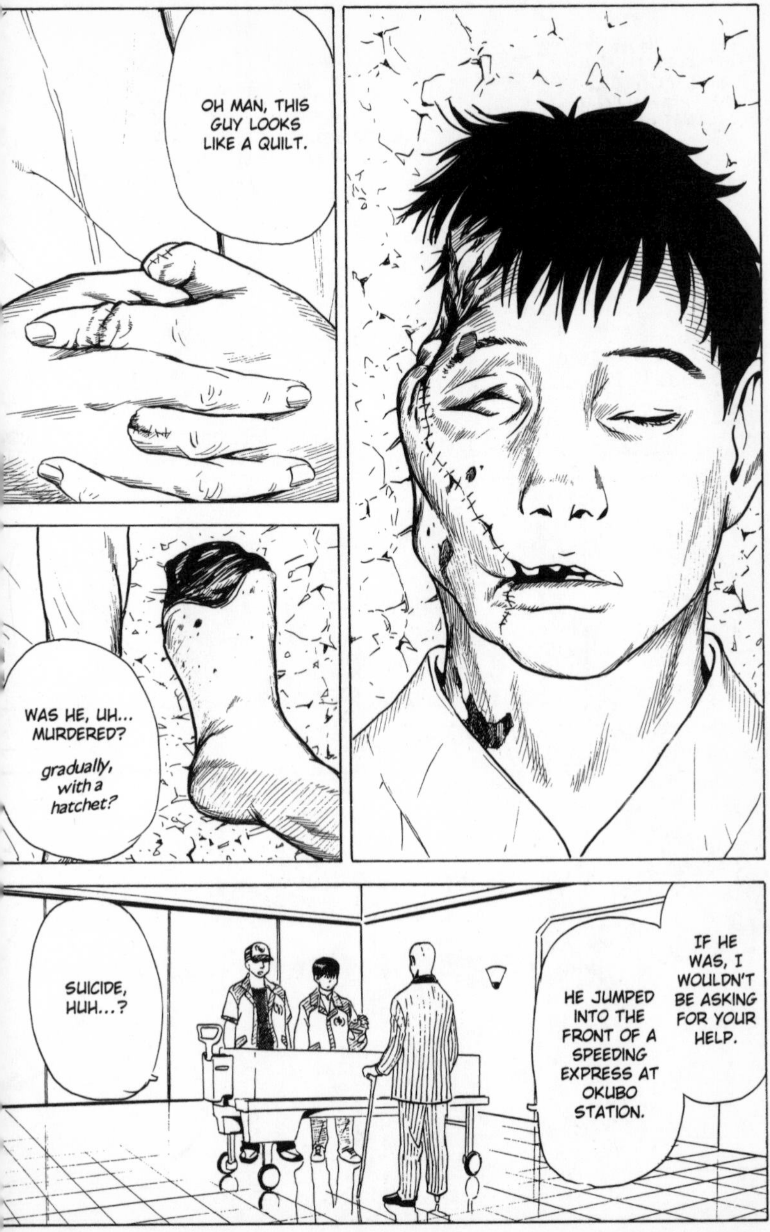
OH MAN, THIS GUY LOOKS LIKE A QUILT.
WAS HE, UH... MURDERED?
gradually, with a hatchet?
IF HE WAS, I WOULDN'T BE ASKING FOR YOUR HELP.
HE JUMPED INTO THE FRONT OF A SPEEDING EXPRESS AT OKUBO STATION.
SUICIDE, HUH...?

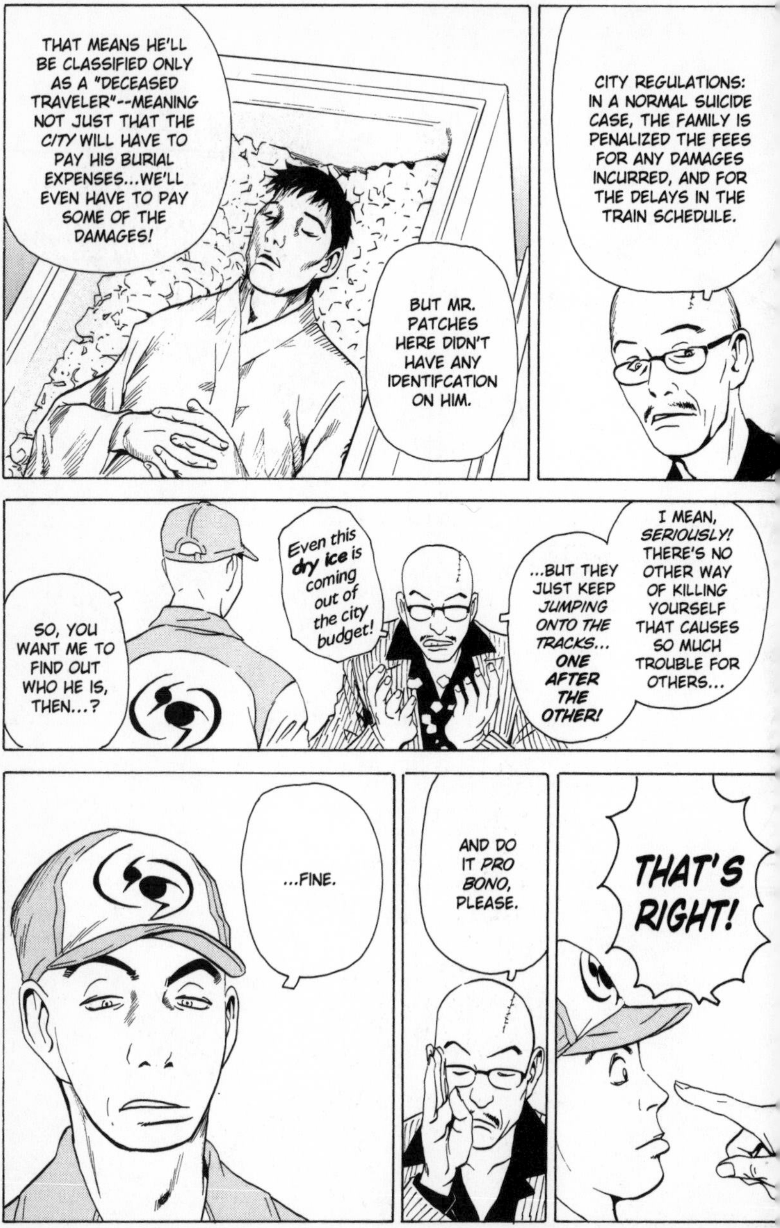
CITY REGULATIONS: IN A NORMAL SUICIDE CASE, THE FAMILY IS PENALIZED THE FEES FOR ANY DAMAGES INCURRED, AND FOR THE DELAYS IN THE TRAIN SCHEDULE.
BUT MR. PATCHES HERE DIDN'T HAVE ANY IDENTIFCATION ON HIM.
THAT MEANS HE'LL BE CLASSIFIED ONLY AS A "DECEASED TRAVELER"--MEANING NOT JUST THAT THE *CITY* WILL HAVE TO PAY HIS BURIAL EXPENSES...WE'LL EVEN HAVE TO PAY SOME OF THE DAMAGES!
I MEAN, *SERIOUSLY!* THERE'S NO OTHER WAY OF KILLING YOURSELF THAT CAUSES SO MUCH TROUBLE FOR OTHERS...
...BUT THEY JUST KEEP *JUMPING ONTO THE TRACKS...* ***ONE AFTER THE OTHER!***
Even this **dry ice** is coming out of the city budget!
SO, YOU WANT ME TO FIND OUT WHO HE IS, THEN...?
THAT'S RIGHT!
AND DO IT *PRO BONO*, PLEASE.
...FINE.

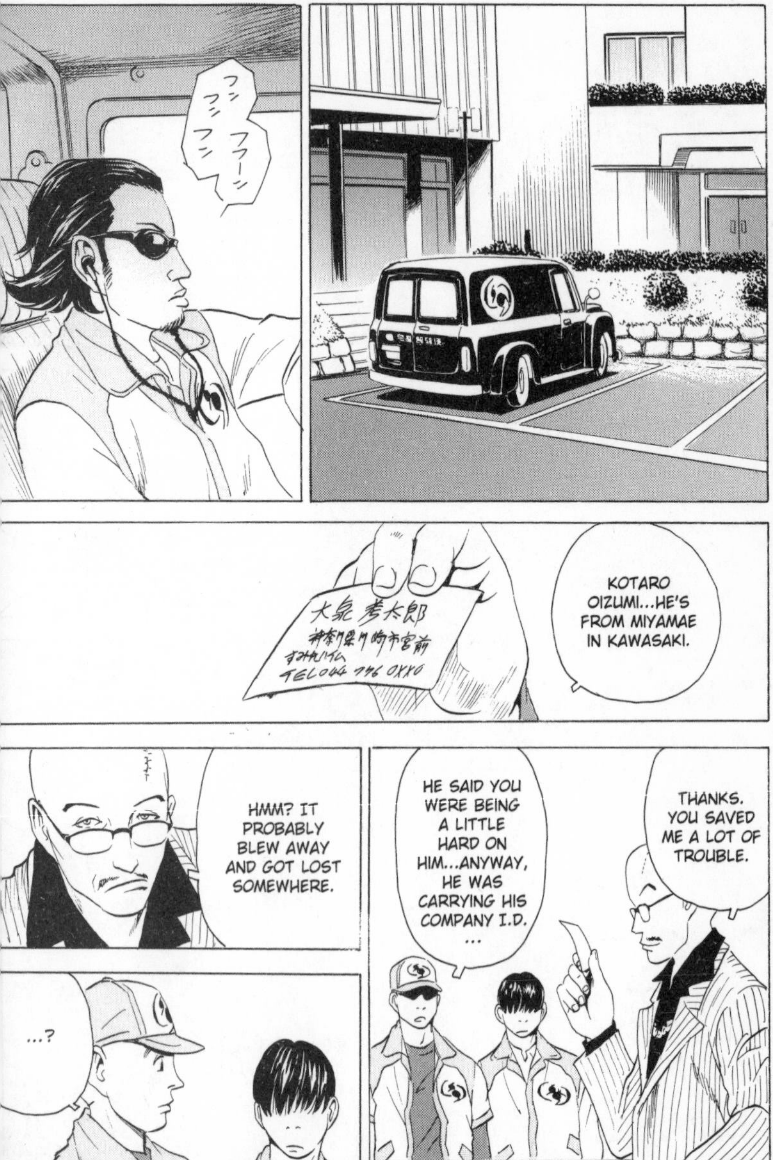
フン フン フン フラーン
KOTARO OIZUMI...HE'S FROM MIYAMAE IN KAWASAKI.
THANKS. YOU SAVED ME A LOT OF TROUBLE.
HE SAID YOU WERE BEING A LITTLE HARD ON HIM...ANYWAY, HE WAS CARRYING HIS COMPANY I.D. ...
HMM? IT PROBABLY BLEW AWAY AND GOT LOST SOMEWHERE.
...?

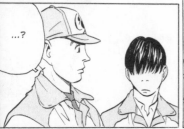

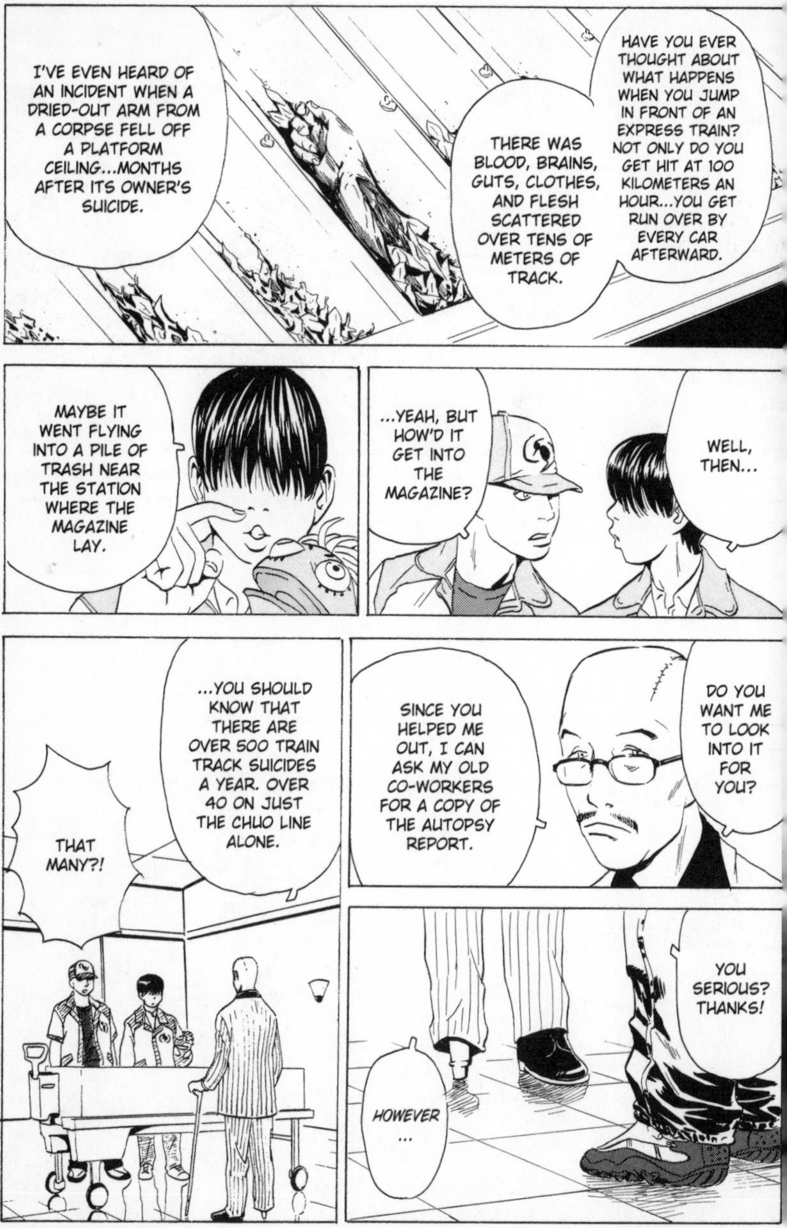
HAVE YOU EVER THOUGHT ABOUT WHAT HAPPENS WHEN YOU JUMP IN FRONT OF AN EXPRESS TRAIN? NOT ONLY DO YOU GET HIT AT 100 KILOMETERS AN HOUR...YOU GET RUN OVER BY EVERY CAR AFTERWARD.
THERE WAS BLOOD, BRAINS, GUTS, CLOTHES, AND FLESH SCATTERED OVER TENS OF METERS OF TRACK.
I'VE EVEN HEARD OF AN INCIDENT WHEN A DRIED-OUT ARM FROM A CORPSE FELL OFF A PLATFORM CEILING...MONTHS AFTER ITS OWNER'S SUICIDE.
WELL, THEN...
...YEAH, BUT HOW'D IT GET INTO THE MAGAZINE?
MAYBE IT WENT FLYING INTO A PILE OF TRASH NEAR THE STATION WHERE THE MAGAZINE LAY.
DO YOU WANT ME TO LOOK INTO IT FOR YOU?
SINCE YOU HELPED ME OUT, I CAN ASK MY OLD CO-WORKERS FOR A COPY OF THE AUTOPSY REPORT.
YOU SERIOUS? THANKS!
HOWEVER...
...YOU SHOULD KNOW THAT THERE ARE OVER 500 TRAIN TRACK SUICIDES A YEAR. OVER 40 ON JUST THE CHUO LINE ALONE.
THAT MANY?!

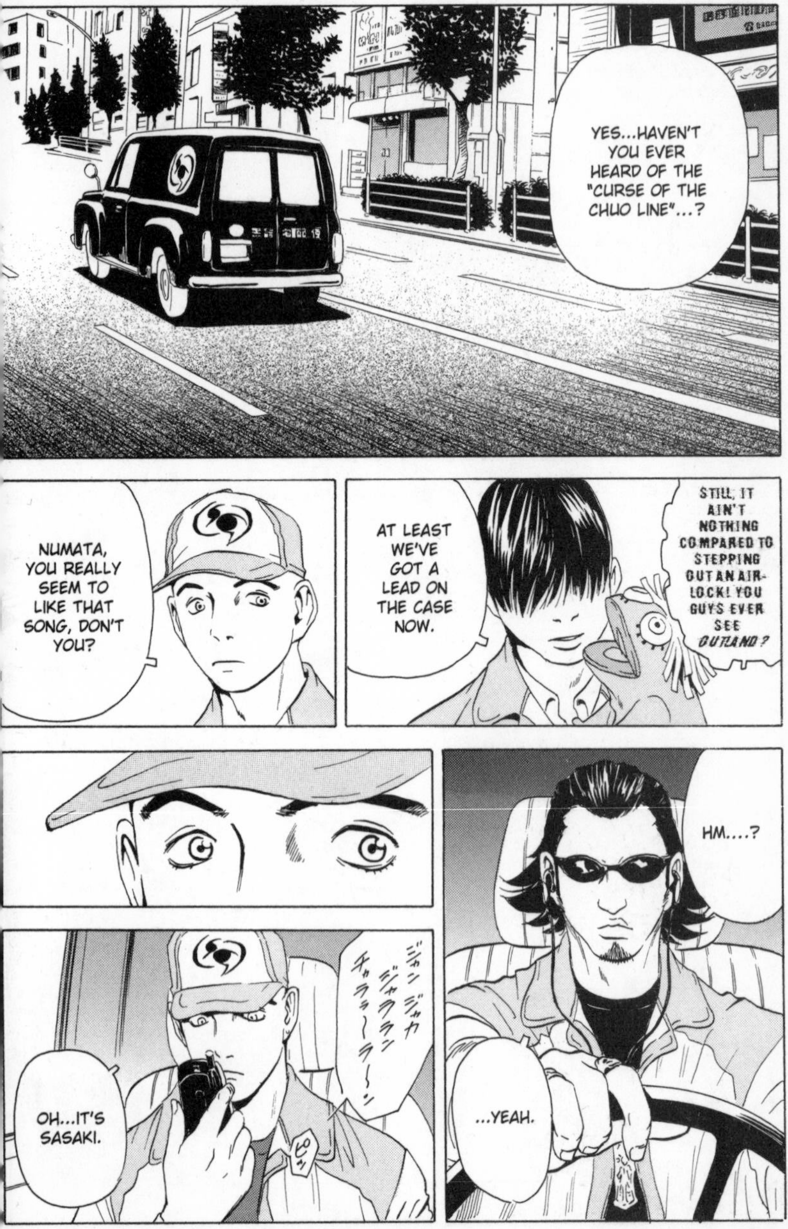
YES...HAVEN'T YOU EVER HEARD OF THE "CURSE OF THE CHUO LINE"...?
STILL, IT AIN'T NOTHING COMPARED TO STEPPING OUT AN AIR-LOCK! YOU GUYS EVER SEE *OUTLAND*?
AT LEAST WE'VE GOT A LEAD ON THE CASE NOW.
NUMATA, YOU REALLY SEEM TO LIKE THAT SONG, DON'T YOU?
HM....?
...YEAH.
ジャン ジャカ
ジャラララン
チャララ～ラ～～ン
OH...IT'S SASAKI.

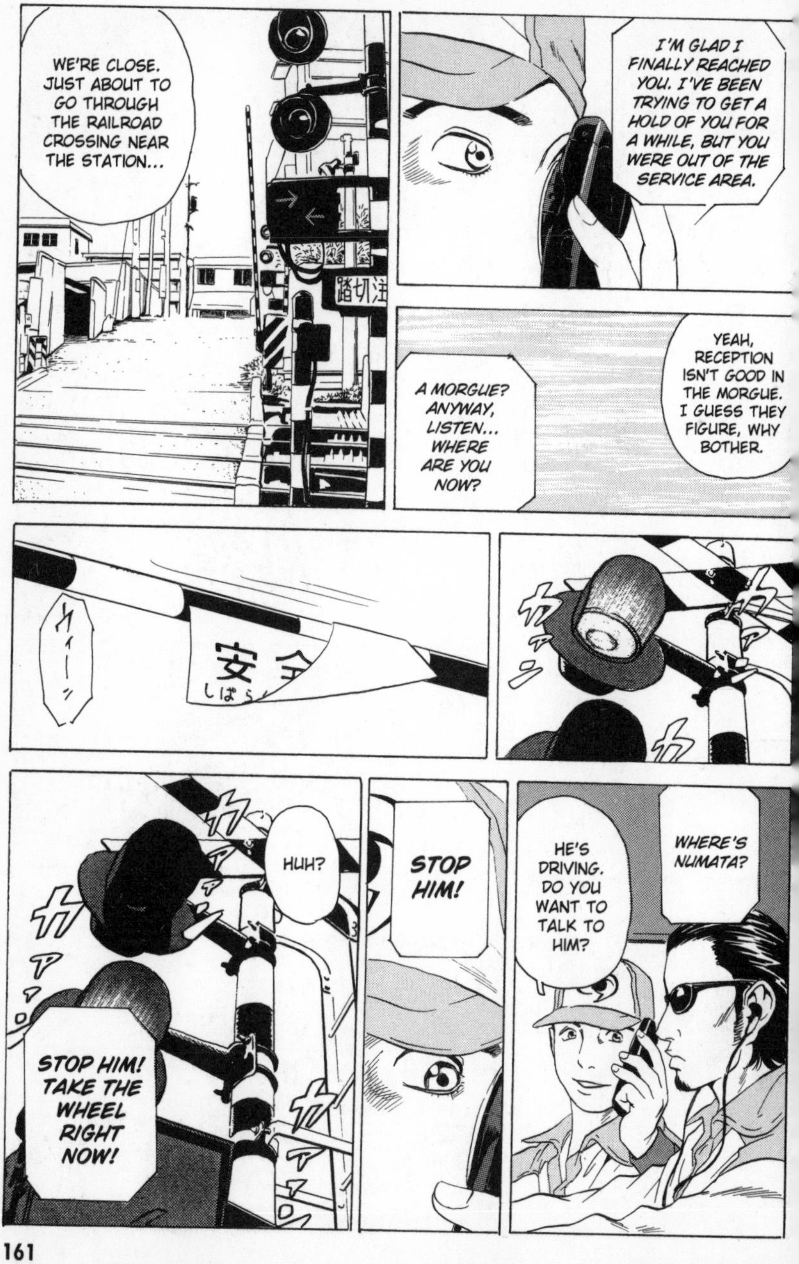
I'M GLAD I FINALLY REACHED YOU. I'VE BEEN TRYING TO GET A HOLD OF YOU FOR A WHILE, BUT YOU WERE OUT OF THE SERVICE AREA.
YEAH, RECEPTION ISN'T GOOD IN THE MORGUE. I GUESS THEY FIGURE, WHY BOTHER.
A MORGUE? ANYWAY, LISTEN... WHERE ARE YOU NOW?
WE'RE CLOSE. JUST ABOUT TO GO THROUGH THE RAILROAD CROSSING NEAR THE STATION...
踏切注
安全
WHERE'S NUMATA?
HE'S DRIVING. DO YOU WANT TO TALK TO HIM?
STOP HIM!
HUH?
STOP HIM! TAKE THE WHEEL RIGHT NOW!

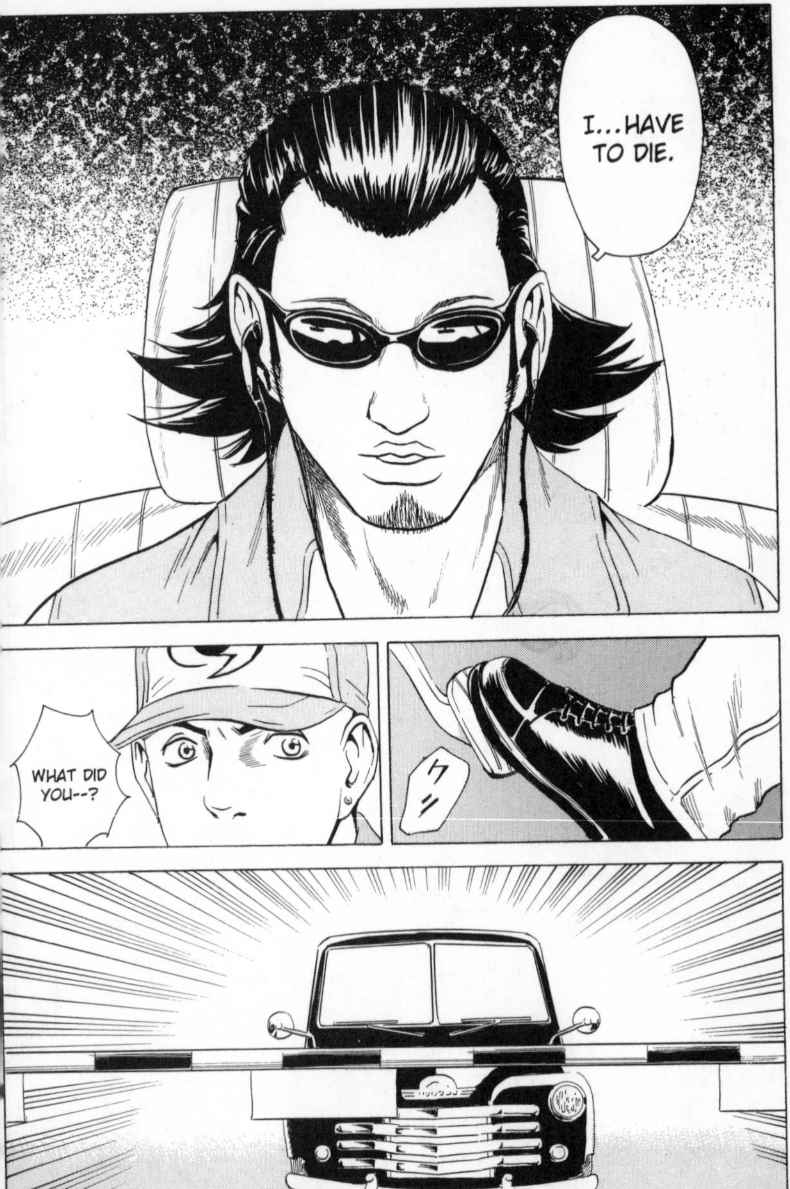
I...HAVE TO DIE.
クニ
WHAT DID YOU--?

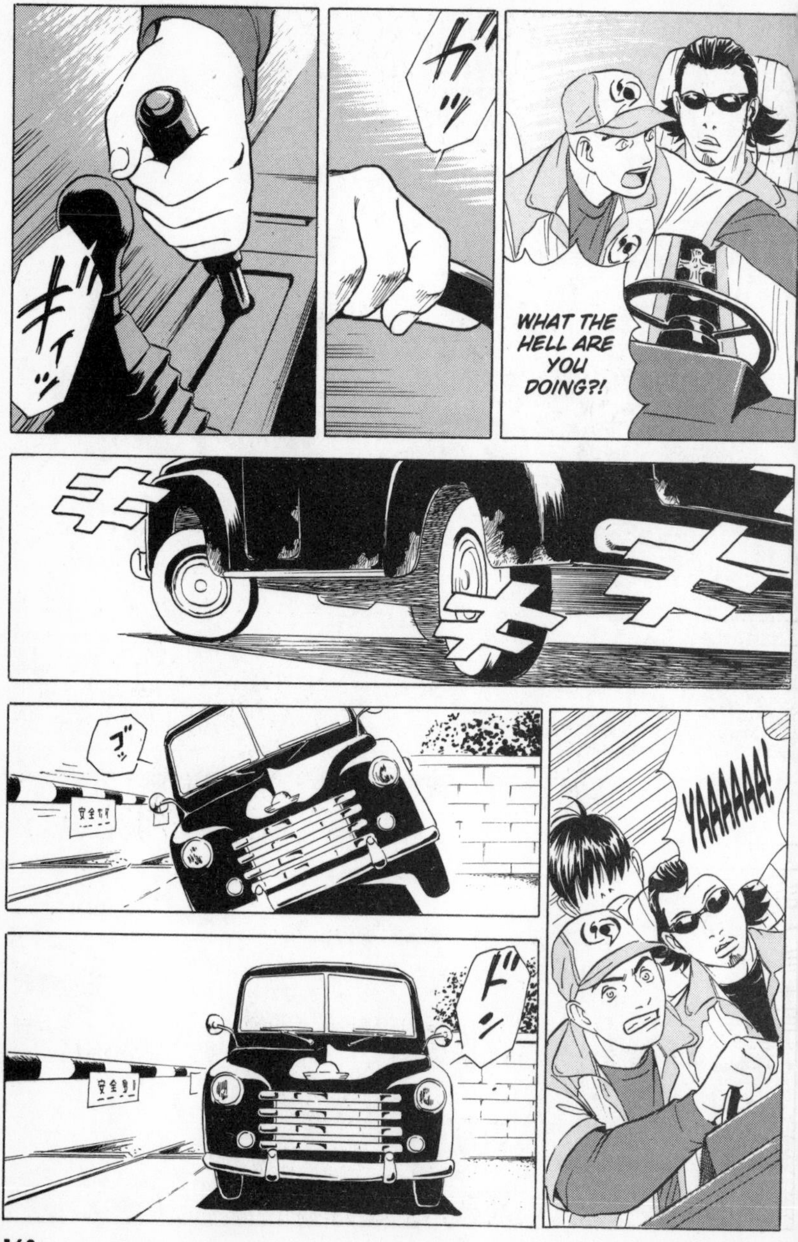
WHAT THE HELL ARE YOU DOING?!
ガッ
ギィッ
キ
キ
キ
YAAAAAA!
ゴッ
ドン

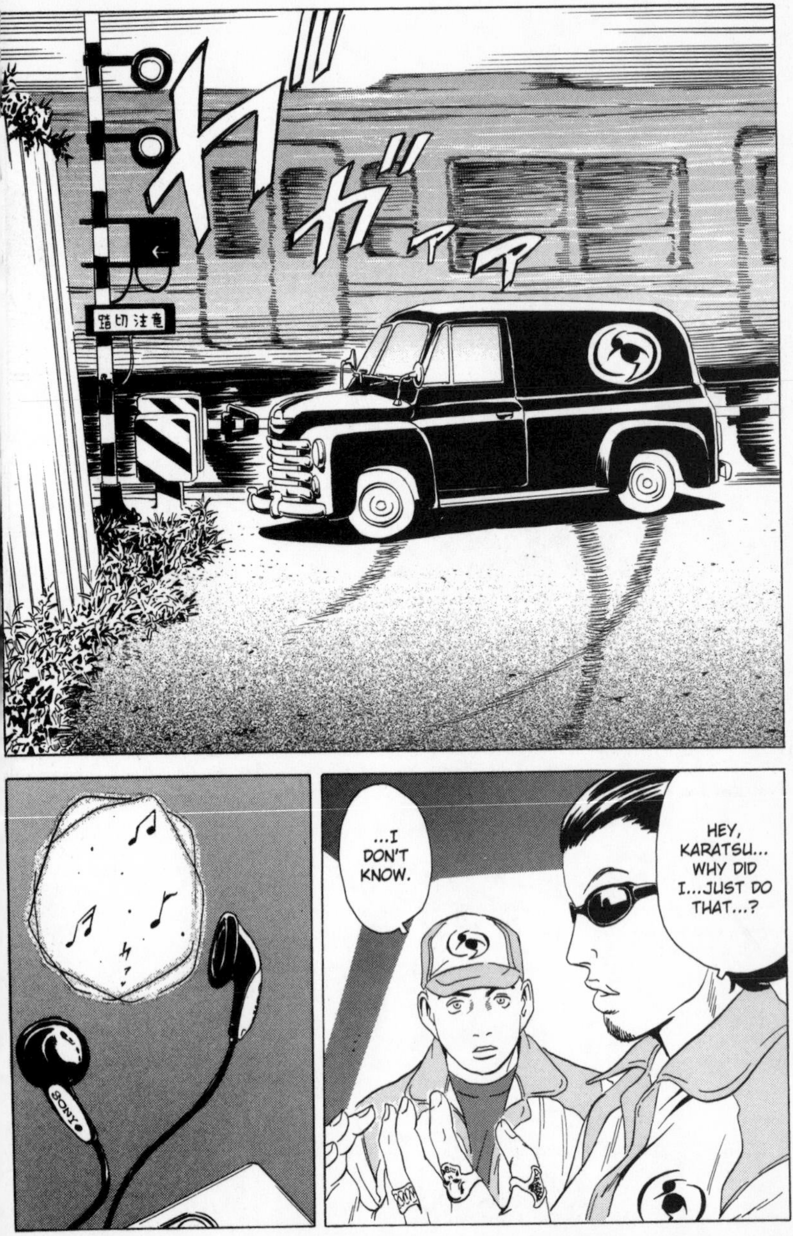
踏切注意
ガァァア
HEY, KARATSU... WHY DID I...JUST DO THAT...?
...I DON'T KNOW.
SONY

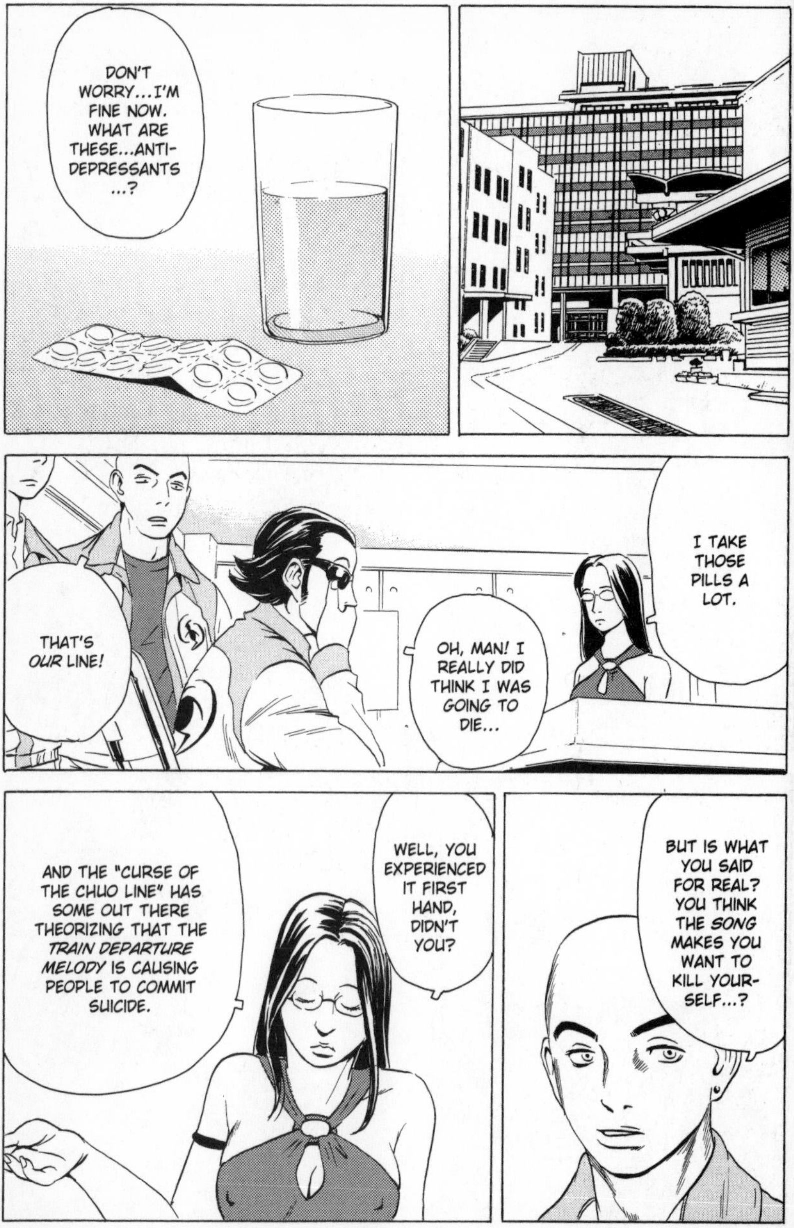
DON'T WORRY...I'M FINE NOW. WHAT ARE THESE...ANTI-DEPRESSANTS ...?
I TAKE THOSE PILLS A LOT.
OH, MAN! I REALLY DID THINK I WAS GOING TO DIE...
THAT'S *OUR* LINE!
BUT IS WHAT YOU SAID FOR REAL? YOU THINK THE *SONG* MAKES YOU WANT TO KILL YOUR-SELF...?
WELL, YOU EXPERIENCED IT FIRST HAND, DIDN'T YOU?
AND THE "CURSE OF THE CHUO LINE" HAS SOME OUT THERE THEORIZING THAT THE *TRAIN DEPARTURE MELODY* IS CAUSING PEOPLE TO COMMIT SUICIDE.

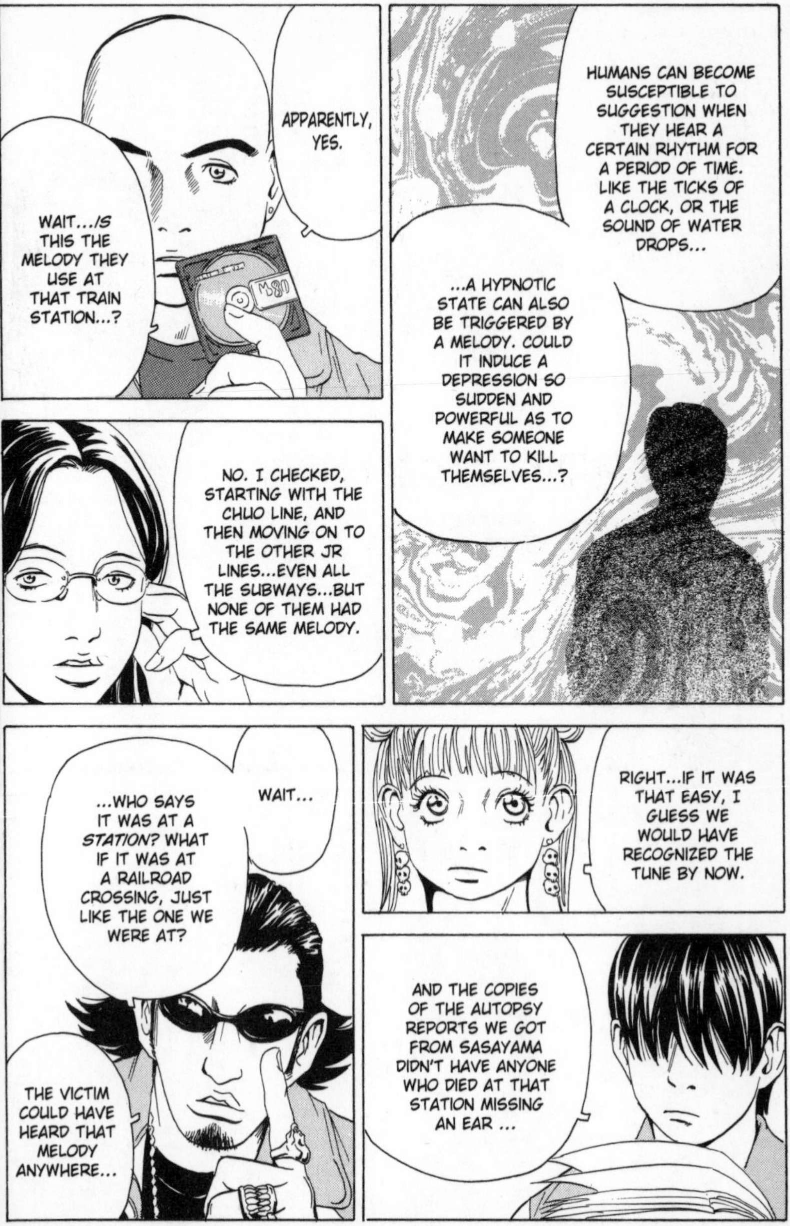
HUMANS CAN BECOME SUSCEPTIBLE TO SUGGESTION WHEN THEY HEAR A CERTAIN RHYTHM FOR A PERIOD OF TIME. LIKE THE TICKS OF A CLOCK, OR THE SOUND OF WATER DROPS...
...A HYPNOTIC STATE CAN ALSO BE TRIGGERED BY A MELODY. COULD IT INDUCE A DEPRESSION SO SUDDEN AND POWERFUL AS TO MAKE SOMEONE WANT TO KILL THEMSELVES...?
APPARENTLY, YES.
WAIT...*IS* THIS THE MELODY THEY USE AT THAT TRAIN STATION...?
M80
NO. I CHECKED, STARTING WITH THE CHUO LINE, AND THEN MOVING ON TO THE OTHER JR LINES...EVEN ALL THE SUBWAYS...BUT NONE OF THEM HAD THE SAME MELODY.
RIGHT...IF IT WAS THAT EASY, I GUESS WE WOULD HAVE RECOGNIZED THE TUNE BY NOW.
AND THE COPIES OF THE AUTOPSY REPORTS WE GOT FROM SASAYAMA DIDN'T HAVE ANYONE WHO DIED AT THAT STATION MISSING AN EAR ...
WAIT...
...WHO SAYS IT WAS AT A *STATION*? WHAT IF IT WAS AT A RAILROAD CROSSING, JUST LIKE THE ONE WE WERE AT?
THE VICTIM COULD HAVE HEARD THAT MELODY ANYWHERE...

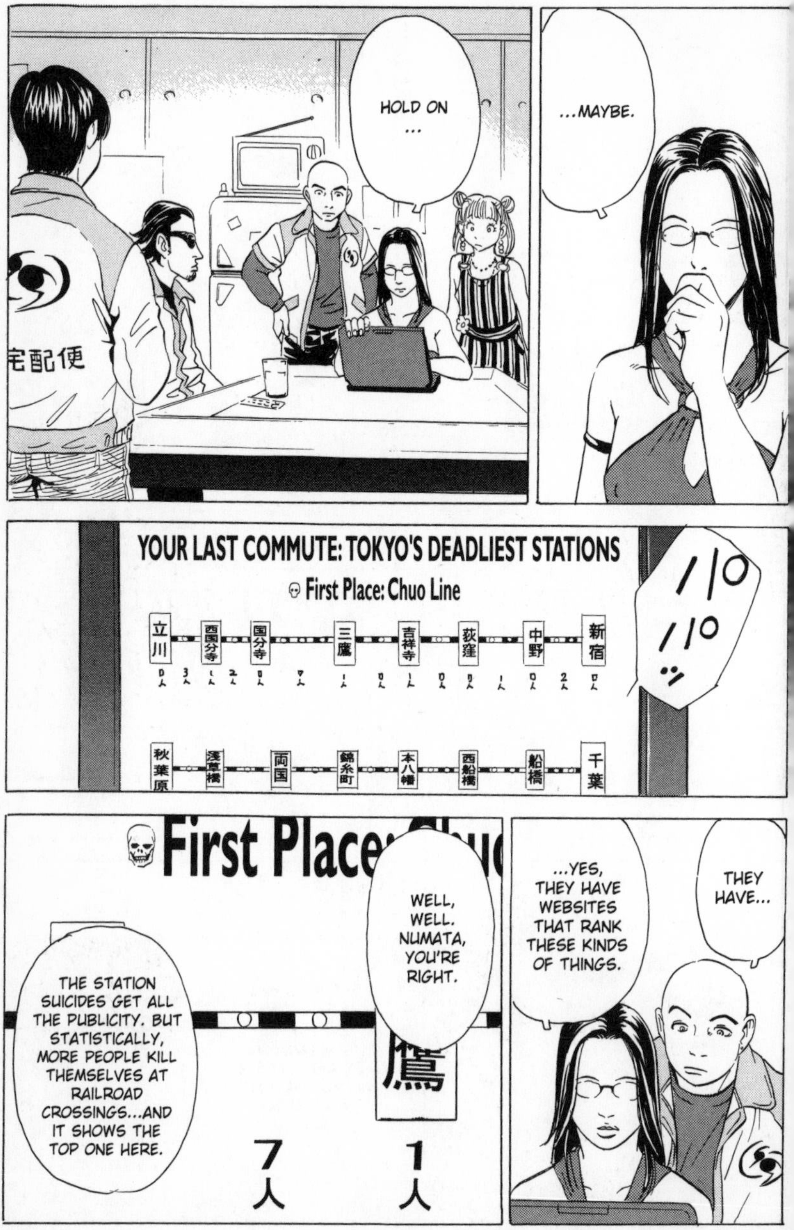
...MAYBE.
HOLD ON ...
パパッ
YOUR LAST COMMUTE: TOKYO'S DEADLIEST STATIONS
First Place: Chuo Line
新宿 中野 荻窪 吉祥寺 三鷹 国分寺 西国分寺 立川
千葉 船橋 西船橋 本八幡 錦糸町 両国 浅草橋 秋葉原
THEY HAVE...
...YES, THEY HAVE WEBSITES THAT RANK THESE KINDS OF THINGS.
First Place:
WELL, WELL. NUMATA, YOU'RE RIGHT.
THE STATION SUICIDES GET ALL THE PUBLICITY. BUT STATISTICALLY, MORE PEOPLE KILL THEMSELVES AT RAILROAD CROSSINGS...AND IT SHOWS THE TOP ONE HERE.
鷹
7人
1人

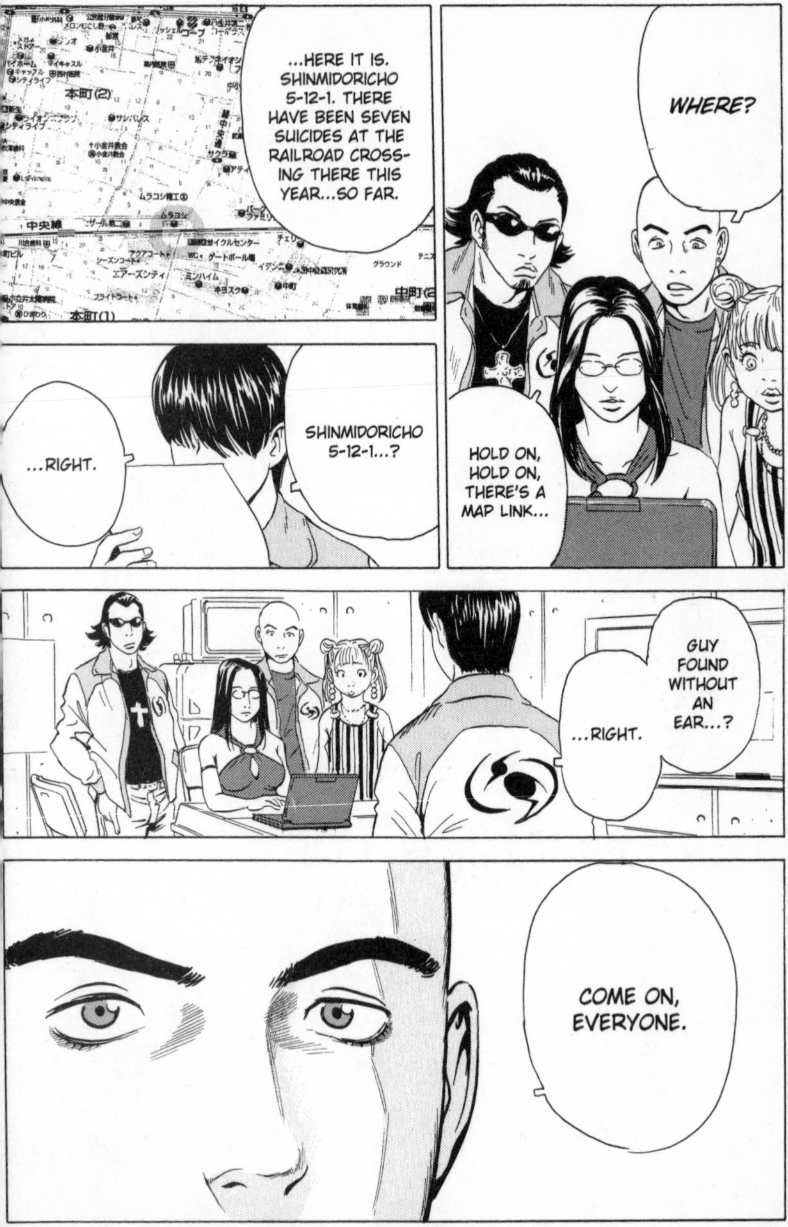
WHERE?
HOLD ON, HOLD ON, THERE'S A MAP LINK...
...HERE IT IS. SHINMIDORICHO 5-12-1. THERE HAVE BEEN SEVEN SUICIDES AT THE RAILROAD CROSSING THERE THIS YEAR...SO FAR.
SHINMIDORICHO 5-12-1...?
...RIGHT.
GUY FOUND WITHOUT AN EAR...?
...RIGHT.
COME ON, EVERYONE.

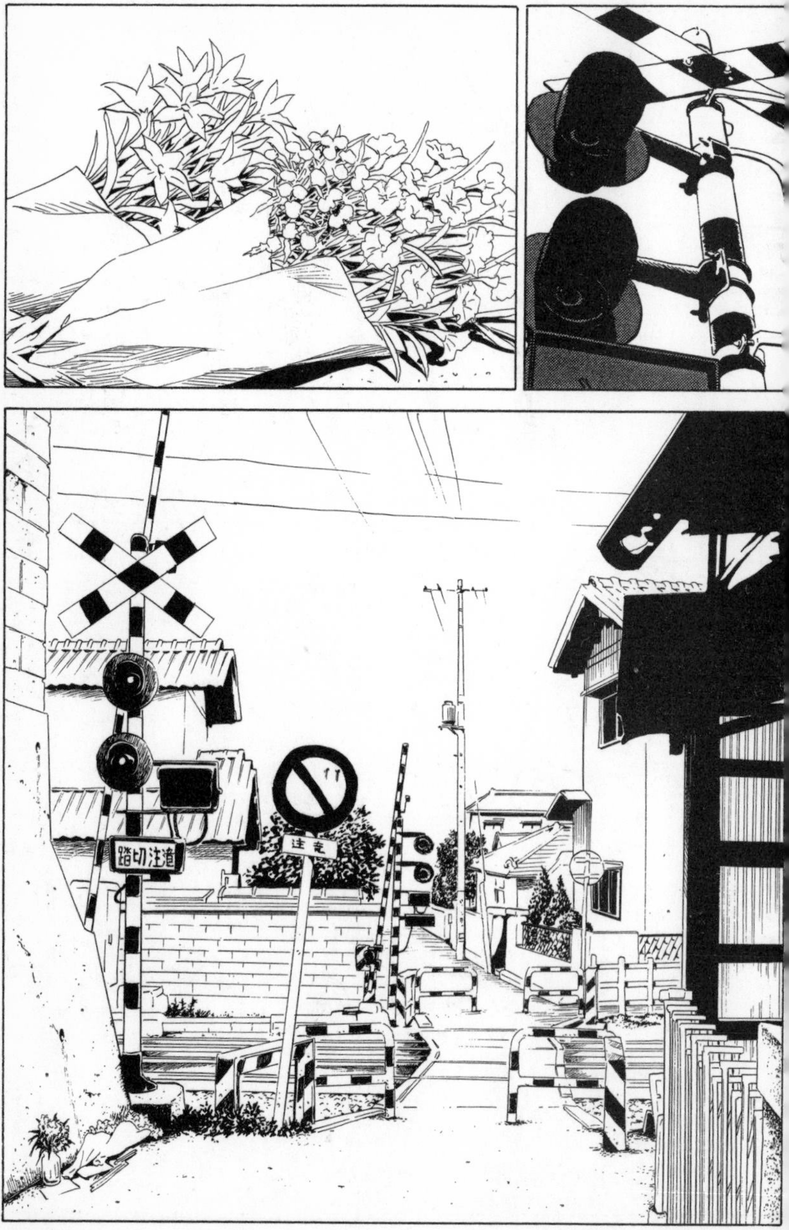
踏切注意
注意

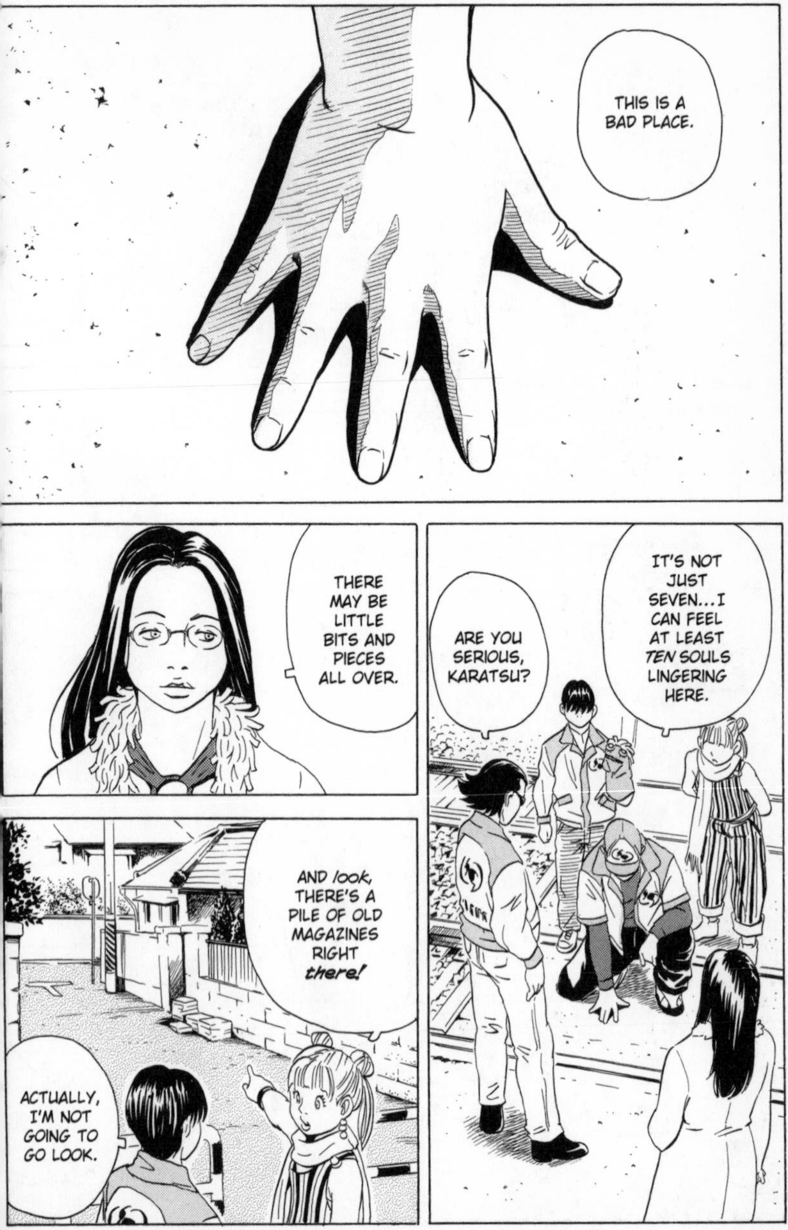
THIS IS A BAD PLACE.
IT'S NOT JUST SEVEN... I CAN FEEL AT LEAST *TEN* SOULS LINGERING HERE.
ARE YOU SERIOUS, KARATSU?
THERE MAY BE LITTLE BITS AND PIECES ALL OVER.
AND *look*, THERE'S A PILE OF OLD MAGAZINES RIGHT ***there!***
ACTUALLY, I'M NOT GOING TO GO LOOK.

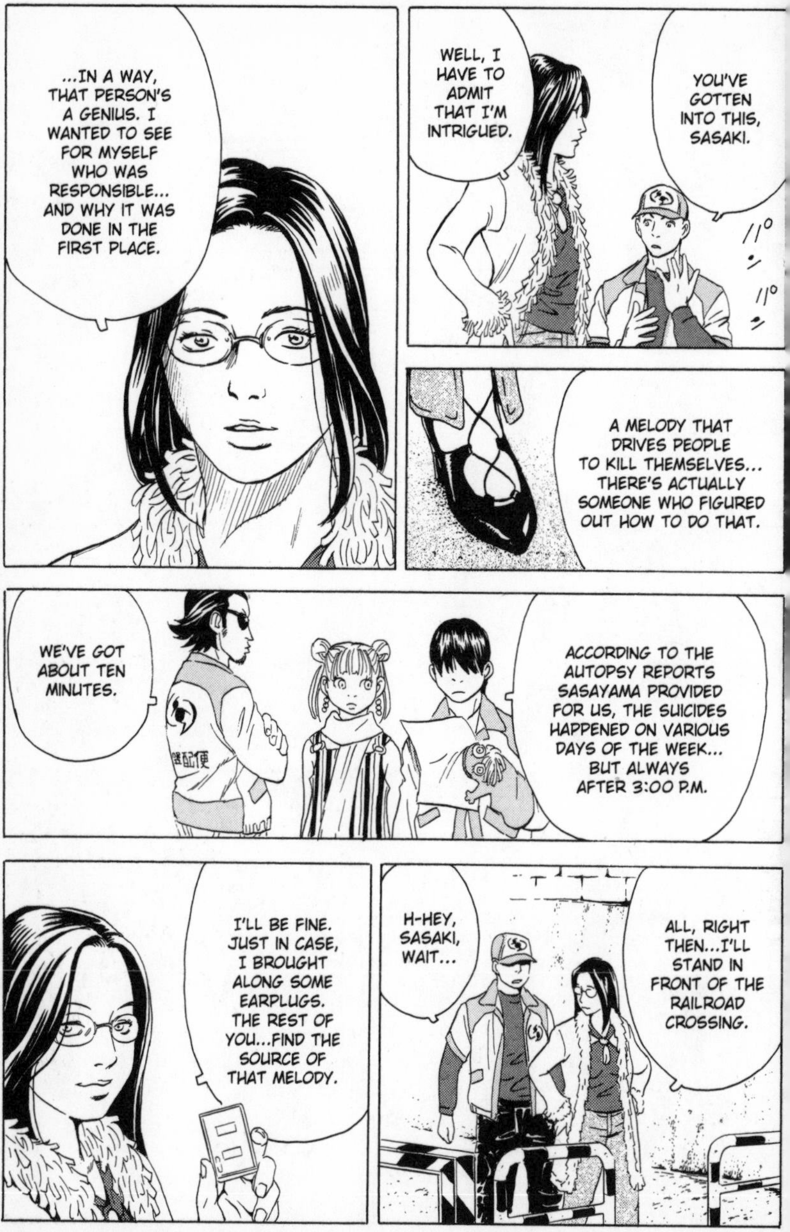
YOU'VE GOTTEN INTO THIS, SASAKI.
WELL, I HAVE TO ADMIT THAT I'M INTRIGUED.
A MELODY THAT DRIVES PEOPLE TO KILL THEMSELVES... THERE'S ACTUALLY SOMEONE WHO FIGURED OUT HOW TO DO THAT.
...IN A WAY, THAT PERSON'S A GENIUS. I WANTED TO SEE FOR MYSELF WHO WAS RESPONSIBLE... AND WHY IT WAS DONE IN THE FIRST PLACE.
ACCORDING TO THE AUTOPSY REPORTS SASAYAMA PROVIDED FOR US, THE SUICIDES HAPPENED ON VARIOUS DAYS OF THE WEEK... BUT ALWAYS AFTER 3:00 P.M.
WE'VE GOT ABOUT TEN MINUTES.
ALL, RIGHT THEN...I'LL STAND IN FRONT OF THE RAILROAD CROSSING.
H-HEY, SASAKI, WAIT...
I'LL BE FINE. JUST IN CASE, I BROUGHT ALONG SOME EARPLUGS. THE REST OF YOU...FIND THE SOURCE OF THAT MELODY.

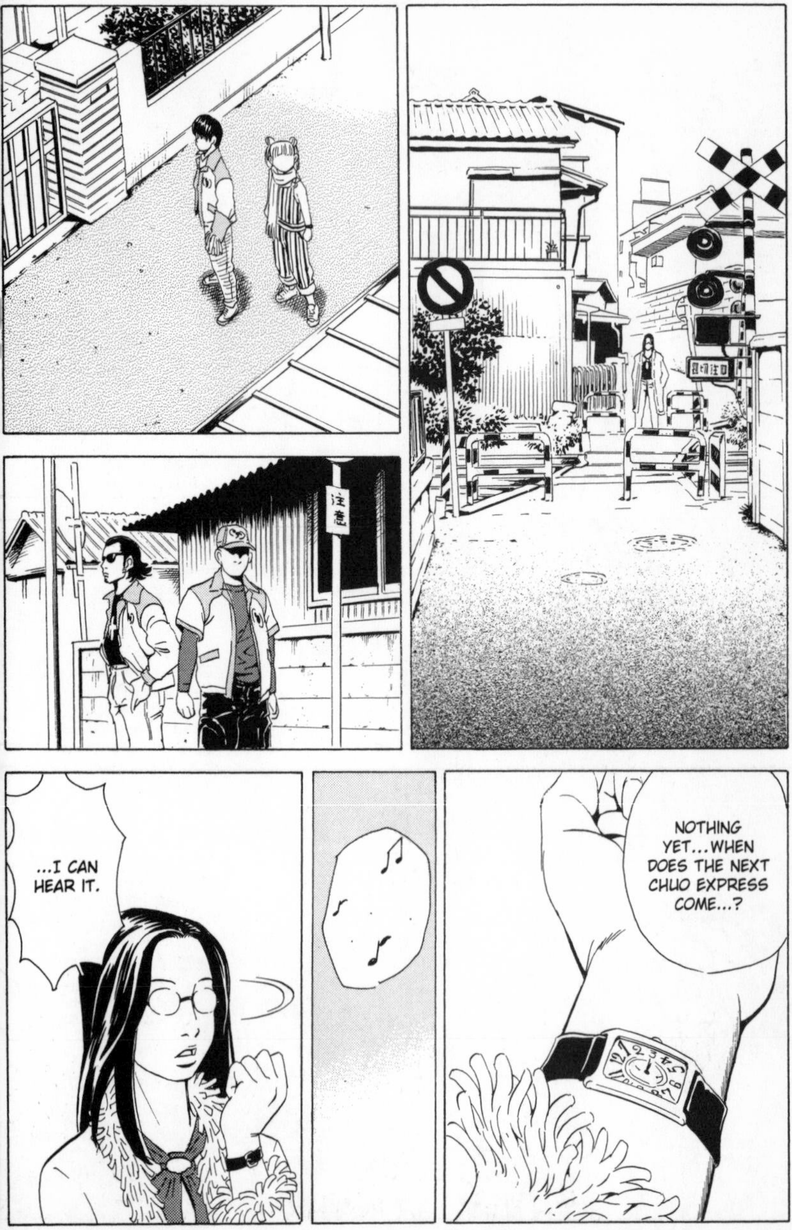
注意
NOTHING YET...WHEN DOES THE NEXT CHUO EXPRESS COME...?
...I CAN HEAR IT.

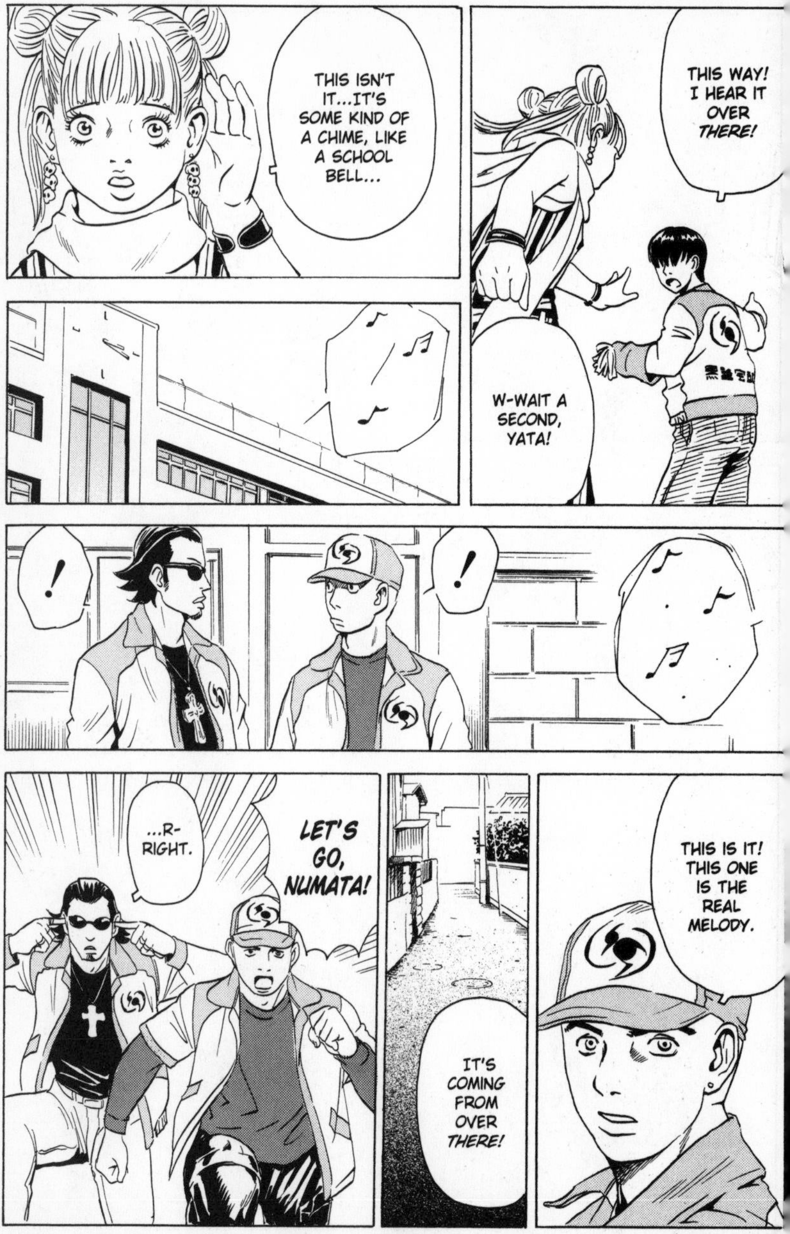
THIS WAY! I HEAR IT OVER THERE!
W-WAIT A SECOND, YATA!
THIS ISN'T IT...IT'S SOME KIND OF A CHIME, LIKE A SCHOOL BELL...
!
!
THIS IS IT! THIS ONE IS THE REAL MELODY.
IT'S COMING FROM OVER THERE!
LET'S GO, NUMATA!
...R-RIGHT.

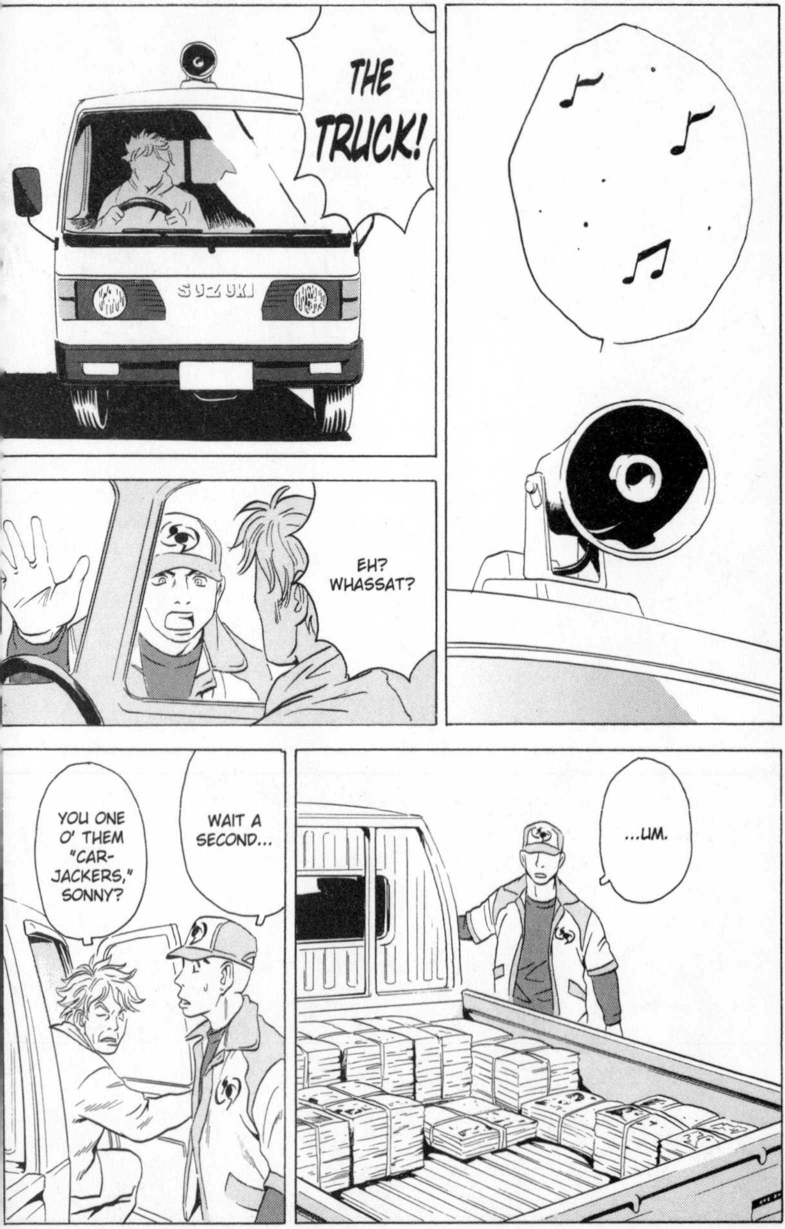
THE TRUCK!
EH? WHASSAT?
...UM.
WAIT A SECOND...
YOU ONE O' THEM "CAR-JACKERS," SONNY?

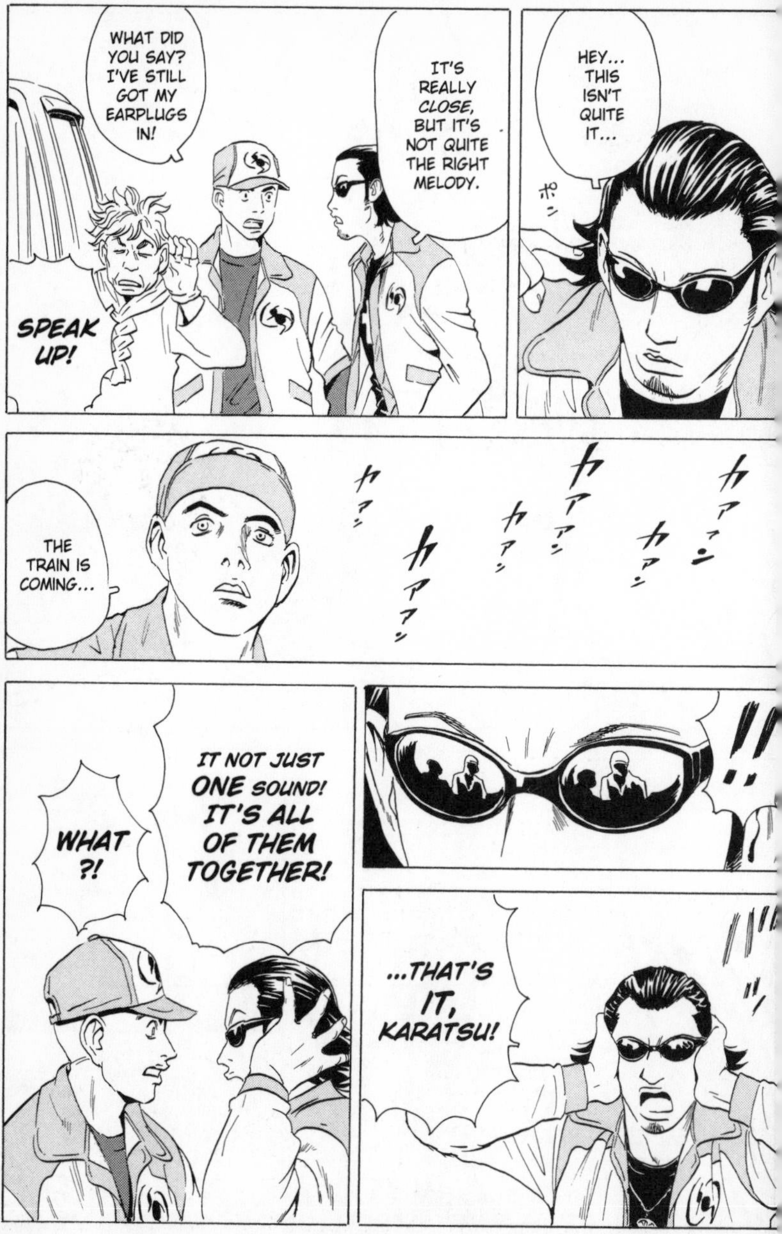

HEY... THIS ISN'T QUITE IT...
ポン
IT'S REALLY CLOSE, BUT IT'S NOT QUITE THE RIGHT MELODY.
WHAT DID YOU SAY? I'VE STILL GOT MY EARPLUGS IN!
SPEAK UP!
カァァン
カァン
カァァン
カァン
カァァン
カァン
THE TRAIN IS COMING...
!!
...THAT'S IT, KARATSU!
IT NOT JUST ONE SOUND! IT'S ALL OF THEM TOGETHER!
WHAT ?!

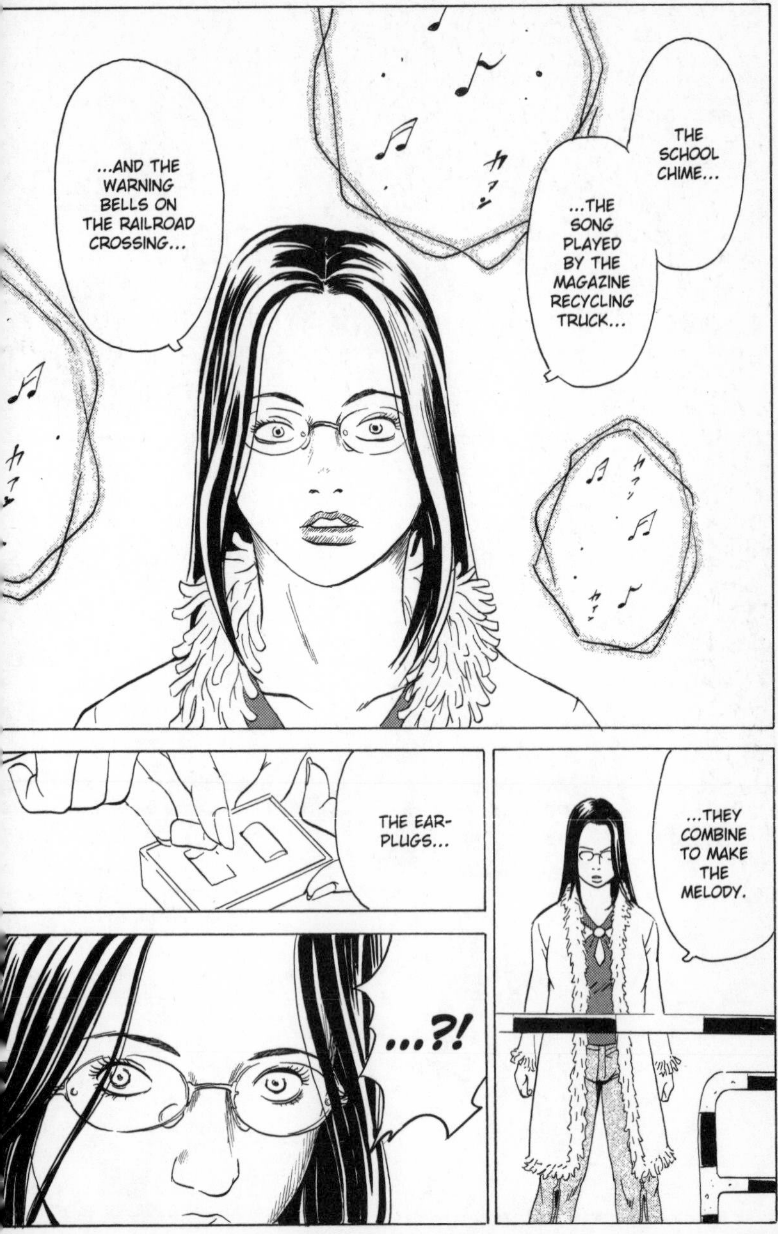
THE SCHOOL CHIME...
...THE SONG PLAYED BY THE MAGAZINE RECYCLING TRUCK...
...AND THE WARNING BELLS ON THE RAILROAD CROSSING...
...THEY COMBINE TO MAKE THE MELODY.
THE EAR-PLUGS...
...?!

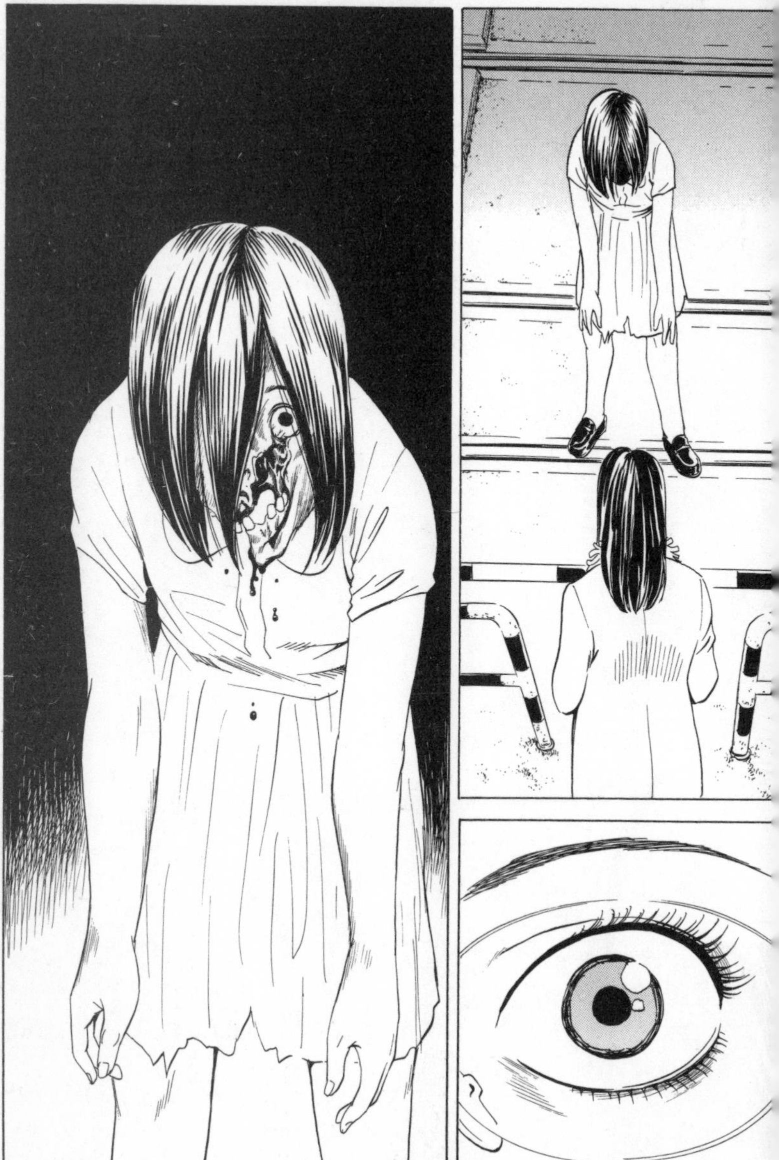

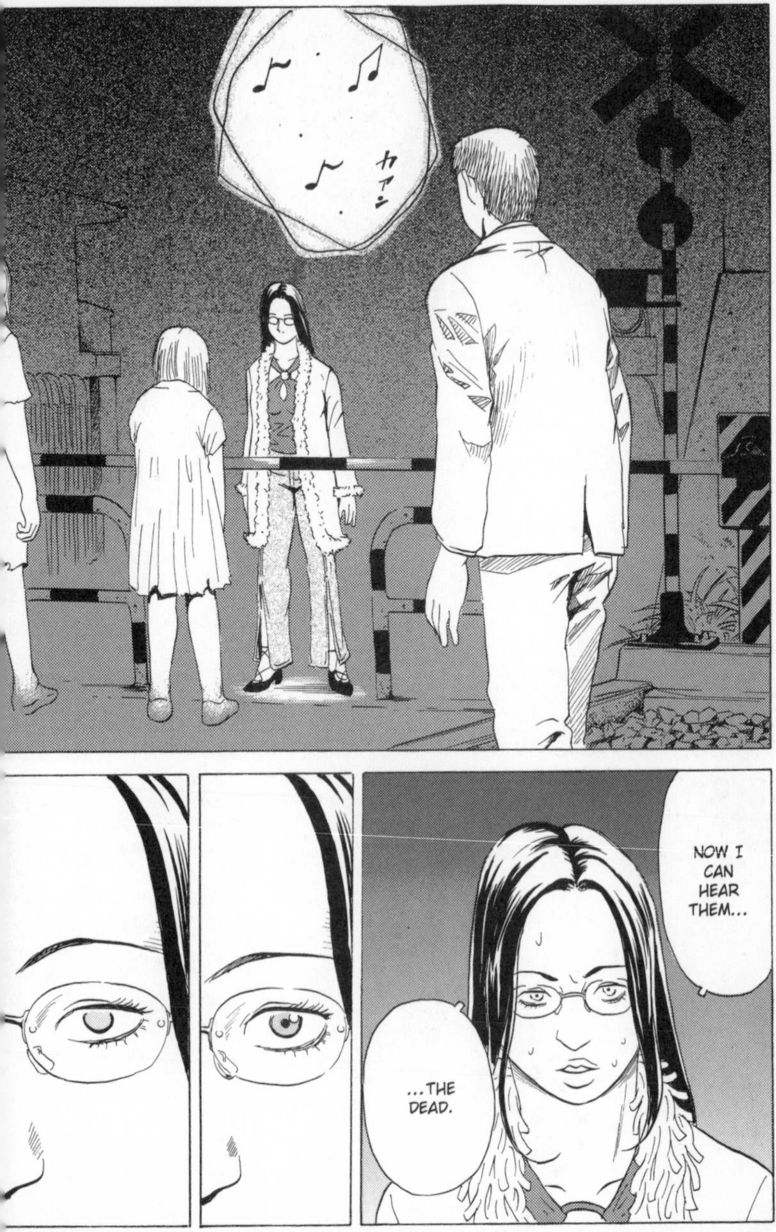
カァン
NOW I CAN HEAR THEM...
...THE DEAD.

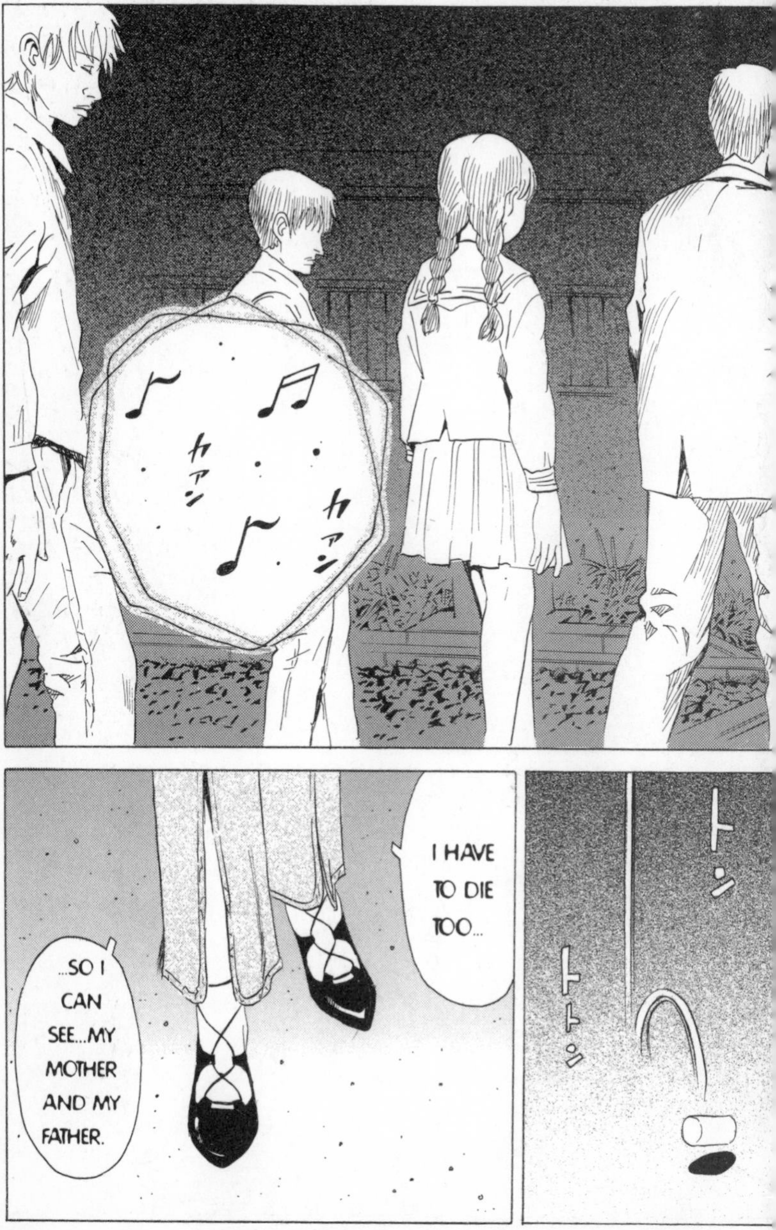
カァン
カァン
トン
トトン
I HAVE TO DIE TOO...
...SO I CAN SEE...MY MOTHER AND MY FATHER.

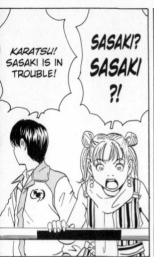

SASAKI? SASAKI ?!
KARATSU! SASAKI IS IN TROUBLE!
STOP!
THEY'RE COMING FROM BOTH DIRECTIONS ...!

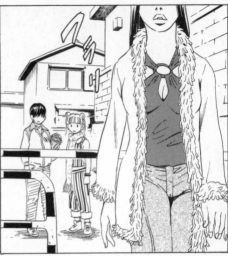

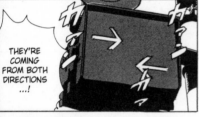

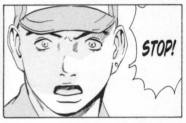

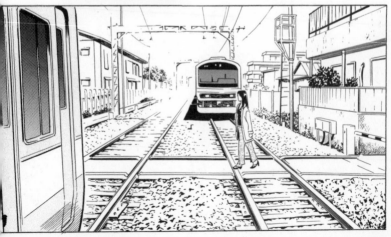

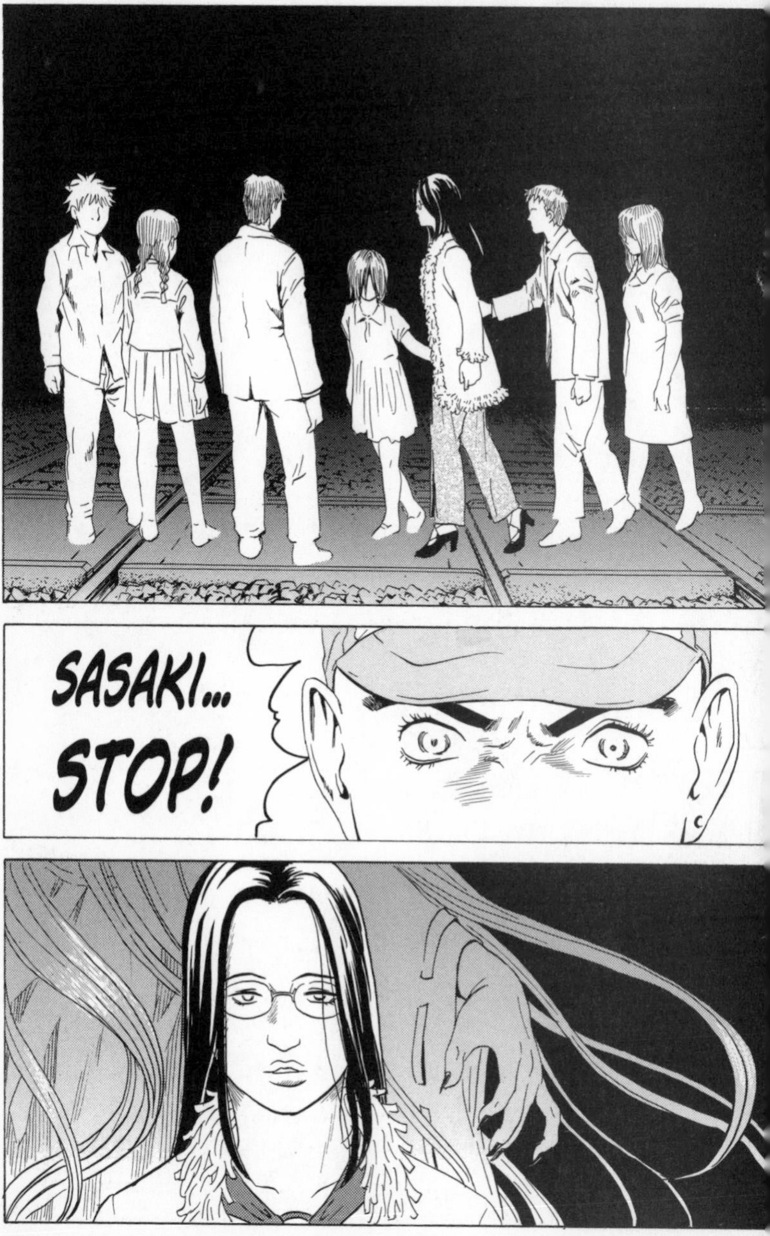
SASAKI... STOP!

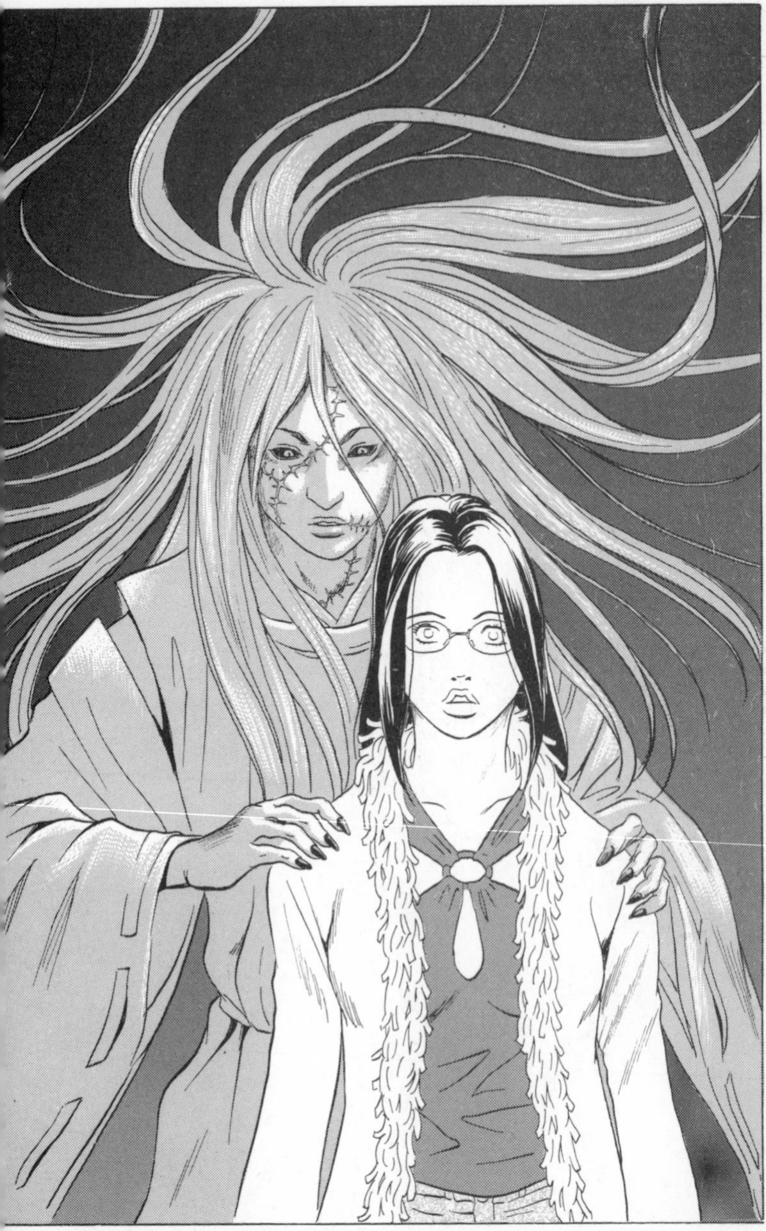

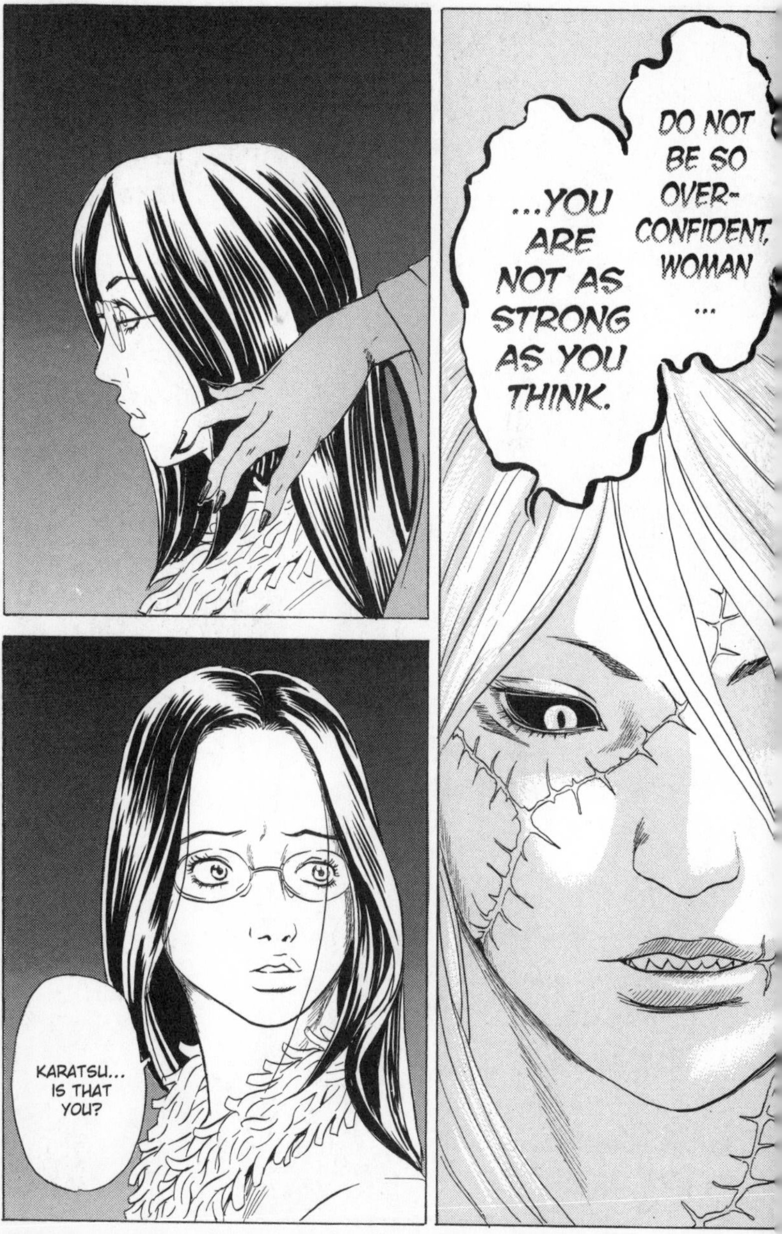
DO NOT BE SO OVER-CONFIDENT, WOMAN ...
...YOU ARE NOT AS STRONG AS YOU THINK.
KARATSU... IS THAT YOU?

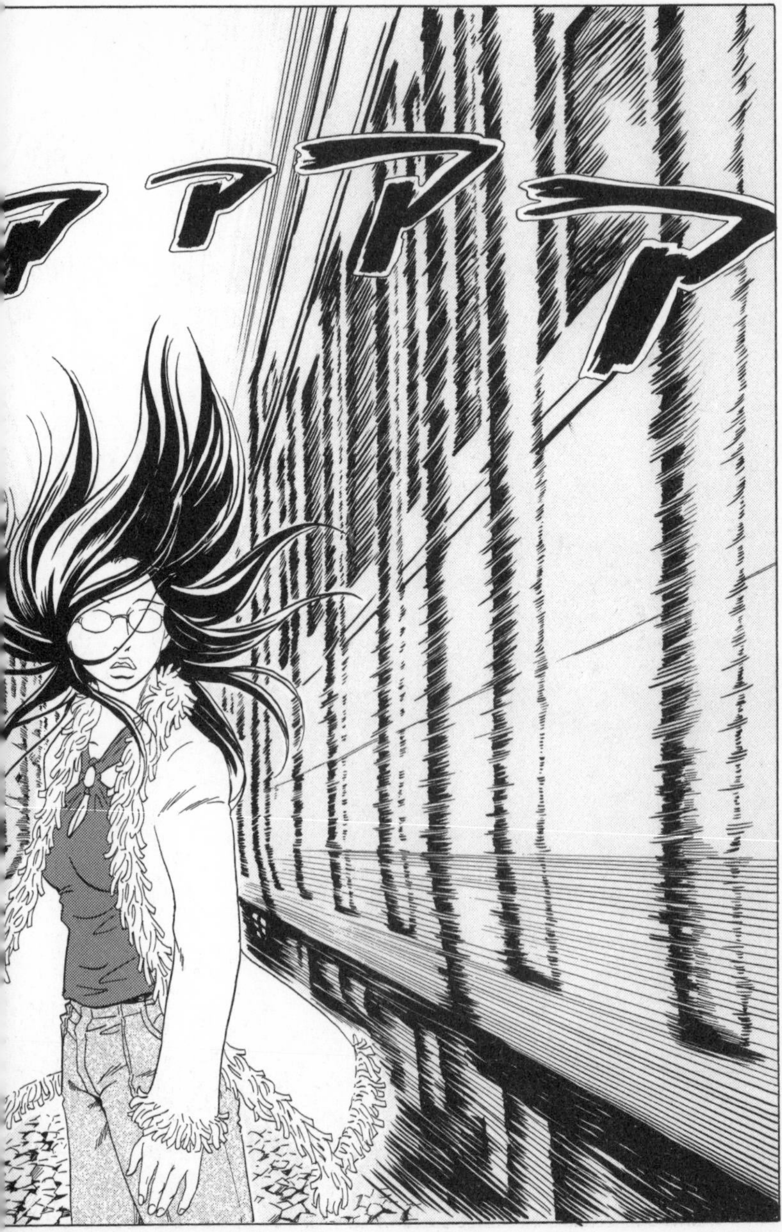
アアアア

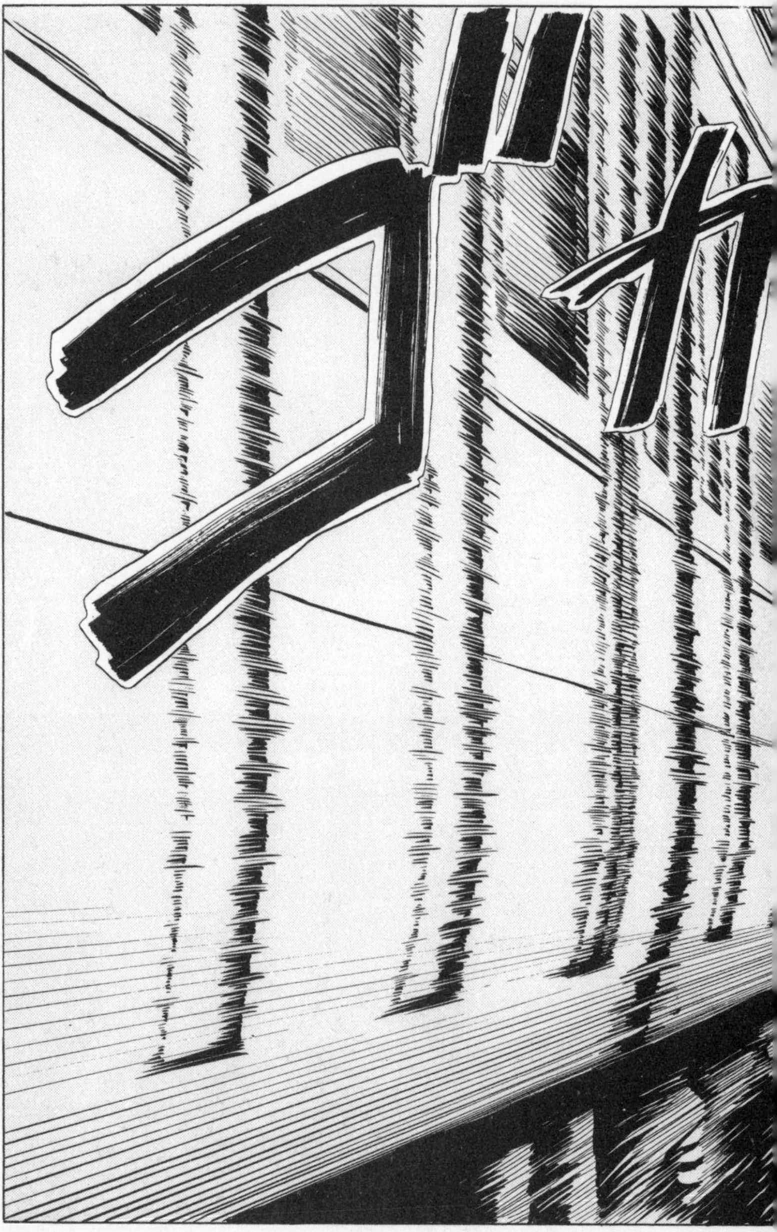
ブオ

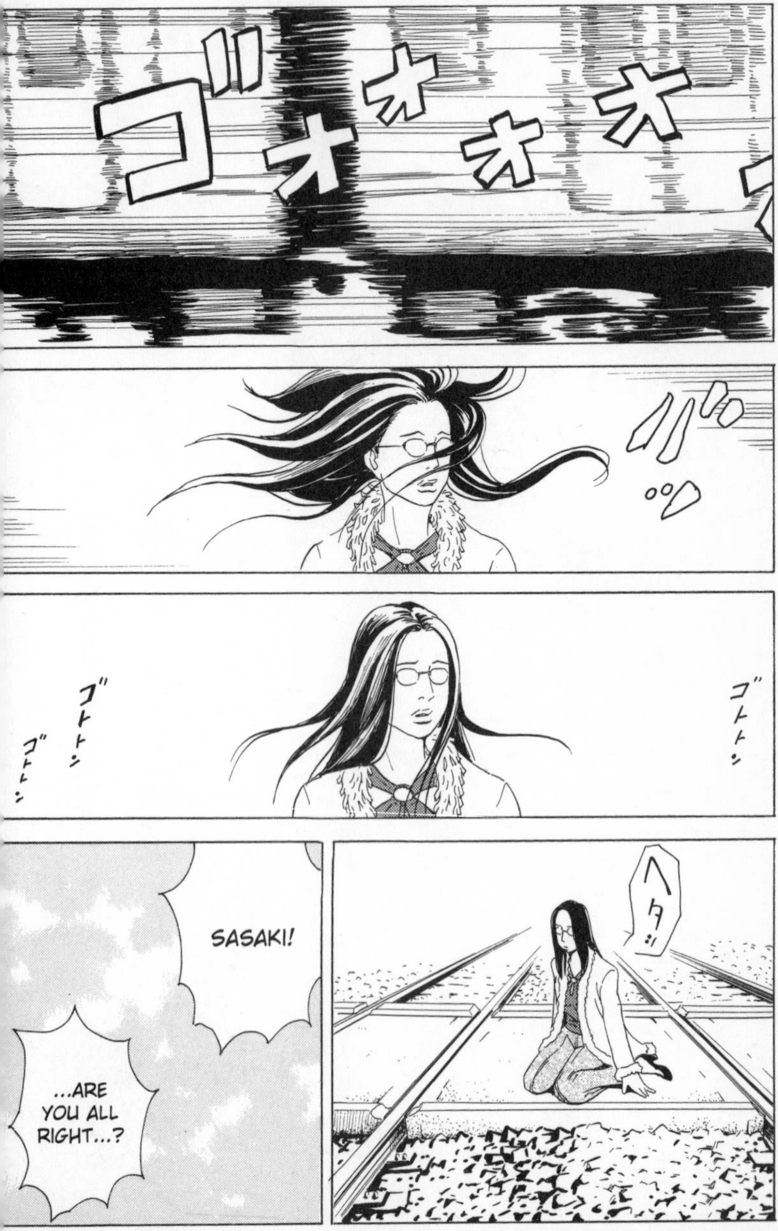
ゴオォオ
バッ
ゴトトン
ゴトトン
ゴトトン
ヘタ
SASAKI!
...ARE YOU ALL RIGHT...?

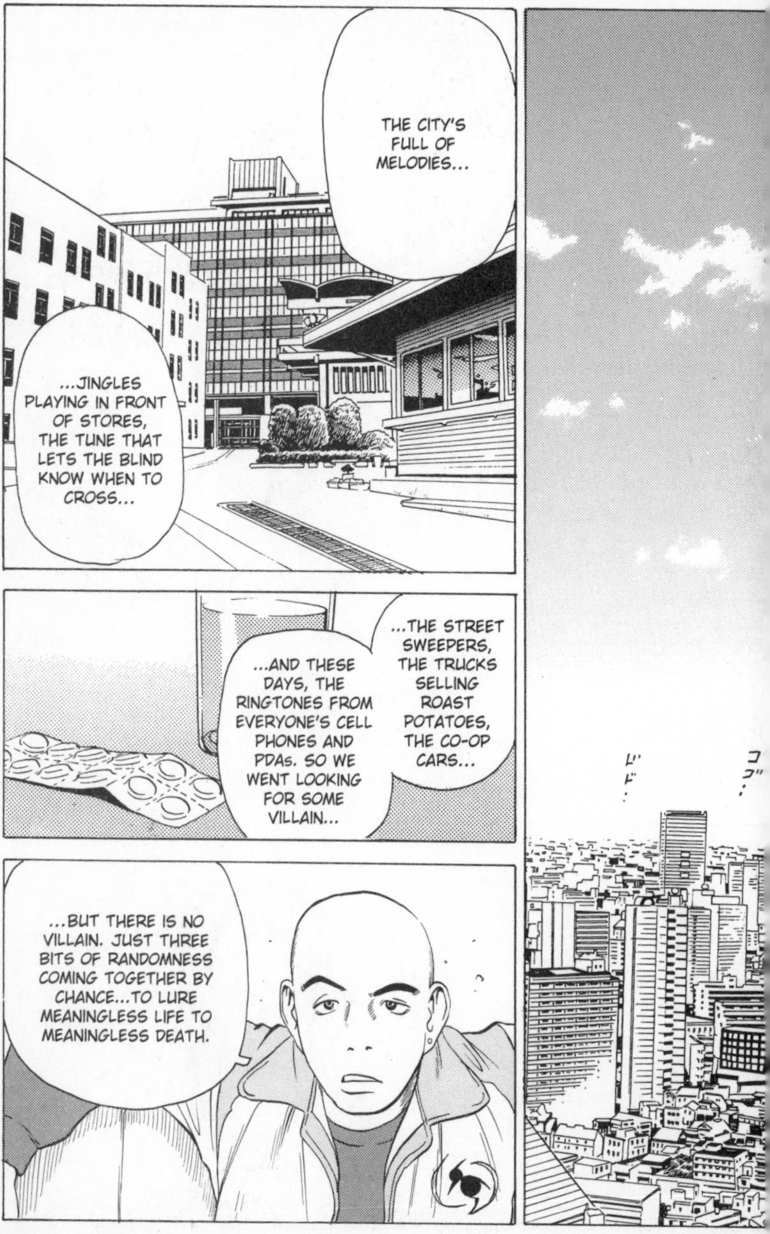
THE CITY'S FULL OF MELODIES...
...JINGLES PLAYING IN FRONT OF STORES, THE TUNE THAT LETS THE BLIND KNOW WHEN TO CROSS...
...THE STREET SWEEPERS, THE TRUCKS SELLING ROAST POTATOES, THE CO-OP CARS...
...AND THESE DAYS, THE RINGTONES FROM EVERYONE'S CELL PHONES AND PDAs. SO WE WENT LOOKING FOR SOME VILLAIN...
...BUT THERE IS NO VILLAIN. JUST THREE BITS OF RANDOMNESS COMING TOGETHER BY CHANCE...TO LURE MEANINGLESS LIFE TO MEANINGLESS DEATH.

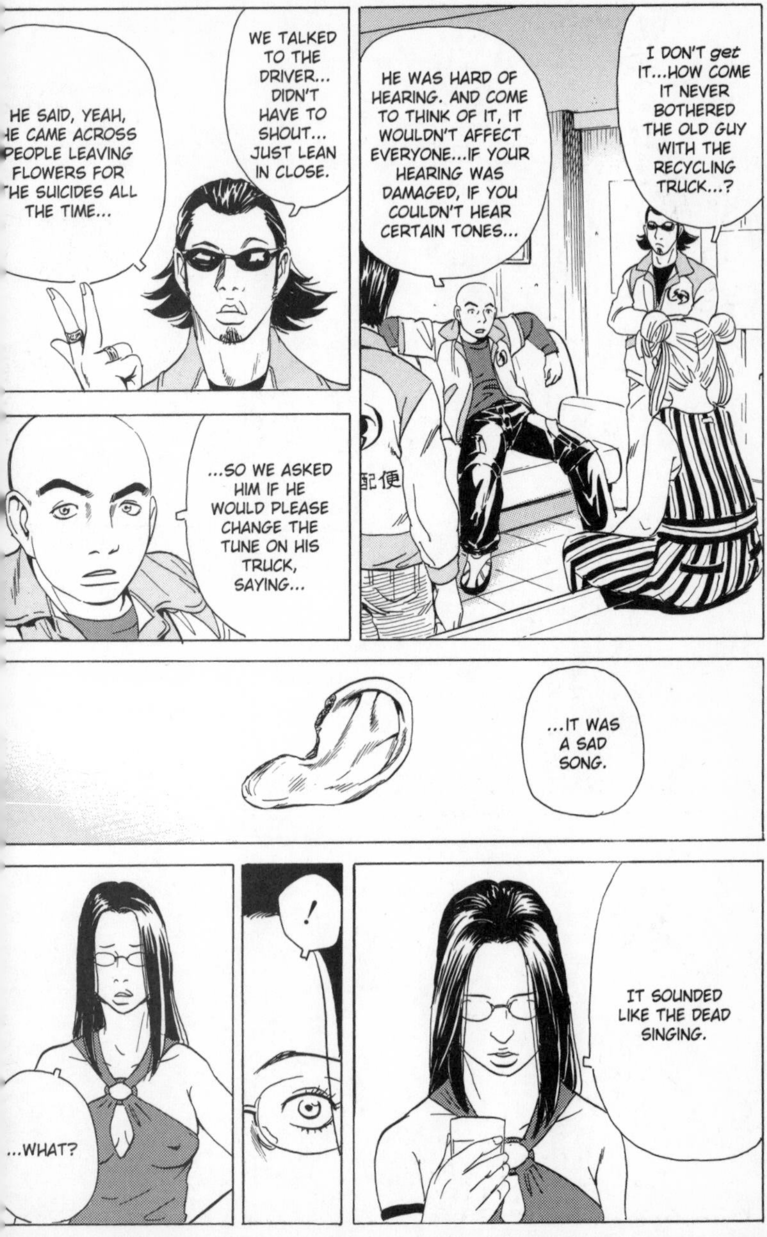

I DON'T get IT...HOW COME IT NEVER BOTHERED THE OLD GUY WITH THE RECYCLING TRUCK...?
HE WAS HARD OF HEARING. AND COME TO THINK OF IT, IT WOULDN'T AFFECT EVERYONE...IF YOUR HEARING WAS DAMAGED, IF YOU COULDN'T HEAR CERTAIN TONES...
配便
WE TALKED TO THE DRIVER... DIDN'T HAVE TO SHOUT... JUST LEAN IN CLOSE.
HE SAID, YEAH, IE CAME ACROSS PEOPLE LEAVING FLOWERS FOR HE SUICIDES ALL THE TIME...
...SO WE ASKED HIM IF HE WOULD PLEASE CHANGE THE TUNE ON HIS TRUCK, SAYING...
...IT WAS A SAD SONG.
IT SOUNDED LIKE THE DEAD SINGING.
!
...WHAT?

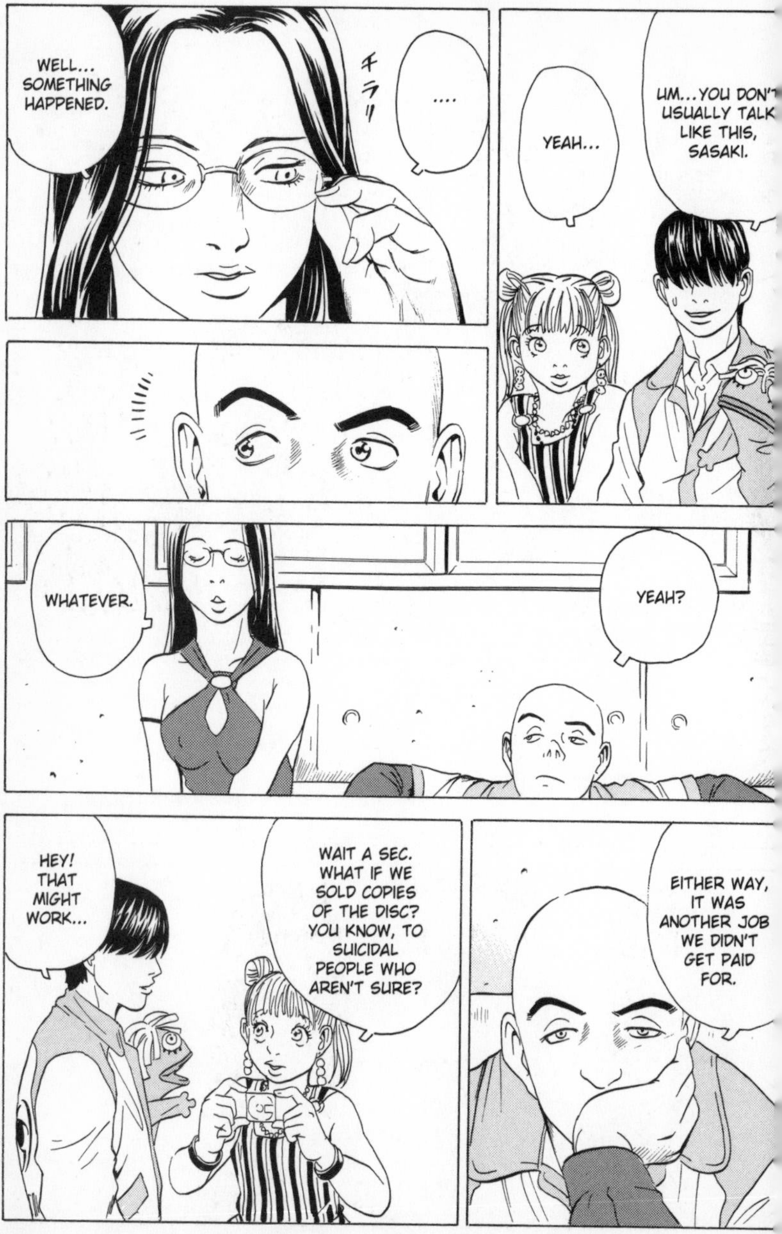
UM...YOU DON'T USUALLY TALK LIKE THIS, SASAKI.
YEAH...
....
チラリ
WELL... SOMETHING HAPPENED.
YEAH?
WHATEVER.
EITHER WAY, IT WAS ANOTHER JOB WE DIDN'T GET PAID FOR.
WAIT A SEC. WHAT IF WE SOLD COPIES OF THE DISC? YOU KNOW, TO SUICIDAL PEOPLE WHO AREN'T SURE?
HEY! THAT MIGHT WORK...

ARE YOU...

...OUT OF YOUR MIND?!

THERE'S ALREADY AS MANY CORPSES...

Um...

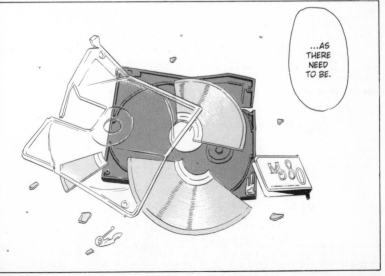

...AS THERE NEED TO BE.

4th delivery: waltz—the end

the KUROSAGI corpse delivery service

黒鷺死体宅配便

eiji otsuka 大塚英志 housui yamazaki 山崎峰水

designer **HEIDI FAINZA**
editorial assistant **RACHEL MILLER**
art director **LIA RIBACCHI**
publisher **MIKE RICHARDSON**

English-language version
produced by Dark Horse Comics

Published by
Dark Horse Manga
A division of Dark Horse Comics, Inc.
10956 SE Main Street
Milwaukie, OR 97222
www.darkhorse.com

To find a comics shop in your area,
call the Comic Shop Locator Service
toll-free at 1-888-266-4226

First edition: March 2007
ISBN-10: 1-59307-594-4
ISBN-13: 978-1-59307-594-1

3 5 7 9 10 8 6 4 2

PRINTED IN CANADA

DISJECTA MEMBRA

SOUND FX GLOSSARY AND NOTES ON *KUROSAGI* VOL. 3 BY TOSHIFUMI YOSHIDA
Introduction and additional comments by the editor

To increase your enjoyment of the distinctive Japanese visual style of this manga, we've included a guide to the sound effects (or "FX") used in this manga-style adaptation of the anime film. It is suggested the reader *not* constantly consult this glossary as they read through, but regard it as supplemental information, in the manner of footnotes. If you want to imagine it being read aloud by Osaka, after the manner of her lecture to Sakaki on hemorrhoids in episode five, please go right ahead. In either Yuki Matsuoka or Kira Vincent-Davis's voice—I like them both.

Japanese, like English, did not independently invent its own writing system, but instead borrowed and modified the system used by the then-dominant cultural power in their part of the world. We still call the letters we use to write English today the "Roman" alphabet, for the simple reason that about 1600 years ago the earliest English speakers, living on the frontier of the Roman Empire, began to use the same letters the Romans used to write their Latin language to write out English.

Around that very same time, on the other side of the planet, Japan, like England, was another example of an island civilization lying across the sea from a great empire, in this case, that of China. Likewise the Japanese borrowed from the Chinese writing system, which then as now consists of thousands of complex symbols—today in China officially referred to in the Roman alphabet as *hanzi*,

but which the Japanese pronounce as *kanji*. For example, all the Japanese characters you see on the front cover of *The Kurosagi Corpse Delivery Service*—the seven which make up the original title and the four which make up the creators' names—are examples of kanji. Of course, all of them were hanzi first; although the Japanese did invent some original kanji of their own, just as new hanzi have been created over the centuries as Chinese evolved.

(Note that whereas both *kanji* and *hanzi* are methods of writing foreign words in Roman letters, "kanji" gives English-speakers a fairly good idea of how the Japanese word is really pronounced—*khan-gee*—whereas "hanzi" does not—in Mandarin Chinese it sounds something like *n-tsuh*). The reason is fairly simple: whereas the most commonly used method of writing Japanese in Roman letters, called the Hepburn system, was developed by a native English speaker, the most commonly used method of writing Chinese in Roman letters, called the *Pinyin* system, was developed by native Mandarin speakers. In fact Pinyin was developed to help teach Mandarin pronunciation to speakers of other Chinese dialects; unlike Hepburn, it was not intended as a learning tool for English-speakers *per se*, and hence has no particular obligation to "make sense" to English speakers or, indeed, users of other languages spelled with the Roman alphabet).

Whereas the various dialects of Chinese are written entirely in hanzi, it is practical to render the Japanese language entirely in them. To compare once more, English is a notoriously difficult language in which to spell properly, and this is in part because it uses an alphabet designed for another language, Latin, whose sounds are different. The challenges the Japanese faced in using the Chinese writing system for their own language were even greater, for whereas spoken English and Latin are at least from a common language family, spoken Japanese is unrelated to any of the various dialects of spoken Chinese. The complicated writing system Japanese evolved represents an adjustment to these differences.

When the Japanese borrowed hanzi to become kanji, what they were getting was a way to write out (remember, they already had ways to *say*) their vocabulary. Nouns, verbs, many adjectives, the names of places and people—that's what kanji are used for, the fundamental data of the written language. The practical use and processing of that "data"—its grammar and pronunciation—is another matter entirely. Because spoken Japanese neither sounds nor functions like Chinese, the first work-around tried was a system called *manyogana*, where individual kanji were picked to represent certain syllables in Japanese (a similar method is still used in Chinese today to spell out foreign names).

The commentary in *Katsuya Terada's The Monkey King* (also available from Dark Horse, and also translated by Toshifumi Yoshida) notes the importance that not only Chinese, but Indian culture had on Japan at this time in history—particularly, Buddhism. It is believed the Northeast In-

dian *Siddham* script studied by Kukai (die 835 AD), founder of the Shingon sect Japanese Buddhism inspired him to crea the solution for writing Japanese still use today. Kukai is credited with the idea taking the manyogana and making sho hand versions of them now known simp as *kana*. The improvement in efficienc was dramatic—a kanji, used previously represent a sound, that might have take a dozen strokes to draw, was now reduce to three or four.

Unlike the original kanji it was based o the new kana had *only* a sound meanin And unlike the thousands of kanji, then are only 46 kana, which can be use to spell out any word in the Japanes language, including the many ordinari written with kanji (Japanese keyboarc work on this principle). The same se of 46 kana is written two different way depending on their intended use: cursiv style, *hiragana*, and block style, *katakan*. Naturally, sound FX in manga are almos always written out using kana.

Kana works somewhat differently tha the Roman alphabet. For example, whil there are separate kana for each of th five vowels (the Japanese order is nc A-E-I-O-U as in English, but A-I-U-E-O except for "n," there are no separate kan for consonants (the middle "n" in the wor *ninja* illustrates this exception). Insteac kana work by grouping together conso nants with vowels: for example, ther are five kana for sounds starting with "k, depending on which vowel follows it—i Japanese vowel order, they go KA, KI KU, KE, KO. The next set of kana begin with "s" sounds, so SA, SHI, SU, SE, SC and so on. You will observe this kind c

nsonant-vowel pattern in the FX listings
r Kurosagi Vol. 3 below.

Katakana is almost always the kind that
ets used for manga sound FX, but on
ccasion (often when the sound is one
ssociated with a person's body) hiragana
e used instead. In Kurosagi Vol. 3 you
n see one of several examples on page
, panel 3, when the liver is extracted with
"ZUBO" sound, which in hiragana style
written ずぼっ. Note its more cursive ap-
earance compared to the other FX. If it
ad been written in katakana style, it would
ok like ズボツ.

To see how to use this glossary, take
example from page 7: "7.4 FX/balloon:
KU – twitch." 7.4 means the FX is the one
page 7, in panel 4 (the "balloon" note, of
urse, means the FX is inside a balloon,
though just as many FX in Kurosagi are
ee on the page). PIKU is the sound these
ana—ピクツ—literally stand for. After the
ash comes an explanation of what the
und represents (in some cases, such as
is one, it will be less obvious than others).
ote that in cases where there are two or
ore different sounds in a single panel, an
xtra number is used to differentiate them
om right to left; or, in cases where right
nd left are less clear, in clockwise order.

The use of kana in these FX also illustrates
nother aspect of written Japanese—its
exible reading order. For example, the way
ou're reading the pages and panels of this
ook in general: going from right-to-left, and
om top to bottom—is the order in which
apanese is also written in most forms of
rint: books, magazines, and newspapers.
owever, if you examine those kana ex-
mples given above, you'll notice something
teresting. They read "Western" style—left-

to-right! In fact, many of the FX in Kurosagi
(and manga in general) read left-to-right.
This kind of flexibility is also to be found on
Japanese web pages, which usually also
read left-to-right. In other words, Japanese
doesn't simply read "the other way" from
English; the Japanese themselves are used
to reading it in several different directions.

As might be expected, some FX "sound"
short, and others "sound" long. Manga represent this in different ways. One of many
examples of "short sounds" in Kurosagi
Vol. 3 is to be found in the example from
41.3 given above: ZUBO. Note the small
つ mark it has at the end. This ordinarily
represents the sound "tsu" (the katakana
form, more commonly seen in manga FX,
is ツ) but its half-size use at the end of
FX like this means the sound is the kind
which stops or cuts off suddenly; that's
why the sound is written as ZUBO and not
ZUBOTSU—you don't "pronounce" the
TSU in such cases.

Note the small "tsu" has another occasional use inside, rather than at the
end, of a particular FX, as seen in 65.6's
TATTATATA—the sound of Yata running
up—here it's at work between two "TA" タ
sounds to indicate a doubling of the con-
sonant sound that follows it.

There are three different ways you may
see "long sounds"—where a vowel sound
is extended—written out as FX. One is with
an ellipsis, as in 52.5's PARA. Another is
with an extended line, as in 15.3's SHAAA.
Still another is by simply repeating a vowel
several times, as in 61.1's IIIIN. You will
note that 52.5 has both the "tsu" and an
ellipsis at its end, even though they would
seem to be working at cross purposes; the
methods may be combined within a single

FX. As a visual element in manga, FX are an art rather than a science, and are used in a less rigorous fashion than kana are in standard written Japanese.

The explanation of what the sound represents may sometimes be surprising; but every culture "hears" sounds differently. Note that manga FX do not even necessarily represent literal sounds; for example 78.1.2 FX: SHIIIN—in manga this is the figurative "sound" of silence. 28.4 FX: GI-RORIN, representing a glare, is another one of this type. Such "mimetic" words, which represent an imagined sound, or even a state of mind, are called *gitaigo* in Japanese. Like the onomatopoeic *gi-seigo* (the words used to represent literal sounds—i.e., most FX in this glossary are classed as giseigo), they are also used in colloquial speech and writing. A Japanese, for example, might say that something bounced by saying PURIN, or talk about eating by saying MUGU MUGU. It's something like describing chatter in English by saying "yadda yadda yadda" instead.

One important last note: all these spelled-out kana vowels should be pronounced as they are in Japanese: "A" as *ah*, "I" as *eee*, "U" as *ooh*, "E" as *eh*, and "O" as *oh*.

2.1 As has been Eiji Otsuka's style throughout *Kurosagi*, all of these titles are again song names. For this volume, the songs are that of Naomi Chiaki. The title of the first story refers to the river ferry that connects Shibamata in Katsushika-ku, Tokyo, with Shimoyagiri, across the Edogawa River (that marks the eastern border of Tokyo proper) in Matsudo, Chiba. The ferry started long ago in the early Edo Period (that is, in the seventeenth century) and today remains the only such service where the boat is still rowed manually by the guides. The original title is *Yagiri no watashi*, "Crossing the Yagiri" or "River Crossing"—no this is not the *watashi* meaning "I" in Japanese, but a homophone spelled with a different kanji. The title of the second story literally means "Applause" but it's also the Japanese title of the US movie *Country Girl* (1954) starring Bing Crosby and Grace Kelly. It's *probably* not pertinent, but an interesting bit of trivia nevertheless. ^_^

7.4 **FX/balloon:** PIKU—twitch

8.2.1 **FX/balloon:** ZU—sound of dragging feet

8.2.2 **FX/balloon:** PETA—sound of feet slapping on floor

8.2.3 **FX/balloon:** ZU—sound of dragging feet

12.2 Japanese anti-Iraq War protest signs in real life often *are* in English as you see here, perhaps for the benefit of the international media (although just as the English expression "Oh my God!" is sometimes portrayed in manga with the stress placed oddly—"Oh MY God"—you will also often see signs that read "No!! War"). The editor saw a few more stylish protests in Japan back in 2003 (this story appeared in July of that year), with skaters in hoodies chalking their slogans on their decks. But all in all, Karatsu has a point on page 13 about the size of the protests—very different from the radical Japanese marches of the 1960s and early '70s that director Mamoru Oshii describes in the semi-autobiographical portions of the novel *Blood: Night of the Beasts*, available, naturally, from Dark Horse.

.4 **FX:** HYUN—sound of the pendulum swinging.

.3 **FX:** SHAAA—hissing sound (like a cat)

.4.1 **FX/balloon:** KOHO—cough

.4.2 **FX/balloons:** GOHO GEHO—cough getting worse

.5 **FX/balloon:** BUHA—coughing up blood

.6.1 **FX/balloon:** GEHO GOHO—coughing

.3 Sasaki uses, as is common in Japan, the English word for "homeless," which is pronounced as *hoomuresu*. Of course, there have been homeless people in Japan for decades (millions of people had at least some experience with it due to WWII), but the editor was shocked in the late 1990s to see tent encampments *inside* the Tokyo subway stations—not only because it seemed such a change from 1980s' confidence and prosperity (during which time there were, of course, also homeless people in Japan), but in that the municipal authorities would allow people to set up shelters there, which would seem unlikely in America.

3.1.1 **FX/balloon:** GAKON—sound of door being pushed open

3.1.2 **FX:** KYU KYU—sound of a squeaky wheel

9.5 I love how Kereellis has the same smile as Yata, Numata, and Karatsu.

19.7 Note the traditional offering to the dead of a bowl or rice, with chopsticks straight up. Foreigners are often warned not to put their chopsticks straight up in a bowl of rice when eating with Japanese (that's what the chopstick rest is for).

20.6 **FX:** GAKU—pratfall/depressed sound

23.3 **FX/balloon:** GACHA—door opening

25.4 **FX/balloon:** JAN JYAKA JIJI JYAAN—ringtone

28.4 **FX:** GIRORIN—glare

29.1 **FX/balloon:** KIN—sound of metal end of cane ringing on floor

29.2.1 **FX:** KA KO—footsteps

29.2.2 **FX/balloon:** KIN—sound of metal end of cane ringing on floor

29.3 **FX/balloon:** SU—reaching into jacket

30.1 **FX:** BA—quickly extending arm

31.6 Tokyo, which is usually thought of as a city, is legally a prefecture unto itself, and is divided into twenty-three wards with a high degree of self-government. Probably the best known of Tokyo's wards outside of Japan (and the editor's favorite) is Shinjuku; the Beastie Boys shot their video for "Intergalactic" in Shinjuku Station, the world's busiest commuter train junction (Michael Gombos is somewhat amazed that they were granted permission to do this, though the effect is classic, as Mike D., MCA, and Adrock dance and throw B-boy gestures into the camera as hordes of confused salarymen walk around them). Although "wards" is the official translation of the Japanese original ku, many of the wards themselves use "city" to refer to themselves in English, and, with individual populations reaching into the hundreds of thousands (Shinjuku alone has 300,000 permanent residents, to say nothing of temporary commuters and shoppers) they indeed qualify.

32.5 FX/balloon: GIRO—glare

33.4 Their "Kurosagi Delivery Service" card (like the sign on their van, they leave the "Corpse" out of it) has the slogan "Any reason, any purpose—moving, fleeing by night, we'll deliver it, no questions asked." The telephone number and e-mail are, regrettably, obscured.

34.1 FX: PUAAN GOGOGO DODO-DO—car and construction sounds

35.3 FX/balloon: PATAN—door closing

35.6 FX/balloon: KI—angry reaction sound

36.5 FX/balloon: DOSA—thud

37.2 FX: SHIBO—lighter igniting

37.6 FX/balloon: KIN—sound of metal tip of cane hitting ground

38.1.1 FX/balloon: KIN—sound of metal tip of cane hitting ground

38.1.2 FX: KO KO KO—footsteps

38.1.3 FX/balloon: KI—sound of metal tip of cane hitting ground.

40.2 FX/balloon: BU—sound of scalpel cutting into skin

40.3 FX/balloon: GU GU—tugging sound

40.4 FX: BOTO—plop

41.1 FX/balloon: SUUU—sound of skin being sliced

41.2 FX: GAPA—sound of chest being opened

41.3 FX: ZUBO—sound of an organ being pulled out

41.5 FX/balloon: SUUU—sound of ski being sliced

41.6 FX/balloon: ZUBU GUCHU—fingers digging into body followed by wet digging sound

42.1 FX: ZURURI—sound of a kidney being pulled out

48.5 FX: KUN KUN—sound of pendulum swinging

49.4 FX: ZURU—sound of a plastic bag being slid out

52.4 FX: PASA—dropping newspaper

52.5 FX: PARA—flipping newspaper page. Note that Tama-chan is the name of a baby seal that first turned up in Tamagawa River in the summer of 2002. The seal continued to appear in various rivers in the Tokyo area for two years, spawned a fandom of its own and had a swarm of media coverage. There were several songs written about it, and some "Tama-chan" character goods even appeared on the market.

52.6 FX: PESHI—putting hand on jar

57.3 FX/balloon: KACHA—keyboard sound

57.4 FX: CHIRA—glancing down at jar

58.5 FX/balloon: PIIPAAPIPU PEPU-PUPIPAA PIPAAPIIPEPO—ringtone

59.3 FX: GOGOGOGO—sound of the car rumbling

9.4 **FX:** GWOOOO—sound of the car being driven

0.5 **FX:** HIIII—sound of a transport plane flying away

0.6 **FX:** IIII—sound of jet engines

1.1 **FX:** IIIIIN—more sound of jets

2.1 Many Americans have voiced concerns about our building bases in Iraq, wondering just how longterm our military presence there will prove to be—but a good *sixty years* after the end of WWII, the U.S. still has literally dozens of bases in Japan, containing 47,000 soldiers, sailors, and airmen. The HQ of all military forces in Japan is located at Yokota Air Base, the site of this scene in the story. It's located in the suburb of Fussa in Saitama Prefecture, about 19 miles west of downtown Tokyo. The controversial presence of the U.S. bases has itself made them the focus of occasional demonstrations, and a ready locale for intrigue and conspiracy stories; perhaps most notably in anime, the film *Blood: The Last Vampire* was set at Yokota.

2.4 **FX:** TA TA TA—jogging sound

3.1 The USAF in fact does adminster the largest mortuary in the American armed forces, but it is located at Dover Air Base in Delaware, under the 436th Services Squadron. Mortuary affairs at Yokota are handled under the auspices of the Honor Guard of the 374th Airlift Wing Services Division.

FX: HYUN HYUN HYUN—pendulum swinging wildly

65.6 **FX:** TATTATATA—Yata running up

65.6.1 This isn't a change—he said *Sesame Street* in the original. A dubbed version of the U.S. show was aired on NHK in Japan for many years, but shortly after this story appeared, a new locally made version (many countries have created such versions to better reflect their own cultures) began showing on TV Tokyo, the network that aired *Neon Genesis Evangelion*!

66.4 Although interrupted by the recent detoriation of relations with North Korea, in the late 1990s and early years of this decade, there was an ongoing effort where the North Korean government cooperated in U.S. efforts to locate the remains of servicemen killed in the Korean War (over 8,000 American soldiers became missing in action in Korea, far more than in Vietnam). From this effort, nearly 200 bodies were found and returned to the United States, passing through Yokota on their way home. This recent example of Yokota being used to handle U.S. war dead possibly inspired Eiji Otsuka to portray it happening today with the Iraq War. It is also true that the mortuary at Yokota was a transshipment point for many of the American casualties during the Vietnam War; an Army surgeon stationed there in the 1960s, Ronald Glasser, gives an account of the period in his acclaimed book *365 Days*. The use of Yokota for dead servicemen from the Iraq War appears to be a literary conceit (or perhaps, an echo of past history) on Otsuka's part; in reality such casualties are often sent first to Sather Air Base at Baghdad International Airport, then to Kuwait, and onward to Dover Air Base, where the actual embalming takes place.

67.3-4 The notion of bodies that are so badly damaged that their dog tags provide the only identification is again something of a throwback to the Vietnam era, as today DNA samples are taken of all military recruits, permitting eventual identification of remains no matter their condition. However, it is true, for example, that looking for ID tags remains part of the mortuary procedure at Sather Air Base in an attempt to establish a tentative identification; final, positive identification is again the responsibility of the 436th Services Squadron at Dover Air Base.

68.1 **FX/balloon:** JIIII—zipper sound

68.4 The idea of placing dead bodies in a pool is probably a reference to the Japanese urban legend (mentioned also in Dark Horse's *Reiko the Zombie Shop* Vol. 2) that some hospitals have a morgue where the bodies are stored in a pool filled with formaldehyde, where attendants stand around with long sticks to keep poking them under again as they bob up.

69.6 **FX:** JAPPO JAPPO—sound of rubber boots sloshing in the pool

71.5.1 **FX:** BIKUN BIKUN BIKUN—corpse twitching

71.5.2 **FX/balloon:** PACHA PISHA—splashing sounds

72.1.1 **FX/white:** BASHA BASHA BASHA BASHA BASHA—loud splashes

72.1.2 **FX/black:** PACHA PACHA—sma** splashes

72.2 **FX:** BATAN DOTAN BATA—Corp** in body bags moving around

72.3 **FX:** GU GUI—face trying to push out of the bag

74.1 **FX:** BURU BURU BURU BURU—hand shaking/waving

75.1 **FX:** PETAN—sound of hand slapping the tile floor as it moves alon**

75.2 **FX:** ZU ZU—dragging sound

75.3 **FX:** BETA—sound of flesh slappir** against tile floor.

78.1.1 **FX:** DO—thud

78.1.2 **FX/white:** SHIIIN—sound of silen**

81.1 **FX:** DOSA—slumping into sofa

81.6 **FX/balloon:** KA—metal end of cane hitting floor

82.3 **FX:** KAN KAN—tapping metal lid** jar with tip of cane

83.2 **FX/balloon:** SU—reaching into jacket

83.3 In 2004, Japan deployed a force of 550 Self-Defense Force soldier** to aid in reconstruction efforts in Iraq—strictly non-combatants, the** were themselves guarded by Australian and Dutch members of the "coalition of the willing." While the SDF troops remained unharmed, number of civilian Japanese did in fact face danger in Iraq, many as NGO (Non-Governmental Organization) volunteers. Seven were kidnapped and two killed—one, in** notorious incident in October 200** beheaded by masked terrorists upon an American flag, his corpse then wrapped in it for people to find. Such gruesome and symbolically charged incidents in real life make the editor reflect upon how much of *Kurosagi* might be called shock value, and how much just stylized truth.

.2 FX: YORO—stagger

.4 FX: GATA GOTON GATAN GATA—sound of Hummer bouncing on the road

.1 FX: GATAKON GOTON—Hummer riding on uneven ground

.4 FX: BATA BATA BATA—sound of his monk robes billowing in the wind

.1 FX: BATA BATA BATA—sound of his monk robes billowing in the wind

.1 FX: MIIIN MIIIN MIIIN—sound of cicadas

.2 FX/balloon: PINPOON PINPOON PINPOON—sound of doorbell

.3 FX: GACHA—sound of door latch

.1.1 FX: DOKA DOKO—sound of club striking bone

.1.2 FX/balloon: BICHA—blood spatter

.3 FX: ZU ZU—hand sliding down wall

.6 FX: CHIKI CHIKI CHIKI—retracting baton

.1 FX/balloon: KIIIIII—door creaking closed

.2 FX/balloon: IIII—continuing to close

.3 FX/balloon: PATAN—door shutting

.1 Is the winged pen nib with the "H" Housui Yamazaki's personal tag?

.1 FX: MEEN MEEN MEEN—sound of cicadas

94.3 FX: GASHA—dropping heavy basket

95.1 FX: PINPOON—doorbell. *Yomiyomi* is a satire on the name of the Japanese newspaper *Yomiuri Shimbun*, which has claimed to have a circulation of as much as 14 million daily.

95.3 FX: GACHA—door opening

95.4 FX: ZORO ZORO—women pouring out of room

96.2 She actually says it this way in the original: *sankyuu booi*—how a Japanese would pronounce the English phrase; most Japanese know enough English to understand it.

96.3 FX/balloon: PATAN—door closing

96.4 FX: KARA—rattle of empty basket falling over

98.3 Japan uses a twenty-four-hour clock, so whereas Americans would say "4 P.M.," they'd say "16." As is the case here, the fact that the number refers to a time of day is made clear by context, or by the use of an English lowercase "h" (as in "16h") or the kanji 時, *ji* (as in 16時).

99.4 FX: CHARAN—dangling pendulum

99.5 FX: HYUN HYUN HYUN—pendulum swinging

99.7 FX/balloon: GACHA—opening door

104.4 FX: DOSA—thud

108.1 FX: KATA KATA KATA—keyboard sound

108.2 FX: PA—picture coming up

108.3 FX: PA—another picture coming up

108.5 **FX:** CHI CHI—giving a tut-tut expression

109.5 **FX/button:** KAKON—pressing key

109.6 **FX:** PA PA PA—multiple images popping up

111.2 **FX:** SHU—spray paint sound

111.3.1 FX/balloon: SHUUU—spraying sound

111.3.2 FX/balloon: SHUUU—spraying sound

113.1 **FX:** JI JI—streetlight buzzing

113.3 **FX:** CHUN CHUN—chirping birds. Note Yata's *Star Wars* gear. You may or may not be aware that Dark Horse has published dozens of original comics set in the *Star Wars* galaxy since 1991—almost, but not quite as long as we've been publishing manga. In fact, Dark Horse has even published *Star Wars* manga—translations of the licensed adaptations of *A New Hope* (by Hisao Tamaki), *The Empire Strikes Back* (by Toshiki Kudo), *Return of the Jedi* (by Shin-ichi Hiromoto), and *The Phantom Menace* (by Kia Asamiya).

113.4 **FX:** KURURI—Puppet turning around

113.6 **FX/balloon:** KARARA—sliding window open

115.2 **FX:** KOTSU—footstep

115.4 **FX:** TA TA TA TA—running sound

115.5.1 FX/balloons: SHU SHUUU—spraying sound

115.5.2 FX/balloon: SHU—spraying sound

115.7 **FX/balloon:** KII—sound of brakes

116.1 **FX/balloon:** WIIIN—power windo rolling down

116.2.1 FX/balloon: GACHA—car door opening

116.2.2 FX: KYORO KYORO—looking around

116.3.1 FX/balloon: SHU—spraying sou

116.3.2 FX/balloons: SHU SHUUU— spraying sound

117.1 **FX:** GOTOTON GOTOTON—trai moving on tracks

117.3 **FX:** KAPA—opening mobile phon

117.4 **FX/balloon:** KASHA—click

118.2 Although he shouldn't worry too much, because, remember, Stev Seagal is also *Hard to Kill* (and also a Buddhist, for that matter). As you may know, Seagal has tw children by his first Japanese wif model Kentaro Seagal and actre Ayako Fujitani, whom *Evangelior* Hideaki Anno directed in his second live-action film, *Shiki-Jits*

118.4 **FX:** BIIIIN—sound of a moped

118.5.1 FX/balloon: KII—brake sound

118.5.2 FX/balloon: GASHA—putting kick-stand down

118.6 **FX/balloon:** TA TA TA—running sound

120.5 **FX:** PASA—flipping open piece of paper

121.4 **FX:** SHU SHU—quick scribbling

122.2 *Oni* is also sometimes translated a "ogre," but, depending on how the reference is used, the connotation of "devil" can seem more appropri ate in English. Sometimes, one might use both at once, as in *Urusei Yatsura*, where Lum is devilish, but her dad is definitely an ogre.

3.1 FX: GACHA—door opening

3.6 FX: CHIRA—peering to the side

4.4 FX/balloons: KON KON KON—knocking

4.6 FX: KACHA—doorknob being turned

4.7 FX: JAKON—telescoping club being extended

4.8 FX: GA—grabbing door

5.1.1 FX: DOKA—impact sound

5.1.2 FX/small: PISHI—floor cracking

6.1 FX: BUN BUN—swinging truncheon

6.2 FX/balloon: SHAKON—toy lightsaber being extended

6.3 FX/balloon: BAKEEN—breaking sound

6.4 Just to note that "Star Peace" wasn't a change by Dark Horse, but a gag in the original.

7.1 FX: BA—jumping into room

8.3 FX: DO DO DO—running sound

8.4 FX: BASHAN—breaking glass

9.2 FX: HYOKO HYOKO—hobbled walking sound

9.4 FX: ZA—coming to a stop

9.5 FX: SU—drawing out cleaver

0.1 FX: KURU—twisting over

0.3 FX: DOKO—impact sound

2.1.1 FX: PYUU—spurting blood

132.1.2 FX/balloon: DOSUN—thudding onto ground

132.3.1 FX/balloon: DO—sound of body hitting ground

132.3.2 FX: PEE POO PEE POO PEE POO PEE POO—sirens

133.6 FX: KATA—turning laptop around

137.3.1 FX/balloon: SHUUU—spraying sound

137.3.2 FX/balloon: SHU SHUUU—spraying sound

138.2 The body has been left in a *koban*, a kiosk typical of the neighborhood police in Japan—hence the sign saying they're out on patrol. Perhaps oddly, you can often find anime- and manga-themed public service announcement posters inside such koban (for example, in the summer of 1996, there was a *Neon Genesis Evangelion* one printed urging people not to waste water—was the idea to use LCL instead?). Hiroyuki Yamaga, co-producer of *Evangelion*, said he never met a cop who wasn't an otaku.

142.1 FX: PINPORO PANPIN PINPOIN—train attention tones

142.2 FX: TANNNN TAAA TATATAAAA TAN TAAA—car horns

142.3 FX: PIIPAPA PIPAPA PPPPOOPAA PIIPIPAPA PIIHA —crossing signal

142.4.1 FX: JAN JACHAAN CHARARAAN JAJAN —phone chatter

142.4.2 FX: PI —phone beep

142.6.1 FX: PINPORO PANPIN PINPORO-PIN—train attention tones

142.6.2 FX: PANPIRO PINPON PIN—train attention tones

142.7 **FX:** PANPIRO—train attention tones

143.2 **FX:** DOGO—impact sound

143.3 **FX:** BAKI GUSHA—breaking and crushing sounds

143.4.1 FX/top: BABA—train speeding by

143.4.2 FX/bottom: BAKI—breaking bone sound

144.2 **FX:** KUN KUN—pendulum swinging

145.1 **FX:** PAKU PAKU—puppet's mouth flapping

146.1 The magazine title, *Young A* (for "Ace") *Weekly*, is a play on two magazines: Kodansha's *Weekly Young* (the original home of *Akira*, and in more recent years hits like *Chobits* and *Initial D*), which actually is famous for its nubile swimsuit covers, and Kadokawa's *Shonen Ace* (in real life a monthly), the current home of *The Kurosagi Corpse Delivery Service* as well as several other manga published in English (including Dark Horse's forthcoming *MPD Psycho*, as well as such titles as *Neon Genesis Evangelion*, *Eureka Seven*, and *Sgt. Frog*). The cover parodies several actual *Shonen Ace* titles, claiming to contain manga such as *Neon Genesis Vangelis* and *Multiple Personality Salaryman*. Note the cameo by Akiba from Housui Yamazaki's other manga *Mail*—Akiba will be making an actual cameo in the next volume of *Kurosagi*.

147.2 **FX/balloon:** POTO—something falling out from between the pages

151.4 **FX:** KASHA—MD recorder being opened

151.5 **FX:** KACHI—hitting record switch

151.6 The Sony MiniDisc, introduced in 1991, was the thing you were supposed to buy to replace your Sony Walkman, but it never really caught on in North America. Unlike portable CD players, MiniDisc players can record as well as play, and provide good audio editing functions. The editor notes that the translator of *Kurosagi*, Toshi Yoshida, was also the producer of the English-dubbed versions of *Inu-Yasha*, *Ranma 1/2, Maison Ikkoku*, and *Jin-Roh* among many others, and made extensive use of the MiniDisc in his work.

153.3 **FX/balloon:** DON—elbow hitting chest. Note that rather than "earring," Karatsu originally said "an ear of bread," which is how Japanese often refer to a piece of bread crust.

154.1.1 FX/black: KATSUN—footstep

154.1.2 FX/white: KIN—metal tip of cane hitting ground

155.1 **FX:** PURAN—dangling sound

158.2 **FX/Numata:** FU FU FU FU-FUU—humming along to music

160.6 **FX/balloon:** JYAKA JYAKA JYARA RAN CHARARARAAN—ringtone

161.4 **FX:** KAAN KAAN KAAN—bells ringing as a train approaches

161.5 **FX/balloon:** WIII—crossbar coming down

161.8 **FX:** KAAN KAAN KAAN—bells ringing as a train approaches

162.2 **FX/balloon:** KUN—pressing on accelerator

63.2 **FX/balloon:** GA—grabbing wheel

63.3 **FX/balloon:** GII—pulling on emergency brakes

63.4 **FX:** KI KI KI—brakes squealing

63.6 **FX/balloon:** GO—mirror touching crossbar

63.7 **FX/balloon:** DON—wheels landing on ground

64.1 **FX:** GAGAAAA—train speeding by

66.3 A charming aspect of Japan is the use of individual melodies, like theme songs, that are played over the loudspeaker to mark arrivals at train and subway stations. Andy Raskin did a story about them that aired on National Public Radio in September of 2003, and you can find an archive of them at the site http://melody.pos.to/.

67.3 **FX/balloon:** PA PA—screen coming up. Note that the screen lists stations on the Chuo line in Tokyo, whose reputation as a method of suicide is in fact quite real (as is the practice of billing the deceased's family). Many Tokyo subway stations have installed transparent anti-suicide walls along the track edges (the trains stop so that their own doors are lined up with doors in the wall, which only then open), but of course this does nothing to prevent suicides at ground-level crossings, such as you see in this story.

71.1 **FX:** PAN PAN—hitting dirt off of hands

75.1 **FX:** PON—taking out earplug

75.3 **FX:** KAAN KAAN KAAN KAAN

KAAN KAAN KAAN—sound of the warning bell for an approaching train

175.5 **FX:** BA—covering ears

178-179.1 FX/balloon: KAAN—warning bell amongst other musical notes

178-179.2 FX/balloon: KAAN KAAN— warning bells amongst other musical notes

178-179.5 FX: TON TOTON—earplug bouncing on the ground

180.1 **FX:** FURARI—a staggering walk sound

180.4 **FX:** KAAN KAAN KAAN—warning bell

184-185.1 FX: GOKAAAAAAA—train speeding by on both sides

186.1 **FX:** GWOOOO—sound of speeding train

186.2 **FX:** BA—sound of last train passing by

186.3 **FX:** GOTOTO GOTOTON GOTOTON—sound of train moving on tracks on both sides

186.4 **FX/balloon:** HETA—sound of Sasaki crumpling to her knees

187.1 **FX:** GOGO DODO—construction noise in the distance

187.3 Such cooperatively run vehicles range from ones shared by farmers to market produce to city dwellers, to colleges providing a shuttle service between dorms and train stations.

189.2 **FX:** CHIRA—peering at Kuro

190.3 **FX:** GAKI BAKI BAKI— stomping and breaking sounds

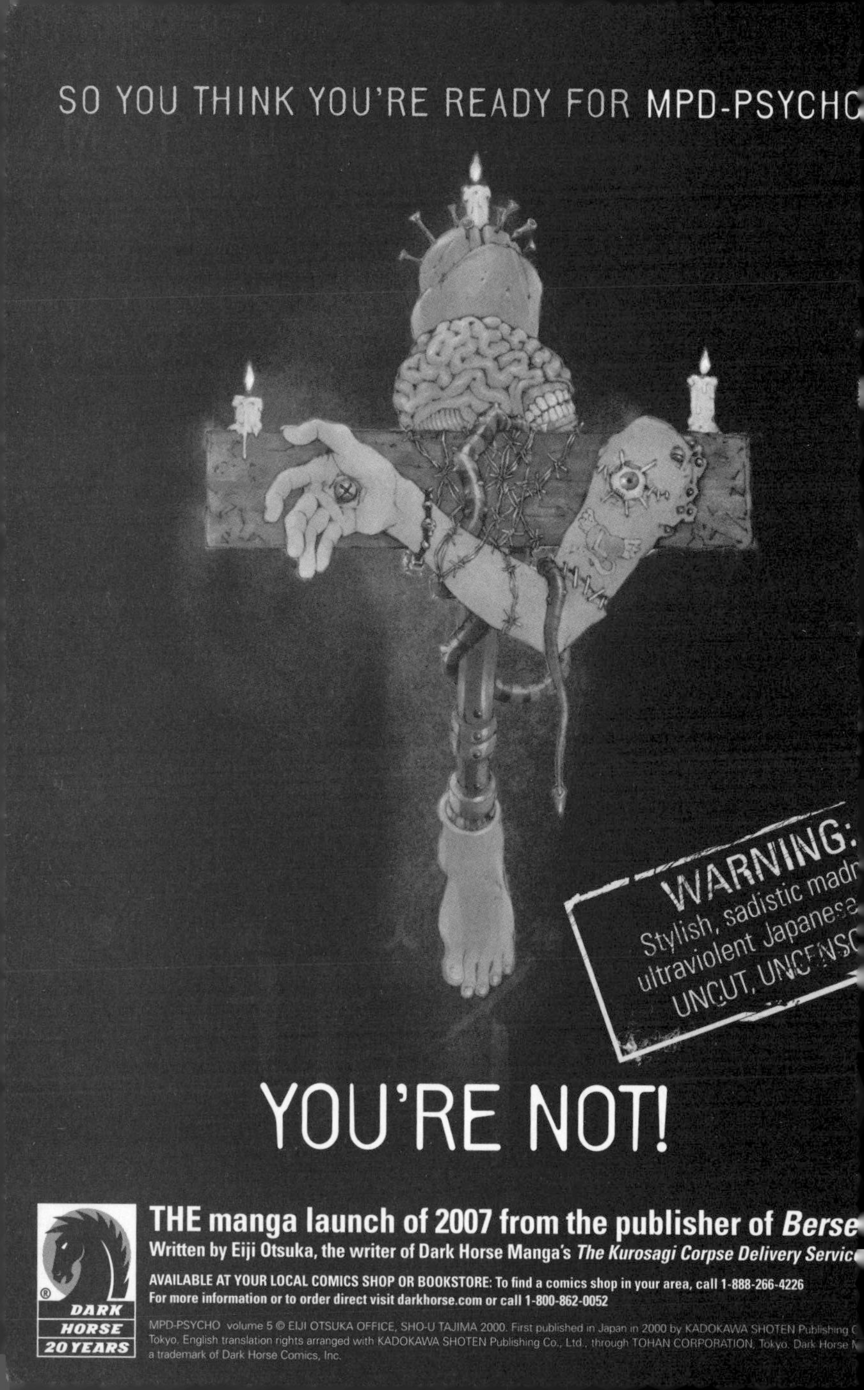

SO YOU THINK YOU'RE READY FOR MPD-PSYCH
WARNING:
Stylish, sadistic mad
ultraviolent Japanese
UNCUT, UNC
YOU'RE NOT!
DARK HORSE 20 YEARS
THE manga launch of 2007 from the publisher of Berse
Written by Eiji Otsuka, the writer of Dark Horse Manga's The Kurosagi Corpse Delivery Servic
AVAILABLE AT YOUR LOCAL COMICS SHOP OR BOOKSTORE: To find a comics shop in your area, call 1-888-266-4226
For more information or to order direct visit darkhorse.com or call 1-800-862-0052
MPD-PSYCHO volume 5 © EIJI OTSUKA OFFICE, SHO-U TAJIMA 2000. First published in Japan in 2000 by KADOKAWA SHOTEN Publishing
Tokyo. English translation rights arranged with KADOKAWA SHOTEN Publishing Co., Ltd., through TOHAN CORPORATION, Tokyo. Dark Horse
a trademark of Dark Horse Comics, Inc.

The first book in a highly successful series of novels from Japan,
Blood: The Last Vampire—Night of the Beasts
is a startling, fast-paced thriller full of chilling surprises.

At Yokota Base in Japan, American soldiers stand guard at the brink of the Vietnam War. Although they fear the enemy outside their base, an even more dangerous enemy waits within—bloodthirsty vampires walk among them! Saya, a fierce and beautiful vampire hunter, leads a team of undercover agents who must wipe out the vampires before they can wipe out the base. But even though Saya is a powerful warrior, her ferocity may not be enough!

ISBN-10: 1-59582-029-9 / ISBN-13: 978-1-59582-029-7 | $8.95

AVAILABLE AT YOUR LOCAL COMICS SHOP OR BOOKSTORE
To find a comics shop in your area, call 1-888-266-4266
For more information or to order direct: •On the web: darkhorse.com •E-mail: mailorder@darkhorse.com
•Phone: 1-800-862-0052 Mon.-Fri. 9 A.M. to 5 P.M. Pacific Time.
BLOOD THE LAST VAMPIRE: NIGHT OF THE BEASTS (KEMONO TACHI NO YORU BLOOD THE LAST VAMPIRE) © Mamoru Oshii 2000. © Production I.G. 2000.
Originally published in Japan in 2000 by KADOKAWA SHOTEN PUBLISHING Co., Ltd., Tokyo. English Translation rights arranged with KADOKAWA SHOTEN
PUBLISHING Co., Ltd., Tokyo through TOHAN CORPORATION, Tokyo. DH Press™ is a trademark of Dark Horse Comics, Inc. All rights reserved. (BL7000)

pressbooks.com

the Ring

Plunge into the depths of manga horror with *The Ring* saga. Based on the best-selling horror novels by Koji Suzuki, these books are perfect for horror and manga fans alike, as well as fans of the hit Japanese and American *Ring* movies!

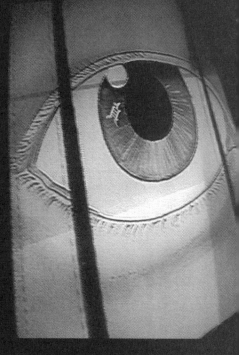

THE RING, VOLUME 0
ISBN-10: 1-59307-306-2
ISBN-13: 978-1-59307-306-0
$12.95

THE RING, VOLUME 1
ISBN-10: 1-59307-054-3
ISBN-13: 978-1-59307-054-0
$14.95

THE RING, VOLUME 2
ISBN-10: 1-59307-055-1
ISBN-13: 978-1-59307-055-7
$12.95

SPIRAL
ISBN-10: 1-59307-215-5
ISBN-13: 978-1-59307-215-5
$12.95

BIRTHDAY
ISBN-10: 1-59307-267-8
ISBN-13: 978-1-59307-267-4
$12.95

AVAILABLE AT YOUR LOCAL COMICS SHOP OR BOOKSTORE! • TO FIND A COMICS SHOP IN YOUR AREA, CALL 1-888-266-4226.

For more information or to order direct visit darkhorse.com or call 1-800-862-0052 Mon.-Fri. 9 A.M. to 5 P.M. Pacific Time.
*Prices and availability subject to change without notice. THE RING 0 © 2000 THE RING 0 Production Group. © MEIMU 2000. THE RING © 1998 THE RING Production Group. © MISAO INAGAKI 1999. THE RING 2 © 1999 THE RING 2 Production Group. © MEIMU 1999. SPIRAL © 1999 SPIRAL Production Group. © 1999 SAKURA MIZUKI. BIRTHDAY © 1999 Koji Suzuki. © 1999 MEIMU. Originally published in Japan in 1999, 2000 by KADOKAWA SHOTEN PUBLISHING Co., Ltd. English translation rights arranged with KADOKAWA SHOTEN PUBLISHING Co., Ltd., TOKYO through TOHAN CORPORATION, TOKYO. English text translated by Digital Manga, Inc. and Dark Horse Comics, Inc. All rights reserved. (BL7042)

DARK HORSE MANGA

STOP!

THIS IS THE BACK OF THE BOOK!

This manga collection is translated into English, but arranged in right-to-left reading format to maintain the artwork's visual orientation as originally drawn and published in Japan. If you've never read comics this way before, take a look at the diagram below to give yourself an idea of how to go about it. Basically, you'll be starting in the upper right-hand corner, and will read each word balloon and panel moving right-to-left. It may take a little getting used to, but you should get the hang of it very quickly. Have fun! If this is the millionth manga you've read this way, never mind. ^_^

1
...
2
THEY TALK TO YOU BECAUSE YOU'RE THE KIND OF GUY WHO CAN'T SAY NO.
3
...YES.
4
RIGHT. SO LET'S TAKE THIS HORRIBLE, STINKING, ROTTING THING BACK TO CAMPUS. QUICK, BEFORE THE COPS NOTICE.
5
BACK TO CAMPUS?!
6
KARATSU, THERE'S NOTHING IN THE HANDBOOK THAT SAYS STUDENTS CAN'T POSSESS CORPSES--OR, IN YOUR CASE, VICE-VERSA.

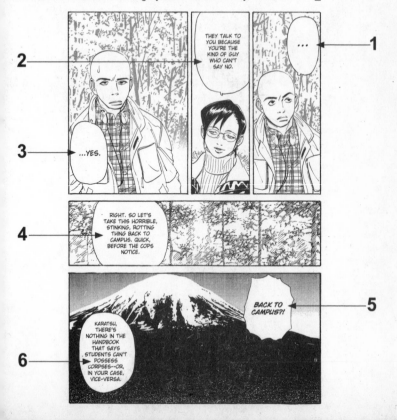